Learning Lessons from WACO

RELIGION AND POLITICS
Michael Barkun, *Series Editor*

Learning Lessons
from WACO

When the Parties Bring Their
Gods to the Negotiation Table

Jayne Seminare Docherty

With a Foreword by Kevin Avruch

SYRACUSE UNIVERSITY PRESS

First Edition 2001
01   02   03   04   05   06   6   5   4   3   2   1

The paper used in this publication meets the minimum requirements of
American National Standard for Information Sciences—Permanence
of Paper for Printed Library Materials, ANSI Z39.48–1984.∞ ™

Library of Congress Cataloging-in-Publication Data
Docherty, Jayne Seminare.
Learning lessons from Waco : when the parties bring theirs Gods to the negotiation table
/ Jayne Seminare Docherty.
p. cm.—(Religion and politics)
Includes bibliographical references and index.
ISBN 0-8156-2751-3 (alk. paper)—ISBN 0-8156-2776-9 (pbk. : alk. paper)
1. Branch Davidians. 2. Waco Branch Davidian Disaster, Tex., 1993. 3. Law
enforcement—United States—Case studies. 4. Conflict management—Case studies. I.
Title. II. Series.
BP605.B72 D63 2001
363.2'3'0973—dc21   2001020954

Manufactured in the United States of America

For those who died or were wounded.
For those who did their best to resolve the standoff.
May we learn the lessons well, and
may we never have another Waco.

Jayne Seminare Docherty holds a degree in religious studies from Brown University (1978) and a Ph.D. in conflict analysis and resolution from George Mason University (1998). She is currently an associate professor in the Conflict Transformation Program at Eastern Mennonite University in Virginia. She is interested in worldview conflicts wherever they may be found and has worked on environmental conflict resolution projects, on community-building initiatives, and with organizations undergoing cultural change. She can be reached at jaynedocherty@aol.com.

Contents

Appendixes:

Illustrations

Figures

Foreword

JAYNE DOCHERTY is part of the first generation of scholars and practitioners educated and trained in the emerging discipline called conflict analysis and resolution, and this book, *Learning Lessons from Waco: When the Parties Bring Their Gods to the Negotiation Table,* tells us just how far this new discipline has come. Conflict analysis and resolution has theoretical and methodological roots in most of the social and behavioral sciences, but at its best it owes allegiance to no one disciplinary vocabulary or methodology. Docherty's professors, the older generation or two of scholars who worked together to help create this new field, all came from some established, named discipline and sometimes had to struggle against the conceptual blinders that disciplinary training so often entails. The earlier generation of practitioners might well have been free of academic blinders—in fact, they were as liable to be suspicious of what "the professors" had to say as any law enforcement officer described by Docherty in this book—but *they* were likely bound by the lessons they learned in the course of their practice-oriented, professional socialization to the field. It is hard for someone coming from labor-management relations to conceive of negotiation in anything but distributive bargaining terms, and hard for someone coming to conflict resolution from therapeutic practices to conceive of parties in conflict except as autonomous individuals susceptible to clinical psychological or psychiatric diagnoses. Docherty approaches the analysis of conflict and conflict resolution on their own terms, and this approach opens the way for fresh conceptions of theory and novel approaches to practice.

This volume is a case study of the American tragedy that unfolded between

February 28 and April 19, 1993, in Waco, Texas, between federal law enforcement agents and members of the Branch Davidians, an unconventional, millennial religious community. Docherty supplements interviews with FBI personnel and the findings of the many official reports, investigations, and expert opinion that followed the events at Waco with a detailed content analysis of the full Davidian-ATF/FBI negotiation transcripts. Her main finding is that the Branch Davidians and federal law enforcement, even while continuing "to negotiate," were looking at the world in utterly different ways, underwriting too often a "negotiation" that was virtually a dialogue of the deaf, resulting in a deep mutual miscomprehension that carried lethal consequences. She calls this "looking at the world" *worldview,* and her book is a case study of just how different worldviews can be from one another, and how important it is to understand the nature of these differences when parties who hold them come into conflict.

The sorts of symbolic, cognitive, and affective processing-package that Docherty calls worldview is what others have referred to as "culture," and the differences she writes about have been called by others (here am I, trained in the discipline anthropology) "cultural differences." But culture is, as Raymond Williams has remarked, one of the two or three most complicated words in the English language, and it comes to social science with formidable baggage, both conceptual and political (1983, 87). It is understandable that Docherty seeks to avoid the many problems associated with culture. Others have despaired of using the term as well, substituting such notions as *discourse, episteme,* or *habitus.* (Still others mistakenly narrow the scope of the culture concept to "values" or "ideology.") Worldview will do as a surrogate so long as it features three important attributes of most contemporary understandings of culture. First, it must never be seen as a static, unchangeable, tradition-bound "thing." This is in fact one of the defects in much of the earlier writing about worldview, making it come across as just that: *a view,* a perspective, as static and fixed (if yet as awe-inspiring, complex, and accomplished) as any massive Western landscape by Albert Bierstadt. Second, worldview must be seen as emergent and contested, in effect "negotiated" by the social actors who hold it and the possibly diverse others with whom they interact. And finally, worldview must not be seen as merely superficial, stylistic variation, a lightly tinged filter that mildly colors our perceptions of the world, but as something that is constitutive of our world. So far as social actors are concerned, worldview (like culture) does not merely embellish social reality: it constitutes it.

On all three counts Docherty succeeds in bringing a fresh understanding to worldview theory, first by emphasizing that one should not speak statically of worldview but processually of *worldviewing*; second, by demonstrating that worldviewing is connected to nothing less than *worldmaking*, often carried on by alternative narratives that jostle, compete, or contradict one another. And finally, Docherty shows that worldviewing is indeed constitutive, not just of variant values, norms, or even appropriate gender and familial relations, as differently understood and accepted by the Branch Davidians and their federal interlocutors, but constitutive right down to the very foundations of alternative rationalities and the ultimate, sacred realities (the "Gods" of the title) that both sides brought to their fateful encounter.

The other part of Docherty's title refers to "learning lessons" from Waco, and it is worthwhile to consider the different audiences who can benefit from this book, and the different lessons that may be learned by each of them.

The first and in many, many ways the most important audience is law enforcement: critical incident response teams and the crisis negotiators among them who come to barricade stand-off situations in the future. Docherty's lesson is that they must add another category of such situations to their typology, different from the bank-robber in a botched robbery who takes hostages and wants to effect an escape; or the ideologically driven terrorist who bargains for the release of imprisoned comrades; or the mentally disturbed estranged husband who takes wife and children hostage in a delusional attempt to hold onto them; or the extremist political activist who wants an interview on *Nightline* and his manifesto published in the *New York Times*. To the existing typology of barricade stand-off situations must be added the unconventional political or religious *community*, often millennial or apocalyptic in beliefs and deeply mistrustful of the state and its agents. One lesson here is not to individuate community members (whose very identity comes from community membership) mistakenly, or "psychologize"—psycho*pathologize*, in fact—their motives or behavior. Law enforcement representatives must be on the lookout, in short, for true worldview differences, come to recognize them (for they will surely reoccur), and understand that the instrumental and "goal-rational" negotiation that may well succeed in *all* the other types of barricade situations mentioned above, may fail in this case. They must understand, in effect, that not everything negotiable is also bargainable.

A second audience who can learn lessons from this book are those negotiation theorists who need to be reminded yet again that worldview (or culture, habitus, discourse . . .) affects the very definition of everything that goes into the negotiation process, from parties to resources to interests and positions. Surely (luckily) not every negotiation involves parties bringing such foundational difference to the table—perhaps only very few ever do. But those that do tend to involve deep rooted or protracted conflicts, and such foundational worldview differences affect much more than negotiating "styles."

A third audience is conflict resolution theorists and practitioners who need to pay careful attention to how Docherty extends Bruno Latour's notion of "symmetrical anthropology." It is not just the Branch Davidians who have a worldview and who brought *their* God to the table; Docherty analyzes at some length the worldviewing of the FBI and other federal agents who brought their own ontologies, schemas, scripts, and metaphors to Mount Carmel. To conflict resolution practitioners one must say: *you* have a culture and *you* are worldviewing too. And if, as a third party, you end up a "worldview translator" between the parties in conflict, never forget that every translation is also an interpretation, and interpretations underwrite the world.

There is, finally, a fourth audience for this book: all Americans who are concerned with religious and political pluralism, tolerance, and the limits of legitimate intrusion by the state into private lives. This is part of what Docherty has called the "never-ending drama of Waco." The lessons to be learned here are matters for long and deep debate. I hope this book is read and studied and discussed at Quantico and in other places where law enforcement crisis teams are trained for the next Waco. But I also hope this book is read by citizens in many other places.

Kevin Avruch

Institute for Conflict Analysis and Resolution
George Mason University

Acknowledgments

THIS PROJECT was my dissertation research and could never have been accomplished without the support and encouragement of my committee: Kevin Clements, Anita Taylor, and Oscar Nudler. The theory of worldview conflict presented here is in large measure a product of dialogue, discovery, and debate among those students and faculty members at the Institute for Conflict Analysis and Resolution (George Mason University) who were as fascinated as I with the problem of worldview conflict. I am deeply indebted to Oscar Nudler, Frank Blechman, Mary Clark, Jarle Crocker, Steve Garon, Nike Carstarphen, Jean Nicholas Bitter, Lisa Schirch, Gretchen Reinhardt, and Carolyne Ashton for their constant support and encouragement during the difficult process of developing a coherent theory out of embryonic ideas. My students and colleagues at George Mason University and Columbia College have also taught me much; it is a privilege to work with such creative, committed, and intelligent people.

Special thanks must be given to Don Bassett, who is both a retired FBI agent and a graduate of the conflict resolution program at George Mason. Don introduced me to members of the FBI Critical Incident Response Group and provided valuable insights into the practice of law enforcement crisis management. Don also arranged for me to participate in two gatherings of the Critical Incident Analysis Group, and the contacts made at those meetings greatly improved my research.

Catherine Wessinger and Jean Rosenfeld helped me reconnect with my religious studies background after almost twenty years of working in other areas. They patiently guided me through the ins and outs of debates in the field of new religious movement studies. They encouraged me to work on connecting scholars and negotiation practitioners, and after my research was completed, they were my greatest source of inspiration and guidance through the publication process.

Finally, I must thank my family. My husband, Tony, provided a "spousal support grant" during my doctoral studies; he gave me emotional as well as financial support and was a constant source of sensible advice. My son, Kevin, went through the doctoral program with me "from six years to six feet" and has been my biggest fan and cheerleader. I am also deeply grateful to my parents (Lou and Esther Seminare) and to my sister and her family (Susan, Ted, Brian, and Mike Greenleaf) for their love and encouragement.

Abbreviations

THE TRANSCRIPTS of the negotiation tapes from Waco are available from the Federal Bureau of Investigation through the Freedom of Information Office. Most are available in electronic format in a variety of software programs. Some are available only in hard copy. Those available in electronic format are difficult to cite consistently because page numbers and line numbers vary depending on the software program. I used electronic transcripts in Word where available and hard copy elsewhere. The transcripts of tapes made off of the original calls to emergency services on February 28 are cited with the prefix 911 followed by the tape number and page number. Thus, tape 6, page 14 of the emergency call tapes would be 911.6: 14. The tapes made by the FBI negotiators are numbered sequentially. I have provided the tape number followed by the page number (e.g., Tape 3: 14).

In-text references to the many government reports, congressional hearing transcripts, and the FBI Critical Incident Logs are abbreviated as follows.

Experts   United States Department of Justice, comp. 1993.
            Recommendations of experts for improvements in federal law
            enforcement after Waco. Government Report. Washington, D.C.:
            U.S. Government Printing Office.
Judiciary   United States Congress. 1996. Committee on the Judiciary.
            Subcommittee on Crime of the Committee on the Judiciary
            House of Representatives and the Subcommittee on National
            Security, International Affairs and Criminal Justice of the
            Committee on Government Reform and Oversight. *Activities of*

Federal Law Enforcement Agencies Toward the Branch Davidians.
104th Cong., 1st sess.

Justice   Richard Scruggs, Steven Zipperstein, Robert Lyon, Victor
Gonzalez, Herbert Cousins, and Roderick Beverly. 1993. *Report
to the Attorney General on the Events at Waco, Texas: February 28 to
April 19, 1993.* Government Report. Washington, D.C.: U.S.
Government Printing Office, October 8.

Logs   Federal Bureau of Investigation. 1993. Waco event log 1; Box
25I/Folder 1. FBI Reading Room (Headquarters), Washington,
D.C., May 24.

Treasury   United States Department of the Treasury. Waco Administrative
Review Team. 1993. *Report of the Department of the Treasury on
the Bureau of Alcohol, Tobacco, and Firearms Investigation of Vernon
Wayne Howell Also Known as David Koresh.* Report. Washington,
D.C.: U.S. Government Printing Office, September.

Learning Lessons from WACO

Introduction

The Never-Ending Drama of Waco

WACO, A TOWN IN TEXAS and now shorthand reference to one of the bloodiest episodes in twentieth-century law enforcement in the United States. Much to the dismay of those who live there, you cannot say the word *Waco* without conjuring images of dead and wounded federal agents and a conflagration in which more than seventy people, including twenty-three children, perished. Between February 28 and April 19, 1993, media images from Waco were seared into our collective psyche, and to the great frustration of many people the story of Waco simply will not go away and seems to have no end.

Making Sense of Waco

Late July 2000

I am diligently preparing this manuscript for final submission to the publisher by August 1. Last month, the Supreme Court remanded a 1994 case against the surviving Branch Davidians to the District Court for resentencing.[1] Last week, the jury recommendations were released in a civil trial brought against the federal government by surviving Branch Davidians and family members of those who died at Mount Carmel. Last night (July 21) I down-

---

1. For a full text of the Supreme Court decision in *Castillo et al. v. United States*, see http://www.cesnur.org/testi/waco77.htm.

loaded the just-released preliminary report of the Special Counsel assigned to investigate government actions in Waco, Texas, in 1993 (Danforth 2000).[2] It is more than seven years after the initial dramatic incidents that changed forever the meaning of the word *Waco*. It is more than five years after the April 19, 1995, bombing in Oklahoma City, an act of domestic terrorism spawned by rage over the events in Waco. The story simply will not end.

Looking at Waco as a Critical Incident

Waco has all of the hallmarks of a *critical incident* as defined by the Critical Incident Analysis Group (CIAG). "A critical incident is any event that has the potential for causing personal trauma and undermining social trust, creating fear that may have impact on community life and even on the practice of democracy. . . . Critical incidents can bring us together or drive us apart. They can alter institutions and institutional relationships. They affect public trust. Ultimately, they confirm or confound our culture" (CIAG 2000).

Critical incidents need not involve violence and bloodshed. The Anita Hill-Clarence Thomas hearings can also be considered a critical incident. What do Waco and the Hill-Thomas hearings have in common? Both were dramatic, short-lived events that have had and continue to have a significant impact on our society as a whole. They are events that have changed the way we think about our collective lives, our social institutions, and our leaders. Because of the Hill-Thomas hearings, we will never think the same way about gender relations in the workplace. Because of Waco, many of us will never think the same way about unconventional religious communities or the power of federal law enforcement agencies. A critical incident, even after the initial trauma is dealt with, continues to impact our institutional practices. Employers around the country have tried to institutionalize new policies and practices regulating gender relations in the workplace. It is not yet clear how Waco will alter law enforcement practices.

2. The full text of the report is available at http://www.osc-waco.org.

Why Waco Defies "Sense-Making" Efforts

The problem with trying to write about a critical incident is that the target keeps moving. Critical incidents by definition produce an onslaught of competing, contradictory, impassioned narratives. They are, after all, critical incidents precisely because their *meaning* is unclear and ambiguous and challenging to our existing beliefs about how the world is organized and how we should behave. It may take decades for a critical incident to settle into our collective consciousness in ways that do not evoke heated debates and high emotion.

Sorting out the "facts" from the "interpretations" is a nightmare. It can also consume phenomenal resources and energy, as demonstrated by this no doubt incomplete list of efforts to pin down the *truth* about what happened in Waco, Texas, in 1993.

• Congress convened two sets of hearings (1993 and 1995) that were broadcast live on national television.

• Currently, a special Senate Subcommittee and the House Government Reform Committee are reinvestigating Waco and both are considering further public hearings.

• The Department of the Treasury convened an administrative review team to examine the actions of the Bureau of Alcohol, Tobacco, and Firearms (ATF) leading up to the February 28 raid.

• The Department of Justice organized a series of inquiries into the events in Waco. These inquiries included a factual review of the operation, a review by a panel of experts, an evaluation by Edward S. G. Dennis Jr., and a report by Deputy Attorney General Philip Heymann.

• The General Accounting Office (GAO) prepared a report on the use of the armed forces in Waco.

• Government agencies conducted a reenactment of the April 19, 1993, raid to ascertain what might have caused flashes on tapes made with a Forward Looking Infrared (FLIR) device.

• The attorney general appointed a Special Counsel (Senator John Danforth) to investigate allegations of government wrongdoing related to the fire that killed the Branch Davidians on April 19, 1993.

This list does not include the normal procedures of processing a crime scene and conducting autopsies. Furthermore, it gives only the official efforts to get at the truth about Waco. A complete list would have to include dozens of investigative reports prepared by members of the media,[3] three documentary films,[4] dozens of books and papers written by academics and activists alike, and uncounted Web sites dedicated to revealing the truth about Waco.

Then there are the legal proceedings resulting from the incident. For many observers, the legal proceedings alone constitute a critical incident, shaking their faith in the judicial system to the core. In 1994, eleven surviving members of the Mount Carmel community were tried on charges of conspiracy to murder federal officers, murdering federal officers, and various firearm offenses. The jury acquitted all of the defendants of the conspiracy and murder charges, and acquitted three Branch Davidians of all charges. Five were convicted of aiding and abetting manslaughter, seven were convicted of using or carrying a firearm during a conspiracy to murder federal officers. One was convicted of possessing an explosive grenade and another of conspiring to possess and manufacture machine guns illegally and of abetting the illegal possession of machine guns (Danforth 2000, 139; also Thibodeau and Whiteson 1999, 309–17).

The jury expected sentences that reflected their concerns that the government had acted improperly and that the Branch Davidians were defending themselves.[5] The presiding judge, the Honorable Walter S. Smith Jr., had other

3. For excellent, frequently updated archives of media reports on Waco, see http://www.cesnur.org and http://www.dallasnews.com/waco.

4. The films range from the highly polemical *Waco: The Big Lie* to the award-winning and critically acclaimed *Waco: Rules of Engagement*. The third film, *Waco: A New Revelation*, directed by the same filmmaker who made *Waco: Rules of Engagement*, helped create the outcry that led the attorney general to appoint a Special Counsel to investigate Waco and the Senate and House to begin new investigations into Waco.

5. Sarah Bain, forewoman of the jury, realized too late that the jury had misunderstood critical portions of the sixty-seven pages of instructions from Judge Smith. She wrote a letter to Judge Smith explaining the jury's reasoning and indicating that the intent of the jury was to give lenient sentences to the Davidians in light of the extreme provocation of the ATF raid. Bain felt so strongly that the Davidians were mistreated in the courts that she became an activist and advocate on their behalf. The text of her letter to Judge Smith can be found at http://www.illusions.com/opf/opf940623.htm.

ideas. Judge Smith began the trial declaring that "the government is not on trial here." He concluded the trial by using sentencing guidelines related to the use of firearms in the commission of a crime to add thirty years each to the sentences of four Branch Davidians and ten years to the sentence of a fifth. The convictions were upheld by the Court of Appeals in 1996, but were overturned by the Supreme Court in June 2000. No criminal charges were brought against any government employees involved in the initial raid, the subsequent siege, or the final effort to drive the Branch Davidians from Mount Carmel.

In civil court, seven groups of surviving Branch Davidians and relatives of those killed at Mount Carmel filed wrongful death suits against the United States and against certain individual Federal Bureau of Investigation (FBI) and Department of Justice employees. The seven cases were consolidated in January 1996, and the trial finally began in June 2000. Why the delay? It is not easy for citizens to sue the government or those acting as part of their government employment. "The United States, as a sovereign nation, is immune from suit *unless it consents to be sued.*" Furthermore, the United States "is [only] liable for the negligent conduct of its employees acting within the scope of their offices, if a private person would be liable under the law of the place (in this case Texas) where the acts complained of occurred" (Wisenberg 2000, emphasis added). In spite of the fact that the government consented to this suit, the defense attorneys retained the right to argue that the defendants were exercising their discretionary duties (i.e., operating on behalf of the state) and were therefore immune from suit. To win their case, the plaintiffs had to prove three things: first, that the discretionary duty exception does not apply when government officials deviate from the plan under which they are operating; second, that the agents in Waco altered the approved government plans on February 28 or April 19 or both; and third, that the alteration of the plans caused the deaths of the Branch Davidians.

The very same Judge Smith whose harsh sentencing of the Branch Davidians was overturned by the Supreme Court was to preside over the civil trial in Waco in spite of Davidian motions asking for a change of venue. This trial was also not one in which the jury would have final say because suits brought against the government are not subject to a jury trial. The jury was to act in an advisory capacity and could only answer the questions as presented by Judge Smith. He asked them to answer the following interrogatories with a simple yes or no:

Did the plaintiffs prove by a preponderance of the evidence that the Bureau of Alcohol, Tobacco and Firearms (ATF) used excessive force on February 28, 1993, in either of the following respects?

1. by firing at Mount Carmel without provocation;

2. by using indiscriminate gunfire at Mount Carmel on February 28, 1993.

Did the plaintiffs prove by a preponderance of the evidence that the Federal Bureau of Investigation acted negligently on April 19, 1993, in one or more of the following respects?

1. by using tanks to penetrate Mount Carmel other than in accordance with the approved Plan of Operations on April 19, 1993;

2. by starting or contributing to the spread of the fire at Mount Carmel on April 19, 1993;

3. by affirmatively deciding to have "no plan to fight a fire" at Mount Carmel, despite Attorney General Reno's directive that required "sufficient emergency vehicles to respond both from a medical and any other point of view."[6]

On July 14, 2000, the jury deliberated for approximately two and one-half hours, and answered "no" to each question, finding in favor of the government.

One week later, the Special Counsel appointed by Attorney General Reno to investigate allegations of FBI wrongdoing on April 19, 1993, and allegations of a subsequent cover up by Department of Justice employees released a preliminary report (Danforth 2000). The conclusions presented are simple, direct, and clear.

The government of the United States and its agents are not responsible for the April 19, 1993, tragedy at Waco. The government:

(a) did not cause the fire;

(b) did not direct gunfire at the Branch Davidian complex; and

(c) did not improperly employ the armed forces of the United States.

Responsibility for the tragedy of Waco rests with certain of the Branch Davidians and their leader, David Koresh, who:

6. My thanks to Stuart Wright for providing me with a hard copy of Judge Smith's interrogatories on short notice. The interrogatories are also included in the Danforth report (Danforth 2000, 143).

(a) shot and killed four ATF agents on February 28, 1993, and wounded 20 others;

(b) refused to exit the complex peacefully during the 51-day standoff that followed the ATF raid despite extensive efforts and concessions by negotiators for the Federal Bureau of Investigation ("FBI");

(c) directed gunfire at FBI agents who were inserting tear gas into the complex on April 19, 1993;

(d) spread fuel throughout the main structure of the complex and ignited it in at least three places causing the fire which resulted in the deaths of those Branch Davidians not killed by their own gunfire; and

(e) killed some of their own people by gunfire, including at least five children. (Danforth 2000, 4–5)

Case Closed . . . Or Is It?

Following the jury finding, the lead government attorney Mike Bradford was quoted in the *Dallas Morning News* as saying, "I hope that this puts to rest concerns about federal law enforcement's activities out there. I think this is a tragedy that has gone on for many years. And I would hope that this does put it to rest" (Hancock 2000). FBI Director Louis Freeh spoke for many in the federal law enforcement community when he said, "The significance of the jury's findings to the courageous federal law enforcement officers who have had to absorb unproven allegations and public criticisms for all these years cannot be overstated."[7] The Department of Justice adopted a muted tone and issued the following statement: "This terrible tragedy was the responsibility of David Koresh and the Branch Davidians, not the federal government. . . . We are pleased the jury affirmed that view" (Mittelstadt 2000).

In the preface to his preliminary report, Senator Danforth writes eloquently of the magnitude of the accusations against the government, which imperil "the existence of public consent, the very basis of government" (Danforth 2000, i). He summarizes the grave consequences of a critical incident such as

7. For a full text of Director Freeh's statement, see http://www.fbi.gov/pressrm/pressrel/press-rel00/freeh071400.htm.

Waco and acknowledges that the less than forthright actions of some Department of Justice employees have fueled the dark suspicions of skeptics. Breaking the "vicious circle of distrust and recrimination" that has resulted from Waco "is essential if we are to rebuild the consent of the governed on which our system depends. We all have a responsibility to distinguish between healthy skepticism about government and the destructive assumption that government is an evil force engaged in dark acts. Government, in turn, has a responsibility to be open and candid, so that light might dispel all suspicion of darkness" (Danforth 2000, iii). Danforth clearly believes that the findings of his staff will enable the country to put Waco to rest.

Other observers vehemently disagree with Danforth and Bradford. Michael McNulty, producer and director of two documentary films about Waco (*Waco: Rules of Engagement* and *Waco: A New Revelation*), was incensed. "I spent seven years of my life gathering evidence, *much of which was not included in the trial,* and these good citizens took two-and-a-half hours to make a decision on this issue" (Mittelstadt 2000, emphasis added). Judge Smith and the lead attorney for the Branch Davidians, Michael Caddell, engaged in a heated exchange over whether the judge's instructions to the jury violated the law and "engineered" the verdict ("Judge Smith's Comments" 2000). Jack Zimmerman, one of the attorneys allowed to enter Mount Carmel during the fifty-one-day standoff to talk with the Branch Davidians about their defense, warned that the trial had not settled the questions related to Waco. "You've got all these unanswered questions that are going to linger. . . . My concern is that we've got extremists who are going to view this as a whitewash. There was really no resolution. The judge didn't let all the evidence in; the jury didn't hear everything" (Mittelstadt 2000).

Filmmakers and attorneys who might have a vested interest in continuing the fight about Waco and "extremist nut cases" are not the only people who think Waco is far from over. In both the civil trial and the Special Counsel investigation, the issues were narrowly framed. Consequently, many observers think that the "real" questions have still not been asked, let alone answered. In some ways, the questions not yet asked are even more volatile and threatening to the social order than are those that the trial and the Special Counsel supposedly answered.

The Questions Not Asked

Danforth's report is abundantly clear about the questions that are not addressed by the inquiry. "On the day that Attorney General Reno appointed me Special Counsel, I said that this investigation would examine whether government agents engaged in *bad acts,* not whether they exercised *bad judgment.* It is an important distinction. . . . While charges of deliberate governmental misconduct justify a far-reaching investigation of this type, there are good reasons why poor judgment—conduct alleged to be careless or imprudent—does not" (Danforth 2000, i, emphasis added).[8] Framed thus, the Danforth report exonerates the FBI and other Department of Justice employees of deliberately evil acts.

The problem with all of the Waco-related investigations conducted thus far is that they are predicated on the assumption that someone must have done something *criminally wrong* to cause such a horrific outcome. If, as I have long suspected, no one on the ground at Waco committed a criminal (i.e., prosecutable) act, then we have an even bigger problem on our hands. Just because nobody committed a crime, we cannot necessarily conclude that nothing is wrong. Among the questions we should be asking as a result of Waco, I would include:

1. Is it acceptable to the American people that normal, established law enforcement procedures, when applied to an unconventional belief community, resulted in the deaths of almost ninety people, including twenty-three children?

2. Have war metaphors ("war on crime" and "war on drugs") altered stan-

8. The Special Counsel was directed to address the following five issues: (1) whether agents of the United States started or contributed to the spread of the fire that killed members of the Branch Davidian group on April 19, 1993; (2) whether agents of the United States directed gunfire at the Branch Davidian complex on April 19, 1993; (3) whether agents of the United States used any incendiary or pyrotechnic device at the Branch Davidian complex on April 19, 1993; (4) whether there was any illegal use of the armed forces of the United States in connection with the events leading up to the deaths occurring at the Branch Davidian complex on April 19, 1993; and (5) whether any government representative made or allowed others to make false or misleading statements, withheld evidence or information from any individual or entity entitled to receive it, or destroyed, altered, or suppressed evidence or information concerning the events occurring at the Branch Davidian complex on April 19, 1993 (Danforth 2000, 2–3).

dard law enforcement practices to the point where they violate the spirit, if not the letter, of the *Posse Comitatus Act,* 18 U.S.C. § 1385, which prohibits the use of the military to enforce the laws?

3. Does responsibility for the ultimate failure of the negotiations (i.e., the "talking" portion of the FBI activities) rest with the Branch Davidians alone, as has been assumed in all of the official investigations conducted thus far?

The first two questions are ethical and political issues that go to the heart of how we see ourselves as a nation. They will not be decided in a courtroom or in some personnel hearing for agents who have been overzealous in their application of law enforcement procedures. Such questions need to be debated and discussed in public forums, with Waco as the goad to our discussion, but not necessarily the focal point of the discussion. The last question is specifically related to Waco and is the basis of the research presented in this book.

Reframing the Problem and Asking New Questions

When I started this research project in 1995, I intended to focus on the "talking" part of the FBI interactions with the Branch Davidians. The first official reports indicated severe problems in the coordination of the tactical and negotiation activities. My reading of the transcripts certainly confirms this problem. Every time the negotiators won a concession from the Branch Davidians, it seemed that the tactical units "punished" the Davidians. However, no official report examines the negotiations themselves more than cursorily. No one in an official capacity has yet asked whether the *negotiations,* if handled differently, could have yielded better results. The Danforth report perpetuates this problem by simply repeating the previous conclusions about the negotiations, conclusions based solely on the statements of FBI personnel and not on any systematic analysis of the transcripts (Danforth 2000, 97–99). I have included this portion of the Danforth report in appendix A for readers interested in comparing the official version of the negotiations with my analysis.

In 1995, when I started my research, this failure to investigate the negotiation activities of the FBI puzzled me. As profoundly as the law enforcement agents seemed to have misunderstood the Branch Davidians, I did not understand how the talks could have been going as well as the negotiators claimed. The assumption that responsibility for the breakdown in negotiations rested solely with the Branch Davidians seemed to be based more on the presumption of Branch Davidian irrationality than on any evidence from the case itself. I had both professional and personal reasons for doubting the "irrationality" of the Branch Davidians.

Spring Semester 1993

As a doctoral student at the Institute for Conflict Analysis and Resolution (ICAR) at George Mason University, I was increasingly concerned that the tools and techniques of conflict resolution were culturally biased and of limited use. Too often, I felt that our practices worked just fine if the parties in the conflict either were or were willing to act as if they were white, Eurocentric, middle class, and preferably male. I was not sure I was learning anything in the classroom that would help me cope with the types of diversity-based conflicts I was seeing in practice. The theoretical focus on "rational analytical problem solving" in our classes seemed to miss the real substance of the deepest and most profound conflicts that confronted us in the field. I say "us" because a number of students and a few faculty members shared these concerns.

Then, in the spring semester of 1993, a visiting professor from Argentina, Oscar Nudler, taught a course that focused on *worldview conflict*. While the drama in Waco unfolded on our televisions, we were building a vocabulary for talking about the problems related to conflicts in which the parties appeared to be speaking different languages and occupying different realities. The potential usefulness of such approaches for dealing with the situation in Waco was not lost on us. The fact that we were junior members of the ICAR community and just building our ideas about a worldview-sensitive negotiation practice kept us from making any contact with the FBI, even as the conflict spiraled to its violent conclusion. I wish we had not been so reticent.

Summer 1974

I was particularly horrified by the April 19 outcome because I could actually imagine life at Mount Carmel. I spent a brief period during the summer of 1974 living in a religious community composed of families and single adults. The community occupied a large building and several other houses in a rural area outside of a small town. We ate in a common dining hall and shared chores on the farm and around the houses as well as child-rearing duties. The community was a place of tremendous peace and solace. The primary focus was prayer and spiritual development. The leader of the community was an older man, considered wise and enlightened by the community members, and we began and usually ended each day listening to his teachings.

In the end, I left the community in part because I was disturbed by how much authority the adults in the community seemed to be handing over to one leader. As someone just leaving home and ready to be out from under parental authority, I was not looking for a substitute father figure. I wondered how adults could be so willing to let someone assume that role in their lives. However, I would not have described the community members as irrational or ignorant or brainwashed. The community included more people with graduate degrees than you commonly find in a group of that size: lawyers, writers, a newspaper editor, numerous professors, and medical professionals. There were also young adults who had been raised in the community. They were intelligent, gentle, and well adjusted. All were there by choice, and all could clearly tell you about their choices and their truth.

I am not comparing the two communities on every score. To my knowledge, the central building block of the community where I lived was the traditional nuclear family. There were no allegations of child abuse or sexual misconduct, and the theology was not apocalyptic. However, the community members were clearly willing to sacrifice other relationships in order to remain in the group. Some members of the group had been rejected by or turned away from their families. Others had been told by their (Catholic) religious orders to choose between this community and their order. As Mount Carmel burned, I thought about how easy it would have been for the media to promulgate a narrative that would make the members of the community where I had lived look crazy. I also thought about how deeply committed these community members were, how calm they were in their faith, and how difficult it would have been to persuade them to leave this home if it meant an end to their community life.

Working on the Project

From the outset, I made some critical decisions about the purpose, scope, and nature of my research. I was *not* interested in identifying criminally guilty parties, if such existed. Identifying criminal actors was, in my view, the role of other investigators. My own sense was that the tragedy of Waco was not that some federal agents acted criminally and carried the entire system of actors along with them in their criminal behavior. Rather, *I suspected the Waco tragedy grew out of many federal agents using standard operating procedures in good faith, but in a situation where those procedures were doomed to fail.*[9] I wanted to figure out whether established negotiation procedures had been confounded by the difficulties inherent in working with parties who do not share a worldview. To address this problem, I looked at the talk portion of the negotiations using a theory of worldview conflict as outlined in chapters 1 and 2. The research methods I applied to the negotiation transcripts are described in chapter 4 and appendix B.

Throughout the project, various people have asked my opinion about the conduct of individual actors. I will not comment on individuals who were at Waco. I will only say that some people carried the military tactics of modern policing beyond bounds that I, speaking as a citizen rather than as a researcher, consider acceptable. Nevertheless, although I am not an attorney, I do not see evidence of prosecutable criminal actions on their part.

I am much more concerned about the fact that our law enforcement bureaucracies appear to lack adequate oversight for keeping such persons out of positions where their zeal and poor judgment result in tragedy. I am even more

---

9. Future investigations may reveal that Delta Force or some other military unit actively participated in the April 19 effort to push the Davidians out of Mount Carmel, or, more likely, that military personnel influenced the FBI to insert the CS gas rapidly rather than in measured amounts over a longer period. Even that discovery will not render this research moot. We still need to answer the following questions: Why did the established law enforcement tactics not work with the Branch Davidians? How did everyone involved in the operation—including the negotiators as well as the HRT, commanders, supervisors in Washington, and the attorney general—reach the point where they were convinced that CS gas was the solution to this standoff?

concerned that law enforcement in this country has become "militarized" in ways that I do not think most Americans support. I want to make it clear that when I talk about a militarized police force, I am not talking about the actual use of the armed services in law enforcement operations. I am referring to the increasing use of paramilitary-type police units and policing tactics by law enforcement agencies at all levels (local, state, and federal). In some ways, Waco was the wake up call for all of us. If we do not heed that call and look long and hard at our current law enforcement practices, I fear that we will see a significant, probably violent breakdown in our government. The people will not consent to be governed by means they consider illegitimate, and our history is one of violent resistance to perceived government excess.

The needed changes in law enforcement practices will have to be crafted from within the law enforcement community. Therefore, I did talk with retired and active FBI agents while conducting my research. My work with them was not on analyzing the Waco negotiations per se, and I did not show them my research as I proceeded. Rather, I asked them to help me understand the standard practices that shaped the negotiation activities in Waco. For some readers, these contacts and relationships will make my work automatically suspect. I, however, am primarily interested in reshaping the practice of law enforcement in general and of crisis negotiation in particular to better work with unconventional belief communities. I did not know how I could accomplish that practical (as opposed to research) work without actually talking with agents, so I did not turn down opportunities to be in dialogue with them. I made every effort to keep my research from being biased in favor of the federal agents, but the reader will have to judge my success in doing so.

So that the reader can make an informed judgment, let me outline my relationships with the FBI. Through the good offices of Don Bassett, a retired FBI agent and graduate of the master's program in conflict resolution at George Mason, I was able to interview formally Gary Noesner and Roger Nisley of the Critical Incident Response Group (CIRG) in Quantico, Virginia. Gary and Roger gave several hours of their time even though neither embraced my work or seemed to think it necessary. Gary was the lead negotiator for part of the Waco standoff and is head of the FBI negotiation unit at Quantico. In addition to a lengthy face-to-face interview, Gary also answered specific questions I had about crisis negotiation practice whenever I phoned him. In his opinion, the negotiations would have worked, or at least worked better than they did, if the tactical activities had not gotten in the way. Roger Nisley replaced Richard Rogers as head of the Hostage Rescue Team (HRT) after Waco and has subsequently become the commander of CIRG with responsibility for overseeing both the negotiation team and the HRT. Like Gary, Roger also indicated that the reorganization of the unit to include a more coherent command structure was probably all that was needed to fix the problems that occurred in Waco.

Also thanks to Don Bassett, I was invited to participate in two conferences hosted by the CIAG. During those conferences, I talked informally with approximately a dozen FBI agents, including Roger Nisley, Gary Noesner, and members of the Behavioral Science Unit.[10] The topics of our conversations included the Montana Freemen standoff, how to foster contacts between the FBI and moderate militia groups, constitutional issues related to domestic terrorism investigations, the use of religious studies scholars as expert consultants, and the Heaven's Gate suicides (which happened to occur at the time of one of the conferences). Some of our conversations were amicable. Some were feisty. All were valuable in terms of giving me a clearer understanding of FBI culture, policies, and practices.

Since completing my research, I have been involved in efforts to foster connections between law enforcement agents and scholars who study new religious movements (NRMs). These efforts have been conducted through the American Academy of Religion (AAR) and have included my participation in the following activities during AAR annual meetings: a panel in 1998 (Docherty 1999), a discussion in 1999 about how to anticipate millennial violence, and observation and discussion of a simulated negotiation presented by FBI negotiators in 2000. I have never been in the paid employ of the FBI or of any other federal law enforcement agency.

10. I learned a valuable cultural lesson at these conferences. Not all of the behavioral scientists were FBI agents, an important distinction within the culture of the bureau. Agents with real "street experience" hold higher status in the bureau than do "civilian" behavioral scientists. Clearly, if the behavioral scientists learn to analyze the complexities of unconventional groups but their lower status as "civilians" keeps their knowledge out of the decision-making process, crisis negotiation practice may still not improve.

What Next?

By 2001, when this book will be on the shelves, the Branch Davidians currently in prison will have received a reduction in their sentences. Danforth will have released his final report. There may have been another round of congressional hearings. God and good fortune willing, we will have gotten past another April 19 without violence. Will Waco have disappeared as an issue? I think not.

However, my *hope* is that we, as a society, will be engaged in a much needed dialogue about the nature of law enforcement and about what constitutes appropriate and inappropriate law enforcement practice. I particularly hope that as the FBI reallocates energy and resources to problems of domestic terrorism, it will give careful consideration to developing a nonviolent *domestic diplomacy* for dealing with unconventional belief communities. Perhaps some of the findings in my research will help in these efforts.

An Overview of the Chapters

In chapter 1, I explain why it is impossible to explain fully the negotiation problems in Waco without carefully examining the worldview differences between the Branch Davidians and the FBI negotiators. However, before analyzing the Waco negotiations as a worldview conflict, I must accomplish several tasks. First, I develop more refined conceptual models of worldviews and worldview conflict in chapter 2, where I lay out some basic terminology and challenge the use of static language (such as *worldviews*) rather than dynamic language (such as *worldviewing* or *worldmaking*). I also examine the connection between storytelling and worldviewing or worldmaking, and I begin connecting worldviews to negotiation.

I must deal with a second conceptual problem before analyzing the Waco negotiations as a worldview conflict. In contemporary society, the worldview of the FBI is, by and large, privileged over the worldview of the Branch Davidians. To examine the Waco negotiations as a situation in which *both* parties brought their gods or ultimate concerns to the negotiation table, we must level the playing field between the Branch Davidian and FBI narratives or worldviews. Otherwise, the FBI worldview is likely to be taken as more real or more in touch with reality than the Branch Davidian worldview. That may be, at some level, an accurate assessment. However, privileging the FBI worldview over the Branch Davidian worldview does not help us understand the problems associated with managing worldview differences and similarities during negotiations. In chapter 3, I propose a *symmetrical anthropology* that treats the secular, scientific worldview of the FBI and the sacred, revelatory worldview of the Branch Davidians as functionally equivalent worldmaking narratives. I demonstrate the usefulness of this symmetrical anthropology by analyzing the stories, taxonomies, metaphors, and institutionalized practices of both the FBI negotiators and the Branch Davidians as they existed prior to the encounter in Waco.

All of the preceding conceptual work helped me to develop a research method for examining the negotiation transcripts. Chapter 4 reviews the research literature on hostage negotiation and the limited attention given to worldviewing in general negotiation research, and describes the worldview-sensitive coding process I used to study the transcripts.

In chapters 5 through 8, I apply the worldview model to four significant problems that plagued the Waco negotiations. I believe the results both illuminate the Waco case and point the way toward improved negotiation practices in dealing with unconventional belief communities. However, I understand the reservations of crisis negotiators, who are quite rightly concerned that theoretically driven and conceptually complex research, such as this case study, defies real-life application. It is all well and good to acknowledge worldview differences between crisis negotiators and barricaded subjects if we have three years to conduct a postincident analysis, but how do we do this type of analysis "on the fly," and how do we use the information we derive to make real decisions about real negotiations as we go? Although acknowledging the legitimate concerns of crisis negotiators, the bulk of chapter 9 is a detailed answer to exactly these questions.

1

What *Really* Happened in Waco in 1993?

WE MAY NEVER KNOW all that happened at the Mount Carmel complex in Waco, Texas, in 1993. The following skeletal account of the confrontation between federal law enforcement agents and an obscure religious sect that had lived in and around Waco since 1935 is all that can be said without deeply offending one of the parties to the conflict.

February 28, 1993. Agents of the ATF stage a raid outside of Waco, Texas. They have an arrest warrant for Vernon Wayne Howell, also known as David Koresh, and a warrant to search the property known as Mount Carmel. Gunfire is exchanged, and a battle lasting approximately ninety minutes ensues. David Koresh is wounded, and an unknown number of Mount Carmel residents are killed or wounded. Four ATF agents are killed and many are wounded. The ATF pulls back. Negotiations begin. The FBI Hostage Rescue Team (HRT) and negotiators are called in. On March 1, the FBI assumes responsibility for managing what has become a siege.

April 19, 1993. After fifty-one days of negotiation, the FBI begins inserting CS gas[1] into the Mount Carmel building. Using loudspeakers, they direct the men, women, and children living there to come out. Tanks make holes in the building. Fires start. The building burns. Almost all of the residents die, including twenty-one children and two pregnant women.

---

1. CS gas is commonly referred to as *tear gas*, a term that minimizes its potentially lethal impact, particularly when used indoors or on young children and pregnant women or when combined with fire, which releases even more deadly chemicals (Kopel and Blackman 1997; Moore 1995; Stone 1993).

The absence of motives, intentions, and in some instances actors (for example, "fires start") is a striking feature of this account. Any effort to describe the motives and intentions of the actors involved in the Waco confrontation evokes heated debate. Who fired first and with what intent on February 28? David Koresh authorized attorney Dick DeGuerin "to represent me in all matters arising out of the *assault* on my home at Mount Carmel on February 28, 1993" (Judiciary 123, emphasis added). Surviving Mount Carmel resident David Thibodeau testified, "helicopters in the back were firing indiscriminately into the building as well according to eyewitness testimony [of community members who later perished in the fire on April 19]. The roof of the tower was riddled with bullet holes shot from the air" (Judiciary 127). On the other hand, an official investigation team concluded, "four agents from the Treasury Department's Bureau of Alcohol, Tobacco, and Firearms (ATF) were killed, and more than 20 other agents were wounded when David Koresh and members of his religious cult, the Branch Davidians, *ambushed* a force of 76 ATF agents" (Treasury 1, emphasis added). Similar controversies arise regarding the motive, intent, and actions of participants if we ask, "Why did the FBI punch holes in the building on April 19?" or "Who or what started the fires on April 19?"

Even apparently simple words and phrases acquire tremendous significance when the events at Waco are discussed. What is the proper name for the group of people living at Mount Carmel? They did not call themselves Branch Davidians. According to Thibodeau, "I always considered myself a student of the Seven Seals. Branch Davidian is something that I really heard on February 28 when the ATF raided" (Judiciary 185).[2] "Seven Seals" is a reference to the New Testament Book of Revelation, which describes a book or scroll sealed with seven wax seals. According to the author of Revelation, when these seals are opened by a mysterious figure identified as "the Lamb," the events leading to the climax of human history will be set in motion. The Mount Carmel community members viewed David Koresh as "the Lamb." Their primary goals in life

2. I use the term *Branch Davidian* interchangeably with terms such as *Mount Carmel community* and *Mount Carmel residents.* I have acquiesced to this imposition of identity on the part of the government, the media, and the general public only because the surviving community members have started referring to themselves as Branch Davidians.

were to deepen their understanding of the Book of Revelation and to await the time for Koresh to open the Seven Seals.

What do we call the property outside Waco? ATF and FBI agents referred to the building as a fortresslike compound. But "the more than one hundred people who lived at Mount Carmel . . . [called it] home . . . 'the anthill' and 'the camp' " (Reavis 1995, 47; also Thibodeau and Whiteson 1999).

How do we describe David Koresh's role in the Mount Carmel community? Most people call him a cult leader who duped and brainwashed his followers. The residents of Mount Carmel called Koresh a teacher and a wise man whose message carried a truth they valued.

Who was Steve Schneider? The FBI identified him as the "second in command" in a military-style hierarchy. Schneider himself resisted this label, and others have said he was David Koresh's student, a pupil whose degree in religious studies made him a particularly valuable aide in disseminating Koresh's message.

What Kind of Conflict Was Waco?

The confrontation in Waco can be examined from many perspectives. However, the raging controversies over language, motives, and intentions surrounding the events in Waco are indicative of deep-rooted conflicts over meaning.[3] To say the Branch Davidians and federal law enforcement agents had difficulty reaching a shared understanding of their February 28 encounter and their ensuing predicament is to state the obvious. Yet this simple observation has profound implications for thinking about whether or how the Branch Davidians and federal agents *might* have been able to create a peaceful out-

---

3. Looking at Waco as a worldview conflict does not replace other analytical frames. Tabor and Gallagher (1995) look at Waco as a clash between secular authorities and unusual religious groups. Moore (1995) and Kopel and Blackman (1997) describe Waco as an example of an increasingly militarized federal law enforcement authority run amok. Waco can also be analyzed as a case study of moral panic and the social construction of deviance (Hall 1995; Lewis 1995; Wright 1995b). Given the central role Waco continues to play in the rhetoric of the Patriot or Citizen Militia movements, Waco can also be examined as a crucial turning point in the development of contemporary citizen resistance to federal authority.

come in Waco. Therefore, it is useful to examine the events in Waco as an example of "a worldview conflict." The lessons learned from such a project may help us in many other situations in which the parties seem incapable of reaching a shared understanding of their problem, let alone a solution with which they can all agree.

What Is a Worldview Conflict?

Nudler claims that conflicts "may be divided into three different kinds: conflicts in which the parties share the *same* world view, conflicts in which they share the same world view only *partially,* and conflicts in which there is *no* [world view] element in common. In our multicultural societies, conflicts of the second, and maybe even of the third, kind seem to be growing" (1993, 4, emphasis in original). If we use Nudler's description, the conflict between federal law enforcement authorities and the Branch Davidians in Waco appears to fall somewhere in the second or third categories. The parties in Waco shared the same worldview only partially, or there were no worldview elements in common. Much post-Waco research has been implicitly or explicitly shaped by this categorization of the conflict (Ammerman 1995; Barkun 1994a; Tabor 1995; Tabor and Gallagher 1995; Thompson 1996, chap. 12).

To anyone working from a social constructionist perspective, the concept of a worldview conflict is obvious. Yet within the field of conflict analysis and resolution, there has been very little exploration of this problem.[4] For conflict analysts and conflict resolution practitioners, the Waco confrontation is a case in which "the obvious" hides a rich vein of unexplored information. Simply stating that the parties' worldview differences heavily impact specific conflicts—such as Waco, the pro-choice versus pro-life conflict, or certain environmental conflicts—does not tell us anything about the dynamics of such conflicts. Nor

---

4. In part as a result of recent preoccupation with " 'the new sexy issue' [of culture] in the field of dispute resolution" (Lederach 1995, 4), some conflict analysts, researchers, and practitioners are beginning to take social constructionist themes more seriously. Of particular note is *Narrative Mediation: A New Approach to Conflict Resolution* (Winslade and Monk 2000), which promises to bring the symbolic world into play in a commonly used form of third-party-assisted conflict resolution.

does it reveal how we might cope with worldview differences while simultaneously helping the parties manage, resolve, or transform their conflict. Such knowledge will emerge only out of the application of a theory of worldview conflict to real cases such as Waco. The transcripts of the recorded negotiations between the FBI and the Branch Davidians as well as other supporting documentation released by the Department of Justice provide a rare opportunity to "observe" parties involved in a worldview conflict as they attempt to negotiate a peaceful resolution to a pressing, complex conflict.

Worldviews as Sources of Conflict

Conflict analysts and conflict resolution practitioners have long described conflict as a multifaceted experience. "To work effectively on conflicts the intervenor needs a conceptual road map or 'conflict map' . . . that details why a conflict is occurring, identifies barriers to settlement, and indicates procedures to manage or resolve the dispute" (Moore 1996, 58). Conflict theorists have pointed to clashing interests (Carpenter and Kennedy 1991; Fisher and Ury 1981; Moore 1996), unmet basic human needs (Burton 1990; Mitchell 1990; Sandole 1990), and miscommunication (Carpenter and Kennedy 1991, 13; Hocker and Wilmot 1995, 10, 22, 38–41; Katz and Lawyer 1985; Moore 1996, 62, 182–90) as sources of conflict. Because practical responses to conflict "are often grounded in a theory that identifies a particular cause of the conflict and suggests prescriptive actions" (Moore 1996, 62), each source of conflict is also addressed in the literature written by and for practitioners of conflict resolution. Interest-based conflicts are considered amenable to integrative bargaining, mediation, and problem-solving processes (Carpenter and Kennedy 1991; Fisher and Ury 1981; Moore 1996; Pruitt and Carnevale 1993). It has been suggested that unmet basic human needs may be addressed through rational analytical problem-solving processes (Burton 1987, 1990; Fisher 1990; Kelman 1990). Other practitioners stress clarifying misunderstandings and improving communication between conflicting parties (Katz and Lawyer 1985). Moore's "Circle of Conflict" (1996, 60–61) illustrates the linkages between causal explanations of conflict and conflict resolution practices (fig. 1.).

Most theorists, researchers, and practitioners acknowledge that clashing values may be the source of some conflicts. However, conflict resolution practi-

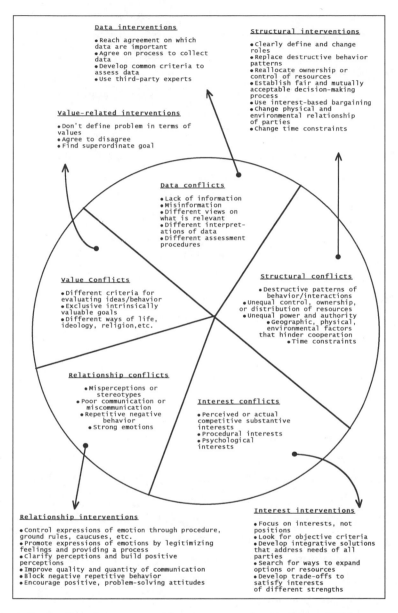

1. Circle of conflict: causes and interventions. Source: Moore 1996, 60–61. Reprinted by permission of Jossey-Bass, Inc., a subsidiary of John Wiley & Sons, Inc.

tioners consider value conflicts highly problematic because such conflicts do not lend themselves to problem-solving processes or to integrative bargaining. Clarifying misunderstandings may actually exacerbate a value conflict as the parties recognize the full extent of their differences (Druckman and Zechmeister 1973; Pruitt and Carnevale 1993, 148). Consequently, practitioners usually try to avoid or work around value conflicts.

Moore advises mediators to reframe value disputes as interest disputes, to identify superordinate goals, or simply to avoid dealing with them (1996, 220). Carpenter and Kennedy encourage practitioners to "work around" or ignore the parties' value differences when values are not a significant factor in the conflict. In cases where the conflict is "over ideologies themselves," they conclude that "chances for constructive negotiation are exceedingly dim" (1991, 201). Others make similar arguments. For example, "when party positions are explicitly related to a negotiator's own belief system (i.e., when there is an 'ideological link'), compromise is unlikely and negotiations will tend to result in either deadlock or capitulation" (Morley and Stephenson 1977, 34). At the very least, aspiring third-party intervenors are told that "values disputes are extremely difficult to resolve, and intermediaries are usually very careful when working with them to ensure that their actions do not increase the parties' intransigence and adherence to hardline positions" (Moore 1996, 216). A review of training literature for police negotiators reveals that the same attitude toward meaning-related conflicts prevails in crisis negotiation. Law enforcement negotiators are taught to avoid, ignore, and work around the barricaded subject's expressions of belief while pushing an agenda of instrumental problem solving and rational decision making.

Is it always possible to avoid so-called value conflicts? Even without evidence from the collapse of negotiations in Waco, I would question both the preceding description of value conflicts and the standard recommendations for working with (or around) those conflicts. First, it may not be possible to separate the value, interest, and needs factors in a specific conflict. Second, in some cases it may be impossible to reframe value conflicts as interest-based conflicts or to identify superordinate goals that minimize the impact of value dissensus. Third, what many people have called value conflicts can be more usefully thought of as conflicts over "naming reality." I deliberately use the term *naming reality* rather than *perceiving reality*. I want to stress that people to some extent "create" their worlds by naming them. They do not simply perceive, more or less accurately, an objectively given and stable reality. The theoretical and research literature hints at but has not fully developed a conceptual framework for understanding conflicts over naming reality.

Druckman and Zechmeister connect value conflicts and cognitive processes in their statement that "many conflicts occur not because of competing interests but because the parties do not share the same conceptualization of the situation. This may occur because of divergent ideologies, values or cognitive structures" (1973, 450). Clark also links cognition and conflict with the concept of a worldview. She describes worldviews as "the ways our minds divide up, order, and arrange the world, unconsciously constructing our thought patterns for us . . . [so that] these become our reality, our inner world" (1989, 160). According to Clark, some conflict behavior is an expression of anger on the part of groups or individuals whose worldviews have been threatened (1989, 325). Carpenter and Kennedy acknowledge the worldview basis of values conflicts when they note, "Our values . . . are the standards by which we judge events and the behavior of other people and by which we decide what is worthy of our support and what deserves our condemnation. . . . Asking someone to adjust his values is like asking him to alter his sense of reality" (1991, 197–98).

Thus, when I refer to Waco as a "clash of worlds," I am neither lapsing into poetry nor engaging in hyperbole. I am talking about a clash of inner worlds, worldviews, senses of reality, or cognitive structures. These worlds, although largely created and maintained through symbolic activities, are very real. Furthermore, inner worlds are not reducible to values even though values are a key component of worldviews. Most conflict resolution practitioners, if pressed, would acknowledge the existence of intractable worldview conflicts, but few have tried to describe or examine carefully conflicts that are grounded in "clashing worlds." Fewer still have tried to delineate processes for working with parties embroiled in worldview conflicts.

Ironically, forty years ago two of the founders of peace studies laid a conceptual groundwork for talking about worldview conflicts. Boulding (1956) described in detail the role of "the image" in shaping human behavior. Rapoport later found the concept of image particularly helpful when thinking about conflicts as debates (1960, 273–88). Both Rapoport and Boulding were part of the cognitive revolution of the 1950s, the goal of which was to "establish meaning as the central concept of psychology" (Bruner 1990, 2). Unfortunately, the cognitive revolution was sidetracked by the advent of the computer age. Boulding and Rapoport, along with many of their peers, began shifting their focus "from the *construction* of meaning to the *processing* of information" (Bruner 1990, 4, emphasis in original). Although the cognitive perspective was not entirely lost during the ensuing four decades, formal game theories, mathematical modeling, and rational-actor models of human behavior took priority. Now scholars are refocusing attention on meaning creation during conflict.

Hunter examines the competing ontological commitments of parties involved in environmental conflicts. Every individual and group has ontological commitments that define "what is," and ontological commitments can differ significantly. One person may vehemently believe trees are inhabited by spirits, whereas another just as fervently denies the very existence of spirits. Out of their respective descriptions of reality or their ontological commitments, "come beliefs, ethics, and psychological dispositions toward risk" (Hunter 1989, 28). This description leads me to speculate that some so-called value conflicts may be traced to divergent ontological commitments.

If parties have ontological commitments, they also appear to have epistemological preferences that can complicate conflicts and conflict resolution processes. Augsburger notes three basic styles used to resolve conflicts.

> The *factual-inductive* method begins with the visible data and selection of important facts and inductively moves toward a conclusion in a linear, sequential reasoning based on logical inferences. The *axiomatic-deductive* method begins with a general principle or value and deduces the implications for specific situations. . . . The *affective-intuitive* method is based on relational, emotional, and personal perceptions of the situation and on the hunches that arise from these perceptions. (1992, 33)

Note that each style of conflict resolution is linked to an epistemological preference—inductive, deductive, intuitive—which raises the possibility that some so-called value conflicts are differences over "correct forms of knowledge" or legitimate epistemologies.

In some cases, ontological and epistemological conflicts may be intertwined. In many public disputes, technical information plays a crucial role in "understanding the nature of the problem and in finding alternatives to a conflict" (Carpenter and Kennedy 1991, 9). Each party brings its own set of "facts and figures" into the discussion, making it difficult to define the problem jointly. Conflict resolution practitioners then emphasize the need for "all sides [to] agree on a common data base before solutions can be developed" (Carpenter and Kennedy 1991, 10). Technical-resource experts may play a central role in helping the parties build that common database. There are, however, inherent tensions between widely shared understandings (or misunderstandings) of scientific knowledge and consensus-based decision-making processes. Ozawa says that "symbolic uses of science, i.e., to legitimate decisions and decision alternatives in order to generate political support and acquiescence, have become dominant functions of scientific advising in public decision making" (1991, 106). This trend, she claims, is largely a consequence of the fact that many people have inappropriately identified scientific knowledge "as a tool for ending dissent" (1991, 106).

I do not completely disagree with Ozawa, but I would also argue that value assumptions, ontological commitments, and epistemological preferences are built directly into any scientific study. This combination greatly complicates conflict resolution in cases where "technical experts" from different disciplines examine the same problem and present competing reports. For example, an ecologist grants existence to complex networks of living organisms. A forester, especially one educated before ecology was integrated into forestry programs, gives priority to individual species. Negotiating a forest management plan is difficult when parties, each claiming to speak for science, are actually competing to impose the ontological commitments of one scientific discipline on the situation.

It would appear that conflicts lumped together under the heading *value conflicts* include a number of different factors: incongruent ontological commitments (Hunter 1989); differing epistemological claims or styles (Hunter 1989; Augsburger 1992); divergent "senses of reality" (Carpenter and Kennedy 1991); distinctive ways of dividing up, ordering, and arranging the world (Clark 1989); incongruent beliefs, ethics, or psychological dispositions (Hunter 1989); competing constructions of a "technical" problem (Ozawa 1991); or some combination of these factors.

Rather than squeezing such a variety of conflicts into the overly narrow category of value conflicts, I suggest they are more usefully collected under a label
that stresses the meaning-creating factors common to all of the problems described above. Following Nudler (1993) and Clark (1989), I use the term
worldview conflicts. Pearce and Littlejohn (1997) prefer the term *moral conflicts*
for studying the same types of conflicts about meaning. Of the researchers who
have examined meaning conflicts, Pearce and Littlejohn come closest to grasp-
ing the holistic and complex nature of what they call moral conflicts and I call
worldview conflicts.

> A moral order is the theory by which a group understands its experience and
> makes judgements about proper and improper actions. It is a set of concepts
> and a set of rules and standards for action. . . . It is the basis for what most peo-
> ple think of as common sense. . . . A moral order thus provides a tradition of
> truth and propriety. . . . [E]very moral tradition holds certain images of order
> inviolate. Any action that threatens the concept of order within the tradition
> will be seen as an abomination, and what is a perfectly acceptable act in one tra-
> dition can be an abomination in another. (1997, 51)

Three ideas in Pearce and Littlejohn's definition deserve careful attention.
First, moral orders or worldviews take the form of *common sense*. They are the
unquestioned, invisible, "given" reality that shapes human perceptions and actions. Consequently, moral orders or worldviews are frequently made visible
only in encounters between persons or groups who have divergent ideas about
what constitutes common sense. Second, conflicting moral orders are frequently understood as *incommensurate*, which is a frightening term to many
who are interested in conflict resolution because it implies that conversations
between conflicting parties may be impossible. However, this outcome need
not be the case. "Incommensurate systems of thought cannot be mapped point
by point onto one another, but they can be compared" (Pearce and Littlejohn
1997, 61). Furthermore, there are cases where it is not necessary to "resolve" all
differences among moral orders or worldviews, but simply to work with or
"manage" those differences so that parties can address other pressing issues. Finally, the connection between moral orders or worldviews and *action* is frequently overlooked. *Worldview* is a term unfamiliar to many negotiators, but

they do recognize the concept of ideology. Consequently, there is a tendency among many practitioners to equate worldviews or moral orders with "mere" ideas. As Pearce and Littlejohn note, however, "actions and ideas are closely tied together; our actions create ideas, and ideas constrain actions. The term *moral order,* then, denotes the pattern of one's compulsions and permissions to act in certain ways and one's prohibitions against acting in other ways" (1997, 54). Understood thus, the concept of worldview conflict points to a model of all social interactions (including conflict) as taking place within a "constructed configuration or a social network . . . composed of symbolic, institutional, and material practices" (Somers and Gibson 1994, 59).

Every Conflict Takes Place in Three Worlds

Theory, however formalized it ultimately appears when presented to the public, is fundamentally a narrative activity. Therefore, I find it helpful to illustrate my theory of worldview conflict with the following real-life story shared by a colleague who specializes in divorce mediation.[5]

> After fifteen years of marriage, John and Susan are in the process of getting a divorce. They decide to use mediation to work out the settlement agreements for their property and custody arrangements for their two children. Although they are willing to use mediation, their relationship remains tense and bitter. During the mediation process, Susan and John use different metaphors for marriage. Susan says *"marriage is a shared journey"* but John claims *"marriage is a contract."* John and Susan are able to reach creative mediated agreements about custody and visitation rights, vacation times with the children, and the distribution of major material assets including their house, bank accounts, and stocks. The only remaining issue is the division of smaller material goods and household furnishings. In what was supposed to be their last mediation session, Susan and John reach an impasse over possession of an inexpensive print they purchased together during their first year of marriage. An item that might be worth twenty dollars at a yard sale becomes the sticking point that threatens to send John and Susan back to an adversarial court process.

5. My research is not about divorce mediation, and I am not a divorce mediator. If I misrepresent any of the finer points of divorce mediation practice, I beg the reader's indulgence.

What do I think is happening here? To account for the particular conflict between John and Susan, I tell the following general story—or employ the following theory—of conflict.

Human beings simultaneously occupy three different "worlds": the material, the social, and the symbolic. Students of social theory will recognize this holistic model as an attempt to combine three observations about human nature. Human beings are animals. Human beings are social and political animals. Human beings are symbol-using animals.

All conflicts—like all human interactions—involve the mobilization of three types of resources: material, social, and symbolic (fig. 2.). If conflicting parties do not mobilize any of these resources, no overt conflict will occur. Although every conflict takes place in all three worlds and involves the mobilization of all three types of resources, the ratio and relative importance of each type of resource in a particular conflict are context and situation specific. To account fully for a conflict, we must study the material, social, and symbolic sources of that conflict. We also need to explain how and why the parties mobilize material, social, and symbolic resources to achieve their goals and objectives during the conflict. To identify potential solutions to the conflict, we need to understand the parties' respective symbolic worlds because the actions they will or will not employ to escalate or resolve the conflict will be determined, as Pearce and Littlejohn suggest, by their symbolically constructed patterns of compulsions and permissions.

Starting with my general story (model) of conflict in three worlds, how do I analyze the case of John and Susan's divorce mediation? When Susan and John began the mediation process, they shared the goal of reaching agreements about the distribution of their resources and about their continued parenting responsibilities. In the material world, John and Susan wanted to work out the division of their possessions while also making provisions for their own support and that of their children. In the social world, they expected to plan for the continuation of their parenting roles and relationship while simultaneously severing their marital roles and relationship. To accomplish this restructuring of social relationships, they needed to work through their bitterness and anger in order to establish the patterns of communication necessary to facilitate their parenting roles.

Mediators know how to deal with conflicts over material goods. If the "di-

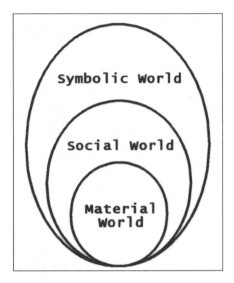

2. Conflict takes place in three worlds.

vide the pie" approach does not work, mediators help their clients "expand the pie" by identifying other resources that can be put on the table (Fisher and Ury 1981; Hocker and Wilmot 1995, 202). Effective mediators help clients name such underlying problems as long-term financial stability or the need for assistance while training to reenter the workforce and help their clients find ways to meet their needs with the available resources. Mediators also facilitate clear communication between clients about their changing roles and relationships (Hocker and Wilmot 1995; Moore 1996). Because Susan and John had a particularly adept mediator, they were able to accomplish a great deal in terms of reaching mutually satisfactory material and social agreements.

Most conflict theorists and many people who train practitioners have, however, largely ignored the symbolic world. This neglect is owing in part to a general failure to recognize and fully appreciate the existence and significance of "symbolic facts" (Cragan and Shields 1995, 18–19). The existence of material facts can be confirmed with the senses. Most people also acknowledge the reality of social facts. They experience themselves as defined, constrained, and empowered by the multiple social relationships and roles they occupy, and they work and live within systems of routinized roles and relationships known as institutions. However, many people only vaguely recognize the existence of symbolic facts. Human symbol-creating and symbol-using activities are deeply embedded in the acquisition and use of language. Because their native language is acquired developmentally, most people rarely recognize the impact of symbolic reality on human interactions. Learning a second language or encountering others who use language that reflects an alternate symbolic world can be a shocking, but enlightening, experience. "Language shock" (Agar 1994) can alert us to the presence of worldview conflict.

John and Susan's use of different metaphors for marriage is a significant indicator of symbolic conflict between them. In Susan's world, couples travel life's road, grow together, and possibly reach a point where their respective life journeys no longer coincide. In John's world, couples make a bargain. They agree to the terms and conditions of their relationship, and there are consequences and penalties to be paid if the contract is severed. Insofar as their contradictory metaphors are tied to competing action schemas, John and Susan will find many of the material and social decisions they must make during mediation very complicated.[6] John wants to penalize Susan for breaking their contract. Susan is seeking affirmation from John of the positive moments they shared during their journey together. For Susan, the print represents a treasured moment of happiness in their shared life. John, by withholding the print, is trying to exact a penalty from Susan for breaking their marriage contract. Neither party is conscious of his or her worldview, and each is deeply puzzled, possibly offended, by the other's worldview. Yet their symbolic conflict jeopardizes their carefully crafted material and social agreements.

Impasses like John and Susan's are often attributed to the parties' irrationality. Many conflict resolution practitioners assume that

> in general parties are able to handle conflict and the resolution process in a rational manner, estimating costs and benefits of various outcomes. . . . A corollary to this assumption, however, is that for various reasons (such as cognitive

6. Cognitive anthropologists have provided useful studies of the connections between metaphors, cultural models, cognitive schemas, and human motivation (D'Andrade and Strauss 1992; Quinn 1991; Quinn and Holland 1987).

factors, group processes, stress) "misperceptions" occur that cause parties to in-accurately interpret various aspects of the conflict. . . . Misperceptions are con-ceived of as examples of faulty reasoning; that is, they are viewed as irrational. (Northrup 1989, 56)

Thus, many observers may consider John and Susan irrational for overvaluing the print.

Conflict resolution practitioners and analysts also tend to assume that emo-tion and irrationality are closely related. Reason is considered good; emotion is deemed bad and dangerous. Most mediators would accept Fisher and Brown's explanation that emotions get in the way of reason (1988, chap. 4). This expla-nation establishes a power differential between people who engage in behavior that is regarded as emotional and those who behave in ways labeled rational. An emotional/rational dichotomy often cuts along gender lines (Lutz 1990). I once heard an army colonel argue he could not comprehend women recruits because they were so emotional. When something went wrong, the women cried, whereas their male counterparts "just kicked something and swore." La-beling crying as emotional but kicking things and swearing as rational behavior disempowered the women. In Western culture, emotions are also thought of as universally shared (primitive) drives and not culturally and socially con-structed events or experiences (Lutz 1988; Wierzbicka 1992, chap. 3). As a re-sult, some parties may be marginalized during conflict resolution processes because of their ostensibly emotional behavior.

In divorce mediation, parties are expected to be emotional or unreason-able. Those divorce mediators who are also trained as therapists may choose to help the parties deal with their emotions. Other mediators typically opt to steer the parties around the emotional aspects of their conflict. In divorce media-tion, we cannot exclude an irrational or emotional party and still continue the conflict resolution process. In public policy or community level conflicts, set-ting aside emotion and working around the "unreasonable parties" is relatively easy. Multiparty dialogue processes may proceed even when some so-called ir-rational parties are excluded. However, Hunter (1989) argues that the source of intractability in public-policy conflicts is often not so much reason versus emotion as it is one system of reason versus another system of reason, with each system of reason grounded in a different set of ontological commitments—which reminds me of another real-life story.

> A four-state, multiyear dialogue process is convened to discuss forest management practices and policies. During the three years of the dialogue process, information is gathered and collated, studies are commissioned and completed, advisory panels that represent all of the stakeholders are established, and numerous opportunities for public input are provided. At the end of three years, the convening body issues a report that many laud as a groundbreaking document. The assumption is that this report will be taken back to each state, where the findings will inform regulatory and legislative follow-up activities. The language of the final report is rich in metaphors. For example, each state is urged to promote forest planning activities that are based on the recognition that "good stewardship is key to a healthy forest and a healthy economy." When the states try to implement the recommendations of the final report, however, the same stakeholder groups that participated in the dialogue process and praised it as a valuable effort to resolve conflicts return to their adversarial positions. Each party accuses the others of misinterpreting the findings of the technical studies commissioned during the dialogue process and of deliberately misrepresenting the agreements that were reached.

What has happened here? The dialogue process successfully facilitated a joint assessment and study of the forest (material) resources that are the focus of this ongoing conflict. Prior to the dialogue, the parties often worked with contradictory and incomplete information. Now they are looking at a shared set of data. The dialogue process has also enhanced interpersonal (social) relationships. However, the parties are now discovering that they attribute contradictory (symbolic) meanings to the same data. The improved personal relationships among the parties do not provide an adequate basis for overcoming their symbolic conflicts. Some people say a healthy forest is a stand of economically desirable trees capable of providing a sustained source of fiber to feed the paper mills. Others argue that a healthy forest includes animals, non-fiber-producing plants, insects, microbes, and a variety of tree species. These two groups look at the same information and draw different conclusions about what it means and how they should act in response to that information. The dialogue process ignored the meaning-creating function of symbolically laden language, such as the healthy forest metaphor. The third-party intervenors have left an extremely important component of this particular conflict unaddressed, thereby making it difficult for the parties to move from agreeing in principle to enacting new policies (Blechman et al. 2000).

Analyzing Waco or Renarrating Waco in Three Worlds

What does my side trip into divorce mediation and participatory public-policy dialogue have to do with Waco? I wanted to demonstrate that conflict is a constructed object of study and practice. The way we conceptualize conflict determines what we observe when examining specific conflicts. The three-worlds model of conflict ensures that we will not neglect the role of ideas, beliefs, and meaning creation when we examine a conflict. Therefore, it provides a conceptual basis for a more complete and holistic analysis of the Waco conflict. If moral orders (worldviews) denote "the pattern of one's compulsions and permissions to act in certain ways and one's prohibitions against acting in other ways" (Pearce and Littlejohn 1997, 54), then how did the incongruent "compulsions and permissions" of the federal agents and the Branch Davidians influence the events in Waco? What material, social, and symbolic resources did the parties in Waco mobilize, for what purposes, and with what consequences?

The Investigation and Raid

Under the leadership of David Koresh, the Branch Davidian community opened several businesses, including at least one enterprise that brought them into the world of gun dealers, the ATF, and the regulation of gun ownership in the United States.[7] The material issues in the conflict were the Mount Carmel

---

7. It cost the Mount Carmel community about $125 per month to support each member of the community, even with their Spartan lifestyle. They ran a number of small businesses, including a stall at gun shows. The Branch Davidians claimed they were purchasing and storing weapons as an investment. Under new government regulations that restricted gun ownership, the weapons were increasing in value, and the community hoped to reap a profit when they resold the weapons. See Thibodeau and Whiteson (1999, 124–31) for a description of the Branch Davidian businesses.

community's possession of particular types of weapons and munitions and their ownership of equipment and parts that would allow them to convert legal (semiautomatic) weapons into illegal (automatic) weapons.

The issue of firearms possession is also a social matter. Declaring specific weapons legal or illegal and requiring citizens to register their weapons with the government are social actions. Some of the problems in Waco may have oc-curred because the changes in gun laws were difficult to understand. Koresh at one point went to the sheriff's office to ask about the legality of some of the weapons. Unfortunately, many local law enforcement agents do not under-stand the increasingly complex federal laws regarding firearms. Furthermore, the enforcement of those laws rests primarily with the ATF rather than with local authorities.

At the same time, in the social world, disillusioned former residents of Mount Carmel mobilized government agencies to investigate the community. Local officials were urged to investigate allegations of child abuse, but their in-vestigation yielded no findings adequate to warrant legal actions against David Koresh or other community members.[8] Opponents also approached the Immi-gration and Naturalization Service (INS) regarding alleged visa violations by foreign nationals living at Mount Carmel. INS investigations were underway at the time of the ATF raid. Finally, those who wanted to see the community dis-banded or Koresh ousted from leadership contacted the ATF regarding alleged violations of firearms laws.

The social conflict *within* the Branch Davidian community was carried out-side the community and into the legal arena through the symbolic activity of telling atrocity tales. "Atrocity tales are first-person accounts by ex-members of culturally dissonant religions" (Downey 1996, 1). Historically, atrocity tales

---

8. Surviving Branch Davidian David Thibodeau insists that children were not physically abused at Mount Carmel (Thibodeau and Whiteson 1999, 116–19), and the Child Protective Services investigation in 1992 was closed because the allegations could not be verified (Thi-bodeau and Whiteson 1999, 121–22). The credibility of Thibodeau's claims is strengthened by his extreme honesty about the more difficult issue of statutory rape with respect to Koresh's sexual re-lationships with young female members of the community (Thibodeau and Whiteson 1999, 113–16). As he points out, however, gathering adequate evidence to prosecute a statutory rape charge is extremely difficult, more so in light of the legitimacy that the Mount Carmel community, including the parents of the girls involved, granted to Koresh's relationships with multiple women.

have been used to discredit culturally unpopular religions, including the Catholic Church and the Church of the Latter-day Saints (Mormon Church) during the nineteenth century and the Unification Church and other "cults" during the 1960s and 1970s (Bromley, Shupe and Ventimiglia 1979; Downey 1996). The objective of an atrocity tale is to provoke a response from the listener by painting a picture of a deviant religion that violates the rights of its members in a number of ways. The alleged atrocities usually fall under the headings of psychological violation of personal freedom and autonomy, physical abuse of members, and disregard for conventional gender and familial relationships. Former members of the Mount Carmel community, such as Marc Breault, incorporated all of these narrative themes into their atrocity tales about the Branch Davidians (Breault and King 1993).

Breault and others also added a theme of criminal activity and potential violence to the atrocity tale, thereby attracting the attention of law enforcement authorities. Past law enforcement experience with violent or potentially violent unconventional groups (Fogarty 1995) made the ATF take warnings about the Mount Carmel community very seriously. There may also have been other social and material pressures on the ATF. Critics have noted that the ATF was videotaping the February 28 raid and that a congressional budget hearing for the agency was scheduled for March 10. A successful dramatic raid would have enhanced their profile and distracted Congress from other problems within the agency (Reavis 1995, 32).

The ATF investigated the material and social issue of firearms possession. They traced the activities of Mount Carmel residents who purchased weapons. They checked invoices, talked with gun wholesalers, and questioned delivery people who had transported arms to Mount Carmel. The ATF also sent an undercover agent into the Mount Carmel community posing as a potential convert. He was told to collect evidence of firearms possession and to gather information about the layout of the Mount Carmel Center. He was also supposed to acquire information about the community's intentions and its daily activities.

All of the material and social information the ATF gathered shaped its agents' response to the Mount Carmel community. It was, however, their symbolic construction of the community's activities that escalated the conflict. The ATF application for a warrant to search the Mount Carmel Center contains relevant material evidence about arms purchases and sales. It also incorporates themes from Breault's atrocity tale. The ATF included in the affidavit numerous references to the "Branch Davidian cult" and the role of David Koresh as a "cult leader." Weaving (material) evidence of firearms purchases together with (social) allegations of sexual improprieties and domestic violence, the ATF produced a (symbolic) narrative about a deviant and potentially a dangerous group led by a manipulative, authoritarian, and violent individual.[9]

How did the symbolic construction of the Mount Carmel Davidians as deviant, dangerous, and potentially violent impact ATF actions? David Koresh and the community were portrayed as a threat in the stories of disgruntled members, the Cult Awareness Network (CAN), and other interest groups. The ATF participated in the creation and promulgation of this symbolic construction of deviance and threat. On the basis of this story, ATF commanders made a tactical decision to serve the search-and-arrest warrant using a dynamic entry raid involving approximately eighty heavily armed federal agents (Wright 1995b).

Stories of past encounters with unconventional groups, combined with a social anxiety about violent and suicidal cults expressed in the frequently repeated story of Jonestown (Hall 1995), clearly influenced ATF actions. For at least one agent, stories of past encounters with so-called cults were very personal. William Buford, who helped plan the February 28 raid, had also participated in "the 1985 siege by ATF and the FBI of the 360-acre Arkansas compound of the white supremacist group The Covenant, the Sword, and the Arm of the Lord (CSA)" (Treasury 38). Law enforcement agents allege that during the protracted CSA standoff the barricaded group destroyed crucial evidence needed by the prosecuting attorneys. This experience, combined with his conviction that a siege at Mount Carmel would trigger a mass suicide, prompted Buford to advocate strongly for a dynamic entry raid in Waco (Judiciary 424, 452–53).

The Branch Davidians knew about the ATF investigation and were tipped off about the raid on February 28. They, no less than the ATF, based their actions on stories they deemed relevant to the situation. A story of righteous self-

---

9. The full text of the affidavit can be found at http://www.constitution.org/waco/affidavt.htm.

defense against unwarranted and violent government invasion of their home led the Mount Carmel community to engage ATF agents in a gun battle. Branch Davidian member Wayne Martin first articulated this narrative while shots were still being fired. He told the emergency services operator, "I have a right to defend myself, they started firing first" (911.1: 10). Throughout the negotiations, Martin and others inside the center used and developed this narrative as a symbolic resource to justify their claims of innocence as well as their allegations of ATF responsibility for the violence. The same narrative theme forms the basis for the wrongful death suit brought by Mount Carmel survivors and Branch Davidian family members.

Many Americans can identify with this particular story, which is a manifestation of an overarching story of self-defense, resistance to tyranny, and defense of private property that is part of mainstream American culture. The Branch Davidian story about the imminent battle between God's chosen people and the forces of evil, although less widely shared, is also not a complete aberration in American culture (Boyer 1992; Fogarty 1995; Hall 1995; O'Leary 1994; Tabor and Gallagher 1995). On the basis of these (symbolic) beliefs, the Mount Carmel residents felt both politically and religiously justified in resisting the ATF raid.

Stabilizing the Barricade Situation

The failure of the ATF raid created a dangerous situation that was then handed over to the FBI Crisis Management Unit on March 1. The FBI inherited a stalemated conflict. The armed residents refused to leave the Mount Carmel Center, and various special weapons units from the ATF and other agencies were stationed outside the center. The tactical units were placed under the command of the HRT, but they could not safely raid the center to end the standoff. On the other hand, federal law enforcement agencies would not back away from the barricade or from their demand for the surrender of David Koresh and others. In addition to the original weapons charges, the community now faced far more serious charges as a consequence of their resistance to the ATF raid, in which four ATF agents died.

The stabilization of the conflict into an armed barricade situation was owing in part to the mediation efforts of Deputy Larry Lynch of the local sheriff's department. The ATF had not made adequate provisions for communication with people inside the center, so Lynch became involved when Mount Carmel resident Wayne Martin phoned 911 during the raid demanding that the police call off their forces. With Lynch's assistance, the ATF and the Mount Carmel residents arranged for a cease-fire and the removal of wounded ATF agents from the Mount Carmel property.

The raid and Lynch's mediation efforts resulted in the following changes in the material world. Four ATF agents were killed, and twenty wounded. Six community members were either killed during the raid or allegedly died later from wounds sustained during the raid. I say allegedly because exact times and causes of death could not be established once the fire on April 19 destroyed forensic evidence. Four Mount Carmel residents were wounded, including David Koresh. The ATF agents, their supervisors, and the Mount Carmel residents experienced natural physiological reactions to a violent confrontation, including hyperventilation as well as elevated heart rates and elevated adrenaline, blood pressure, and blood sugar levels (Gilmartin and Gibson 1985). A perimeter had been established around the Mount Carmel Center, and law enforcement personnel were attempting to control access to the area. They were also mobilizing more weapons and equipment, such as armored personnel carriers. The Mount Carmel residents were making defensive preparations for another raid. Both the police and the community members were attempting to establish their internal communication systems, although both were hampered by resource problems.

These material changes had repercussions in the social world. Biological changes in the ATF agents and the Mount Carmel residents impacted their behavior. In barricade settings, "the extreme instability brought on by the physiology of the situation deteriorates the thinking processes" (Gilmartin and Gibson 1985, 46). Both the barricaded subject and the officers "are highly reactive to changes in their immediate environment. A hypersensitivity to visual and auditory stimuli can be expected to bring about extreme behavioral responses" (Gilmartin and Gibson 1985, 46). Because law enforcement officers are more frequently exposed to situations that induce these physiological changes, they develop coping mechanisms. These mechanisms are not foolproof, but police officers are typically able to pull back from confrontation and establish a barricade situation that allows for efforts to resolve crisis situations without further violence. The barricade experience is usually a new one for the civilians involved, however. Their ability to manage their natural physiological responses is much lower. Thus, the Branch Davidians' fearful and threatening responses to the presence of media helicopters overhead (911.3: 24ff.) and to armed ATF agents reentering the Mount Carmel property to remove injured agents (911.2: 11–20) can be traced in part to changes in their physiological states.

The deaths and injuries sustained by individuals on both sides of the barricade also had profound social implications. The ATF agents, no less than the Mount Carmel residents, were members of a tightly knit community. The death of any police officer has social and psychological repercussions that reverberate throughout the law enforcement community. The loss of four agents in a single incident was a devastating blow to the ATF, and responses of grief and anger over their deaths complicated the establishment of a barricade-negotiation situation. The Mount Carmel residents were also trying to make sense of the deaths of their community members. Furthermore, because of his injuries, the acknowledged leader of the community was sometimes unavailable to talk with negotiators.

There were problems with the communication systems on both sides of the barricade. Some problems were caused by equipment failure. Others were the result of negligence, as when the ATF left their communication station unmonitored. In the early hours of negotiation, while they were trying to arrange for the evacuation of injured ATF agents from the Mount Carmel property, Lynch was on one phone with Wayne Martin while on another phone with the ATF communications center. Personnel in the ATF communications center failed to respond to Lynch on numerous occasions. Meanwhile, Koresh and Steve Schneider were in periodic, but irregular, communication with the ATF via another phone line, and Koresh was making calls to the media on a cellular phone that was plagued by failing batteries.

Without clear lines of communication, it was extremely difficult to establish the roles and relationships necessary to negotiate even the most pressing problems, such as the removal of the wounded ATF agents from the Mount Carmel property. Judging from the transcripts of the 911 tapes, both parties wanted to evacuate the agents as quickly as possible. However, mutual mistrust complicated the negotiations. The ATF would not send unarmed personnel onto the Mount Carmel property. Koresh and others in the center feared the ATF would use the recovery of the wounded agents as a cover for another attack. The ATF and community members each attributed the delays in getting medical aid to the wounded agents to the other party's lack of cooperation, which set the stage for continued suspicion and mistrust between the parties.

The violence of the raid also severely damaged any previous working relationship between Mount Carmel and the ATF. Koresh and other Mount Carmel residents claimed during the negotiations that they had known about the ATF investigation and knew the identity of the undercover agent who had been attending Bible studies with the community.[10] Koresh thought he had made clear his willingness to talk with the ATF[11] and felt betrayed by the raid. For their part, the ATF agents were shocked by the violence of the Mount Carmel community's response to their effort to serve a legal and valid search-and-arrest warrant.

In spite of these problems, the Mount Carmel residents and the ATF (with the help of other police agencies) managed to establish a relatively stable barricade situation. The wounded agents were removed from the Mount Carmel property, and the wounded residents were offered medical care on the condition that they leave the property, which they refused to do. By the time the FBI negotiators arrived, authority and responsibility for the negotiations had shifted from Lynch to the ATF. The task of building relationships based on empathy and trust between the police and the barricaded subjects had commenced under the direction of ATF agent Jim Cavanaugh. Indeed, Cavanaugh

10. For evidence that others in the Mount Carmel community were aware of the undercover operation, see the testimony of David Thibodeau (Judiciary 174) and his more complete account in Thibodeau and Whiteson 1999, 142–46.

11. The 1995 congressional hearings contain extensive testimony that Koresh offered to talk with ATF agents about any alleged violations and invited the ATF to visit Mount Carmel to examine the community's weapons and property. The ATF did not act on the offer, which was made through Henry McMahon, a firearms dealer who dealt with Koresh (Judiciary 163), and confirmed by ATF agents (Judiciary 262).

was so successful in building positive relations with Koresh and Schneider that they resisted the move to hand over negotiating responsibility to the FBI (Tapes 4 and 5).

Fifty-one Days of Negotiations

The material boundaries had been established, and the social relationships were being constructed. In the symbolic world, however, the FBI and the Mount Carmel residents were in profound disagreement over the problem they confronted.

> What the FBI viewed as a complex Hostage/Barricade rescue situation drawn directly from their Crisis Management Program strategy manual, Koresh and the Branch Davidians saw as the beginning of the end of the world. Although there was conversation back and forth between Mount Carmel and the government agents during the prolonged standoff, neither side proved willing or even capable of bridging the great gulf between those two very different understandings of the situation. (Tabor and Gallagher 1995, 99–100)

I agree with Tabor and Gallagher regarding the presence of a very large "gulf of misunderstanding" separating the Branch Davidians and the FBI. However, I would say the situation was more complex than Tabor and Gallagher describe. There were, after all, negotiation successes during the fifty-one days of conversations, and the successes demand explanation no less than the ultimate breakdown of negotiations. Based on careful analysis, I argue that the Waco transcripts and other documents indicate that some FBI negotiators creatively attempted to adapt their negotiation strategies to the Waco situation. I also find evidence in the transcripts to support the claim that the Branch Davidians and some FBI negotiators made efforts, some of which were successful, to bridge the "gulf of misunderstanding" that plagued the negotiations. An analysis of the transcripts that is informed by a theory of worldview conflict can explain a great deal about the outcome of the negotiations in Waco. Furthermore, such a case study can yield generalizable lessons regarding the management, resolution, and transformation of worldview differences during negotiation processes.

An Overview of the Waco Negotiations

The negotiations in Waco can be broken down into three phases, each phase marked by the dominant negotiation strategy employed by the parties.

Phase One (February 28-March 4): Bargaining

This relatively short period was marked by extremely intense interactions between the parties, both in terms of the number of hours they were engaged in conversation and the sense of urgency conveyed in their conversations. If we judge solely by the number of negotiation accomplishments, the bargaining phase was the most successful period during the fifty-one-day standoff. It was also one of the most disappointing for the FBI negotiators. The Branch Davidians and law enforcement agents negotiated a cease-fire, arranged for the evacuation of the dead and wounded ATF agents, and began negotiating to end the standoff. All of this was accomplished on February 28. By March 3, the parties had cooperated in removing twenty-one children from Mount Carmel. Tragically, these children were the only ones who left Mount Carmel during the entire fifty-one days of negotiation. On the other hand, the negotiations faltered when an agreement to "trade" the national broadcast of a one-hour sermon by Koresh for the immediate surrender of the entire Mount Carmel community collapsed because Koresh announced that God had told him to wait. The community, according to Koresh's vision, was not to surrender until further instructions from God. By March 3, FBI spokespersons were expressing deep disappointment with Koresh's "betrayal" of the negotiated agreement, and the conversations between the Branch Davidians and the FBI negotiators reflected increasing tensions and communication difficulties.

When the planned surrender failed to materialize, the Branch Davidians tried to explain why they *could not* leave Mount Carmel until God told them to do so. After a period of intense debate (March 2–4), both parties adopted persuasive strategies.

Phase Two (March 5–15): Persuasion

Both parties introduced more persuasive tactics during phase two. Unfortunately, neither party found the other very persuasive.

The FBI organized their persuasive efforts around the following themes. Convince the parents who had sent their children out that they were needed on the outside by their children (Justice 129). Continue reassuring the Mount Carmel residents that they would be treated fairly if they came out (Justice, 129). Use the twice daily press conferences both to reassure the Branch Davidians of fair treatment and to use psychology to get the Branch Davidians to doubt Koresh's leadership (Justice 129). Negotiate with Steve Schneider and try to drive a wedge between Koresh and his "second in command" (Justice 129). Entice Koresh to come out by implying weaknesses in the case against him and discussing the opportunities he would have to expand his following and to promote his views through book and movie deals (Justice 129).

During phase two, the Mount Carmel residents increased their resistance to the FBI's original bargaining framework while also adopting a persuasive strategy of their own. One part of their strategy involved "sharing their message" with the agents in order to convince them that the Branch Davidians were telling the most important truth the world had ever heard. Koresh announced, "God has strengthened me for this one last thing, for one last opportunity, and that is for you and all of the agents and all of these individuals who are risking their, not just their carnal lives, but the lives hereafter, [to hear His message]" (Tape 26: 6). The second part of their persuasive strategy involved trying to convince the FBI that bargaining was not the correct way to frame their negotiation encounter. As part of this persuasive strategy, the Branch Davidians became less cooperative with the bargaining process that the FBI was promoting.

Difficulties arose during phase two because the FBI was never fully committed to a *balanced* persuasive negotiation process. They did not feel obligated to listen to the Branch Davidians' persuasive arguments regarding the appropriate negotiation process, and they were even less interested in listening to the Branch Davidians' persuasive argument about the End Time. Although individual negotiators made a concerted effort during phase two to understand the

Branch Davidian worldview and to craft arguments that would make sense to the Mount Carmel residents, these attempts were sporadic. The negotiation team did not engage in a systematic effort to map and understand the Branch Davidian worldview as it was made manifest during the negotiations. Nor did they clearly analyze the Branch Davidians' proposed process of "diplomatic negotiations" in place of bargaining. Instead, the official negotiation posture was based on using persuasion and influence to convince the Mount Carmel residents to participate in the FBI's original strategy of bargaining.

By March 15, the exchanges between the FBI negotiators and the residents of Mount Carmel resembled a dialogue of the deaf between two street corner preachers; each on his own corner, shouting at the apostate on the other corner in an effort to convert him to the one true faith. Frustrated with this impasse, the on-scene commander ordered the FBI negotiators to stop listening to Koresh's "Bible babble" and to get the negotiations refocused on substantive issues amenable to bargaining.

It was also during phase two of the negotiations that the now infamous disagreements between the tactical units and the negotiators became most problematic. Standard crisis negotiation procedures require the careful coordination of negotiation efforts with such tactical activities as cutting off the electricity, using psychological pressure tactics, and moving tactical units closer to the barricaded subject. This coordination broke down in Waco, and the mixed nature of the messages being sent to the Branch Davidians became more apparent during phase two. By March 15, the balance between coercion and persuasion had tipped in the direction of coercion.

Phase Three (March 16-April 18): Coercion Meets
Obstinate Resistance

This period was marked by an escalation of coercive tactical measures and increased intolerance among the negotiators for what they considered the Branch Davidians' "nonsensical" language. Ironically, this was also the period during which the negotiators experimented with unusual and creative negotiation processes. They allowed face-to-face negotiations with Steve Schneider and Wayne Martin on the Mount Carmel property, tried to use the local sheriff and Koresh and Schneider's defense attorneys as third-party intermediaries, and permitted the defense attorneys to enter Mount Carmel. All three of these activities were deviations from standard barricade negotiation procedures. All three experimental efforts had the potential to work well with a barricaded community motivated by unconventional beliefs. Unfortunately, inappropriate tactical maneuvers cut short or undermined such efforts. Furthermore, the negotiators never fully committed to the most creative and potentially useful third-party intermediary options made available during this period. The negotiators sent an audiotape prepared by biblical scholars Phil Arnold and James Tabor into Mount Carmel, but refused Koresh's request to speak directly with Tabor and Arnold. Of all of the potential intermediaries, Tabor and Arnold were the two who most clearly "spoke the language" of the Mount Carmel community (Carstarphen 1995).

The pace of negotiations, measured in terms of the number of hours per day spent in direct conversation, decreased significantly during the third phase. The Branch Davidians were more focused on discerning God's will than on engaging in negotiations with people who refused to take them seriously. They also set negotiations aside during their traditional Passover observances. The end of Passover was a time of great hope for the community because Koresh announced that God had instructed him to translate the Seven Seals of the Book of Revelation, a long-awaited event in the Mount Carmel community. Koresh assured everyone that after he had translated the Seven Seals, the entire community would exit Mount Carmel and surrender to authorities.

Unfortunately, the FBI neither shared in the Branch Davidians' hope nor believed that their hope was authentic. The Branch Davidians' inconsistent participation in negotiations (as defined by the FBI) annoyed the agents, and the glacial pace of the negotiations had already frustrated them. Their frustration was increased by confusion over the surrender plans. The defense attorneys had announced that the Branch Davidians would surrender immediately following Passover, thereby raising expectations among the FBI agents. Then on April 14, Koresh announced a "new revelation" directing him to translate the Seven Seals *before* surrendering to authorities. Given their heightened expectations, Koresh's promise to surrender felt to the negotiators like one more delaying tactic rather than a significant breakthrough. Consequently, the FBI commanders and negotiators did not take Koresh seriously when he said he was working on the translation.

A shift toward ever more coercive negotiation practices (e.g., bullying, be-rating, and debating) occurred toward the end of phase three. In keeping with common practice in a crisis negotiation, tactical commanders had been explor-ing options for a nonnegotiated solution to the standoff even as the negotiators were engaged in efforts to bargain with and persuade the Branch Davidians. On April 12, FBI officials in Washington met with Attorney General Janet Reno to brief her on their proposed plan to insert CS gas into Mount Carmel, thereby forcing the residents to exit. Between April 12 and April 18, the nego-tiators continued to talk with the Branch Davidians, encouraging Koresh to complete the Seven Seals and arranging to supply him with necessary equip-ment such as a typewriter ribbon. Meanwhile, the FBI commanders and HRT were making plans for the April 19 tactical operation that resulted in the final conflagration in which seventy-four Branch Davidians died.

2

Understanding Worldview Conflicts

IDENTIFYING PARTICULAR CONFLICTS as worldview based rather than interest based is akin to a first-time museum visitor's distinguishing French impressionist paintings from those of the Dutch masters. Unlike the uninitiated museum visitor, a person trained in art appreciation can explain the differences between schools of painting. If practitioners of conflict resolution want to move beyond the stage of simply "knowing a worldview conflict when they see one," they must articulate a conceptual model of worldviews and worldview conflicts.

"Conceptual models which, in simplified and therefore comprehensible form, try to represent certain aspects of reality are basic in any attempt at theory" (von Bertalanffy 1968, 200). I would probably be a bit less grandiose than von Bertalanffy in making claims about representing reality. However, I agree that developing and presenting to others a conceptual model of worldview conflict is a useful exercise. First, the discipline of thinking analytically and systematically about a set of related concepts and questions helps clarify my own story about the world of conflict. Readers can then decide whether my story resonates with their own experience. Second, building a conceptual model of worldview conflict directs attention to specific "component parts" of the total system of ideas. These parts can then be worked into a coherent research project examining the data from Waco. By bringing *an* order (not *the* order) to the ideas about worldview conflict, a conceptual model imposes discipline on the researcher and the research design process. To develop a conceptual model of worldview conflict, we need to identify the features or characteristics peculiar to those conflicts. It makes sense to begin by clarifying the term *worldview*.

Developing a Model of Worldviews
and Worldview Conflict

A worldview is not a thing. The term *worldview* denotes a *concept* that at-tempts to articulate the consequences of human activities that are individual as well as collective, psychological as well as social. Goodman (1978) comes closest to this active understanding of worldview when he talks about world-making. Having made the distinction between a "thingified" conceptual term and the activities to which it refers, I should also note that *worldview* is not the only noun used to reference the activities I want to discuss. Worldviews have also been called cosmologies (Douglas 1996), cognitive maps (Laszlo et al. 1993), images (Boulding 1956), mindscapes (Maruyama 1992), symbolic uni-verses (Berger and Luckmann 1966), world hypotheses (Pepper 1961), as-sumptive worlds (Frank 1973), moral orders (Pearce and Littlejohn 1997), or just plain worlds (Goodman 1978).

Worldview is not only a noun attempting to capture actions; it is also a con-cept that challenges many of the defining categories of modern life. *Worldview-ing* is a process that defies the contemporary separation of individual and social phenomena. Hence, many scholars—including psychologists, anthropologists, sociologists, political scientists, and religious studies experts—study the ongo-ing processes of worldview formation, maintenance, and revision. Worldview-ing encompasses cognitive (psychological) processes such as categorization, boundary establishment, and the creation and use of scripts or schema. World-views are validated through intersubjective (social) processes of meaning nego-tiation. Worldviewing is a universal activity, even though worldviews differ significantly from one community to another.

Temporarily conceding the use of a noun to describe actions, let me return to the question: What is a worldview? Nudler defines a worldview as a complex "entity" that includes the following interrelated elements:

- An *ontology*—or a theory about the nature of what exists in the universe.
- A *theory of world order*—or beliefs about how what exists (the elements in the universe) relate to each other.
- An *axiology*—or a value theory about which parts of the universe are more or less important than other parts.

• An *epistemology*—or beliefs about how and to what extent it is possible to know about what exists (Nudler 1993, 4)

Palmer says *worldview* "refers to the fundamental cognitive orientation of a society, a subgroup, or even an individual" (1996, 113). Then he adds that a worldview "encompasses natural philosophy . . . fundamental existential and normative postulates or themes . . . values (often conflicting), emotions, and ethics; it includes conventional cognitive models of persons, spirits and things in the world, and of sequences of actions and events; it includes social scenarios and situations, together with their affective values, contingencies and feeling states" (1996, 114). With the exception of "action scripts," Nudler's definition captures Palmer's ideas in a more concise form.

Keeping in mind that "a world view has all the complexity of life itself" (Palmer 1996, 114), and focusing on worldviewing actions, I suggest that in order to delineate any worldview (including our own), we need to know how the person or group under scrutiny answers the following questions.

• What is real or true? (*Ontology*)
• How is "the real" organized? (*Logic*)
• What is valuable or important? (*Axiology*)
• How do we know about what is? (*Epistemology*)
• How should I or we act? (*Ethic*)

Again, there are problems with this definition. First, we can never fully "know" anyone's worldview, including our own. The questions listed above are answered in the unconscious more than in the conscious mind. They are *lived* answers rather than articulated principles or formulas. Second, worldviewing activities take place in dialogue with the *context* within which people live. Changes in context raise new, different, and previously uncontemplated problems that may lead people to alter their worldviews. Therefore, worldviews are usefully thought of as emergent and dynamic systems. They are also best studied by looking at people's unreflective actions and unconsciously chosen language, rather than at their deliberately crafted statements of values, opinions, and ideologies. In chapter 3, I demonstrate ways to "reveal" the worldviews of two communities (the Branch Davidians and the FBI negotiators) by analyzing their stories and institutionalized practices. First, however, I want to consider the connections between worldviews and conflict.

In keeping with my earlier emphasis on worldviewing rather than on world-views, I find it useful to think of people as managing worldviews rather than as sharing worldviews. "People do not simply 'have' beliefs"; they "think *in groups*, from a particular *perspective or mindset*" (McGee 1984, quoted in Pearce and Lit-tlejohn 1997, 52, emphasis in original). So, too, people do not have worldviews; they collaborate with others to view or make the worlds in which they live. Therefore, every human interaction involves the management of worldviews.

When people limit their social encounters to other people raised in the same community or culture, worldview management is relatively simple. In the late twentieth century and early twenty-first century, however, few people live in cultural isolation. Contact with others who construct the world differently is becoming a routine human experience. Daily cross-cultural encounters or "border crossings" occur "around such lines as sexual orientation, gender, class, race, ethnicity, nationality, age, politics, dress, food, or taste" (Rosaldo 1989, 208), not to mention religion. These experiences challenge previously stable versions of reality. It is no longer easy for socially and politically dominant groups to maintain the double-sided illusion that they are "people without cul-ture," whereas those who occupy subordinate or marginal positions in society "have cultures" that mark them as different from the unmarked norm (Rosaldo 1989, 198).

Routine encounters with groups who do not share or who explicitly reject the dominant worldview direct our attention to the worldviewing activities by which *every* group constructs, maintains, and transforms its own commonsense version of the world. Everyone has culture; everyone engages in worldviewing. Or, more appropriately, everyone engages in *worldmaking*. Like Goodman, I am "not speaking in terms of multiple possible alternatives to a single actual world but of multiple actual worlds" (1978, 2). Therefore, the problem presented by worldviewing differences is not one of reconciling competing more or less accurate world versions with the "real" world. The challenge of our time is learning how to manage, negotiate, or navigate through multiple worlds.

In a world "crisscrossed by border zones, pockets, and eruptions of all kinds" (Rosaldo 1989, 207), the impact of worldviews on social conflict demands at-tention. People who engage in cultural border crossings manage their world-view differences and similarities more or less successfully and with little or no fanfare every day. The tacit processes by which people manage their worldview differences and similarities become visible when they *fail*, rather than when they succeed.

Conflicts, then, may be classified according to how well the parties accomplish the task of worldview management (fig. 3). Some conflicts involve parties who start with very similar worldviews or successfully manage their differences. In other conflicts, parties start with divergent worldviews and succeed partially in managing those differences. Finally, there are those conflicts in which the parties appear to occupy incommensurate worlds. They start with dissimilar worldviews and never achieve a workable worldview détente. Furthermore, these conflicts become self-sustaining. The more contact the parties have with one another, the more focused they become on their differences (Druckman and Zechmeister 1973, 450; Pearce and Littlejohn 1997, 68–70).

Because the negotiation of worldview differences and similarities is an ongoing process, parties in protracted and complicated conflicts may manage some of their worldview difficulties better than others. Consequently, they may appear to move up and down the scale of worldview divergence illustrated in figure 3. We can hypothesize that parties with divergent worldviews who are embroiled in a protracted conflict are able to reach agreement on specific issues when they effectively manage their worldview differences and similarities. When parties have not adequately managed their worldview differences and similarities, even the smallest problem can block agreement.

Worldviewing and Conflict Resolution

Acknowledging the presence of worldviewing in all conflict encounters directs attention to typically unconscious "negotiations over reality." Thus, worldviewing can be incorporated into a conceptual model of conflict resolution by separating "negotiating reality" from "issue-specific negotiations" (fig. 4.). Parties who successfully manage their worldview differences are able to participate effectively in processes such as negotiation, mediation, facilitated problem solving, or other efforts to promote the cooperative management, resolution, or transformation of a specific conflict. Parties who fail to manage their worldview differences must divert attention to negotiating reality rather than to solving an immediate problem. In most cases, parties move back and forth between the two activities without being aware of the interrelated processes.

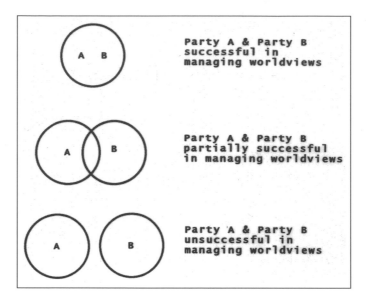

Party A & Party B
successful in
managing worldviews

Party A & Party B
partially successful
in managing worldviews

Party A & Party B
unsuccessful in
managing worldviews

3. Managing worldviews during conflict.

Moore's concepts of consensual and dissensual conflict can be adapted to the nested model of negotiating reality and issue-specific negotiation just described. Interest-based (consensual) conflicts are marked by "a consensus . . . between parties about competition for the desired end result" (Moore 1996, 215). The parties agree that the conflict is about distributing scarce resources and agree that "enough different interests exist to facilitate a trading process to minimize losses on all sides" (Moore 1996, 215). From a social constructionist perspective, we would say the parties have negotiated a reality that supports their efforts at issue-specific negotiation. From a worldview conflict perspective, we would say the parties are successfully managing their worldviewing differences and similarities, and can therefore engage in interest-based negotiation. Value (dissensual) disputes, on the other hand, "focus on such issues as guilt and innocence, what norms should prevail in a social relationship, what facts should be considered valid, what beliefs are correct, who merits what, and what principles should guide decision makers" (Moore 1996, 215). Parties involved in dissensual conflict may have immediate issues that need to be handled. However, their dissensual conflict is indicative of a failure to nego-

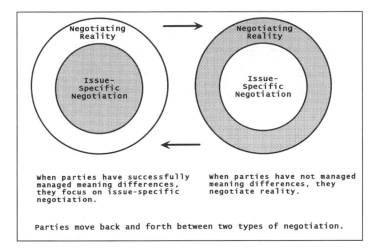

4. Issue-specific negotiation occurs within a negotiated reality.

tiate a reality adequate to support interest-based negotiation or joint problem solving. In no case can issue-specific negotiation or the management of consensual conflict take place outside of a negotiated reality. The management of consensual conflict is dependent on the management of dissensual conflict. Yet researchers, theorists, and practitioners of conflict resolution routinely ignore crucial aspects of managing dissensual conflict such as problem definition and agenda setting. Authors who focus most directly on explaining processes for resolving conflicts usually do not discuss problem identification and definition (Hocker and Wilmot 1995; Mitchell and Banks 1996; Pruitt and Carnevale 1993). Nor is the topic of apparent concern to those who explain how to design dispute or conflict management systems (Blake and Mouton 1984; Costantino and Merchant 1996; Ury, Brett, and Goldberg 1989). The impression is that negotiation, mediation, and other conflict resolution processes take place within an uncontested, given reality. When these authors do address the need to identify and define a problem in need of resolution, they speak as though these reality-defining processes occur prior to and outside of the issue-specific negotiation process.

Thinking of negotiating reality and issue-specific negotiation as simultaneous, interpenetrating processes permits researchers and practitioners to formulate critical questions. For example, how successfully do parties need to negotiate reality in order to engage effectively in issue-specific conflict resolution processes? Do parties negotiate reality even when they are engaged in issue-specific negotiations? If so, do some subprocesses of negotiation demand a more stable worldview détente than others? For example, is it possible for parties to negotiate reality while searching for an arena, defining issues, and setting the agenda, but less possible for them to negotiate reality while engaged in bargaining?

To anyone familiar with negotiated order theory, figure 4 will appear rather commonplace. Negotiated order theory, associated with the work of Strauss (1978), examines "the interpretive nature of multiple realities in organizing, and the dual relation between organizational structure and ongoing interactions among individuals in organizations" (Geist 1995, 48). Particular negotiation encounters, such as labor-management negotiations or negotiations between nurses and doctors over patient care, are studied as interactions that occur within an organizational structure that is itself a *negotiated order*. Negotiated order theory attempts to demonstrate that structures and institutionalized roles, rules, and regulations constrain individual action even though such structures are simultaneously maintained, transformed, and (re-)created through human interaction.

My dual model of negotiation has much in common with negotiated order theory as it has been applied to the study of organizations. However, it would, I believe, be a mistake to conclude that figure 4 is nothing but a picture of negotiated order theory. Negotiated order and negotiated reality are not identical concepts, and researchers using negotiated order theory to frame research projects have been forced to stretch their concepts to incorporate competing realities.

Negotiating reality forces people to address their ontological and epistemological differences, whereas negotiating order involves reaching agreement on roles, rules, and relationships. A negotiated reality may be implicit in the negotiated order of an organization or community, but the negotiation of reality has not been the focus of negotiated order theory research. Only recently have scholars started to question the negotiations of *meaning* by which structural contexts (the social world) and negotiation contexts (organizations) are established in the first place. They are beginning to ask, "[W]hose order is being negotiated" (Geist 1995), and what organizational constraints prohibit some conflicts from ever reaching negotiation (Littlejohn 1995)? Their conclusions are not surprising. Within organizations, conflicts over meaning tend to be repressed and marginalized. "Moral differences are covered up by the hegemony of dominant moral orders, in which less powerful groups, who may have opposing ideologies are marginalized or silenced" (Littlejohn 1995, 102). The fact that some negotiated order researchers are beginning to look at these questions is an important development. However, it is not clear that negotiated order theory can encompass these new problems and issues without radically stretching the core concepts on which the theory is based. As long as the focus is on *order*, there may be a built-in bias toward the assumption that order involves the imposition of a single, hegemonic worldview.

In the larger social arena, worldview conflicts are even more complicated. The same repressive forces at work inside organizations operate in this arena to negate the worldview challenges offered by marginalized social groups. For example, the media proffer an oversimplified and inaccurate picture of all Citizen Militia and Patriot groups as "nuts in the woods with guns" or white supremacist hate mongers. In Europe, farmers and workers who have reservations about the European Union are dismissed as "economic Luddites." In both cases, people with an alternate naming of the world discover there is no established forum within which to raise their concerns. Groups whose alternative worldviews are repressed may withdraw into isolated enclaves, or they may engage in illegal activities as a means of protest. Even those who choose isolation may discover that their alternative lifestyle engenders negative responses from society at large. When marginalized social groups that are pushing to raise worldviewing issues finally do get the attention of leaders, it is often within the context of a crisis. Farmers confront police in France, and the Freemen face off with the FBI in Montana. For the police, managing the crisis is supposed to be an exercise in minimizing violence while moving the discussion into a more appropriate forum. The FBI in Montana and the police in France seek to move the parties into their respective court system, only to discover that the protesters consider the courts to be part of a reality that needs to be renegotiated. Similarly, the Branch Davidians did not question simply the negotiated *order* by which the courts would operate if they surrendered to the legal system. They questioned the very legitimacy of the courts, and they did so on the basis of an alternate naming of reality.

Recognizing that people negotiate reality and not just organizational order points to the formidable power associated with *naming* a problem or conflict. Participants in issue-specific conflict management practices need to address the exercise of problem-naming power. Yet this activity falls outside the traditional parameters of issue-specific negotiation. Naming a problem as worthy of issue-specific negotiation—that is, getting a problem or conflict on the agenda—is an exercise in negotiating reality. It is not simply a question of negotiating institutional or organizational relationships and rules. Problem naming or agenda setting is a much-neglected issue with important implications for handling worldview conflicts.

Naming the conflict is only one example of the way negotiating reality impacts issue-specific negotiation. How do we begin to articulate the processes of worldviewing and the impact of worldviewing on conflict dynamics? Once parties with divergent worldviews are embroiled in a conflict, how do their negotiations of reality impact their issue-specific negotiations? We must attempt to answer these questions when constructing a conceptual model of worldview conflict.

Narrative and Conflict

People do not walk around with their worldviews plastered to their foreheads. We cannot simply ask someone involved in a conflict, "What is your worldview, and how does it impact your stated position?" So how do we recognize a worldview conflict, and how do people manage their worldview differences and similarities? How do they negotiate reality? Narrative is one essential expression of worldviewing, and worldview conflicts are marked by competing and ostensibly irreconcilable stories.

The field of conflict analysis and resolution is built on the premise that "conflict is a natural and inevitable part of all human social relationships. . . . Conflict is not deviant, pathological, or sick behavior *per se*" (Laue 1987, 17). From an etic or outsider's perspective, this may be an accurate statement about the nature of social systems. From an emic or insider's perspective, conflict is experienced as an extraordinary "breach of regular, norm-governed social rela-tions" (Turner 1974, 38). Perhaps it is useful for third-party intervenors and those interested in cultivating the positive, creative aspects of conflict to argue that "conflict is not the opposite of order" (Laue 1987, 17). When trying to un-derstand the behavior of parties involved in a conflict, however, we must not forget that they experience their circumstances as a violation of established order.

When a breach of social norms occurs in a public arena and is "seen as the ex-pression of a deeper division of interests and loyalties than appears on the sur-face" (Turner 1981, 146), a crisis ensues. The crisis escalates and expands. "Sides are taken, factions are formed, and unless the conflict can be sealed off quickly within a limited area of social interaction, there is a tendency for the breach to widen and spread until it coincides with some dominant cleavage in the widest set of relevant social relations to which the parties in conflict belong" (Turner 1981, 146). Anthropologists have documented the many ways that social groups attempt to repair a breach of norms and reintegrate the group (Avruch, Black, and Scimecca 1991; Gulliver 1979; Turner 1974; Watson-Gegeo and White 1990). During a crisis, group leaders mobilize formal and informal "adjus-tive and redressive mechanisms" in efforts first to halt expansion of the breach and then to reintegrate the social group (Turner 1981, 147). However, opposi-tion leaders may emerge to resist reintegration, and the consequence of a breach of norms may be either reintegration of the group or schism. If reintegrated, the group may have undergone a number of significant changes as a result of the cri-sis. If the final result is schism, the group splits into two or more new groups.

The adjustive and redressive mechanisms mobilized in response to a breach of social norms are material, social, and symbolic. To understand the impact of worldviewing on parties caught up in a social conflict, we must examine all three types of resources. For example, Iraq's invasion of Kuwait was a breach in the norm-governed social relations between nations. After the Iraqi transgres-sion, the international community had three basic response options—diplo-matic negotiations, economic sanctions, and military engagement. Each option required the mobilization of different material, social, and symbolic resources, and each option required careful coordination of multiple actors. How did the community of nations collectively settle on military engagement as the "cor-rect" response to the Iraqi breach of norms?

The coordination of a cooperative multinational military response was possible only after the international community arrived at a shared explanation for the breach and a common understanding of what was required to reintegrate the community of nations. People name a conflict and coordinate responses to a breach of norms by employing rhetoric. Rhetoric, or "the use of symbolic means of inducing cooperation in beings that by nature respond to symbols" (Burke 1969b, 43), takes many forms. Narrative is among the most powerful forms of rhetoric, and war rhetoric relies very heavily on storytelling to mobilize popular support. President Bush garnered domestic and international support for a military response to the invasion of Kuwait by using a "terrorist narrative" to reframe "the Persian Gulf conflict from a conventional military confrontation to a fight against terrorism" (Winkler 1995, 36).[1] The terrorist narrative negated Iraqi claims that they had legitimate grievances against Kuwait and made the Iraqi leadership solely responsible for the hostilities. It also demonized Saddam Hussein by portraying him as a rogue menace to world order, legitimated the role of the United States as protector of an innocent hostage/victim (Kuwait), and justified Bush's refusal to negotiate with and offer concessions to Iraq. Once the public validated the terrorist narrative, there was a remarkable shift in public opinion regarding the need for military action against Iraq (Winkler 1995, 43, 45, 47).

Why, after trying out a number of different rationales for intervention in the Persian Gulf crisis, did Bush succeed in mobilizing support by using the terrorist narrative? Clearly the *content* of the narrative held appeal for the public, but some of the appeal also had to do with the narrative *form* of the argument. Because all conflicts are experienced as violations of established social norms, they evoke stories (Augsburger 1992; Avruch 1991; Black 1991; Lederach 1995; Watson-Gegeo and White 1990; White 1991). According to Bruner, "when you encounter an exception to the ordinary, and ask somebody what is happening, the person you ask will virtually always tell a story that contains *reasons* (or some other specification of an intentional state)" (1990, 49, emphasis in original). Storytelling helps people make sense of the unusual by explaining the intentions of the actors and describing "a possible world in which the en-

1. For an alternate but not incompatible analysis of Bush's rhetorical use of narrative during the Persian Gulf crisis, see Lakoff's examination of the fairy tale of the just war (1992).

countered [exceptional behavior] is somehow made to make sense or to have 'meaning' " (Bruner 1990, 49). In other words, a story ascribes motive and intent to the actors and describes a world in which those attributed intentions make sense. During periods of conflict, telling stories helps people *name* the conflict, ascribe *blame* for the conflict-causing breach, and *frame* appropriate and inappropriate responses to the conflict.

How do people coordinate their stories about a conflict? Bormann uses the unfortunate term *fantasy* to describe the stories people weave to explain events as the consequence of "people with certain personality traits and motivations making decisions, taking action, and causing things to happen" (1996, 89). Using Bormann's concept, Bush's terrorist narrative was a fantasy that attributed the Persian Gulf crisis to Saddam Hussein's evil intentions and deviant personality. The dramatic quality of fantasies evokes in the audience an emotional response and a sense of involvement. They are invited to identify with the hero and to denigrate (blame) the villain. When people share a fantasy, they experience "symbolic convergence." They see the world in the same way. Symbolic convergence leads to shared motivations. People come to define (name) the problem the same way and to envision (frame) the same processes for responding to the problem. Symbolic convergence is necessary for cooperative action. Some stories promote symbolic convergence by dividing groups into heroes and villains, and such stories validate the coordination of the "millions of cooperative acts" that go into implementing the ultimate expression of human division, war (Burke 1969b, 22).

Worldview Conflicts and Narrative

Fisher offers the root metaphor *Homo narrans* as an extension of Burke's definition of "man" as the "symbol-using (symbol-making, symbol-misusing) animal" (W. Fisher 1987, 63). Human beings tell stories because it is in their nature to do so, and in telling stories they make their worlds. Stories guide the way people shape and reshape the material world. For example, the story of the forest as a farm led people to reshape the forest itself through practices such as clear-cutting and monocultural replanting. "Stories are symbolic actions that draw upon and define social reality" (Sillars 1991, 154). Thus, the forest as a farm story also provided a conceptual foundation upon which to build social institutions such as the Forest Service and schools of forestry. Narrative, then, interpenetrates all three worlds: the material, the social, and the symbolic.

When stories are told and retold by many people—as opposed to idiosyncratic stories recounted by one person—they become the symbolic cores around which organizations, communities, and civilizations shape their collective lives. At the organizational level, stories may take the form of "organizational autobiographies" (Czarniawska 1997) that establish a negotiated order. At the community or societal level, shared stories become the "myths" or "grand narratives" (Hayles 1995) that define reality. Here, I am using the term *myth* "to denote stories that express in narrative form the central values of the society and the way it views what the world is and means" (Ellwood 1996, 8). This definition is strictly functional and does not judge the truth or fiction of a community's organizing narratives. In modern, secular societies, myth has become a tainted concept. Few people recognize that history, as taught in most schools and commemorated in public celebrations, fulfills a mythic function by providing "exemplary models for significant human activities" (Baird 1971, 78). Whether labeled myth or history, the central organizing narratives of any community connect past, present, and future generations by allowing a community to repeat and retrieve its common destiny (Polkinghorne 1988, 135). Thus, it is useful to think of the central organizing narratives of any community as *worldmaking stories*.

A worldmaking story expresses the authoritative claims of the community that legitimates it. In that respect, *all worldmaking stories, whether overtly sacred or ostensibly secular, function as myth or sacred narrative*. Claims about ultimate truth and authority are implicit in every worldmaking story. Viewed as a worldview conflict, Waco was a clash of ultimate authorities. The Mount Carmel residents brought an apocalyptic, biblically based worldmaking story to the negotiations. The FBI negotiators invoked a secular scientific story of "the way things really are." The different *types* of authority invoked by the Branch Davidians and the FBI should not, however, divert attention from the functional similarity of their worldmaking stories.

While I was working on this project, a colleague asked, "So, what *do* you do when one of the parties brings God to the negotiating table?" A better question is, "What do we do when the *parties* bring their *gods* to the table?" Using the term *gods* to mean something akin to one's "ultimate concern" or "ultimate authority," and examining the function of competing worldmaking stories, I argue that the FBI—no less than the Branch Davidians—brought their gods to the table.

With Baird, I am defining religion as the ultimate concern of an individual or group. An ultimate concern is "a concern which is *more important than anything else in the universe for the person involved*" (Baird 1971, 18, emphasis in original). Because this definition focuses on the human actors, we need not address the truth or importance of the object of ultimate concern. I am not interested in ascertaining which party brought "the one true God" to the table in Waco. I am interested in understanding the impact of ultimate concerns on negotiation processes. What happens to well-intentioned efforts to resolve conflict when the parties bring competing gods or apparently incommensurate ultimate concerns into the discussion? In moral or worldview conflicts, "actions that one side thinks will defuse the situation or even resolve the conflict are perceived by those on the other side as demonstrating the perfidy of the first and obligating them to respond by continuing or intensifying the conflict" (Pearce and Littlejohn 1997, 68). Or, in the words of another colleague, "When the gods get involved in human affairs, things get really messy."

The mess begins with the problem of identifying a conflict in the first place. Identifying a breach of norms is an interpretive process subject to negotiation. When communities telling divergent worldmaking stories meet, they lack a common authoritative base from which to identify a breach of norms. *Naming* a conflict becomes highly problematic. There are many cases in which one party—usually the less powerful—feels that a breach of norms has occurred, but the conflict never makes it onto the agenda. However, some breaches of normative relationships, such as the deadly encounter between ATF agents and the Mount Carmel community, are so blatant they demand recognition. Then the problem is deciding which (whose) norms were violated.

Even when conflicting parties agree that a particular event constitutes a breach of regular, norm-governed social relations, they may understand quite differently the norms that were violated. The parties develop competing *blaming* narratives to explain their current impasse—which is what happened in Waco.

Federal law enforcement agents portrayed the ATF raid and subsequent gun battle with the Mount Carmel residents as a violation of normative expectations regarding obedience to the law and peaceful cooperation with law enforcement officials. They described the Branch Davidians as a bizarre cult living a dangerous and deviant lifestyle. According to the agents, the Mount Carmel residents caused the breach when they violently resisted the *legitimate* exercise of police authority. The appropriate redressive and adjustive response was for the Branch Davidians to surrender to government authorities, have their day in court, and take whatever punishment they had coming.

The Branch Davidians, on the other hand, told a story of the February 28 raid in which the ATF violated normative expectations regarding individual liberty and limitations on the government's use of excessive force against its own citizens. By staging a military-style raid on a private residence, the ATF violated the spirit if not the letter of the *Posse Comitatus Act* of 1878.[2] According to the Mount Carmel residents, their resistance to the raid was a *legitimate* exercise of their right to self-defense. Surrendering to law enforcement officials and having their day in a court run by the same government guilty of violating established norms had little appeal for the Branch Davidians. Their rejection of (il)legal law enforcement authority was further complicated by their apocalyptic expectations. Believing themselves in the final days before the establishment of God's kingdom on earth, the Mount Carmel residents had little incentive to cooperate with secular authorities.

In each blaming narrative, there is also a *framing* story that delineates the narrator's proposals for resolving the current crisis. Framing stories carry indications of desired outcomes and descriptions of appropriate processes for managing the conflict. The framing stories offered by the parties are highly problematic in worldview conflicts. When a conflict occurs within a single community, tacit agreement about worldmaking stories facilitates the shared acceptance of blaming and framing stories, and the parties are able to frame a

2. The *Posse Comitatus Act*, which has become a rallying point for many groups concerned about the militarization of federal law enforcement, prohibits the use of the army (later extended to air force and navy) for purposes of domestic law enforcement. References to *posse comitatus* issues (i.e., misuse of military resources by law enforcement agencies) should not be confused with membership in Posse Comitatus organizations, which recognize no authority above the county level and have been associated with white supremacist movements (Barkun 1994b). Members of these organizations have come into regular, sometimes violent, conflict with federal authorities over taxes and weapons (Aho 1990; Corcoran 1990; Coulson and Shannon 1999, 192; Sargent 1995). The Mount Carmel community was not associated with an active Posse Comitatus group.

process for managing the conflict. If the process works effectively, the parties are able to agree on adjustive or redressive responses to the breach of norms that generated the conflict. If the process is ineffective, the community undergoes schism.

Framing the process for resolving the conflict in Waco was difficult because the conflict was *between communities;* the parties did not have a tacit agreement about appropriate blaming or framing narratives. For the federal agents, the proper resolution involved moving the Branch Davidians into the court system. There, they would face the original weapons possession charges and new charges related to the February 28 shoot-out. For the Mount Carmel residents, the proper resolution was less clearly defined. There was no institutionalized forum in which to address all of their concerns. They demanded a full investigation of the ATF actions on February 28, but remained unclear about whom they would trust to carry out such an investigation. On the other hand, they simply wanted the federal authorities to go away and leave them to continue their study of the Seven Seals and their preparation for the imminent end of the world. The February 28 raid was significant to them primarily as a harbinger of the Second Coming. God would resolve the conflict in His court, where He would sit in judgment. The U.S. government, the ATF, and the FBI would be the defendants.

When communities organized around divergent worldmaking narratives come into conflict, they have difficulty managing that conflict because each party finds the naming, framing, and blaming stories of the other party baffling or offensive. The parties look at the same event and name differently the breach of norms or source of conflict. Each party blames the other for the conflict. Each party acts in good faith to frame a conflict management process. Yet both parties misinterpret the peacemaking efforts of the other party, often taking goodwill gestures as conflict escalatory moves that obligate retaliation or a hardening of positions. In most cases, parties who are unsuccessful at signaling their willingness to talk never reach the negotiation table. Therefore, many parties experiencing difficulties with worldview management never engage in formal conflict resolution processes. What happens when—in spite of the problems associated with naming, framing, and blaming—parties who are troubled by worldview management problems are compelled by circumstances to engage in an issue-specific negotiation process? The Waco negotiation tapes provide a rare opportunity to observe parties trying to resolve an immediate problem while also attempting to cope with their naming, framing, and blaming differences.

Contending Narratives, Narrative Reason,
and Conflict Resolution

Some conflict resolution scholars and practitioners recognize the role of narrative in conflict resolution and the problem of power struggles between parties who wish to privilege one narrative over another. When multiple narratives are offered, they are often combined as frame and embedded narratives (Prince 1987, 25, 33). The frame narrative sets the parameters of discussion, and embedded narratives are constrained by those parameters. When a mediator invites the parties to tell their stories, there is a real risk that the first story told will create a *frame narrative* within which the other parties must speak. If one party in a conflict is allowed unilaterally to establish the frame narrative, the other parties are forced to compose embedded narratives that logically connect with the world created by the frame narrative. Cobb argues that in mediation the first speaker to tell a story does "more than just 'take their turn'—they construct the semantic and discursive space on which all subsequent speakers must stand by providing a set of coherent relations between plots, characters, and themes" (1993, 250). It is not coincidental that in almost 75 percent of a set of community mediation cases examined by Cobb and Rifkin (1991), the first story told framed the agreement.

The conflicting parties are not the only people who make worlds through narrative. The frame narratives of third-party intervenors can shape a conflict resolution process so as to exclude parties from the table. For example, efforts to apply collaborative planning to environmental conflicts are typically organized using a narrative about stakeholders and interest-based parties (Crowfoot and Wondolleck 1990; Susskind 1994; Susskind and Cruikshank 1987; Wondolleck 1988). The interest-based stakeholder narrative recognizes actors who hold discrete, quantifiable, instrumental interests. According to this frame narrative, legitimate actors in forest management conflicts may include timber-dependent communities, owners of sawmills, or backpackers who use the forest for recreational purposes. The forest itself is not recognized as a legitimate actor. Instead, the forest is defined as the scene within which actors move and upon which they act. Within the interest-based stakeholder narrative, stories connected to the "forest is a farm" metaphor are privileged over stories that incorporate the "planet is a living being" metaphor. Consequently, groups who want to include the forest as an actor find themselves excluded from collaborative-planning processes because third-party intervenors and the other parties consider them irrational. The internal logic, ontology, and epistemology of a story that includes the planet as a living being stand in opposition to the internal logic, ontology, and epistemology of stories that include the planet only as scene or setting for the actions of human or animal actors. When groups that advocate alternative naming, framing, and blaming stories are included in the collaborative decision-making process, they are marginalized by the requirement that they restructure their own stories to fit within the frame narrative.

Moving from the comparatively calm arenas of community mediation centers and environmental dispute resolution processes, we can see that the negotiations in Waco involved a variety of contested frame narratives. Furthermore, the power to name the world was not evenly distributed between the parties. The power imbalance in the symbolic world directly impacted the material and social outcomes in Waco, and the narrative power imbalance between the FBI and the Branch Davidians in Waco reflected a larger worldview conflict. The worldmaking stories that were told by the Mount Carmel community and the FBI negotiators can be thought of as specific manifestations of more comprehensive grand narratives. Although there were idiosyncratic elements in their story, Mount Carmel residents used themes taken from a rich and dynamic apocalyptic tradition when narrating their world. The FBI negotiators, on the other hand, used narrative themes and symbols from social science research, most notably psychology, to create and maintain their world. The encounter in Waco was not the first—nor will it be the last—confrontation between one group espousing a religious symbolic world and another advocating a secular-scientific symbolic world.

During the Waco standoff, the media, the federal authorities, and society at large privileged the secular-scientific symbolic world. So unbalanced was the power to define the world that some observers have cited Waco as evidence of the government's outright hostility to religion: "Throughout its history, the FBI has been as active in enforcing America's socio-religious orthodoxy as it has

been in pursuing actual dangerous criminals. . . . The State distrusts all loyalties other than to itself. Let a religion generally accede to the State's goals and
it will flourish; let it run crosswise to them, however innocently, and its adherents, like Antigone, will find that they have committed 'the crime of piety' "
(Clifton 1994, 3–4). Lawrence Sullivan, writing as an expert consultant for the
Department of Justice, was moved to ask, "Is the federal assault on this religious community near Waco, Texas, together with its ensuing standoff and fiery
end, emblematic of the trivialization of religion in official America?" (1993, 3).
Waco is a particularly violent example of conflict between a religious group and
secular authorities. This case, although shocking in its violence, also startled
many people by pitting a "fanatical" religious group against the "legitimate"
secular authorities inside the United States. In the minds of many, such a conflict was not supposed to happen in a "modern" society, and when it did happen, they were left without conceptual tools that would help them make sense
of the conflict.

3

When Worlds Collide

IN ORDER TO STUDY WACO as a worldview conflict, we need to avoid privileging the FBI's modern secular narrative over the Branch Davidians' religious narrative. The foundational narratives of the FBI and of the Mount Carmel residents must be treated as *functionally equivalent worldmaking stories*. Therefore, the "gods" of secular society must be uncovered and named—no easy task. Most of us are steeped in modern assumptions about knowledge and reason. "The adjective 'modern' designates a new regime, an acceleration, a rupture, a revolution in time. When the word 'modern,' and 'modernization,' or 'modernity' appears, we are defining, by contrast, an archaic and stable past," "a 'yesteryear' absolutely different from today" (Latour 1993, 10, 35). One of the greatest alleged differences between this yesteryear and the modern era is epistemological. The modern era was established when revealed (sacred) knowledge was replaced by scientific (secular) knowledge.

Religion and religious sensibilities could not be entirely banished from modern culture. However, the ancient gods, who were active in history, were replaced by a "crossed-out God" relegated to the private, spiritual domain (Latour 1993, 32–35). Waco was a confrontation between the Branch Davidians, for whom God acts in history, and FBI agents, for whom religion is an individual, private concern. For the Branch Davidians, the Waco standoff was a confrontation between God and the evil powers of a secular state that refused to be governed by God's law. For the FBI negotiators, the Waco standoff was a confrontation between the legitimate powers of the state and a group deluded by religious fervor or duped by a con man using religion as a cover for immoral and criminal activities.

Starting with the argument that the FBI and the Branch Davidians both brought their gods to the table forces us to confront the general failure among academics to subject modern society to the same type of scrutiny applied to allegedly primitive or premodern societies. Anthropologists study foreign collectives by tackling everything at once. They produce holistic portraits of societies that may include such diverse subjects as "the distribution of powers among human beings, gods, and nonhumans; the procedures for reaching agreements; the connections between religion and power; ancestors; cosmology; property rights; plant and animal taxonomies" (Latour 1993, 14). The study of modern society, on the other hand, is parceled out to the various social science disciplines. This division of labor confounds efforts to examine social phenomena that play out simultaneously in the symbolic, social, and material worlds.

Anthropologists holistically study conflict and disputing processes in other cultures. The study of conflict in modernized societies is typically divided among such disciplines as sociology, political science, public policy, international relations, peace studies, law, counseling, psychology, and organizational development. Anthropologists readily link interpersonal conflict and war by exposing the ways in which the members of a community transfer their symbolic representations of conflict between the interpersonal and the intergroup level (Boggs and Chun 1990). In contrast, those who study conflict in modern societies struggle to explain the connections between labor-management disputes and class conflict (Rubenstein 1993) or the relationship between a fight involving high school students of different races or ethnicities and societal-level racial conflicts (Dugan 1996). In the modern context, an effort to link structural explanations of conflict to interpretive explanations is greeted as a novel and difficult undertaking (Ross 1993a, 1993b).

It is tempting to conclude that conflict in modern society is different from that in premodern societies. However, the differences may have more to do with the manner in which researchers conceptually construct "conflict" and "society" in the modern and premodern settings than with any inherent distinction between modern and premodern experiences of conflict. To adopt a symmetrical approach when studying a conflict between a group with a secular worldview and a group with a religious worldview, we must assume that "if one is willing to study sacred spears and stones in archaic cultures, it is absurd to suggest that it is illegitimate to consider the religious significance of nationalism or defense systems for modern man" (Baird 1971, 26). Symbolic, world-making activities are as pervasive in secular modern societies as they were in re-ligious, premodern societies.

Just as premodern and modern societies are categorized separately and studied differently, so too are religion and science conceptually divided. Most contemporary scholars would agree that a religious system "is a cluster of sacred symbols, woven into some sort of ordered whole. . . . For those who are com-mitted to it, such a religious system *seems* to mediate genuine knowledge, knowledge of the essential conditions in terms of which life must, of necessity, be lived" (Geertz 1973, 129, emphasis added). By contrast, science is rarely thought of as a cluster of symbols woven into an ordered whole. Many people assume that science does not create worlds, but simply examines *the world* as it exists. For the most part, people in contemporary society have accepted the no-tion that "scientific discourse aspires to objectivity, but religious symbols are by nature participatory, enactive, involving [and] grounded in authoritative ac-counts of great foundational force that generate and govern the world" (Paden 1988, 69).

An evenhanded examination of the symbolic worlds of both the FBI and the Branch Davidians is derived from a symbolic realism (Brown 1989) that de-bunks the claim that religion is a meaning-making enterprise, whereas science is a truth-discovering enterprise. However much scientific discourse may aspire to objectivity, science is no less dependent than religion on "authoritative ac-counts of great foundational force that generate and govern the world." Thus, we can acknowledge that forestry, as an applied science, rests on a foundational forest-farm narrative. Gaia-inspired ecology rests on a foundational narrative that renames the environment as an actor rather than as a scenic element. The sense-making or worldmaking aspects of science and religion, however differ-ent their content and internal logic, are products of similar cognitive and social processes.

The faithful "citizens" of scientific-secular and religious symbolic worlds even respond similarly to "deviant" behavior and "heretical" truth claims. Ac-cording to Geertz, when religious symbols "are uncriticized, historically or philosophically, as they are in most of the world's cultures, individuals who ig-nore the moral-aesthetic norms the symbols formulate, who follow a discordant style of life, are regarded not so much as evil as stupid, insensitive, unlearned, or in the case of extreme dereliction, mad" (1973, 129). We can argue that David Koresh was called "the wacko from Waco" or "the Mad Man in Waco" (Bailey and Darden 1993) or "Vern [Howell, a.k.a. David Koresh], weird asshole" (Lewis 1994, xii) because he challenged an uncriticized secular-scientific symbolic world. In Java, "the insane and flagrantly immoral are . . . said to be . . . not yet human" (Geertz 1973, 129). The FBI treated the residents of the Mount Carmel community, particularly the women, as less than fully responsible adults. David Koresh and the Mount Carmel community ignored the symbolically formulated moral-aesthetic norms of modern society and lived a discordant lifestyle, so the FBI, the media, and the majority of the American people assumed they must be mad, deluded, and irrational.

Creating a Symmetrical Anthropology

To counteract the privileging of the FBI's modernist worldmaking narrative over the religious worldmaking narrative of the Branch Davidians, I am advocating a symmetrical anthropology. According to Latour, a symmetrical anthropology must be "capable of confronting not beliefs that do not touch us directly—we are always critical enough of them—but the true knowledge to which we adhere totally" (1993, 92). I propose building this symmetrical anthropology on the basis of worldview analysis, and I suggest looking to stories, taxonomies, metaphors, and institutionalized practices as carriers of both religious and secular worldviewing or worldmaking.

When narrative analysis is used to interpret the worldviewing of particular groups, it is helpful to distinguish different types of group stories. Foundational stories, which help a group establish its identity, can be thought of as organizational or group autobiographies. Groups also tell stories to explain the world as they experience it. Naming the self and naming the world are related activities, and these stories are often woven together. Individual and collective identities are formed through interaction with the world. If a person becomes a Branch Davidian, it is in response to a worldmaking story that establishes becoming a Branch Davidian as rational behavior.[1] Given a different worldnaming story,

---

1. My use of the word *become* begs the question of how one adopts, rejects, or accepts the worldview of one's birth community. Adult baptism, confirmation, and the Jewish bar mitzvah or

that person would become a Roman Catholic, an atheist, or a Buddhist. If a person becomes a negotiator with the FBI, it is in response to a naming of police work, crime, and criminology that validates becoming an FBI negotiator.

Other groups are a part of every community's world, and the stories a group tells about itself determine in large measure the stories it tells about other groups. If we believe that being a Branch Davidian is the morally correct response to an evil world, we will judge accordingly those who do not share this belief. If we believe that negotiating "rationally" is sensible behavior, we will deem irrational those people who do not negotiate within our definition of rationality.

Once groups have narrated the two-sided relationship between self and world (including other groups), they also develop stories that guide their actions in the world. These stories separate good from evil, effective from ineffective, and rational from irrational behaviors. The stories may differ in quality from group to group, but not in function. For example, the Branch Davidian action stories focus on issues of good and evil because their naming of the world and self directs attention to the problem of acting in a biblically righteous manner in an evil world. The FBI negotiators' action stories are more analytical in character, with the emphasis on determining effective, goal-oriented behavior that achieves a peaceful end to barricade standoffs.

Stories are complex expressions of a group's worldview, but other forms of language also carry worldviewing assumptions. For example, human groups make, negotiate, and communicate their worlds and their identities through categorization (Abrams 1990; Abrams and Hogg 1990; Baird 1971; Gusfield 1989, 29; Hogg and McGarty 1990; Lakoff 1987). Anthropological linguists construct folk taxonomies of various cultural domains (diseases, plants, foods, medicines, etc.), and ethnographers generally ask informants to classify terms in a domain. They do so because "these classifications are assumed to . . . rep-

---

bat mitzvah ceremonies all mark an adult *decision* to "become" that to which one was born. Many of the Mount Carmel residents who died on April 19 were second- and third-generation members of the community. However, those born in the community and those who had moved there more recently were by their own accounts united in their *choice* to be at Mount Carmel in 1993. Also see Thibodeau's account of life at Mount Carmel before and during the standoff (Thibodeau and Whiteson 1999).

resent a speaker's conception of how the world is organized" (Lehrer 1974, 19). As with stories, taxonomies reflect the primary focus of the groups that employ them. Taxonomies are also tied to a group's stories about the world, self, and other. An FBI negotiator has a more elaborate taxonomy of barricaded subjects and their motivations than does a police officer without negotiation training. A Branch Davidian has a far more elaborate taxonomy of God's actions in the world than does the average Christian, who does not think of God as taking direct action in daily human affairs.

Groups also link concepts and objects in ways other than categorization. I have alluded to one such linkage, metaphor, in many of my earlier examples of worldview conflict. Susan and John, the divorcing couple described in chapter 1, used different metaphors for marriage. Parties embroiled in conflicts over natural-resource management use different metaphors to name the natural world or some part of it, such as the forest. Groups who participated in a multi-year dialogue process on forest management use the same healthy forest metaphor, but interpret it differently. What exactly is a metaphor, and why does Nudler argue that metaphors as well as stories are windows onto someone's worldview (1993, 4)?

Metaphors link two concepts together by employing familiar entities or systems to give shape to unfamiliar entities or systems. By drawing an analogy between the (relatively) known and the (relatively) unknown, metaphors guide perception, action, and reasoning. Metaphors help make sense of the new and unfamiliar by extending knowledge of the familiar. Because our actions are dependent on the way we name the world, metaphors function as a form of action model as well as shorthand descriptors of ontological and logical beliefs. The metaphors built into the language of a community can reveal a great deal about the way that community names the world. Metaphors are also powerful conceptual tools that, when acted on, reshape the material and social worlds. For example, the European settlers in North America started with a "forest is a wilderness" metaphor, later opted for a "forest is a mine" metaphor, and most recently settled on the "forest is a farm" metaphor (Docherty 1996b). Before the "forest is a farm" metaphor was widely validated, there was no conceptual basis on which to build forestry schools (often located in colleges of agriculture) or to create the U.S. Forest Service (located in the Department of Agriculture). There was also no conceptual basis for the practices of clear-cutting and monocultural replanting.

Metaphors exhibit themselves in worldview conflicts in at least three ways. First, a worldview conflict may be driven, in part, by disagreements over the meaning of a shared metaphor. For example, foresters who advocate a farming practice more like a nineteenth-century farm may be in conflict with those who advocate an agribusiness approach to forestry, even though they share the "forest is a farm" metaphor. Second, a worldview conflict may involve disputes over which metaphor is appropriate for a particular situation. Many current conflicts over forest management can be understood, in part, as rooted in disagreements over whether or not the "forest is a farm" metaphor provides adequate guidance for the practice of forestry. Third, a worldview conflict may involve strong disagreements over whether or not a metaphor is literal or merely figurative speech. Individuals and communities become blind to their own metaphors and to the creative process captured in metaphoric language. In some logging communities, "forest is a farm" may be taken as absolute truth, an objective statement of the way the world really is. Anyone who challenges the practice of forest farming threatens the true believers' sense of reality and identity. When a conflict involves communities that have literalized distinctly different metaphors, communication becomes almost impossible. Members of one community may dismiss metaphors of great significance in another community as babble or nonsensical language.

Worldmaking language is also enacted in the institutionalized practices of a group, and every form of practice is an attempt to alter existence by bringing it into conformity with the group vision. "In practice . . . there is always the attempt to make coherent a given world of ideas" (Oakeshott 1994, 260). A medical doctor trained at the Mayo clinic and a Chinese herbalist both take actions to treat their patients. In so doing, however, each has a different vision of the person and of what constitutes health and illness, as well as different established practices for moving the patient from a state of illness to a state of wellness. Purposeful activities clearly rely on a dual vision of what is and what should be. It is easy to see how the FBI negotiators' practices fit this model. For the negotiators, the given reality of an armed barricade "needs to be" transformed by negotiating the barricaded subject out from behind the barricade and into the court system. However, practice is not limited only to goal-directed actions. Communities founded on sacred narratives also act to change the world from what is to what should be. Religious communities enact the sacred ideal in their daily lives, even when that means violating the conventions of a profane world and risking persecution.

Using stories, taxonomies, metaphors, and institutionalized practices, I set out to uncover the worldviews of the FBI negotiators and the Branch Davidians as they existed prior to their encounter in Waco. Worldview analysis is an interpretive process, subject to all the risks associated with interpretation. I have tried to minimize the risk of misinterpretation by looking at what people do as well as what they say. I have also examined multiple information sources to reduce chances that a story is idiosyncratic rather than legitimized by the group. Nevertheless, any worldview analysis should be taken as tentative, subject to change, and the result of a dialogue between the worldview of the analyst and that of the group being analyzed.

The FBI Negotiators' World:
Creating a Field of Practice

When first established as a field of practice, police negotiation of barricade situations was called hostage negotiation.[2] Many practitioners still use the term *hostage negotiation,* in spite of changes in the types of situations being negotiated. Police negotiation was developed in response to highly visible incidents of hostage taking in which the barricaded subjects held one or more persons against their will in order to force authorities to fulfill certain demands. Hostages were threatened with harm if the hostage takers' demands were not met. As hostage negotiation practices became available to a larger number of police departments, they were increasingly applied to situations in which the

2. Where I have quoted directly from a source, I have provided citations. However, the major ideas and concepts presented are so commonplace in the field of law enforcement crisis negotiation that I have not tried to list specific references for every idea. I am grateful to the FBI negotiators and retired negotiators who helped me understand their field of practice and provided me with a copy of the note-taking guide used in the negotiation course at the FBI Academy.

barricaded subjects were not making instrumental demands. Therefore, some negotiators now use the term *crisis negotiation* to describe their practice.

The formalized practice of police crisis negotiation was greatly advanced in 1973, when the FBI established a training program for hostage negotiators at the FBI Academy. Institutionalizing any practice involves codifying and refining the knowledge base for the discipline as well as delineating standard practices. Crisis negotiators cannot approach each barricade situation as a unique confrontation any more than a doctor can approach each ear infection as a unique illness. The establishment of crisis negotiation as a distinct field of police work involved creating taxonomies of cases and connecting each type of case to an appropriate response. Police negotiators use three diagnostic taxonomies to bring conceptual order to a barricade crisis. First, the negotiators conduct a threat assessment to determine the level of threat posed to the captives. The negotiators sort pure-type hostage situations from other types of barricade crises as part of an effort to separate negotiable from nonnegotiable cases. Second, the negotiators use psychological diagnostic categories to make sense of the individual barricaded subject. Finally, they use linguistic categories to interpret the communication of the barricaded subject.

Distinguishing Negotiable from Nonnegotiable Barricade Situations

The distinction between hostage negotiation and crisis negotiation is not a semantic tempest in a teapot. Separating pure-type hostage situations from other barricade crises has improved police decision making by clarifying the differences between barricade crises in which negotiations are likely to work and those in which negotiating poses a greater threat of violence to the people involved. According to the current FBI negotiation-training program, less than 10 percent of barricade crises involve hostage takers making clear demands. In most cases, the so-called hostages are held for *expressive* rather than for *instrumental* reasons. In these cases, the person being held is more likely to be a victim than a hostage. The captor has often specifically selected the captive based on a current or past relationship. The captive may have been chosen for execution or as a witness to the captor's suicide. The instrumental/expressive classification schema used at this level serves "as a general template through which negotiators determine the type of crisis negotiation situation they are facing and the subsequent strategies employed for obtaining a resolution" (Hammer and Rogan 1997, 9).[3]

Does this mean that any situation in which the barricaded subject has a prior relationship with the captive is nonnegotiable? No. Subjects exhibiting expressive rather than instrumental motives are assessed for potential violence against their captives (Fuselier, Van Zandt, and Lanceley 1991). Police also factor in the possibility that the barricaded subject is seeking to commit "suicide by cop" by pushing the police to kill him (Van Zandt 1993). Threat assessment is a continuous process during a barricade situation, and a great deal of effort has gone into helping law enforcement officials recognize when a situation demands immediate tactical action rather than negotiation (Fuselier, Van Zandt and Lanceley 1991).

Naming the Actors Involved in a Barricade Crisis

Once a decision is made to negotiate, diagnostic focus shifts to the barricaded subject. Researchers and practitioners of crisis negotiation have cooperated to develop taxonomies for categorizing hostage takers. Some of these taxonomies address motive and are employed as supplements to the diagnostic distinction between a pure-type hostage situation and an expressive barricade crisis. For example, Cooper divides hostage takers into six categories: political extremists, fleeing criminals, institutionalized persons, wronged persons, religious fanatics, and mentally disturbed persons (Hammer and Weaver 1989, 9). Goldaber (1979) sorts perpetrators into individuals prone to suicide, persons seeking revenge, and temporarily distraught or seriously disturbed persons who seize hostages to eliminate a current problem. The earliest taxonomy of barricaded subjects was Hacker's (1976) division of hostage takers into crusaders, criminals, and crazies. Subsequent researchers and practitioners have further refined Hacker's broad categories, giving the greatest attention to the "crazies."

Using psychological categories, the police negotiator shifts attention to di-

---

3. The following articles develop the instrumental/expressive classification scheme: DiVasto, Lanceley, and Gruys 1992; Fuselier 1986b; Van Zandt and Fuselier 1989.

agnosing the barricaded subject's mental health. Police negotiators routinely cite the research indicating that mentally disturbed subjects are involved in more than half of all hostage-taking incidents (Borum and Strentz 1992; Fuselier 1986a). The implication is that barricade incidents are caused at least in part by the preexisting mental illness or personal crisis of the barricaded subject. Consequently, police negotiators and the psychologists who act as their consultants routinely diagnose barricaded subjects during a crisis situation (Rueth 1993). Law enforcement journals also contain articles such as "The Inadequate Personality as a Hostage Taker" (Strentz 1993), "The Borderline Personality: Negotiation Strategies" (Borum and Strentz 1992), "Negotiating with the Hostage-Taker Exhibiting Paranoid Schizophrenic Symptoms" (Strentz 1986), or "The Antisocial Personality as Hostage-Taker" (Lanceley 1981). The use of psychological diagnostic categories is further institutionalized through training programs for police negotiators. Those who develop and assess training programs believe "effective negotiation training courses include a focus on the psychological classification of the hostage taker. This classification allows negotiators to understand the 'style' and motivation of the subject, and therefore, [to] choose a negotiation strategy appropriate for the situation" (Borum and Strentz 1992, 6).

Once crisis negotiators have decided that a situation is negotiable and have described or tentatively named (diagnosed) the barricaded subject, how do they name themselves and their coagents or allies? The actors outside the barricade include the police negotiators, intelligence and technical support staff, and tactical teams such as the special weapons and tactics (SWAT) team or the hostage rescue team. Each specialized unit is organized with clear objectives and its own command structure (Botting, Lanceley, and Noesner 1995; Fuselier 1986a, 1986b; Hillmann 1988; McMains and Mullins 1996). An on-scene commander coordinates the special units (fig. 5.).[4]

An oft-repeated adage among police negotiators is, "negotiators do not command, and commanders do not negotiate." The commanders are expected

---

4. I am summarizing what is sometimes called the "East Coast model" of crisis negotiation. There is also a "West Coast model," popularized in Los Angeles, in which the negotiators are integrated into the tactical structure (personal conversation with Gary Noesner, FBI negotiator). The East Coast model has been adopted and promoted by the FBI.

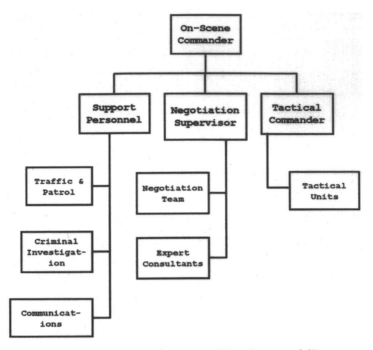

5. Crisis negotiation command structure ("East Coast model").

to "maintain a holistic view of the crisis situation" and make decisions "based on objective assessments . . . [that] incorporate the full range of available assets, to include negotiations, tactical, investigative, and others" *(FBI Law Enforcement Bulletin* 1992, 18). FBI negotiators and HRT personnel most commonly use a judicial metaphor to describe the role of the on-scene commander during a standoff. Like a judge, the commander listens to the case for tactical action, as presented by the HRT commander, listens to the case for continued negotiation, as presented by the lead negotiator, and then renders a "decision," which the HRT and the negotiators carry out cooperatively.

Narrating the "Plot" in Barricade Negotiations

How do crisis negotiators hope to make the barricade drama play out? Ideally, the negotiators, commanders, and tactical units will manage the situation cooperatively so that the barricaded subject peacefully surrenders to authorities. The goal is to move the barricaded subject and his or her concerns or issues into more normalized settings such as the courts or mental health-care facilities. Police negotiators assume that barricaded subjects may be disturbed or suffering from a psychological disorder, but also that they can be rendered predictable and manageable using the correct diagnostic knowledge and appropriate clinical responses.

Yet the police cannot unilaterally narrate the sequence of events in a barricade crisis. The barricade drama plays out as an interactive improvisation with the barricaded subject. Diagnosing the subject's psychological state does not provide adequate information to guide the negotiators' responses to the subject's actions and demands. The police also need interpretive tools in order to select effective responses to the subject's actions and language. Miron and Goldstein classify the communication (language and action) of barricaded subjects along a continuum from instrumental to expressive:

> By an instrumental act, we will mean any action on the part of a perpetrator which has some recognizable goal which the perpetrator seeks to have fulfilled and which will constructively benefit him. . . . By expressive acts we will mean all those acts which serve only to display the power or significance of the perpetrator—acts which appear to be senseless in that there is no obvious way in which the perpetrator can stand to gain anything or in which the act is clearly self-destructive. (1979, 10)

Using this classificatory schema, a barricaded bank robber demanding a getaway car is acting instrumentally, but a barricaded subject demanding to speak with the president is acting expressively, probably to enhance his or her sense of self-worth or importance. Miron and Goldstein never intended the instrumental/expressive categories to be used in a dichotomous fashion, however. Many barricaded subjects use both instrumental and expressive communicative behaviors. Police negotiators use the instrumental/expressive categorization at this level of analysis as an interpretive lens for getting at the "real" meaning of a barricaded subject's actions. With this interpretive device, they are able to select communicative responses that will guide a particular barricaded subject from crisis to calm and change the situation from an armed barricade to a more normalized arena for working out problems. Selecting the best response involves matching police language with that of the barricaded subject.

The ideal of police negotiation is to use Miron and Goldstein's interpretive tools in combination with the psychological taxonomy in order to tailor police responses to the subject. For example, negotiators are told that the real needs of barricaded subjects who exhibit symptoms of a borderline personality disorder "are more expressive than material. In other words, borderlines bargain for support and recognition rather than material items, such as money or vehicles" (Borum and Strentz 1992, 9). Negotiators who understand these characteristics of the barricaded subject "provide support and empathy—thus responding to the *real* needs of the subject—and eventually resolve the incident by making nominal concessions" (Borum and Strentz 1992, 9, emphasis in original). In similar fashion, police negotiators are reminded that paranoid hostage takers can be arrayed along a continuum from most disturbed to least disturbed. The police negotiator is instructed to select communication strategies according to the subject's level of disturbance. Negotiators can use problem-solving approaches with a barricaded subject who is a paranoid personality, but not with one who is paranoid schizophrenic (Fuselier 1986a, 2). Specific instructions are provided for interacting with subjects diagnosed as having inadequate personalities or antisocial personalities or suffering from clinical depression (Fuselier 1986a).

Why do police negotiators assume that barricaded subjects can be moved from crisis to calm? Because they believe human beings balance two distinct states of being and behavior: emotionality and rationality. People may swing more toward emotion or more toward reason in response to external events, but most people occupy a middle range or a normal functioning level between extreme emotion and overly cold, detached rationality. Police negotiators see the barricaded subject as highly emotional and out of control. Therefore, ending a barricade standoff involves moving the subject from an overly emotional to a more rational state (fig. 6.). The skills used to calm the subject and manage him or her toward rational behavior include active listening, empathizing, building rapport, and influencing or persuading (fig. 7.). The ultimate goal is to change the subject's behavior.

Like any other conflict resolution practice, police crisis negotiation is an effort to "make talk work" (Kolb 1997) and to avoid more costly, potentially dangerous responses to the problem at hand. However, crisis negotiation is a talking practice that takes place in an environment fraught with potential violence. The crisis negotiators coordinate their activities with the tactical units in order to send nonverbal reminders that talking is not the only option open to police. At some point, the decision regarding whether to continue talking may be taken out of the negotiators' hands, which raises questions about the negotiators' coordination with their allies.

How are the tactical and negotiation units coordinated? On what grounds does a commander make objective assessments regarding tactical and negotiation activities? In theory, the units are coordinated with reference to a common goal (Docherty 1996a). However, the goal is not always clear. Are the police primarily committed to negotiating a peaceful end to the crisis or to enforcing the law? The answers to these questions are ambiguous and are renegotiated among the police units in the context of each crisis. The answers depend on a complex mix of factors related to the multiple priorities of police work.

The first priority for the police during a barricade situation is preservation of lives, followed by apprehension of the subject and recovery and protection of property, in that order. Preservation of lives is accomplished by containing the situation, calming the barricaded subject, and negotiating a nonviolent end to the siege. However, not all characters in the barricade drama are considered equally deserving of protection. Protection is given first to hostages, then to innocent citizens caught in the area, then to police or federal agents, and last to suspects or criminals (McCarthy 1993).

Assigning different values to the characters in the barricade drama helps commanders determine whether a situation is negotiable. In the absence of an immediate threat of violence, priority is given to negotiation. The tactical units (SWAT and HRT) support the negotiators, and the commanders coordinate the activities of each unit to enhance the possibility of a negotiated settlement (Hillmann 1988). If the hostage taker kills or makes believable threats to kill one or more hostages, immediate action is required. Protecting the lives of hostages, innocent citizens, and law enforcement agents may require "neutralizing" the barricaded subject. In nonnegotiable situations, the

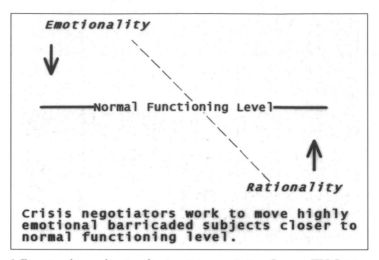

Emotionality

——————Normal Functioning Level——————

Rationality

Crisis negotiators work to move highly emotional barricaded subjects closer to normal functioning level.

6. Emotionality and rationality in crisis negotiation. Source: FBI Crisis Negotiation Unit.

negotiators step into a support role, and priority is given to tactical activities (Fagan and Van Zandt 1993). Negotiators may stall in order to give the tactical units time to prepare, gather intelligence for the tactical team, distract the subject during an assault, or talk the subject into a position that allows police snipers a clear shot.

Analyzing the FBI Negotiators' Worldview

Worldviewing is a holistic activity, and worldview analysis is a tricky undertaking. People do not establish their ontologies, logics, ethics, epistemologies, and axiologies separately. Yet it is useful to analyze the worldviewing dimensions of a community's language as if worldviews were constructed out of isolated component parts. Teasing out the "parts" of a worldview directs attention to factors that might otherwise go unnoticed. It is also helpful to situate a community's worldmaking narratives in relation to the stories validated by the society within which they work. As with any interpretive process, a worldview analysis should never be mistaken for the holistic process of worldviewing.

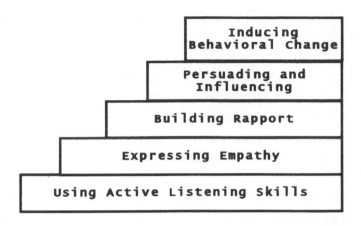

7. Crisis negotiators' stairway to changing barricaded subject's behavior. Source: FBI Crisis Negotiation Unit.

The Ontology and Logic of FBI Negotiation Practices

Dualism is a "theory which admits in any given domain, two independent and mutually irreducible substances" (Runes 1960, 84). There are several indications in the previous stories that police negotiators organize the world using a *dualistic logic*. For police negotiators, human actors are categorized as normal or abnormal. In casual conversation, police negotiators refer to barricaded subjects as bad guys. The police are, of course, the good guys. In a similar dualistic fashion, human motives are labeled as instrumental or expressive. Furthermore, police negotiators equate instrumental behavior with reason and expressive behavior with emotion.

Here, the police are working within a wider cultural framework that describes reason and emotion as mutually exclusive and qualitatively distinct states of being. As I noted in chapter 1, many other practitioners of conflict resolution also disempower some parties in a conflict by relegating their behavior to the allegedly inferior realm of emotion. In most barricade negotiation cases, this approach may not be problematic. When negotiating with a barricaded community that is organized around an alternative logic, however, the emotional/rational dualism may make negotiation impossible. There is no room in figure 6 for *competing rationalities*, a problem I address in detail in chapter 6.

In combination with their dualistic logic, police negotiators rely on an *essentialist ontology*. The true character of a person and the wellspring of his or her actions are located in his or her essential character. Bad guys are inherently different from good guys, who are rational and normal. Developing diagnostic taxonomies of hostage takers is symptomatic of "individual approaches to criminology which see criminals as self-evidently different from normal people" (Powell 1989, 3). In crisis negotiation, the result has been a critical focus on the "abnormal actor" who is involved in "a special form of conflict interaction in which the participants are actively engaged in coercive competition" (Rogan and Hammer 1995, 555). The other party to the interaction (the police) remains unexamined, and the interactive process itself is largely ignored as a possible cause of the subject's behavior.

The level of legitimacy accorded the dualistic and essentialist ontological narratives of police negotiators was apparent in the relative attention given to competing experts during the Waco negotiations. Two members of the FBI Behavioral Science Unit factored the apocalyptic beliefs of the Mount Carmel community into their analysis of the Waco standoff. Agents Pete Smerick and Mark Young wrote, " 'In traditional hostage situations, a strategy which has been successful has been negotiations coupled with ever increasing tactical presence. In this situation however, it is believed this strategy, if carried to excess, could eventually be counter productive and could result in loss of life' " (Justice 180). Smerick and Young discussed in detail the impact of contextual factors, as opposed to the inherent psychological conditions of individual Branch Davidians, on the Mount Carmel community's response to FBI actions. They were telling a worldmaking story about parties who interactively influence one another's interpretations of events and actions. In similar fashion, biblical scholars James Tabor and Phil Arnold offered to act as interpreters of the Branch Davidian worldview, only to have the FBI decline their offer (Carstarphen 1995; Tabor 1995; Tabor and Gallagher 1995). The essentialist narrative won out over the contextualist and interpretive counternarratives offered by Smerick and Young and Tabor and Arnold. The FBI turned to experts who provided clinical diagnoses of Koresh because they assumed that pinning down a diagnosis was the most useful approach to managing a complex barricade situation. Furthermore, the FBI negotiators continued to pursue this diagnostic approach, even when the wildly contradictory diagnoses offered by the experts rendered the formulation of a coherent negotiation strategy extremely difficult, perhaps impossible.

The following list of the different ways in which Koresh was diagnosed gives some idea of the difficulties created by the diagnostic process. Koresh was possibly suffering from a seizure disorder. Koresh had antisocial and narcissistic personality traits and delusions of grandeur. Koresh showed no evidence of being actively psychotic. Koresh was *not* suffering from delusional beliefs. Koresh was a con artist with narcissistic tendencies. Koresh was self-directed, hedonistic, and manipulative. Koresh was suffering from rampant, morbidly virulent paranoia. Koresh was suicidal. Koresh was *not* suicidal. Koresh was a functional, paranoid-type psychotic (Justice 159–179). For the most part, the other residents of Mount Carmel received little diagnostic attention from the FBI negotiators and outside consultants. The FBI acknowledges that a video made by the Mount Carmel residents during the fifty-one-day siege shows people who "spoke in a calm, assured tone" and whose overall appearance was not that of "a bunch of 'lunatics' " (Justice 205). At the same time, team members described the Mount Carmel residents as having "low self-esteem" (Justice 206) and usually dismissed them as duped, deluded, brainwashed cult members whose actions and language did not even merit careful analysis.

The Epistemology of FBI Negotiation Practices

Powell laments that "most of the professional literature on barricade and hostage negotiations is written by psychiatrists or police with experience in clinical psychology" (1989, 2). He is right to be concerned that psychology is being made to serve the ideological interests of the state during hostage negotiations (1989, 6). However, he oversimplifies the situation by conflating psychiatry and psychology, and by failing to acknowledge that police negotiators are appropriating a limited portion of psychological discourse and methods. The fields of psychology and psychiatry are riddled with complex internal conflicts over the nature of reality, the definition of mental illness, useful ways of naming and understanding psychological crisis, correct forms of knowledge about psychological phenomena, and the most effective ways to respond to people who are in distress. In appropriating psychological constructs and psychiatric diagnostic categories, police negotiators have tended to align themselves with the subset of the fields of psychology and psychiatry that most closely shares their own ontological, epistemological, and logical assumptions about the world.

In 1980, the American Psychological Association (APA) adopted a new classification system of mental disorders. This classification system was codified in the *Diagnostic and Statistical Manual of Mental Disorders, Third Edition,* or DSM-III (the 1987 revision is known as DSM-III-R). In spite of critical concern that DSM-III inappropriately "medicalizes deviance," the new diagnostic manual has been readily incorporated into the judicial system, where it is used "when questions are raised about a defendant's mental capacities, intentional states, or cognitive abilities" (Kirk and Kutchins 1992, 8).

Several institutional factors led to the rapid adoption of DSM-III. The APA actively promoted DSM-III, and they marketed Structured Clinical Interview forms to be used with DSM-III-R (Kirk and Kutchins 1992, 53). These forms simplified and standardized diagnostic interviews by providing "a progression of questions to be asked of patients . . . [whose] responses . . . were then matched with the diagnostic criteria that systematically allocated symptom patterns into specified diagnostic categories" (Kirk and Kutchins 1992, 53). DSM-III has been described as an attempt to reduce the "art" of diagnosis and therapeutic intervention to a mechanical exercise of "technical rationality" (Kirk and Kutchins 1992, 220). Armed with DSM-III-R and appropriate materials, clinical social workers, psychologists, and other mental health practitioners who are not physicians gained legitimacy and a sense of power from their newfound ability to make psychiatric diagnoses using scientific jargon (Kirk and Kutchins 1992, 196).

In similar fashion, law enforcement negotiators felt increasingly free to use diagnostic categories to describe barricaded subjects. They continue to do so even though many mental health professionals consider it a "fundamental attribution 'error' " when "constructions like 'psychopathology' and 'depression' [are invoked] to classify or explain infrequent, non-normative, non-typical, or even unusual conduct" of an individual (Wiener and Marcus 1994, 228). Even with DSM-III categories, diagnoses should not be rendered on the basis of a single incident or episode in a person's life. Yet law enforcement negotiators and their expert consultants are not the only ones who use DSM-III categories so quickly. Many third-party payers (e.g., insurance companies) encouraged the adoption of standardized diagnostic categories by refusing to pay for treatment unless the patient had been diagnosed according to DSM-III (Hoffman 1992). Consequently, mental health professionals continue to apply diagnostic labels quickly, even in the absence of adequate supporting information.

In spite of the many pressures to adopt DSM-III categories as descriptions of objective reality, many people remain critical of the entire diagnostic exercise. Sociologists criticize DSM-III because it ignores the social context within which deviance labeling takes place. "An expanding list of mental disorders that contains everything, including low intelligence, tobacco dependence, antisocial personality, schizophrenia, caffeine intoxication, and childhood misconduct, offers an ideology for understanding a potpourri of dysfunctional or devalued behaviors as medical disorders rather than as diverse forms of social deviance" (Kirk and Kutchins 1992, 238). DSM-III categories mask the fact that "the concept of mental illness . . . cannot be disentangled from moral judgments," and those who depend on these categories ignore the historical evidence that such judgments "can be misused to take dissenters out of circulation by circumventing due process of law" (Frank 1973, 9).

Many psychologists and even some psychiatrists criticize DSM-III for shifting the analytical emphasis from causes to symptoms. DSM-III represents "a radical departure for American psychiatry, which had accepted as a first axiom that its first task was to identify and treat causes, not symptoms" (Kirk and Kutchins 1992, 77). Again, this emphasis has the effect of decontextualizing the patient, whose symptoms are treated in isolation from the social milieu in which the problematic behavior originated or manifested itself.

People exhibiting polar opposite symptoms are labeled with the same diagnosis because their social worlds are not taken into account. "For example, an individual who reports depressed mood (says he is 'sad'), who manifests psychomotor retardation, reports low energy, hypersomnia and weight gain, is diagnosed with major depressive syndrome, as is an individual with psychomotor agitation and reports insomnia, weight loss, feelings of worthlessness, and indecisiveness" (Wiener and Marcus 1994, 219). When the individual patient is viewed in isolation, many important aspects of his or her condition are obscured. Someone may say "I feel helpless" but mean "I feel incompetent," or the person may be making a statement about his or her social reality and mean "I am powerless to act because another will not allow me to act" (Wiener and

Marcus 1994, 219). Without any information about the patient's social environment, diagnoses based on the patient's statements are tentative at best.

When police negotiators use psychological concepts, there is a double filtration process between the experience of the subject being diagnosed and the diagnosis. First, the subject's experience or behaviors are filtered through the diagnostic categories established by psychological professionals. Then, both the psychological diagnosis and the behavior of the subject are filtered through the lenses of law enforcement practice. Additionally, law enforcement practice is itself shaped by labeling practices that define categories of persons and actions as deviant, criminal, and in need of control (Ferrell and Sanders 1995; Goode and Ben-Yehuda 1994). Any exploration of the worldmaking activities of law enforcement negotiation necessarily involves an examination of police appropriation of psychological categories to advance their own practice. The first questions to ask are: If DSM-III and the categories contained therein are so controversial, why do police negotiators use them, and why do they feel most comfortable with expert consultants who use diagnostic language?

The FBI preference for working with experts who used medical terminology to diagnose Koresh can be better understood if one examines the epistemological premises that guide law enforcement negotiators. Police negotiators lean toward epistemological realism. They assume "that the object of knowledge enjoys an existence independent of and external to the knowing mind" (Runes 1960, 93). Therefore, there is a natural affinity between police negotiators and those mental health professionals who are willing to dichotomize actors as normal or abnormal and who locate the source of deviant behavior in the individual. FBI negotiators in Waco did not seek out mental health professionals who question the epistemological, logical, and ontological assumptions on which DSM-III rests, even though approaches used in constructivist psychotherapies (Neimeyer 1993) and narrative therapy (Combs and Freedman 1990; White and Epston 1990) would have offered more useful insights and practical recommendations during the Waco standoff. Likewise, in Waco, the FBI found "little useful information" in the advice that religion experts and theologians offered (Justice 186).[5] I would argue it was not the information that was useless.

---

5. FBI personnel have also told me that religion scholars offered "little useful information" during the 1996 Freemen standoff in Montana. Unless the significant worldview differences be-

Rather, the underlying constructivist worldview of religion scholars did not easily mesh with the preexisting objectivist worldview assumptions common to police negotiators.

The Axiology and Ethic of FBI Negotiation Practices

Police negotiators' ontological, logical, and epistemological worldview assumptions act together to shape police negotiation practice. The stories police negotiators tell about what is real, how the real is organized, and how we can know about what is real provide the basis for answering the following question: What should police negotiators *do* in response to a barricade situation? In the modernist symbolic world, effective practice rests on accurate knowledge, and police negotiators impose order on a potentially chaotic situation by psychologizing the barricaded subjects (Docherty 1996a; Hammer and Weaver 1989; Powell 1989). Because diagnosis implies prescription, psychology also influences police negotiation practice once a diagnostic label is placed on the subject. Just as police negotiators look to DSM-III for analytical categories, so they turn to clinical psychology to guide their development of negotiation practices. Counseling strategies used in clinical psychology, like the negotiation strategies employed by police, rest on the assumption that disturbed subjects can be moved from highly excited (emotional) to calm (rational) states of being. Consequently, police negotiators have readily adapted to their own situation such practices as establishing rapport, empathetic listening, and active listening.

Actions are tied to values as well as to knowledge. To outsiders, it may seem ironic to argue that crisis negotiation is part of a "new diplomatic ideal in police practice—which resides alongside the authority to use force" (Powell 1989, 7). Nevertheless, law enforcement agents experience crisis negotiation as significantly more diplomatic than other options for managing a barricade situation. From their perspective, the uneasy alliance between diplomacy and enforcement necessitates the construction of an axiological framework capable of

---

tween religious studies experts and FBI negotiators can be managed effectively, there is little hope that the FBI negotiators will avail themselves of expertise that may help avoid tragic outcomes in future confrontations between federal law enforcement agents and unconventional religious groups (Docherty 1999).

guiding commanders as they choose between negotiated and tactical solutions. What are negotiators to do when they face a situation in which diplomacy contradicts one or both of the primary missions of police work: to enforce the law and to protect the public? The narrative construction of differently valued characters provides a framework within which the police can answer the question: Should we negotiate with this particular barricaded subject?

The World Made by the Mount Carmel Community

The Mount Carmel community also told worldmaking stories, although their stories were not couched in the same rational, scientific jargon the FBI negotiators favored. "At whatever level of size or degree of complexity, a community exists wherever a narrative account exists of a *we* which has continuous existence through its experiences and activities" (Carr 1991, 163). Unconventional religious and political groups, like social movements (Fine 1995), are particularly concerned with telling stories that emphasize their separation from "others" who do not share their visions, values, or beliefs.[6] Czarniawska (1997) compares group narratives to autobiographies and agrees with Bruner's definition of an autobiographical story as "an account of what one thinks one did in what settings in what ways for what felt reasons" (1990, 119). The statement "I was under stress at work, and lashed out at my husband when I got home" is a relatively simple autobiographical act by Bruner's definition. A written autobiography is a more complex autobiographical narrative. An oral tradition collectively told, retold, and refined by a particular group is also autobiographical. The first autobiographical act of any human collective is a tale of origin or explanation of the group's existence, purpose, and founding. Tales of origin define the group "we" in relation to one or more others.

---

6. I am not claiming that narrative is the only means by which social groups construct a sense of identity. " 'Community' . . . seems to imply simultaneously both similarity and difference. The word thus expresses a *relational* idea: the opposition of one community to others or to other social entities" (Cohen 1985, 12). Contained in the concept of community is the notion of a boundary, and "the manner in which [boundaries] are marked depends entirely on the specific community in question" (Cohen 1985, 12).

The Branch Davidian Tale of Origin

From the outset, the Mount Carmel community named itself in relation to the other of mainstream Seventh-day Adventism. All but seven of the adults living at Mount Carmel in 1993 had been raised in the SDA tradition or in one of its offshoots. Seventh-day Adventism emerged out of the Great Disappointment when William Miller's prediction that the Second Coming of Christ would occur on October 22, 1844, proved inaccurate. Ellen G. White, who remained faithful to Adventist teachings after the Great Disappointment, became the prophet of the SDA Church. White preached a return to keeping the Sabbath on Saturday rather than on Sunday, dietary restrictions, and "an aloofness from, and distrust of, government" (Reavis 1995, 55). However, White's most important teaching was known as "present truth" or "new light." " 'Present truth' means truth for the time, which is *progressively* revealed to God's remnant people in the last days" (Tabor and Gallagher 1995, 48–49). White's followers proclaimed her the teacher for the current age, the bearer of the present truth.

After White's death, her followers faced a dilemma not unlike that faced by Jesus' disciples. Was White the last teacher before Christ's return? Or would there be other prophets bringing more new light teachings before the end? The SDA Church leadership has not proclaimed a successor to Ellen White, but many groups within the SDA community have anointed new prophets and proclaimed new versions of the present truth. White's present-truth doctrine placed the Adventist community on a path of sectarian division and redivision.

In the early twentieth century, Victor Houteff was among those who laid claim to the role of teacher of the present truth (Pitts 1995, 23). Houteff "insisted that [White's] call for purification applied to the Adventists themselves in his day" (Tabor and Gallagher 1995, 34). He "implied that the Seventh-day Adventist doctrines and teachings were deficient" (Pitts 1995, 21), thereby offending the SDA Church leaders, who were also worried about Houteff's claim "that the biblical prophets clearly taught that the Kingdom of God was to be a literal, physical, millennial rule on earth, centered in Palestine" (Tabor and Gallagher 1995, 35). The Mount Carmel community was founded in 1935, when Houteff and a group of his followers moved to a site seven miles northwest of Waco (Pitts 1995, 25). They named their home Mount Carmel, and when Houteff was ejected from the SDA, they took the name Davidian Seventh-day Adventists. At some point during the intervening decades, the original property was sold and the community moved to the "New Mount Carmel" northeast of town, which was the location of the 1993 confrontation with federal agents. In spite of the physical relocation, the residents of the new Mount Carmel were the descendants—some of them biologically, others only theologically—of Houteff's community.

From the time Mount Carmel was founded in 1935, the SDA Church was the primary target of the community's message of reform. "Houteff addressed neither all people nor even all Christian denominations. He spoke exclusively to the Seventh-day Adventists because only they were allegedly prepared to understand the implications of his teachings, and if they heeded the new message, the forces to bring history to a conclusion could be set in motion" (Pitts 1995, 24). This focus remained the same even into the Koresh era. The Mount Carmel community claimed that the SDA Church had become complacent and had lost its will to focus on God's command in the End Time. Mount Carmel was maintained by its residents to serve as a gathering place for those people willing to make the sacrifices required of true believers. The community was home to those who wanted to study the Bible, prepare for the Second Coming of Christ, and live in radical obedience to God's plan as it was revealed in Scripture, the signs of the times, and the teaching of current-day prophets.

The Mount Carmel community also continued, in a more radical form, the SDA tradition of defining itself in contrast to the world. The deeply ingrained suspicion of state authority, rejection of worldly ways, and elevation of a Bible-centered lifestyle that marked early Adventism were dramatically emphasized in the Mount Carmel community. In contrast to both the SDA Church and the world, the community did not celebrate Christmas or Easter. "Like the Puritans, they believed that Christmas marked an unscriptural, pagan holiday, rooted in Roman festivals for the sun" (Reavis 1995, 60). At first, the community maintained its own school system, and during the Houteff era they also ran a denominational college (Pitts 1995, 27–28). "Students began each day facing two flags, one Davidian, one American and reciting that 'As Christian students in America . . . we pledge our hearts, our minds, our hands, our all, first to the flag of God's eternal kingdom, and to the Theocracy for which it stands, one people made up of all nations, and bound by the cords of everlasting love, liberty, purity, justice, peace, happiness and life for all' " (Reavis 1995, 61). Even after economic difficulties forced them to close the school and college, the community kept its children as separate as possible from the outside world.

Mount Carmel residents did work outside the community, although their goal was always to minimize their reliance on the outside world (Pitts 1995, 26). The community even created its own money system and sustained itself by instituting a "second tithe" to pay for practical community needs such as health insurance, the school, and old-age care (Pitts 1995, 27). Whatever interaction community members had with the outside world, religious rituals, Bible study, and a special diet were daily reminders of their separation from that world.

The End Time and the Realization of the Davidian Purpose

The passionate commitment of the Mount Carmel community cannot be understood apart from their sacred narrative and their absolute faith in God's active and ongoing revelation of truth. The Mount Carmel community subscribed to a premillennialist prophecy of the End Time that was not unique to their community (Boyer 1992; O'Leary 1994; Tabor and Gallagher 1995). According to premillennialist teachings, the end of the world will unfold as follows.

- The present age will show increasing apostasy.
- There will be a seven-year period of tribulation.
- There will be a Rapture, in which believers will be taken up into heaven.
- The Antichrist may appear in the middle of the seven years.
- Christ will return during the final battle of Armageddon, where the Antichrist is defeated.
- Judgment Day will follow, and believers will be saved for an eternal reign with Christ, but the unsaved will be lost to Satan.
- There will be a new heaven and new earth. (adapted from Chandler 1993, 226)

Many people equate the apocalypse with despair, assuming that an apocalyptic vision negates the possibility of meaningful action. However, as O'Leary notes, "the predicted End of the world does not simply reduce people to passive spectators; the tragic drama of Apocalypse offers . . . *those who are persuaded* . . . a role in the cosmic drama" (1994, 87, emphasis added). The Mount

Carmel residents were convinced that God expected them to play an instrumental role in the creation of a new heaven and new earth. God's plan was fully laid out in Scripture, particularly in the Book of Revelation and the Prophets, and the Mount Carmel community had privileged access to God's plan. Therefore, they had a unique part to play in the fulfillment of that plan. This group autobiography sustained the Mount Carmel community through six decades, including various crises of leadership and economic setbacks (Pitts 1995). It also laid the foundation for Koresh's rise to leadership in the 1980s.

In Davidian theology, the key to understanding the entire Bible and the meaning of current events as part of God's plan for the world is unlocking the Seven Seals presented in the Book of Revelation. The Seven Seals can be "unlocked" or interpreted only by a mysterious figure known as "the Lamb." When that happens, the events leading up to God's final judgment will be set in motion. So it is not just a question of knowing what is happening or is going to happen. Understanding and correctly interpreting the Book of Revelation is necessary to *initiate* God's sacred plan for the End Time. In mainstream Christian theology, the Book of Revelation is not taken literally, and the Lamb is understood as a reference to Jesus. For the Mount Carmel community in 1993, David Koresh was "the Lamb" who held the key to the Seven Seals.

Koresh claimed to have had a vision while visiting Israel in 1985. During this encounter with God, he was given direct personal knowledge of God's plan for the world. According to Koresh, his experience was similar to Moses' encounter with the Burning Bush. He heard directly the voice of God and was transported to heaven, where he was shown great mysteries. The voice stayed with him and guided him in his reading and interpretation of Scripture. With divine assistance, Koresh was to act as God's messenger. To him would fall the special task of opening the Seven Seals.

Tabor and Gallagher, biblical scholars who are not Branch Davidians, claim "one can hear a marked difference in the existing tapes of his [Koresh's] Bible study sessions before and after 1985. In the earlier materials Koresh clearly knows the texts of the Bible well, but his teaching is routine . . . even dull at times" (1995, 59). Later, his teaching was filled with energy, and he showed "great skill in weaving together many dozens of complicated images and concepts" (1995, 59). However, it does not matter whether outsiders authenticate Koresh's claims. What matters is the fact that the Mount Carmel community granted Koresh's claims a level of legitimacy they had denied other aspiring leaders of the community.[7] When George Roden, Koresh's rival for leadership in the 1980s, began ending prayers "in the name of George B. Roden, amen," the community rejected him soundly (Reavis 1995, 81). Koresh preached the imminent coming of Christ, argued that the world had already entered the period of tribulation, and claimed God had given him the present truth or new light for this age, and the community validated his claims. The Mount Carmel community did not think of Koresh as perfect or sinless, but they did believe he had access to perfect knowledge. Furthermore, it was knowledge they highly prized.

In the Mount Carmel community, unlocking the Seven Seals was not an intellectual exercise; it was a way of life. "Koresh often said he had been sent both to 'explain and to do the Scriptures.' In other words, the Davidians believed that opening these seals involved not only explaining their mysterious meaning but also bringing about the events they prophesied" (Tabor and Gallagher 1995, 54–55). Doing the Scriptures meant placing God's new laws for the coming Kingdom above the laws of the state and the laws of man. For the Mount Carmel community, the New Light Doctrine that Koresh had introduced was both a revelation of God's new law and a significant part of the role they were to play during the End Time. "Drawing on the Book of Revelation, Koresh asserted that in his role as a messiah he became the perfect mate of all the female adherents. Central to his messianic mission . . . was the creation of a new lineage of God's children from his own seed. The children created through these unions would erect the House of David and ultimately rule the world" (Bromley and Silver 1995, 58–59).[8]

This belief had a significant impact on the FBI efforts to negotiate the "re-

7. Mount Carmel residents also spoke of the change in Koresh's preaching after his visit to Israel. Catherine Matteson talked about the " 'perfect picture of the Bible' " that " 'God [had] planted in his brain' " (qtd. in Reavis 1995, 97). Clive Doyle also testified to changes in Koresh's teaching after the trip to Israel, and another member of the community talked about the " 'kind of a spirit in the room' " when Koresh spoke. She compared listening to Koresh with " 'having a religious conversion experience all over' " (qtd. in Reavis 1995, 97).

8. For a more complete explanation of the Mount Carmel beliefs regarding celibacy, polygamy, and gender relations in the End Time, see Tabor and Gallagher 1995 (67–76) and Thibodeau and Whiteson 1999 (107–16).

lease" of the children in Mount Carmel. All of Koresh's biological children who were in residence at Mount Carmel perished on April 19. The Branch Davidians did not place these children of the New Light in the same "innocent bystander" category with the other children in the community. The community's steadfast refusal to send Koresh's children out of Mount Carmel is rooted in their internal logic and the prophetic validity they granted to Koresh's New Light Doctrine.

The community radically altered gender relations, family patterns, and the concept of marriage in response to the New Light Doctrine. In this respect, they were like many other alternative religious movements.[9] It might even be argued that the Book of Acts and Paul's teachings regarding marriage and celibacy reflect experimentation with alternative modes of social, economic, and family organization by a "new religious movement." What others saw as deviant behavior the Mount Carmel residents experienced as a faithful response to God's direct revelation of a new law.

Analyzing the Branch Davidian Worldview

The Ontology and Logic of the Mount Carmel Community

Christian apocalyptic narratives are based on the twin premises that time must have a stop and that evil "will be justified and made sensible in the ultimate destiny of the cosmos" (O'Leary 1994, 33). It is extremely difficult for any community to live continuously in a state of anticipation regarding the End Time. Like most millennialist sects, the Mount Carmel community experienced periods of heightened apocalyptic expectations interspersed with periods of relative calm. After Houteff's death, his wife (Florence) set April 22, 1959, as the date for the Second Coming. Hundreds of Branch Davidians who lived outside the Mount Carmel community sold everything and gathered at

---

9. It is not at all unusual for alternative religious movements to advance radically new ideas about gender relations, family, and sexual behavior. See Pitzer 1997 for papers examining these issues in historical communities. Also see S. Palmer 1994 for an examination of gender roles in NRMs.

Mount Carmel to await the establishment of God's earthly kingdom (Pitts 1995, 30–32). After this "Lesser Disappointment," the remaining community reorganized with Ben Roden as leader.[10] Roden laid the groundwork for the Koresh era by focusing the community on the task of understanding and fulfilling the prophecies of the last days in order to *usher in* the kingdom of God.

In 1993, the Mount Carmel community was once again experiencing a heightened sense that the End Time was drawing near. As part of their apocalyptic expectations, the residents were strongly committed to the following ontological claims. Satan exists. God exists. Satan and God act in the world through human institutions and individual people. Time is linear and will come to an end. The end is fast approaching. The Bible holds God's word. Prophets are given to every era to interpret God's word for that time.

There is a dualistic logic at work in the Branch Davidian worldview. The world is organized into good and evil, the saved and the damned, believers and unbelievers, agents of God and agents of Satan. Even the linear organization of time can be seen as a form of dualism. There was a beginning; there will be an end. The current time is sinful; God will bring a sacred time.

Although the FBI negotiators and Branch Davidians share a dualistic logic, the Branch Davidians do not hold to a combined essentialist and dualist ontology regarding human nature. No one is inherently good or inherently evil. For the Branch Davidians, *all* humans are fallen, but no one is permanently bound to his or her fallen nature. Each individual can be saved by submitting to God's will. The exercise of free choice is what separates the saved and the damned, the agents of God and the agents of Satan. During the Waco negotiations, the Mount Carmel residents invited the FBI negotiators to choose God's law over man's law. The negotiators resisted these invitations as situationally inappropriate conversion efforts. The Branch Davidians, they said, were disrupting the "real" negotiations with their proselytizing. However, for the Mount Carmel residents, proselytizing *was* the truly important business at hand. With the Second Coming looming on the horizon, all else was trivial by comparison, even the task of peacefully resolving the barricade standoff.

10. For a history of the changing leadership at Mount Carmel, see Pitts 1995.

The Epistemology of the Mount Carmel Community

For the FBI, truth is waiting to be discovered through scientific research and careful analysis of reality. Therefore, good practices or right actions are framed in relation to accurate knowledge about the human psyche and social institutions. For the Branch Davidians, perfect knowledge of the past, present, and future has already been revealed by God in Scripture. After Koresh's experience in Israel, the key to unlocking that perfect knowledge was available to those who would listen. Truth is discerned through processes of prayerful reflection, meditation, and Bible study. These epistemological differences greatly complicated FBI and Branch Davidian efforts to manage their worldviewing differences during the Waco standoff.

The Ethic and Axiology of the Mount Carmel Community

Every worldview has an axiology, a means of sorting what is believed to exist into categories of more- and less-valuable entities. The Mount Carmel community valued faith, God, the Bible, true prophecy, and a radical obedience to God's will. They dismissed many things deemed valuable by mainstream society, and they readily sacrificed creature comforts that most people consider necessities, such as indoor plumbing. The Branch Davidians turned much of the axiology of mainstream society on its head, which complicated the negotiations. For example, when the FBI negotiators made a videotape of the children who had exited the property, they sent this tape into Mount Carmel to demonstrate that the children were well, but missed and needed their parents. The Mount Carmel residents were appalled to see their children drinking sodas, eating candy, and watching television shows they considered inappropriate. A videotape that was intended to reassure the community that the children were well cared for and safe had quite the opposite effect. The FBI failed to account for the Branch Davidians' value system and axiological commitments.

The Branch Davidians' belief in the imminent end of the world heightened their sense of God's immediate and direct action in history. In response to the question "How should we act?" the Mount Carmel community answered, "With *radical obedience* to God's *new* law, the law that will hold sway in God's coming kingdom." By definition, God's law must be radically different from the laws of man. Therefore, like other communities caught up in the fervor of apocalyptic expectation, the Mount Carmel community felt called to engage in practices that mainstream society considered deviant.

For any type of group, we can say, "the group as a whole may enter into an antagonistic relation with a power outside of it, and it is because of this that the tightening of relations among its members and the intensification of its unity, in consciousness and action, occur" (Simmel 1955, 91). For "world-transforming movements" or groups (Shupe and Bromley 1983) who are determined to bring a new divine law to a corrupt world, the effect of outside rejection is intensified by their internal logic. The way one discerns the "new divine law" is in part by the amount of opposition it evokes from a corrupt and sinful world. See, for example, Barker's (1983) study of the ways deprogramming efforts actually strengthened the Unification Church. Hence, the more condemnation that the evil forces of the worldly powers heaped on Koresh's teachings, the more legitimate the message was in the eyes of the community.

Was the Problem Worldview Similarities or Worldview Differences?

When the standoff between the FBI and the Mount Carmel community is first confronted, it is natural to notice the extreme differences in their symbolic worlds. Closer examination reveals underlying logical similarities. For example, both the FBI and the Branch Davidians espoused dualistic visions of a world divided along the lines of good and evil. This similarity raises an interesting question. Was the conflict in Waco driven by the parties' worldview differences or by their worldview similarities? Or did some fatal combination of similarities and differences fuel an escalatory conflict that resulted in tragedy? Once we start looking for similarities between the two groups, they become readily apparent. Both the FBI and the Mount Carmel community believed the use of guns and other deadly weapons was justifiable under specific circumstances.

Both groups brought their ultimate concerns to the negotiation process. Both groups had similar constructions of their own identities, each seeing itself as the "defender of truth." Clearly, worldview conflicts should not be conceptualized as pure dichotomies. Conflict may be driven as much by similar beliefs as it is by competing beliefs.

4

Managing a Crisis Between "Citizens of Separate Worlds"

MOST CONFLICTING PARTIES plagued by severe worldview management problems never make it to the negotiation table. In Waco, however, the FBI and Branch Davidians were forced into a negotiation process by the ATF raid and by the Branch Davidian response to that raid. What happened when they got to the table? Not surprisingly, given their preexisting worldmaking narratives, the FBI and the Mount Carmel community named very differently the February 28 "breach of norms" that sparked their conflict. They also told divergent blaming stories about the February 28 confrontation. Yet, in spite of their naming and blaming difficulties, both parties tried to frame and implement a negotiation process in order to end their armed standoff.

Obviously, their negotiation efforts were not completely successful. On the other hand, they were not a total failure. Thirty-five people left Mount Carmel during the fifty-one-day standoff. The dead and wounded ATF agents were evacuated from the property. The FBI sent milk for the children, medicine for the wounded, telephone equipment, and a video camera into Mount Carmel. The parties successfully arranged for two defense attorneys to meet with the Branch Davidians, and they engaged in highly unusual face-to-face negotiations on the Mount Carmel property. So we can hardly conclude that the FBI and the Branch Davidians were totally incapable of managing their worldview differences in order to handle specific issues or problems. On the other hand, there is enough evidence of worldview management difficulties at Waco to warrant a research project designed to "observe" the impact of worldviewing (negotiating reality) on the parties' efforts to resolve their confrontation using issue-specific negotiation. (See fig. 4 in chapter 2.)

We must "watch" the parties interact in order to observe the impact of worldviewing on issue-specific negotiation. Given the rarity of issue-specific negotiations between parties who have not managed their worldviewing differences and the unlikely presence of research-oriented observers to such a process, it is not surprising that little attention has been given to this research problem. And given the fact that I began my research project two years after the confrontation in Waco, the reader might ask how I could possibly watch the parties in action. Fortunately, the FBI followed the standard practice of recording the negotiation sessions, so there is a record of the interactions between the parties.

The FBI also maintained Critical Incident Logs (hereafter, "logs") to facilitate information sharing among the law enforcement units (HRT, command, negotiations, and technical support) involved in the standoff. The negotiators used the logs to summarize the most important information from each negotiation session. The log entries, which are labeled with date and time, are easily coordinated with the transcripts. Reading the transcripts alongside the logs, I was able to follow the actual conversation between the parties while also "eavesdropping" on the FBI negotiators' *interpretation* of "what counted" or had merit in the conversation.

The Mount Carmel residents did not keep logs. However, one of the worst kept secrets in law enforcement, even immediately after April 19, is the fact that the FBI managed to use sophisticated listening devices to record conversations inside Mount Carmel. The tapes made from the listening devices may provide a similar window into the Branch Davidian interpretation of the negotiations. Unfortunately, the Department of Justice has declined to release the listening tapes for public scrutiny or scholarly research.[1] On the other hand,

---

1. In March 1996, I submitted a request for the "bug" tapes, or for transcripts of the tapes, under the Freedom of Information Act. At that time, they were unavailable. Since then, the Department of Justice has released portions of the tapes during various court proceedings and investigations. These segments have been used to bolster the claim that the Branch Davidians set the fires on April 19. To my knowledge, no one has been permitted to analyze the full content of the bug tapes.

the Branch Davidians were quite forthright in their rejection of the FBI's naming, framing, and blaming stories, probably a consequence of their preferred focus on negotiating reality. Whatever the reason behind them, the Branch Davidians' attempts to negotiate reality with the FBI allow us to draw tentative conclusions about their interpretations of the negotiation efforts on the basis of the negotiation transcripts alone.

Defining Concepts

If we are going to study the interrelated processes of *issue-specific negotiation* and *negotiating reality*, we must first define these terms and explain how the processes are interrelated in practice and research.

What Is Negotiation?

Fisher and Ury argue that "like it or not, you are a negotiator. Negotiation is a fact of life. People negotiate even when they don't think of themselves as doing so" (1981, xi). Negotiation is taught in business schools, law schools, dispute and conflict resolution programs, special workshops, and training programs. Within the emergent discipline of conflict analysis and resolution, negotiation research is by far the most developed subfield. Despite all of the attention given to negotiation, however, there is no commonly accepted definition of the term itself.

As with any field of practice, the guiding metaphor we adopt to describe negotiation shapes our research, theories, and negotiation practices. Negotiation has been described as: bargaining, joint choice, joint research, joint construction of a future, a drama, a search for justice, and interactive problem solving (Spector 1996). For many researchers, negotiation is equated with bargaining (Carnevale and Hilty 1992; Fouraker and Siegel 1963; Iklé 1993; Pruitt and Lewis 1977; Rubin and Brown 1975); and the "negotiation is bargaining" metaphor has profoundly affected both the theoretical analysis of negotiation and the development of negotiation tactics (Sergeev 1991, 59).

However, not all bargaining is the same, and not all bargaining research begins with identical assumptions. The narrowest research looks only at quantifiable, tradable commodities with an eye to identifying the bargaining zone "within which it is better for both parties to agree than not to agree" (Bazerman and Neale 1992, 73). Other researchers and practitioners distinguish between integrative and competitive bargaining and look at nonmaterial "goods" as well as at material resources when thinking about bargaining. Gulliver proposes a very broad concept of bargaining as "the presentation and exchange of more or less specific proposals for the terms of agreement on particular issues" (1979, 71).

In spite of the differences among bargaining-oriented research, there is one overarching similarity. Research on bargaining behavior "posits a rational actor model of negotiation which characterizes effective negotiation as the result of rational discourse between contending parties" (Hammer and Rogan 1997, 10). This same rational-actor model is extended to research that focuses on problem solving (Burton 1987; Bush and Folger 1994). Unfortunately, overemphasizing the rational behavior of parties who are engaged in bargaining, negotiating, or problem solving tends to obscure the ways in which those parties also negotiate reality. Although Gulliver's definition of bargaining has appeal, the "negotiation is bargaining" metaphor is nevertheless overly narrow to capture the full experience of negotiation. Negotiation also includes activities such as persuasion, debate, problem solving, adaptive learning, and joint decision making (Cross 1996; Druckman 1977; Gulliver 1979; Hopmann 1995; Kelman 1996; Walcott, Hopmann, and King 1977). For the purposes of my work, I assume that issue-specific negotiation exhibits the following characteristics.

• Negotiation involves communication that takes many forms, including "persuasion and haggling . . . bargaining and debate . . . and using rhetoric to clarify issues and to persuade" (Druckman 1977, 41). Communication also includes the strategic use of silence and a refusal to interact with the other party.

• The process of issue-specific negotiation is goal directed and future oriented.

• Negotiation involves at least two parties who work on resolving their conflict without compulsion by a third party.

• The relationship of the negotiating parties is marked by a combination of shared and divergent interests, goals, and objectives.

• Bargaining may best be thought of as the end goal of other negotiation activities (Lewicki et al. 1994, 177–79).

• "In negotiation there are two distinct though interconnected processes going on simultaneously: a repetitive cyclical one and a developmental one" (Gulliver 1979, 82). Consequently, negotiation has both an interactive and a developmental quality.

Gulliver explains this last point by using the analogy of an automobile in motion. The repetitive cycles of moving wheels, pumping pistons, opening and closing valves, and firing spark plugs move the vehicle through space. In negotiation, says Gulliver, repetitive cycles of communication move the process of negotiation through a series of overlapping sequences or phases. The phases of negotiation are: (1) searching for an arena for negotiation, (2) formulating an agenda, (3) exploring the range of the dispute, (4) narrowing the differences between the parties, (5) determining a viable range of outcomes, (6) bargaining, and (7) ritually confirming the agreement (Holmes and Sykes 1993, 41). Moving through the phases is not always a neat linear process, and parties involved in negotiation may have to backtrack through previous phases when they encounter problems. For negotiations to succeed, however, they must ultimately move through each phase. According to this model of negotiation, the key to ultimate success is engaging in interactive processes that promote the parties' collective progression through the requisite phases.

I return to this two-phase model of negotiation when I explain how it has influenced crisis negotiation. First, however, I want to examine the concept of negotiating reality, a concept that is not easily incorporated into existing models of negotiation.

What Is Negotiating Reality?

What I call negotiating reality has also been described as the social construction of reality (Berger and Luckmann 1966) and "the fitting together of individual lines of action" (Blumer 1969, 82). The product of negotiating reality has been described as "a conflict-riddled, negotiated order" (Denzin 1992, 161) and a social order that is "made visible in everyday interchanges between people . . . incomplete . . . and revisable through negotiations" (Powell 1989, 17). The focus is on action as the wellspring of social structure and on symbolic action rather than unthinking responses to stimuli.

Joint actions emerge when "participants fit their acts together, first by identifying the social act in which they are about to engage and, second, by interpreting and defining each other's acts in forming the joint act" (Blumer 1969, 70). Joint actions are usually facilitated by the fact that "most of the situations encountered by people in a given society are defined or 'structured' by them in the same way" (Blumer 1969, 86). Tannen talks about " 'structures of expectations' " developed out of "one's experience of the world in a given culture (or combination of cultures)," and through which "one organizes knowledge about the world and uses this knowledge to predict interpretations and relationships regarding new information, events, and experiences" (1993a, 16). From this perspective, social reality is always being negotiated as people interpret, define, and mutually coordinate their actions.

The task of negotiating social reality can be more or less difficult depending on the extent to which people share meaning systems or symbolic worlds. In Waco, two socially negotiated realities, or worlds, collided. Each world was legitimate in the eyes of its adherents. Each world contained a rich array of scripts (Schank and Abelson 1977), schemas (Holland and Quinn 1987; Lakoff 1987), scenarios (Palmer 1996), and frames (Goffman 1986; Minsky 1975) that gave rise to coherent structures of expectations. Each world also rested on truth claims deemed offensive by "citizens" of the other world. Consequently, the participants in the encounter between federal agents and the Mount Carmel community did not define their shared experience in the same way. Their lines of action did not readily fit together, and collective action was greatly complicated by their inability to structure their actions jointly. This inability raises an important question about negotiation.

How Are Issue-Specific Negotiation and Negotiating Reality Connected?

General negotiation research. Most negotiation researchers do not even place the problem of a negotiated reality on their map of research problems. Negotiation research is, for the most part, steeped in assumptions that presume the parties may have different perceptions of reality, but not that the parties may live in or make different realities. The arenas in which negotiation research is conducted tend to reinforce this blindness to worldmaking activities. Negotiation is often studied in a business environment or in a university using simulations. In both settings, the parties share expectations or scripts that shape their interactions. They do not need to negotiate reality because everyone involved knows (and accepts) the rules for that arena.

Fortunately, some scholars are beginning to expand the map of research problems in ways that allow us to look at negotiating reality. These researchers have linked the concept of framing as "the construction of shared meanings that typify social and cultural contexts" to the study of negotiation (Putnam and Holmer 1992, 129; also see Drake and Donohue 1996).[2] In so doing, they have laid a foundation for a connection between negotiating reality and issue-specific negotiation. Even with this new line of research, it may take years for findings to impact the research and the practice related to crisis negotiation.[3]

Communication scholars are among those taking the lead in making a connection between negotiating reality and issue-specific negotiation. It is no accident that many of these researchers have turned to hostage negotiation transcripts as a fertile data source because the recorded negotiations provide ample materials for analysis. More important, however, the context of hostage negotiations creates unique opportunities to observe the simultaneous negotiation of reality and the negotiation of particular issues. Police negotiators and

2. Readers interested in this type of research might begin with the following sources. Geist (1995), Conrad and Sinclair-James (1995), and Littlejohn (1995) use negotiated order theory to focus on reality negotiation problems. Gibbons, Bradac, and Busch (1992) examine the role of meaning construction in persuasion during negotiation. Wilson and Putnam (1990) and Roloff and Jordan (1992) look at the projection, protection, and maintenance of "face" as part of the negotiators' constructed and negotiated identities. Donohue and Ramesh (1992) and Duck (1994) study the construction of negotiation relationships, and Bochner, Cissna, and Garko (1991) and Duck (1994) look at the management of meaning during negotiation.

3. One example of this type of research involves expanding on Morley's observation that "the end point of the [negotiation] process is a set of *rules*. . . . [and] there may also be an agreed *story* about what has happened, and why" (1986, 303). Research on negotiating the rules of negotiation has not been applied to crisis negotiation, no doubt because the police use coercive power to define the parameters of negotiation, and the barricaded subject usually acquiesces to the rules of negotiation laid out by the police. Most researchers also assume that the power to establish the rules by which a barricade negotiation will be conducted rests primarily or entirely with the police. However, in Waco and subsequent barricades involving the Freemen in Montana and the Republic of Texas, resistance to the rules of negotiation was a clear manifestation of the parties' worldview management problems. In such cases, the assumption that the police can unilaterally set the rules of negotiation may be a significant hindrance to peaceful resolution.

barricaded subjects do not have a prior relationship, and their interactions are not part of a prescribed script located within a stable social context. Furthermore, their intentions are coercive—including the goal of coercing the other party into one's own reality. Consequently, the barricaded subject and police negotiator must quickly establish a relationship adequate to support negotiation, frame the process by which they will negotiate, and articulate a mutually acceptable power relationship. All of these reality negotiation tasks are accomplished in conjunction with an issue-specific negotiation process.

The scholars who are studying hostage negotiation transcripts hope to improve crisis negotiation practices and to transfer to other arenas the lessons learned from studying barricade negotiations. Unfortunately, their work appears to be having little direct influence on the training of crisis negotiators, and the crisis negotiation literature does not reflect any awareness of the reality negotiation problem.[4]

Crisis negotiation research and training. Crisis or hostage negotiation literature comes in two varieties: papers written by and for practitioners and academic studies of crisis negotiation transcripts.[5] The literature written by practitioners is largely disconnected from the body of general negotiation research. Even the hostage negotiation research most directly tied to police agencies appears to have a limited influence on training materials.

A recently published book on crisis negotiation has started to bridge the gap between general negotiation research and crisis negotiation practice: McMains and Mullins's 1996 *Crisis Negotiations: Managing Critical Incidents and Hostage Situations in Law Enforcement and Corrections.* However, the authors clearly favor a very practice-oriented wing of academic writing on negotiation

---

4. The absence of practitioner interest in the reality negotiation problem was particularly true prior to 1993. It is important, when the performance of the negotiators in Waco is examined, to place them in historical context and focus on the standards of practice that prevailed at that time.

5. Academic research on crisis negotiation can be grouped under three broad headings. There is a school of communication-based research that builds on Strauss's negotiated order theory and on other communication-based frameworks for studying and explaining interaction (Donohue and Roberto 1993, 1996; Hammer and Rogan 1997; Powell 1989; Ramesh 1992; Rogan 1990; Rogan and Hammer 1995). There is phase research (Abbott 1986; Holmes 1997; Holmes and Sykes 1993), and, finally, there is a small set of research based on symbolic convergence theory (Covert 1984; Ramesh 1992).

(Fisher, Ury, and Patton 1991; Ury 1981), research that equates bargaining and negotiation (Putnam and Jones 1982; Rubin and Brown 1975), and research conducted in management or business environments. There is no reference to social constructionist research that might raise issues of a negotiated reality. More disturbingly, in four hundred pages, the authors fail to acknowledge the growing body of communication-based research on barricade and crisis negotiations. In the absence of theoretical and analytical contributions from academic researchers, crisis negotiation literature often takes the form of anecdotal accounts of "lessons learned" during highly visible incidents (Fagan and Van Zandt 1993; Fuselier, Van Zandt, and Lanceley 1989, 1991; Van Zandt and Fuselier 1989).

When theoretical frameworks are employed in the practitioner literature, the authors write as if the theories they are using have been proven valid (Hare 1997). For example, the most favored theoretical framework is a combination of Miron and Goldstein's distinction between expressive and instrumental acts with diagnostic categories from psychology and psychiatry. The result is a crisis negotiation practice that "focus[es] on assessing perpetrator behavior according to the two-part taxonomy of instrumental and expressive acts" (Hammer and Rogan 1997, 14), while simultaneously diagnosing the barricaded subject for particular illnesses such as paranoia, borderline personality disorder, and schizophrenia (Borum and Strentz 1992; DiVasto, Lanceley, and Gruys 1992; Lanceley 1981; Miron and Goldstein 1979; Strentz 1986).

Although the instrumental/expressive taxonomy and the use of psychiatric diagnoses have proven helpful in many barricade situations, it is not at all clear that these analytical frameworks are universally applicable. They provide an inadequate conceptual model for understanding and negotiating with barricaded communities motivated by unconventional beliefs. Furthermore, there is growing recognition that Miron and Goldstein's expressive/instrumental continuum of action has, in practice, been transformed into a dichotomous schema for classifying events (Hammer and Rogan 1997). The insight that all communication carries multiple messages, so that an act may be both instrumental and expressive in nature, is in danger of being lost.

Crisis negotiation practice and training materials are also influenced by Gulliver's two-process model of negotiation. Police negotiators are trained using prescriptive models that advocate engaging in nonbargaining interactions to establish a basis for bargaining. On the microlevel of interaction, police negotiators are trained to use active listening, indirect questioning, I-messages, embedded sentences, and therapeutic communication practices (Froman and Glorioso 1984; McMains and Mullins 1996, chap. 6; Miron and Goldstein 1979; Slatkin 1996). Crisis negotiators are also instructed to develop a relationship with the barricaded subject, instill doubt in the subject about his or her current choice, use techniques of persuasion and influence, adopt active listening skills, and build rapport with the subject (McMains and Mullins 1996, appendix A). All of these activities are promoted as necessary to reach the point at which the barricaded subjects will engage in bargaining and rational problem solving. Crisis negotiators are being taught to recognize the developmental phases in crisis negotiation (Abbott 1986; Donohue et al. 1991; Holmes and Sykes 1993; Rogan 1990), but it is not at all clear that they are being taught to think reflectively about the connection between their interactive work with the barricaded subject and the sequential development of the negotiation process. There seems to be an assumption in the training literature that good interactive techniques will always and automatically yield the desired sequential phase development.

An Early Research Design Discarded

Based on the models and theories just described, I began my Waco negotiation research project with the following assumptions. Negotiation research, in general, ignores the problem of negotiating reality even though there are some conflicts in which this problem cannot be ignored. Negotiations, when they progress smoothly, do so because the parties effectively use interactive communication processes in order to move successfully through the requisite phases or stages beginning with arena and problem identification and ending with ritual closure. I theorized that problems with negotiating reality are likely to disrupt *both* the interactive processes and the phase development when parties are attempting to negotiate a specific issue or problem.

Thus, using the Gulliver (1979) model as applied to crisis negotiation by Holmes and Sykes (1993), I articulated two interrelated research questions. First, did worldview management problems disrupt the cyclical process of negotiation interaction in Waco? If yes, how? Second, did the disruption of the cyclical process of negotiation prevent the development of normal negotiation phases in Waco? If yes, how?

I then experimented with a two-level coding process. First, I coded seventy-five sequential transcripts using a set of predefined indicators of worldview management problems, including the parties' use of competing metaphors and their continuing reliance on divergent naming, framing, and blaming stories that resist transformation or resolution. I then attempted to code a clean copy of the same transcripts using the phase indicators developed by Holmes and Sykes (1993).[6] When comparing the two sets of coded transcripts, I expected to see increased indications of worldviewing difficulties whenever there was an effort to move the negotiations into another phase. I expected this problem because when parties move from one phase of negotiation to the next, they must affirm what they have accomplished thus far and reach agreement about the next task at hand. Both the affirmation of past accomplishments and the designation of next steps involve framing activities and are therefore likely to direct attention to worldviewing problems.

I discovered that in the Waco transcripts the phase development was so disrupted as to be almost nonexistent. Very small phase development patterns were embedded in apparent chaos. For example, the negotiations over sending in milk and the negotiations about sending some of the children out of Mount Carmel eventually progressed according to the phase model suggested by Gulliver (1979) and by Holmes and Sykes (1993). However, the surrounding negotiation over ending the standoff rarely settled into clearly sustained discussion focused on a single task or phase and obviously never resulted in a successful outcome.

Indeed, throughout the negotiations, the Branch Davidians were particularly reluctant to move beyond phase one (searching for an arena for negotiation) or phase two (formulating an agenda). This may sound odd to the reader, and it was certainly puzzling to the FBI negotiators. Whereas the negotiators assumed that the arena for negotiation was a barricade standoff and the agenda

6. These phases are: (1) searching for an arena for negotiation, (2) formulating an agenda, (3) exploring the range of the dispute, (4) narrowing the differences between the parties, (5) determining a viable range of outcomes, (6) bargaining, and (7) ritually confirming the agreement (Holmes and Sykes 1993, 41).

was moving the Branch Davidians from behind the barricade into the court system, the Branch Davidians contested both of these assumptions. On the other hand, the Branch Davidians were puzzled and frustrated by the way the FBI negotiators simply could not or would not hear that Davidian concerns for justice, fairness, and the preservation of their own sense of reality went beyond just ending the current standoff. I finally concluded that if I wanted to say anything more than "the negotiations failed to develop through the requisite phases," I would have to refine further my conceptual model and coding schema.

A Simplified Research Design

In the end, I decided to keep the research questions simple. Starting with the nested model of issue-specific negotiation taking place within a negotiated reality (fig. 4 in chapter 2), I asked the following questions: What activities comprise negotiating reality? What activities comprise issue-specific negotiation? What types of language are used to negotiate reality? What types of language are used during issue-specific negotiation? I hypothesized that the coded transcripts would reveal those periods when worldviewing seemed particularly disruptive to the development of negotiation phases. These portions of the transcripts would be made visible by the fact that the FBI and the Branch Davidians were each trying to engage in a different activity, or they were using different languages, or both.

Mapping Activities and Languages onto the
Nested Model of Negotiation

The activities and languages of negotiating reality. I have talked about naming, framing, and blaming as worldmaking activities used in response to conflict. These activities rely on the rhetorical use of symbolic and narrative language. For example, the terrorist narrative President Bush used in response to the Iraqi invasion of Kuwait was effective because it named a conflict-generating breach of norms, allocated blame, and framed a process and resolution that appealed to Bush's domestic and international audiences. The power of the terrorist narrative rested on the symbols it invoked (a rogue terrorist, innocent victim/hostage, and righteous protector). However, the power of the symbols was greatly heightened by a narrative structure that created a heroic role (protectors of the innocent) for the United States and its allies, as well as images of a desirable outcome to the confrontation (good triumphing over evil).

The activities and languages of crisis negotiation. Police negotiators have identified activities involved in crisis negotiation. Some of these activities are microlevel *negotiation tactics* such as listening actively, using I-messages, questioning indirectly, and composing embedded sentences. Other activities are *negotiation strategies* such as defusing intense emotions, developing a relationship with the subject, building rapport, instilling doubt in the subject about his or her current choice, and persuading the subject that other options meet his or her needs. Researchers point to other activities such as facework that practitioners have only vaguely articulated.

Crisis negotiators have also identified as instrumental and expressive the types of language used to accomplish these activities. I have joined other researchers in substituting the term *relational* for the term *expressive*. Within crisis negotiation models, expressive language is considered largely extraneous to the negotiation process. That is to say, negotiators are instructed to work with or around expressive language in order to get to the "real" (instrumental) languages of bargaining and problem solving. In fact, however, researchers have documented crisis negotiators and barricaded subjects actively using so-called expressive language for two purposes. They use relational language to build rapport and relationships with the other party, and they use identity language to preserve and defend their own "face" and that of the other party.

Putting the model together. The activities and languages associated with negotiating reality and issue-specific negotiation can be mapped onto the nested model of negotiation (fig. 8.). This refined and clarified model points to particular *indicators* of negotiating reality and issue-specific negotiation. Using these indicators, I was able to code the Waco negotiation transcripts for six types of *language:* narrative [NARRAT], symbolic [SYMBOL], instrumental [INSTRUM], relational [RELAT], and identity [IDENT]. Ritual greetings, chitchat, and statements that were interrupted before the speaker said anything of substance were coded as null [NULL]. Readers interested in more detailed definitions of each language type will find more information in appendix B.

Limitations of the coding process. The coding process is clearly interpretive

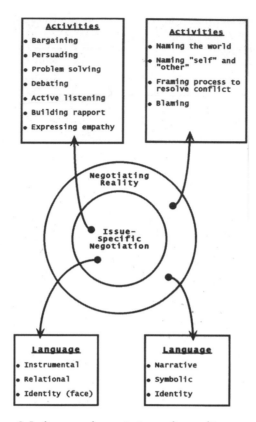

8. Indicators of negotiating reality and issue-specific negotiation.

and is not in any way intended to classify definitively a statement as symbolic *or* narrative *or* instrumental in nature. For one thing, the coding categories are not discrete. A single statement almost always includes more than one type of language. I used the coding process as a tool of self-discipline, a means of introducing rigor into my reading of the transcripts. By focusing attention on the types of language being used, I had a better chance of approaching the material with the same basic questions in mind each day.

I coded transcripts for six forms of language, focusing the coding at the level of a complete "turn" taken by a given speaker. However, my original question was about both meaning making (reflected in language) and negotiation progress (reflected in activities). Coding for activities must focus on larger sections of the transcripts because working on an activity involves communicative exchanges between the parties over a sustained period. In the end, I concluded that a line-by-line coding for activities would not yield the information I was seeking. Instead, I opted to focus on a selected set of transcripts and a limited range of activities. How did I select the transcripts that received detailed analysis?

Selecting among the transcripts for activities. Based on reading through the complete set of transcripts several times, I concluded that the negotiations in Waco were essentially finished by March 15. (See my overview of the negotiation phases in the introduction.) By that time, the parties were locked in a recursive loop of talking past each other, and they were turning to more coercive (FBI) and resistant (Branch Davidian) strategies. Therefore, I decided to focus my intensive analysis on the period from February 28 through March 15. I coded transcripts after March 15 insofar as they contained exchanges related to the four activities on which I opted to focus my analytical work.

I further refined my analysis by focusing on four critically important activities in any negotiation process: establishing a relationship between the parties, bargaining, framing the negotiation process, and reaching and ratifying an agreement. Why did I select these processes for attention? First, during the short period between February 28 and March 15, both the Branch Davidians and law enforcement negotiators made a clear effort to establish a good working relationship, and they had some success using bargaining processes to accomplish specific tasks. They also appeared to reach an agreement for a complete surrender by the Branch Davidians, and they spent considerable time planning the "ritual of surrender," only to have the agreement break down. Second, the Branch Davidians expended an increasing amount of energy during this period trying to frame the negotiation process. The FBI, by and large, rejected the Branch Davidian framing efforts as irrelevant because in their opinion this situation was clearly a hostage-barricade negotiation. If I ignored the Branch Davidians' framing efforts in my analysis, I would privilege the FBI framing of the problem and thereby violate my own commitment to adopting a symmetrical anthropology (chapter 3) when dealing with worldview conflicts.

Therefore, I opted to focus analytical attention on framing in addition to the activities (building rapport, bargaining, and planning for a surrender) that both parties supported to some extent.

I hoped that the coding process would help me determine whether world-viewing problems contributed to the collapse of the negotiations, and if so, how. I adopted the following working questions.

• Did worldviewing differences disrupt the process of establishing a relationship between the barricaded subjects and the FBI negotiators in Waco? If yes, how?

• Did worldviewing differences disrupt the use of bargaining processes in Waco? If yes, how?

• Did worldviewing differences disrupt the process of establishing (framing) a mutually acceptable negotiation process in Waco? If yes, how?

• Did worldviewing differences undermine the March 2 agreement and subsequent efforts to resolve the standoff? If yes, how?

Demonstrating the Benefit of Coding for Symbolic and Narrative Language

Coding the following conversation between David Koresh and an FBI negotiator demonstrates the value of looking at narrative and symbolic language in worldview conflicts.[7] Koresh and the FBI negotiator are discussing the problem of sending children out of Mount Carmel.

> PN03: . . . You immediately started letting the children come out of the compound because some of them are concerned and afraid and they don't un-

---

7. With three exceptions, I have assigned numbers to the law enforcement negotiators, rather than use names. My goal is to uncover and critique the unspoken assumptions of crisis negotiation as it is currently practiced, not to pinpoint any one negotiator for criticism. I refer to only three negotiators by name: Larry Lynch (a deputy with the local sheriff's office), Byron Sage (the first FBI negotiator on the scene), and Jim Cavanaugh (the ATF agent who assumed the role of negotiator in the immediate aftermath of the February 28 raid). The identities of these men have been so widely discussed in subsequent official reports, books, trials, and media accounts that maintaining their anonymity serves no purpose.

derstand everything that's going on. And I think that that's been real good. And I would—

DAVID [KORESH]: They're unable to make at this point a real decision in regards to . . . you know, choosing good and evil, so to speak.

PN03: Right . . . and I want us to continue with that. I would like to see you continue sending out—

DAVID: We're going to, we're going to.

PN03: Okay, good.

DAVID: You know, we're, like I say, we're at the point now to where, you know, my father, my God, our God, you know, whether we, acknowledge him or not. Our God is keeping a very strict and close eye on every movement that's being made. (Tape 33: 41–42)

Using *only* the established categories of instrumental, relational, and identity language and marking all other language as NULL, I would probably code the preceding passage as follows.

[IDENT INSTRUM RELAT] PN03: . . . You immediately started letting the children come out of the compound because some of them are concerned and afraid and they don't understand everything that's going on. And I think that that's been real good. And I would—

[NULL] DAVID: They're unable to make at this point a real decision in regards to . . . you know, choosing good and evil, so to speak.

[INSTRUM RELAT] PN03: Right . . . and I want us to continue with that. I would like to see you continue sending out—

[INSTRUM] DAVID: We're going to, we're going to.

[RELAT] PN03: Okay, good.

[IDENT] DAVID: You know, we're, like I say, we're at the point now to where, you know, my father, my God, our God, you know, whether we, acknowledge him or not. Our God is keeping a very strict and close eye on every movement that's being made. (Tape 33: 41–42)

The negotiator's opening statement reinforces the positive value of bargaining for the release of the children [INSTRUM], builds a positive identity for Koresh as a reasonable person who cares about the children [IDENT], and expresses the parties' shared concern for the well-being of the children [RELAT]. All of these messages reflect established crisis negotiation strategies. Identify a problem that can be resolved cooperatively through bargaining or problem solving. Engage the barricaded subject in the task by building his positive identity as a reasonable person capable of rational decision making. Build rapport with the subject by articulating shared concerns, goals, and commitments.

Adding the symbolic and narrative categories, we see that the FBI negotiator's opening statement also holds symbolic and narrative content. The negotiator accomplishes his instrumental, relational, and identity objectives by telling a snippet of a story about scared and confused children [NARRAT]. Koresh opts to respond to the narrative rather than to the instrumental message and begins his own story about the children as immature moral agents [NARRAT and SYMBOL]. The FBI negotiator redirects the conversation to the immediate problem of releasing children [INSTRUM] and makes a clear relational claim on Koresh [RELAT]. Koresh responds with an instrumental assurance and an acknowledgment of the relational claim. However, he then continues with *his* primary concern, explaining to the FBI negotiator the larger theological and religious implications of the current standoff. In so doing, he invokes God as a witness to current activities in Waco [NARRAT and SYMBOL].

Negotiators are told to "match" their language to that of the barricaded subject, but matching is presumed to occur along the instrumental-expressive (relational) continuum. In this case, the negotiator sets an instrumental tone by focusing attention on the children who have already left Mount Carmel. Koresh responds with a symbolic explanation of *why* the children should be sent out of a dangerous situation, but the FBI negotiator ignores that language to persist with the instrumental focus on getting more children out of harm's way.

This pattern was consistent in the Waco negotiations, in which some FBI negotiators dismissed the Branch Davidian symbolic language as "Bible babble."[8] Without any attention to symbolic and narrative language, David

---

8. The diplomacy of the negotiators kept them from using this pejorative phrase when talking directly with the Branch Davidians, even though they used it among themselves. As time wore on, however, some of the negotiators came close to using this type of dismissive language, and from the outset most of the negotiators made it abundantly clear that biblical language was not relevant to the task at hand.

Koresh's explanations for why the children were being sent out of Mount Carmel are coded as NULL language. Yet Koresh's symbolic and narrative language contains a wealth of information about the Branch Davidian worldview. This information could have been used to create a coherent rationale for ending the standoff, a rationale grounded in the worldmaking narrative of the Branch Davidians and therefore more likely to accomplish the task at hand.

Coding for six types of language illustrates that messages the FBI negotiators considered strictly instrumental or expressive also contained implicit symbolic references. This situation was particularly apparent when the FBI negotiators attempted to use persuasion. For example, when trying to convince Scott Sonobe to assume a leadership role within the Mount Carmel community, the negotiator referenced a symbolic construction of the world in which men are the protectors of women and children.

> [SYMBOL IDENT RELAT] PN01: You know, a lot of people, the little kids who can't talk for themselves, all the women who are scared. You know, they're counting on the men to be strong, to lead them out. You know what I'm saying? (Tape 18: 4)

The negotiator was trying to build up Sonobe's face. As a man, he was also expressing rapport. "We men have to take seriously our duties to protect those who are weaker." A woman negotiator would probably not be able to use this persuasive argument credibly. Furthermore, this effort at persuasion will work only if the person to whom it is addressed also believes that men must protect women and children from danger. The listener must also agree that remaining inside Mount Carmel puts the women and children in greater danger than exiting the property.

Unaware of their own use of symbolic language, the FBI negotiators viewed this utterance and others like it as an effort to encourage Sonobe by beefing up his resolve. When Sonobe and others at Mount Carmel failed to respond positively to these efforts, the negotiators attributed this failure to the psychological traits or conditions of the Branch Davidians. They were described as either brainwashed or suffering from low self-esteem (Justice 206). Without a recognition of their own symbolic construction of the situation, the FBI negotiators did not consider the possibility that Sonobe and others failed to respond because they did not accept the negotiators' basic assumptions about the world. In this specific case, many Branch Davidians concluded that the women and children were safer at Mount Carmel than they were out in "the world."

What Constitutes Instrumental Language?

During the Waco standoff, the FBI negotiators encountered frequent resistance to their implicit symbolic references, which leads me to speculate that the category I am calling symbolic language is a *comparative category*; it exposes worldviewing differences. If everyone involved in a conversation and those observing it (or coding the transcripts) share a meaning system, then the category of symbolic language will be pushed into the background because no one presents an alternate set of symbols.

Recognizing the ease with which worldmaking language can disappear in the absence of persons who contest the shared reality of a group forced me to reconsider the relativism of all of my coding categories. Who, I wondered, said that language focused on getting everyone in Mount Carmel out from behind the armed barricade was instrumental? I concluded that the category of instrumental language does not exist separately from a particular worldmaking narrative. The FBI would agree that language focused on ending the standoff was instrumental in nature. The Branch Davidians, on the other hand, would probably see as instrumental all language focused on getting the FBI to recognize the legitimacy of Davidian biblical teachings.

Anyone coding the transcripts must adopt a standpoint or position from which to identify instrumental language. Thus explodes the myth of researcher neutrality. In the absence of a neutral position from which to work, the researcher is obligated to delineate her standpoint clearly. For coding purposes in this case, I have assumed that instrumental language was directed toward solving particular problems related to the safe conclusion of the standoff. I say this not because I privilege the FBI perspective over the Branch Davidian perspective. It is strictly a reflection of my own interests in doing this research. I want to understand why the Waco negotiations broke down because my primary practical objective is to develop analytical frameworks and negotiation practices that are more likely to succeed when law enforcement agents confront communities motivated by unconventional beliefs. If my goal were to understand the dynamics of religious conversion efforts during a barricade standoff, I would adopt the Branch Davidian perspective. I would code as instrumental all language related to Branch Davidian efforts to persuade the FBI negotiators that they were participating in an encounter of cosmic significance for the imminent apocalypse.

5

Establishing Relationships Across a Worldview Divide

FBI NEGOTIATORS ARE INSTRUCTED to build rapport and relationships of trust with barricaded subjects, which, they are told, can be accomplished through active, empathetic listening. The model of communication on which this practice is based is rarely articulated. When it is made explicit, it becomes apparent that crisis negotiators are being taught to view communication largely as a mechanical process of sending and receiving messages. A textbook on crisis negotiation identifies seven components of communication: (1) a sender who encodes a message; (2) the message itself; (3) the channel to convey the message; (4) the receiver who must decode the message; (5) noise that may interfere with the message; (6) feedback or the receiver's response; and (7) the context that helps determine appropriate and inappropriate messages (McMains and Mullins 1996, 145). Of these communication components, only "the context that helps determine appropriate and inappropriate messages" touches on meaning creation or worldviewing problems. Unfortunately, this aspect of communication theory remains largely undeveloped in the crisis negotiation literature. The FBI training materials treat communication activities as tools to be employed in order to control the behavior of the barricaded subject. In this model of communication, the concepts of rapport and trust are detached from any understanding that communication does more than just exchange information or convey feelings. *Communication is also a process by which people cooperatively create meaning by naming the context within which they are operating.*

Police Negotiators and Barricaded Subjects Negotiate
Identities to Build Relationships

"How actors create a climate for negotiation is an important process in itself" (Powell 1989, 42), a process that is much neglected in crisis negotiation practice. The practical guides to hostage negotiation emphasize the mechanics of isolating, containing, and communicating with barricaded individuals. Inadequate attention is given to the communicative processes by which "antagonistic actors activate identities sufficient to initiate and maintain negotiation work, achieve the symmetry required for negotiation, and bring dangerous situations to a peaceful close" (Powell 1989, 42).

To correct this conceptual gap, Powell (1989) identifies six tasks that must be accomplished in order to initiate bargaining or problem solving. He also documents some of the means by which police negotiators consciously and unconsciously accomplish these tasks. The parties must recognize that they are interdependent and facing a shared future. They must identify a negotiable object or shared focus around which they can articulate differing objectives and engage in cooperative action. They must designate a mutually recognized meaningful disagreement about the negotiable object or shared focus. They need to create congruent functional identities as negotiators. In those cases where negotiators are acting on behalf of constituents or larger organizational entities, each party needs to recognize the other's representative identity.[1] Finally, negotiators must establish personal identities that allow them to confidently engage in a cooperative encounter that will result in mutual commitments. Implicit in Powell's work is the fact that parties in conflict are negotiating reality as they accomplish these six tasks. In other words, they cooperatively name self and other, and name the world (or at least their immediate context) in ways that enable them to engage in issue-specific negotiations.

Four of Powell's six tasks involve naming self and other. The parties must present and mutually affirm their respective identities as persons (personal identities), as representatives of larger groups (representative identities), as le-

---

1. Powell describes negotiators who act on behalf of others as activating *categorical identities*. I find this terminology unclear and confusing, so I use *representative identity* wherever he would use *categorical identity*.

gitimate negotiators (congruent functional identities), and as persons facing a shared future (interdependent identity). What do these four dimensions of identity entail? How are they interrelated? How are they enacted during typical crisis negotiations, and how did the unique features of the Waco standoff disrupt the enactment of the parties' identities, thereby interfering with their negotiation efforts?

Presenting Personal Identities

In typical barricade negotiations, the parties begin their encounter with no prior relationship. Therefore, police and barricaded subjects are forced to make declarations regarding their personal identities, and each party presents a personal identity that will advance his or her goals and interests. Police negotiators declare themselves to be trustworthy, fair, willing to cooperate, and concerned about the safety of the hostage taker as well as of the hostages. The barricaded subject's presentation of self changes over time. Early in the negotiations, a barricaded subject usually projects an image of someone who is in control, strong, and potentially dangerous. As it becomes apparent that his or her immediate goals are unattainable, the barricaded subject begins to display a more cooperative, trustworthy, and conciliatory persona. This change in demeanor is a logical response to the power imbalance between the parties because the police can easily overwhelm a typical barricaded subject, and he or she knows it.

In Waco, the power imbalance between law enforcement agents and the barricaded subjects was ambiguous. The Branch Davidians possessed or were rumored to possess a large quantity of high-powered weapons. They had also demonstrated their willingness to use weapons against law enforcement agents. Therefore, the tactical commanders mobilized armored personnel carriers (APCs) to protect agents assigned to exposed positions. Feeling threatened by the "tanks" on their property, the Branch Davidians responded with combative rhetoric. Their verbal threats validated the tactical commanders' fears and evoked more menacing postures from the tactical units. Thus, the relative *balance* of power in Waco fueled conflict escalatory interactions that complicated the establishment of positive personal identities and a relationship of trust.

Whereas most barricaded subjects drop their tough rhetoric as the barricade is stabilized, the Branch Davidians vacillated between conciliatory language and violent posturing. Their pugnacious statements were intended to make the FBI think twice about using the military equipment they were bringing to Mount Carmel. The Branch Davidians' presentation of self did not follow the "normal" pattern for a barricade standoff, and the FBI negotiators already assumed the residents of Mount Carmel were psychologically unstable. Consequently, the Davidians' mercurial self-presentation led some negotiators to question whether members of the community were reliable negotiating partners. A problem located in the worldmaking interactions between the parties was thereby attributed to the "flawed character" of one party, with negative consequences for the entire issue-specific negotiation process.

In typical crisis negotiations, police and barricaded subjects also attempt to make a chaotic and dangerous situation more predictable by imposing identities on one another. It is certainly safer for the barricaded individual to assume that all police officers are hostile. Therefore, he or she does not readily separate the individual police negotiator from his or her role identity as a law enforcement officer. Police negotiators actively promote a softening of their role identity by presenting themselves as caring persons in search of a diplomatic solution to a dangerous situation. Only over time do barricaded subjects allow police negotiators to mobilize personal identities that mitigate some of the hostility inherent in their role identities as law enforcement agents.

Police negotiators are able to bring forth their personal identities because they are not rigidly constrained by a prenegotiated institutionalized *script*. The concept of a script is most closely associated with the work of Schank and Abelson (1977). A script can be described as "a commonly assumed temporal ordering for some kind of event, for example, 'meal in a restaurant', 'trip to the beach' " (Bothamley 1993, 477). Scripts work, in part, because they identify specific roles and the activities associated with those roles. Thus, it does not matter which person acts the part of a waiter in the restaurant. As long as someone assumes that role and as long as that role is validated by the participants, they can cooperatively enact the "meal in a restaurant" script. Unlike persons having a meal in a restaurant, police negotiators and barricaded subjects must improvise their interactions.

Although there are no institutionalized and frequently repeated scripts to guide police negotiators and barricaded subjects, there are proto scripts. Popular culture contains enough examples of barricade negotiations that most people have a vague (and often inaccurate) idea of how these situations are likely to play out. Police negotiators also have a preferred script, which they hope to entice the barricaded subject into enacting. In Waco, the Branch Davidians resisted the FBI negotiators' script because they saw their negotiations with law enforcement officials as embedded in and shaped by the larger drama of the imminent Second Coming of Christ. On the other hand, the FBI rejected the Branch Davidians' End Time script. The existence of competing scripts disrupted the establishment of relationships capable of supporting a negotiation process.

Even when they are working with complementary proto scripts, the actors in a barricade situation are simultaneously creating the social context of their encounter (an armed barricade) and negotiating their identities (barricaded subject and police negotiators), which greatly complicates their problem-solving endeavors. To work together, the parties must be able to predict one another's actions and responses. Without clear role identities and a script, parties in barricade situations are forced to rely very heavily on personal identities when trying to predict behaviors and responses. Hence, the police interview anyone they can find who knows the subject in order to formulate a clearer sense of his or her personal identity (Fuselier, Van Zandt, and Lanceley 1991; McMains and Mullins 1996, 259–80). They supplement information about the barricaded subject with psychological taxonomies that categorize hostage takers according to their motivations and personality types. In Waco, however, the barricaded "subject" was a community of diverse people motivated by shared unconventional beliefs. Constructing individual profiles for each member of the community was impossible, and the negotiators knew virtually nothing about the community as a collective social unit.

In their search for information about a barricaded subject, police negotiators make every effort to identify credible sources (McMains and Mullins 1996, 277–79). In Waco, however, much of the information given to the FBI negotiators was tainted. The Branch Davidians had been brought to the attention of the ATF by disaffected former group members. During their investigation, the ATF consulted with other estranged community members, families who were worried about loved ones living at Mount Carmel, and anticult organizations. The same atrocity tales that led the ATF to investigate the Mount Carmel community and to stage the February 28 raid continued to influence the FBI negotiators, and they ignored more reasoned assessments of the group's motives and behaviors.

The situation in Waco was further exacerbated by an internal inconsistency in crisis negotiation practice. Police negotiators attempt to establish rapport with barricaded subjects by finding common ground with them as persons. At the same time, they assert worldnaming control by using psychological taxonomies to impose identities on barricaded subjects. Getting to know persons as individuals implies an effort to "get inside their heads and understand how they see their own circumstances" (Duck 1994, 89). The use of psychological taxonomies, on the other hand, treats a barricaded subject as "an object for us as observers" (Duck 1994, 89). Setting aside any moral repugnance we might feel at objectifying another human being, the practice of imposing an identity on a barricaded subject is risky. Oversimplified imposed identities do not predict the full range of motives that guide a person's actions. Furthermore, barricaded subjects resist—sometimes violently—being reduced to bundles of traits. In rare cases, a barricaded subject may accept an imposed identity without resistance. More typically, identities are contested, argued, and stabilized through mutual consent.

In Waco, the Branch Davidians were unable to communicate the full range of their personal identities to the FBI negotiators. This failure was not owing to a lack of effort; it was a consequence of blind spots in the FBI negotiators' worldmaking narratives. The following statements by Steve Schneider and Wayne Martin were typical of statements made by many members of the Mount Carmel community. They include a great deal of information about the Branch Davidians' sense of self, information that the FBI negotiators in Waco largely ignored.

> STEVE: Larry, all I ever wanted, like the rest of these people, is eternal life. This world everybody ends in death. This world is really a cemetery, whether it's disease or whatever else. A person lives their life, they come to an end. . . . We would like to see that the whole world has an opportunity. That's . . . what we're all about. We're about what the Bible speaks from one end to the other end. . . . That's what we're all about. I want to see you make it, I want to see myself make it. I mean we were here studying that book to know exactly what God— (911.6: 14)

WAYNE: Well, you know, sometimes, ah, it's hard to make people realize where we're coming from. We're people that try to live out the Bible. . . . And we thought that in America we had a right, a constitutional right to our religious beliefs. . . . Now . . . we don't think that's possible anymore. (911.6: 22–23)

The psychologizing practices of police negotiators lead them to "conceive of the self as being defined by *individuality*" (Abrams 1990, 92). This approach "generally disregards the possibility that *group membership itself may confer identity*" (Abrams 1990, 92, emphasis added). In a normal barricade setting, where the police confront an individual or possibly a small group of individuals, police taxonomies are problematic because they reduce persons to bundles of traits. In Waco, where the police were negotiating with a community of barricaded subjects, psychological taxonomies were problematic because they obscured motives that were grounded in social or group identity rather than in an individualized sense of self-identity.

Affirming Representative Identities

"The interpersonal structure of negotiations is raised to another level of complexity when actors elaborate their agreements and disagreements to include larger organizational contexts" (Powell 1989, 29). Personal identities may be offered in an attempt to separate persons from their roles. Representative identities are, by contrast, an expression of roles. Negotiators use their representative identities when speaking for the larger corporate groups of which they are a part. Representative identities allow a person to make promises on behalf of a group and to tap into group resources to meet negotiated obligations. On the other hand, representative identities can also constrain the negotiator because his or her constituents may need to ratify or reject any agreement, a common problem in many negotiation arenas. Representatives of labor and management each answer to constituencies or superiors, and those who represent interest-based stakeholder groups in public-policy dialogues answer to larger communities. Representative identities are both constraining and empowering. A negotiator's ability to mobilize other actors and institutional resources to implement any agreement adds to his or her strength and credibility as a negotiator. However, the constraints imposed by his or her constituency may make the negotiator less flexible. Astute negotiators use their representative identities to their own advantage. For example, negotiators attribute their lack of flexibility to pressure from their bosses or constituents, or they pressure the other party by implying that those same bosses or constituents will act in unpredictable and dangerous ways if an agreement cannot be reached.

In most barricade situations, only the police negotiators have representative identities. Two exceptions to this general rule are prison uprisings and terrorist hostage takings. In prison uprisings, crisis negotiators recognize the need to identify and help legitimize inmate leaders who are capable of negotiating an end to the crisis (Fagan and Van Zandt 1993; Fuselier, Van Zandt, and Lanceley 1989; Van Zandt and Fuselier 1989). In terrorist hostage takings, the police isolate the barricaded subjects, which disrupts the subject's ability to communicate with his or her constituency or leaders and weakens the sense of obligation to the larger group. "Once the subject has been away from a support system for days or weeks and emotional and physical exhaustion sets in, that person may be more willing to accept the rationale . . . [that] their demands have been heard, their cause has been 'aired' to the world, and therefore, killing hostages would only serve to discredit them and their cause in the eyes of the public" (Fuselier and Noesner 1990, 6). Disrupting the terrorist hostage taker's representative identity weakens his or her ability to negotiate and strengthens the police negotiator's persuasive efforts.

In most barricade situations, the subject is an isolated individual who has no representative identity with which to manipulate the negotiation process, and police negotiators take full advantage of this imbalance in representative identities by typically placing themselves as a buffer between their bosses (commanders, chiefs, and higher authorities in the police department) and the barricaded subject. When a barricaded subject's demands are denied, the police negotiator softens the blow by indicating that he (the police negotiator with a positive personal identity) is also constrained by the limitations imposed by his superiors. The bosses become an obstacle to negotiating an end to the barricade, and the barricaded subject and the police negotiator work cooperatively to craft a solution to their shared problem (i.e., resolving the standoff in a way that satisfies "the bosses").

In Waco, *both* the Branch Davidians and the FBI negotiators had representative identities that needed to be articulated and managed. In fact, the Branch Davidians mobilized two forms of representative identity. The FBI negotiators recognized one and rejected the other. Both the FBI negotiators and the Branch Davidians acknowledged the need to identify legitimate leaders to negotiate for the Mount Carmel residents, but, unfortunately, the parties did not always share an understanding of what constituted a legitimate negotiator because they were telling different stories about the internal dynamics and organizational structure of the Mount Carmel community.

Even more disruptive to the negotiation process was Koresh's argument that he also answered to a boss. Just as the FBI negotiators accounted to their commanders, so Koresh answered to God. Just as the FBI negotiators claimed to be constrained by orders from their commanders, so Koresh was constrained by orders from God. Not believing Koresh was God's representative and rejecting the assertion that God spoke directly to him, the FBI negotiators refused to validate this representative identity claim. Unfortunately, they overlooked the fact that the Mount Carmel community affirmed Koresh's status as God's messenger. Their behaviors and motivations were explicable only in terms of this belief. Yet the FBI negotiators opted to view Koresh's representative identity claim as a mere stalling tactic. In so doing, they ignored important information that they could have used to formulate more effective negotiation strategies for dealing with the Branch Davidians.

Establishing Congruent Functional Identities and an Interdependent Identity

When negotiators forge congruent functional identities, they acknowledge themselves as complementary entities who are participating in coordinated exchanges (Powell 1989, 27–28). Faced with a barricaded community, the FBI negotiators in Waco felt compelled to simplify the negotiation process by identifying those persons who were capable of negotiating and those who were not. Part of this process involved identifying legitimate group leaders.

A second part of the simplification process was identifying those persons the FBI considered inherently *incapable* of acting as negotiators. As a result, children were not considered legitimate negotiating partners even though the negotiators spoke with some of the children in Mount Carmel. To a large extent, the women in the Mount Carmel community were also ignored. The FBI negotiators will strenuously object to this statement, arguing that they spoke with women in Mount Carmel on numerous occasions. That is true. However, the negotiation transcripts make it clear that the FBI negotiators interacted very differently with the women in the community than they did with the men. I touch on this issue again as I examine the worldviewing problems in Waco, but a more complete study needs to be made of the problems associated with having an overwhelmingly male law enforcement agency attempt to negotiate with female members of an unconventional community that is being publicly ostracized for its experimentation with unconventional gender relations.

Two worldmaking narratives account for the FBI's selective validation of congruent negotiating partners. First, the FBI adopted many of the claims found in anticult narratives. They assumed that Koresh as a single charismatic leader ruled the community with the assistance of a cadre of deputies (the "mighty men"). Second, they projected a command-and-control organizational structure onto the Mount Carmel community. They assumed that their negotiating partners were organized with a clear distinction between leaders and followers and that leaders had the right to "order" followers to take specific actions. Both of these FBI worldmaking narratives provoked continuous worldnaming disputes when they were flatly contradicted by the Branch Davidians.

The Branch Davidians and FBI negotiators were also hampered by worldviewing disagreements regarding time. A sense of interdependence implies a temporal scale against which the relationship is measured. In typical crisis negotiations, the police and barricaded subjects have a very short-term relationship. They are interdependent for the duration of the barricade crisis. In other settings, negotiating parties have a much longer and more complicated interdependent identity. In Waco, the FBI negotiators and Branch Davidians were unable to agree to a time scale against which to measure their interdependence. Consequently, their interdependent identity was never stabilized—a serious problem that I address in more detail shortly.

Worldnaming and Establishing Negotiating
Relationships As Interrelated Processes

Overall, when the Branch Davidians and FBI negotiators were able to manage their naming of the world cooperatively, they succeeded in enacting identities and building relationships capable of sustaining negotiations. When they were unable to manage their worldnaming differences, the processes of constituting identities and establishing a relationship were disrupted because naming self and other and naming the world are two sides of the same worldviewing activity. People cannot name themselves without naming the world, and they cannot name the world without naming themselves and others in relation to the world. If two parties name the world very differently, all forms of identity are more difficult to establish, and all forms of interaction are more complicated.

Duck argues that *"the ability of two persons to behave with one another socially is defined, limited, and circumscribed by their comprehension of one another's meaning system.* To put it more accurately, the nature of a given person's relationship to someone else is defined in terms of the extent to which that person construes or understands the way the other thinks" (1994, 90, emphasis added). Perfect sharing of meaning is not necessary, but meaning must be managed in any interpersonal encounter.

Taken together, Duck and Powell point to the importance of conducting research that examines the ways in which "each person interprets and responds to the acts of another, monitors the sequence, and compares it to his or her desires and expectations" (Bochner, Cissna, and Garko 1991, 26). Unfortunately, most negotiation research neglects the role of meaning management in significant ways. First, researchers assume that the actors are all acting "rationally" and that the negotiating parties are operating in a situation in which meaning is shared, but interests diverge. Second, most negotiation research also focuses on situations in which identities, roles, and the rules of negotiation are already established and ratified by the parties. For example, in the case of labor-management negotiations, the parties have a preexisting relationship and share many basic assumptions about the world. The parties' identities and the parameters of the negotiation encounter are established prior to specific bargaining sessions. In barricade negotiations, however, the parties must create a previously nonexistent relationship *and* stabilize a temporary arena for interaction. Negotiating reality and negotiating a particular problem are interlocking and largely simultaneous processes in such situations.

Police negotiators do a grave disservice to themselves and to the barricaded subjects if they overlook the fact that the "development of relationships . . . [is] affected not by some growth of closeness or emotions, nor by the acquisition of information, but by one person's organized (re)construction of the other and the social consequences of that (re)construction" (Duck 1994, 91). To fashion a relationship sufficient to support negotiation activities, police and the barricaded subjects need to do more than just share information and express positive rapport. They must exercise worldnaming power through the use of narrative and symbolic language, and they must exercise that power cooperatively.

Worldnaming power is the capacity to "define what is good or bad, acceptable or unacceptable, right or wrong, and is manifest in the sanctioning of modes of conduct" (Ramesh 1992, 37).[2] In negotiation, worldnaming power is the ability to activate identities, name negotiable objects or a shared focus, articulate a meaningful disagreement, and frame a process for managing conflicts. In successful crisis negotiations, the parties cooperatively exercise worldnaming power to build a shared reality (the barricade) and name a negotiable problem (dissolving the barricade). In any negotiation, the parties need not share an image of the world. In fact, aspects of the parties' respective images of the world may be the focus of continuing disagreement between them. However, negotiators must share enough meaning that each can articulate the other's naming of the world even if they continue to disagree over the nature of reality. In Waco, the Branch Davidians were much better at articulating the FBI negotiators' image of the world than vice versa. Unfortunately, both parties were more interested in asserting worldnaming control than they were in cooperatively exercising worldnaming power.

Worldnaming control is the capacity to exercise one's worldnaming power unilaterally in order to "label events/acts/people" (Ramesh 1992, 45). Although each party in a negotiation might strive for worldnaming control,

2. Ramesh uses the term *ideological power* rather than *worldnaming power*. Working in a multidisciplinary environment, I find the term *ideology* overburdened with competing meanings and inferences. The term *worldnaming power* captures Ramesh's intentions without the same risk of sidetracking discussion into old arguments about the nature and meaning of ideology.

power is rarely so unevenly distributed as to place complete narrative control in the hands of a single party. Even in typical barricade negotiations, where the police can utilize superior firepower to support their exercise of worldnaming control, the hostage taker has some rhetorical and conceptual resources with which to resist the police negotiators' naming of the world. Through their conversation, police negotiators and barricaded subjects collaborate in the exercise of worldnaming power. They manage the differences in their images of the hostage taker and in their expectations regarding negotiation processes. They do so through dialogue because talk is the "primary process through which humans construct and communicate images of the world. . . . It is by means of talk and symbols that humans present one another with both direct and indirect evidence of how they think about life, themselves, each other, the world, and everything in it" (Duck 1994, 18). In Waco, the parties sometimes used talk to name their world cooperatively, but more often they used talk to advocate for competing worlds.

Waco Successes and Difficulties

The Parties Cooperatively Exercise Worldnaming Power

When congruent functional identities have been established, "there is a sense of shared consequences and accountability rather than a simple sense of opposition" (Powell 1989, 29). Congruent functional identities are frequently established and cemented by specific negotiation successes. Police negotiators are taught to look for small issues to negotiate with a barricaded subject. Each success builds the foundation for negotiating larger problems. Successes are often celebrated verbally, as when Lt. Larry Lynch reacted to the evacuation of ATF personnel from the Mount Carmel property.

> LYNCH: Alright standby. What we have now, is, is just a . . . standoff. Alright. Everybody kind of calm down. But take a deep breath and see what develops next. Thanks for all your help. We couldn't have done it without ya' Wayne. We've saved some people. OK? . . .
> WAYNE: OK.

LYNCH: Alright, we've gone this far. We've done this, we've done this to-gether. Let's stay hooked. OK. You and me. We'll get through it. (911.3: 21)

Notice that Lynch defined the situation (a standoff) in a manner that encompassed both parties as negotiators. He also verified the value of Martin's previous negotiation efforts, and he allocated to both parties the praise and credit for the success.

Establishing congruent functional identities is an essential part of fashioning interdependence. Both functional and interdependent identities are created when "negotiators recognize that their actions have consequences for them as a unit" (Powell 1989, 26). Because functional and interdependent identities depend heavily on a shared naming of the world, police negotiators and barricaded subjects must negotiate reality even in the midst of crisis. For example, on February 28, when Wayne Martin phoned 911, he named a problem and demanded that the police treat it as a negotiable object or shared focus of problem-solving action. More than that, however, he based his demand on a distinct image of the world.

> [INSTRUM] UNIDENTIFIED FEMALE: 9–1–1. What's your emergency? 9–1–1. What's your emergency?
>
> [INSTRUM] UNIDENTIFIED MALE [WAYNE MARTIN]: There are men—seventy-five men around our building . . . shootin' at us. . . . [The 911 dispatcher turns the call over to Lynch.]
>
> [INSTRUM RELAT] LT. LYNCH: Yeah, this is Lieutenant Lynch, may I help you?
>
> [INSTRUM RELAT SYMBOL] [WAYNE MARTIN]: Yeah, there're seventy-five men around our building and they're shootin' at us at Mount Carmel. . . . *Tell them there's children and women in here and to call it off.* (911.1: 1–2, emphasis added)

Why did Martin receive a quick and positive response to his demands? In part, because Lynch was acting in accordance with his role as the deputy responsible for 911 calls, but also because he shared or at least accepted Martin's naming of the world. Specifically, Lynch responded positively to Martin's classification of women and children as persons in need of protection, which is an example of parties coordinating their actions on the basis of shared or similar categorical beliefs about the world.[3]

Having recognized Martin's image of the world, Lynch was able to use Martin's own worldmaking narrative to frame the current problem as amenable to negotiation.

> [RELAT INSTRUM] LT. LYNCH:[4] Wayne, tell me what's happening Wayne, this is Lynch at the sheriff's office. . . . Talk to me Wayne, let's get this thing resolved, Wayne.
>
> [SYMBOL INSTRUM] WAYNE MARTIN: We got women and children in danger.
>
> [RELAT SYMBOL INSTRUM] LT. LYNCH: Okay, Wayne . . . Talk to me Wayne, let's, let's take care of the children and the women. Wayne, let's not do anything foolish that we'll be sorry for, talk to me Wayne, I can't help you if you won't talk to me. Wayne, Wayne, please talk to me Wayne, let's work it out. (911.1: 8)

"Let's take care of the children and women." With one sentence, Lynch acknowledged Martin's categorization system, validated Martin's worldview, and reinforced Martin's identity as a "male protector." "Let's." With a single word, Lynch indicated that he shared the male protector identity with Martin, affirmed their positive relationship, and committed himself to working with Martin to resolve the current crisis. Then Lynch advanced the claim that reasoned talk (not shooting) was the appropriate process through which responsible male protectors could act in the current situation to protect women and children from further danger.

Worldviewing is manifested in actions as well as in talk. Lynch and Martin apparently agreed that a cease-fire was the most pressing problem. Hence, they both adopted problem-solving behaviors. Lynch initiated contact with the ATF (911.1: 4), and Martin provided Lynch with information about the events unfolding at Mount Carmel and continued to press his demand for a cease-fire. Once they had adopted problem-solving behaviors, their language was almost

---

3. The importance of categorization cannot be overemphasized. In chapter 6, I discuss the problems that occurred when the FBI negotiators and Branch Davidians were unable to coordinate their categorizations of sacred objects and tradable commodities.

4. The transcripts were clearly prepared by different people and vary in the way they reference speakers. In identifying speakers, I use what the transcripts show.

entirely instrumental and relational. They shared information, made demands and requests for assistance, suggested ways of handling the problem they faced, and offered reassurances of their intentions to cooperate.

In the midst of their cooperative effort, Lynch and Martin encountered a moment of opacity when they discovered discrepancies in their images of a cease-fire. At that point, they turned once again to symbolic language.

> [INSTRUM SYMBOL] LT. LYNCH: Okay that, alright are you, are you ready to come out and give up? Are you ready to terminate this Wayne?
> [INSTRUM SYMBOL] WAYNE MARTIN: We want a cease-fire, we'll talk. (911.1: 12)

The use of symbolic language did not persist because Lynch accepted Martin's limited vision of a cease-fire. In their next substantive discussion regarding future actions, Lynch said, "Okay, we're working on it so just . . . hang loose, do not return fire Wayne, okay? Just kind of hold what you got till we get the situation settled and your [sic] willing to talk to 'em [ATF]? Will you visit with 'em?" (911.1: 17). Immediately following this exchange, Martin began actively passing the word to others at Mount Carmel to stop firing (911.1: 17). Prior to this, he had made no effort to control the actions of anyone else at Mount Carmel. His contributions to the problem-solving effort had been restricted to sharing information and expressing demands. Later, Lynch conceded the definition of cease-fire more explicitly by responding with an "Okay" when Martin said, "So, hold their fire . . . leave the property, and we'll talk" (911.1: 22).

Thus, Lynch and Martin cooperatively replaced an image of cease-fire that included surrender of the Branch Davidians with one that required the withdrawal of ATF agents from the Mount Carmel property. Having managed their worldviewing differences, Martin and Lynch could collaborate on implementing an end to active hostilities. These exchanges over the meaning of cease-fire stand out as brief moments of symbolic communication within an overwhelmingly instrumental encounter. Similar worldview coordination occurred during negotiations over evacuating the dead and wounded ATF agents from the property and arranging for children to leave Mount Carmel. Such excursions into noninstrumental language demonstrate the role of meaning management even in urgent crisis negotiation situations.

Meaning management was also a significant factor in the establishment of relationships between the negotiators and the Branch Davidians. Negotiating personal identities is part of negotiating reality and may be initiated in several different ways. The police negotiator and barricaded subject "may make convincing announcements of personal identities which show them as reliable actors" (Powell 1989, 32). Any self-proclaimed identity must, however, be accepted by the other party. It is only when "these positive attributes of personal identity are mutually acknowledged [that] they support the construction of interdependent futures" (Powell 1989, 32). Negotiations over personal identity do not end with direct declarations. Personal identities are established over time and as a consequence of communication that is not directly related to resolving the current standoff. Police negotiators deliberately attempt to identify interests and life experiences they have in common with a barricaded subject. Consequently, on the afternoon of February 28, under circumstances few would consider appropriate for idle social chat, Lynch asked Martin about his family.

> WAYNE: Larry, you know I have children here . . .
>
> LARRY: Okay, how old are they Wayne? How old are your kids?
>
> WAYNE: It's hard to keep up with them.
>
> LARRY: You have that many? . . . God, see, all I can afford is two kids, Wayne. I couldn't, that's all I can take care of. I couldn't afford anymore. How many kids do you have out there? (PAUSE)
>
> WAYNE: Well, you know, we've always been very reluctant to give out numbers.
>
> LARRY: No, okay, okay. That's fine. I'm just, it's more than 2 then hun. . . . Uhm, how old are they? Different ages?
>
> WAYNE: Oh yeah. They range.
>
> LARRY: What's your oldest? I've got one that's 20.
>
> WAYNE: Yes, I've got one in his 20's.
>
> LARRY: Okay, okay. What's your youngest?
>
> WAYNE: I've got one that's 4.
>
> LARRY: Oh, okay. That's quite a spread. . . . Quite a spread. Well, that's

what we want to do. We want to make sure they're okay, and that, you know, that you can go on and do, you know, how, ya want to do out there, but we need to bring this particular incident to a close. And you know . . . we don't want to see your children get hurt or you get hurt or David. Uhm, you know, we just want to get everybody squared away. (911.6: 21–22)

This type of rapport building is exactly what police negotiators have in mind when they talk about using expressive language and strategic self-disclosure to build a personal relationship with the barricaded subject. Contrary to the crisis negotiation literature, however, it is evident that such side trips into noninstrumental interaction entail more than simple expressions of personal warmth or common interests. Lynch and Martin's exchange helped them present identities separate from their respective roles as a law enforcement officer and barricaded subject, and established a point of rapport between them. However, this exchange had the potential either to advance or to disrupt the negotiations over ending the standoff. Lynch used the shared fact of parenthood to make a case for a negotiated solution to the current standoff, but the topic of parenthood also introduced a potentially disruptive worldview (reality negotiation) problem. Martin's personal identity as a parent led the discussion dangerously close to the controversial issues of Branch Davidian gender and family relations. Martin warned Lynch away from the sensitive topic of the number of children at Mount Carmel. When Lynch indirectly referred to alleged irregularities regarding Branch Davidian children, he acknowledged Martin's prior refusal to discuss these problematic issues and quickly moved the conversation back to safer topics. In this exchange, Martin and Lynch enriched their personal identities while also establishing a shared understanding about dangerous topics or issues to be avoided in future conversations. They built rapport while naming the world.

The parties in Waco also succeeded, even under chaotic circumstances, in establishing representative identities to support their negotiations. Although barricaded subjects do not usually have representative identities, Lynch recognized the fact that the situation at Mount Carmel was different. Very early in the encounter, he attempted to verify Martin's authority to negotiate on behalf of the community.

LT. LYNCH: . . . Wayne will you be the person that we talk to. . . ?

WAYNE MARTIN: These are my orders.

LT. LYNCH: Will you be the person that, that I, that we talk to Wayne, to get this thing resolved?

WAYNE MARTIN: Yeah. (911.1: 22)

Representative identities can change over time, particularly in volatile situations, and Martin removed himself from the role of negotiator once communication was established between Koresh and the ATF (911.16: 15). Both parties must validate any change in representative identity, and Martin had to repeat his announcement regarding the change in his representative identity several times before Lynch acknowledged it.

WAYNE: As I was explaining to [FBI negotiator Byron Sage], I don't want to interfere with the negotiations going on between David and Cavanaugh. However, I will, to the best of my ability, be your eyes and ears as far as people leaving this building.

LARRY: Okay, great, that's what we need. . . . All your negotiations now have moved over with Cavanaugh . . . and Steve . . . and David. (911.17: 12–13)

The FBI Asserts Worldnaming Control
Within a Changing Context

Lynch and ATF officer Jim Cavanaugh were able to negotiate complicated and dangerous issues (a cease-fire, the evacuation of dead and wounded ATF agents, and the removal of children from Mount Carmel) with the Branch Davidians. Theoretically, such early negotiation successes should have laid the groundwork for a continuation of instrumental problem-solving efforts. Instead, the FBI negotiators who arrived in Waco on March 1 encountered a barricaded community that vacillated between cooperating with issue-specific negotiation endeavors and attempting to engage the FBI negotiators in Bible studies. By March 3, exasperated negotiators and FBI commanders were accusing Koresh of negotiating in bad faith and behaving irrationally.

What happened? On the one hand, the law enforcement community unilaterally changed negotiators, altered the agenda, and reframed the negotiation process. On the other hand, the Branch Davidians recovered from the initial shock of the February 28 raid and started pondering the significance of their violent encounter with the ATF. Simultaneously, new criminal charges were lodged against the Branch Davidians as a result of the shoot-out. All of these changes made negotiating reality an extremely pressing problem. Unfortunately, it was a problem the FBI negotiators attempted to ignore, even though they needed to engage the Branch Davidians in a cooperative worldnaming exercise in order to answer such questions as: Who are the parties? What are the issues or problems? How should negotiations be framed? Instead, they opted all at once to change negotiators, redefine the objective of the negotiations, restrict the use of symbolic and narrative language, and impose a bargaining framework on the negotiation process. The Branch Davidians' resistance to these combined changes obstructed the issue-specific negotiation process.

Changing negotiators. Allocating responsibility for negotiating the Waco standoff to the FBI was more than just a change in individual actors. Replacing ATF negotiators with FBI negotiators was the equivalent of substituting one of the negotiating parties. A good analogy would be a company that undergoes a corporate merger in the midst of renegotiating a labor contract. The new parent corporation is a powerful and unknown player whose policies, procedures, and preferences can significantly alter the negotiations. The new parent corporation also inherits the "baggage" of the previous owners, and they cannot simply assume they will be viewed positively by the other party. At the very least, such a modification needs to be clearly explained to everyone involved, but this explanation was not given in Waco. ATF officer Jim Cavanaugh went off duty in the late evening on February 28, and FBI negotiator PN02 stepped in to continue the negotiation process. PN02 identified himself as FBI only after the Branch Davidians resisted cooperating with the new negotiator because they wanted to continue working with Cavanaugh. Even then, the change in negotiating partners was treated very lightly.

MR. KORESH: And see, I did everything in my power to avoid you gentlemen coming and doing what you did.

PN02: I have to apologize to you because . . . I'm not with ATF and I . . . wasn't involved in that process. I don't know all the background to that.

MR. KORESH: Well, Jim's with ATF.

PN02: Right, but I'm just telling you I, I don't, I don't want to give you the sense that I know all of the background of this because, because I don't. (Tape 4 and 5: 55

Federal officials in Washington worked out their own agreement about control and responsibility for the Waco situation, but the negotiators in Waco failed to communicate and explain that decision to the barricaded Branch Davidians. Law enforcement officials presumed they had the right to make these changes without consulting with the Branch Davidians. Legally, they were correct. Procedurally, they were incorrect. In any negotiation, everyone involved needs to ratify changes in negotiating parties. Furthermore, after such a change, time must be allotted for the parties to reestablish their relationships and identities and to rename the negotiable object or problem around which their issue-specific negotiations are oriented.

Changing the negotiable object or problem to be addressed. Because the FBI introduced new actors and new agenda items simultaneously, it is difficult to determine whether the Branch Davidians truly disliked PN02 or he simply became one object of their resistance to the use of bargaining as a process for ending the standoff. The Branch Davidians clearly felt PN02 was more persistent than Cavanaugh in pursuing a speedy end to the siege. They also considered this single-minded focus on reaching a final resolution to the standoff extremely annoying.

As further discussed in the next chapter, the FBI negotiators were presented with an incomplete account of the earliest negotiations, an account that was already shaped by the worldmaking narratives of the first negotiators on the scene. Consequently, negotiators from Quantico incorrectly concluded that the parties had already identified ending the standoff as the central negotiable problem and that they had reached an agreement that bargaining was the appropriate process for accomplishing this shared objective.

How did this problem develop? Police negotiators are not trained to recognize worldviewing differences or worldview management transactions. Therefore, after the changeover in negotiators, no effort was made to identify the worldview management successes that had permitted Cavanaugh, Lynch, Schneider, Koresh, and Martin to arrange a cease-fire, evacuate the dead and wounded ATF agents, and begin removing children from Mount Carmel. Nor did anyone mark the worldview management difficulties encountered in the immediate aftermath of the raid and gun battle. Recording such information would have alerted the FBI negotiators to the limited nature of worldview coordination between the federal agents and Branch Davidians. By March 1, the parties in Waco had cooperatively identified removing children from Mount Carmel as a shared problem amenable to negotiation and cooperative action. They had not yet agreed that getting all of the Mount Carmel residents to surrender to federal authorities was a shared objective.

Greater awareness of the processes by which parties in a crisis barricade situation negotiate reality would also have alerted the FBI negotiators to the worldviewing dynamics within the Mount Carmel community. While law enforcement agencies were reallocating authority for the Waco situation, the Mount Carmel residents were collecting their thoughts, recovering from the natural biobehavioral stress responses induced by the raid and shoot-out, and beginning to articulate an organized narrative about the meaning of their current situation. Between March 1 and March 3, the Branch Davidians' narrative about the February 28 raid gained coherence as they collectively interpreted that experience. Locating their current predicament in relation to the imminent Second Coming of Christ, the Mount Carmel residents developed a much clearer answer to the worldviewing question, "What should we do in this situation?" Or, put in the negative, "What are we prohibited from doing in this situation?"

No longer facing such immediate crises as establishing a cease-fire and evacuating dead and wounded ATF agents from Mount Carmel, the Branch Davidians confronted the problem of determining the long-term consequences of the ATF raid and their own violent response. This problem was a different type of issue altogether—one that was difficult to construct as a negotiable object because the nature of the problem was changing even as the parties tried to resolve their differences. Most notably, new criminal charges were lodged against the Branch Davidians as a result of the shoot-out.

It is important to acknowledge that the FBI had limited control over deciding the charges that would be leveled against participants in the February 28 confrontation. Attorneys from the Department of Justice were responsible for these decisions. Because the nature of criminal charges and the timing of their announcement can greatly impact a barricade negotiation, better coordination between the crisis management team and the office of the U.S. attorney would have helped the negotiators in Waco.[5]

Barricaded subjects "make demands based upon the situational milieu" (McMains and Mullins 1996, 70); therefore, changes in the Waco context led to changes in "demands." I have placed the term *demands* in quotation marks because the concept of a clear demand accompanied by a deadline and threats of violence (McMains and Mullins 1996, 72–74) is largely inapplicable to the Waco standoff. The Branch Davidians were acutely aware they could face the death penalty. They also feared that once removed from Mount Carmel, the entire community would be destroyed. If, as they believed, the Mount Carmel community was destined to play a significant role in God's plan for the world, the destruction of the community could not be taken lightly. Consequently, the Branch Davidians became more focused on negotiating reality at precisely the time that law enforcement negotiators were attempting to focus on bargaining and problem solving. The result was a continuous worldnaming contest over legitimate and illegitimate language.

Limiting narrative and symbolic language. To negotiate reality, the Branch Davidians used narrative and symbolic language. The FBI negotiators did not recognize the need to negotiate reality and routinely countered narrative and symbolic language with relational and instrumental responses. This difference transformed opportunities for the parties to exercise worldnaming power cooperatively into contests over worldnaming control. Some of these contests were overt. The parties engaged in an ongoing argument over legitimate language because the FBI negotiators dismissed the Branch Davidians' biblically based language as irrelevant to the negotiation process. The parties also debated the appropriate way to frame their negotiation process, a problem that I address in the next three chapters.

5. A little-known confrontation with another radical religious group—the Covenant, Sword, and Arm of the Lord—was much better served by the U.S. attorney in Arkansas. In that case, the U.S. attorney (Asa Hutchinson) went out of his way to ensure that the rights and dignity of the community members were protected (Coulson and Shannon 1999, 294).

These worldviewing conflicts were obvious and prolonged. Less blatant, but no less deleterious in their impact on negotiations, were the missed opportunities to build relationships between the parties. Determined to frame the negotiation process as composed only of instrumental and expressive interactions, the FBI negotiators overlooked the Branch Davidians' attempts to use narrative and symbolic language in order to build personal rapport with them. For example, Schneider believed that FBI negotiator PN02 shared many of his own deeper concerns about truth, God, and the ultimate meaning of the world.

[NARRAT SYMBOL RELAT IDENT] MR. SCHNEIDER:I want to live forever. Ever since I was a very small child—I've always like yourself looked up at the stars and wondered why is this—where are we going, how did we get here, what's this vast expanse about?

[NULL] PN02: Yeah.

[NARRAT SYMBOL IDENT] MR. SCHNEIDER: Why is this earth a cemetery, everything dies here, plants, people, animals, 6,000 years of woe and human history. We get a little bit of pleasure but we're never satisfied and fulfilled and relatives can be taken out of your life, friends, accidents. God, what's going on?

[NULL] PN02: Yeah.

[SYMBOL NARRAT IDENT] MR. SCHNEIDER: Who are you, God?—But I've never really claimed to know God. I tried it the Christian routine for the majority of my life and in honesty, I mean, I've never really known God but I've always wanted to know God.

[NULL] PN02: Um-hum.

[NARRAT IDENT SYMBOL] MR. SCHNEIDER: (Indiscernible) claim to know him now, but I do see something about a book that's very logical and clear and this man also has opened up very deep sciences, physics, astronomy and these are the things that not many have gotten to hear recently but those that have gotten to sit down and study (indiscernible) would have gotten to the place where you'd have gotten to hear those things and would have been totally astounded—

[INSTRUM RELAT] PN02: You know, I've just been handed a note that David—I guess David did a radio interview and that's, that's been completed. It—you know, I—how, how is he feeling with his injuries? (Tape 4 and 5: 6–7)

The negotiators in Waco were comfortable establishing personal rapport and identities by discussing shared interests, hobbies, hometowns, or children.

Most of them were clearly uncomfortable when the Branch Davidians attempted to discuss the meaning of life. Working within the strictures of crisis negotiation procedures, which stress avoiding discussions of religion, truth, or philosophy (Judiciary 325; Van Zandt 1997, 145), PN02 responded with non-committal verbal indications that Schneider had his attention. However, he obviously classified Schneider's conversation as meaningless in relation to the "real purpose" of the negotiation. PN02 did not recognize that Schneider was trying to establish rapport by way of common concerns over the meaning of life. When PN02 became too uncomfortable or too frustrated with the conversation, he cut Schneider off by abruptly reintroducing instrumental and relational language and activities. This pattern of communication became routine in Waco, particularly when the FBI negotiators attempted to impose a rational bargaining process on the negotiations.

Imposing a bargaining process. While introducing new actors, altering the definition of the negotiable object or problem to be addressed, and limiting the use of narrative and symbolic language, the FBI negotiators also began framing the negotiations as a bargaining exchange. I address this problem more fully in the next chapter, but for now it is important to note that the Branch Davidians resisted this description of the negotiation process. Contrary to the FBI negotiators' perceptions, such resistance did not constitute an attempt to renege on earlier agreements. Nor was the Branch Davidians' resistance an indication of instability, irrationality, or bad faith. Careful examination of the earliest records reveals that the initial negotiation successes in Waco were accomplished through processes other than bargaining. Lynch and Martin did not bargain with one another before cooperating to arrange a cease-fire, and the Branch Davidians did not treat removing the dead and wounded ATF agents from Mount Carmel as a problem appropriately addressed through bargaining. For the Branch Davidians, the use of bargaining was not a foregone conclusion, but a framing issue that was still open to debate.

The Parties Compete to Narrate Interdependence
and Identify a Negotiable Problem

Police negotiators endeavor to establish a sense of interdependence with barricaded subjects that is organized around the short-term goal of peacefully ending a dangerous situation. This definition of the problem seems so logical that few participants or observers recognize the assumptions about reality on which it rests. Interdependence organized around a single, short-term goal is measured against a limited temporal horizon and judged against a clear definition of success or failure. As the barricaded subject and police negotiator dissolve the barricade confrontation, they also dissolve their relationship. If they accomplish this task without violence, they congratulate themselves (collectively) for their success.

A short-term, goal-directed relationship is only one possible description of interdependence between negotiating parties, however. In other settings, parties have ongoing relationships. For example, during a divorce mediation involving a couple with children, the parties are simultaneously dissolving their relationship as a couple and reaffirming their interdependence as parents. Changing the expected duration of the relationship, redefining the problem, and altering the definition of success can lead to a different but no less powerful sense of interdependence between the parties.

In Waco, three stories of interdependence competed for priority during the fifty-one days of negotiations (fig. 9.). Each story measured the interdependence of the parties along a distinct temporal horizon. Each story included its own cast of actors. Each story identified particular goals and related sets of issues that needed to be addressed during the negotiations. Each story measured success differently. What were these stories, and which party favored which story?

The first story, preferred by the FBI, measured the interdependence of the parties against a short time frame. According to this story, the relationship between the Branch Davidians and FBI would last only as long as the barricade situation. In this narrative, the cast of characters in Waco consisted of the Branch Davidians and the FBI—the ATF having been removed from the scene. The shared goal of the actors was to dissolve the barricade safely. The measure of success was getting the entire Mount Carmel community to leave the property without any further violence. Failure would include a mass suicide of the community or further violence between the community and law enforcement agents. This narrative encompassed the FBI negotiators' underlying concern about enforcing the law because the objective was to move the Branch Davidians into the legal system. There, they would be tried for their part in the February 28 shoot-out with the ATF.

Short Term	Medium Term	Long Term
Narrative Time Frame		
Relationship lasts as long as the standoff.	*Relationship* lasts through the process of assessing blame for the February 28 confrontation.	*Relationship* lasts at least through the end of secular history, probably into eternity.

Actors:
Branch Davidians   FBI
	Actors:
	Branch Davidians ATF FBI
	    [God] [Dept. of Justice]
		Actors:
		Koresh & Branch Davidians ATF & FBI
		[on behalf of] [on behalf of]
		          God U.S. government

Negotiable Problem: Peacefully end the standoff.	*Negotiable Problem:* Construct equitable processes for determining consequences of February 28 confrontation.	*Negotiable Problem:* Handle current crisis in keeping with God's plan for the world.
Measures of Success: Branch Davidians surrender. Conflict moves to the courts.	*Measures of Success:* Branch Davidians treated fairly in courts. ATF held accountable.	*Measures of Success:* Every individual involved has opportunity to choose between God's will and the demands of secular authorities.
Narrator: FBI	*Narrator:* Branch Davidians	*Narrator:* Branch Davidians

9. Three narratives of negotiator interdependence competed for supremacy in Waco.

Noticeably missing from the FBI's preferred story were the Branch Davidians' concerns about equity and justice. Where the FBI negotiators assumed that issues of justice would be dealt with in the courts, the Branch Davidians saw a legal system that was unfairly stacked against them. The Branch Davidians understood they had to answer for their actions on February 28, but they insisted on placing three other issues on the table: they wanted a full investigation of ATF activities on February 28; they wanted that investigation conducted by a trustworthy organization; and they wanted guarantees that ATF agents would be held legally accountable for the deaths of Branch Davidians.

In raising the issue of equity, the Branch Davidians introduced a medium time frame into the narrative of interdependence. The cast of characters was also changed because the Branch Davidians insisted that they and the ATF remained interdependent, even after the FBI assumed responsibility for managing the standoff. Ending the standoff peacefully depended on guarantees that justice would be fairly administered to both parties involved in the February 28 encounter. As a result, the temporal horizon against which the Branch Davidians measured the parties' interdependence extended at least through whatever court cases, hearings, or investigations would occur once the barricade situation was resolved. Success required credible guarantees that they would be treated fairly and that the ATF would be held accountable for the February 28 raid.

In this narrative, the precise role of the FBI negotiators was unclear. Obviously, the Branch Davidians were speaking with FBI negotiators, but the ATF remained the subject of their greatest concerns, which may help explain some of their resistance to changing negotiators. The Branch Davidians did not want the other party to walk away from the disaster they had jointly created on February 28. It also raises the possibility that the FBI might have been more effective had they assumed a mediator rather than a negotiator role. By entering the confrontation in Waco as replacements for the ATF, the FBI became identified with the ATF even as the negotiators sought to detach the FBI from responsibility for the February 28 fiasco.

Had the short and medium time-frame narratives been the only competing narratives of interdependence in Waco, negotiations would have been difficult enough. Unfortunately, the Branch Davidians were also working within a very long time frame. For the Branch Davidians, interdependence with the ATF and the FBI occurred within a sacred as well as a secular context. In this story, the February 28 raid thrust the Branch Davidians and the ATF into a relationship as interdependent actors in God's plan for the world. This long-term construction of interdependence was not even on the edges of the FBI negotiators' worldviewing map. Envisioning interdependence within the sacred context also introduced an actor the FBI negotiators preferred to ignore, God. For the Branch Davidians, God was always a significant actor in the negotiations because they located their own actions in relation to God's will. In the Branch Davidians' long-term narrative of interdependence, God actually brought issues and goals to the table. Ending the standoff without violence was not the sole measure of success, although it was one factor to be considered. Ending the standoff while ensuring justice for the parties was also important, but not in itself an adequate measure of success. Ultimately, success would be measured in relation to how well the parties advanced God's plan for the imminent Second Coming of Christ.

Identifying a negotiable object and meaningful disagreement. Why does it matter that the parties in Waco were narrating their interdependence against different temporal scales? Each timescale implied a different definition of the negotiable object or problem in need of solution. For the FBI negotiators, the purpose of the negotiations was to get everyone safely out of Mount Carmel *while enforcing the law.* For the Branch Davidians, the objective was to get everyone safely out of Mount Carmel *if they could negotiate an equitable resolution of the conflict started on February 28 and if God approved.* The devil, as they say, is in the details. Or, in this case, the devil was in the contingency clauses.

Constructing a successful negotiation in Waco required that the parties frame the conflict in a manner that incorporated, acknowledged, or in some way addressed all of the contingency clauses. Reconciling, coordinating, or managing the worldviews implicit in their respective statements of the problem depended on the ability of the FBI negotiators and the Branch Davidians to name the world cooperatively—i.e., to negotiate reality. Specifically, the parties needed to address one another's ultimate concerns and values. The FBI organized their goal-directed negotiation efforts with reference to values of law enforcement. The Branch Davidians organized the same goal-directed activities with reference to values of justice and divine law. In other words, the parties answered to different gods. In the next three chapters, I address how the parties in Waco attempted to negotiate reality or resisted negotiating reality. It remains to be seen whether it is even possible for parties who are separated by such profound worldviewing differences to negotiate reality in a manner that supports successful issue-specific negotiations.

Efforts to Define Interdependence Cooperatively

Narratives can be combined in a number of ways, and parties who bring different narratives of interdependence to a negotiation are not forced to choose only one story about their relationship. In Waco, each party made some effort to combine its preferred narrative(s) of interdependence with those of the other party. The Branch Davidians accepted the goal of ending the standoff peacefully. However, they refused to adopt the short-term narrative as the only one relevant to the situation in which they were embroiled. With their medium-term narrative of interdependence, they placed additional concerns on the table. In order to persuade the Branch Davidians to dissolve the barricade, the FBI negotiators attempted to reassure them that they would be treated fairly in the courts. In other words, the FBI negotiators validated one portion of the Branch Davidians' concerns about fairness, but they never adequately validated the Branch Davidians' concern that the ATF needed to be held accountable for their actions. At best, they offered vague reassurances that people in Congress were calling for an investigation of the ATF. They also promised the Branch Davidians that the FBI and Department of Justice officials would conduct a thorough investigation of the February 28 confrontation. Because the FBI tactical teams were locating military vehicles on the Mount Carmel property and FBI spokespersons were painting a negative portrait of the Branch Davidians in the press, the Branch Davidians did not consider this latter promise very convincing. As for the Branch Davidians' long-term narrative of interdependence, the FBI negotiators rejected it completely.

Does this mean the parties in Waco could never have established an interdependent identity and cooperatively named the world in a manner that would have supported issue-specific negotiations to end the standoff? Not necessarily. It does, however, imply that the FBI negotiators' current crisis negotiation practices provide inadequate tools for establishing relationships with barricaded communities motivated by unconventional beliefs. Warmth and personal regard are not enough to support the processes of establishing interdependence, identifying a negotiable problem, and enacting identities capable of supporting issue-specific negotiations. The parties must also cooperatively exercise their worldnaming power in order to build a relationship as negotiators. Furthermore, if the negotiations are framed to include an extended temporal horizon and actors other than those who are on the scene, all of the necessary actors must be incorporated into the relationship. The attorney general, members of Congress, and the U.S. attorney for Waco were parties who might have helped resolve the Waco standoff if they had been brought into the negotiations. That, however, would have required a significant rewriting of the FBI's crisis management scripts,[6] and the FBI negotiators appeared unaware that they were even working from scripts, let alone that they might have the power to rewrite them.

---

6. I use the plural "scripts" because it is not at all clear that the HRT, commanders, and negotiators were actually working with a single, unified script. Elsewhere, I have argued that simply reconciling the script differences *within* the FBI would likely have resulted in a better outcome in Waco (Docherty 1996a).

6

"If You Release Some of Those Youngsters . . . We Will Play the Tape"

Negotiation as Bargaining

FBI NEGOTIATORS assigned to the Critical Incident Negotiation Team (CINT) at the FBI Academy in Quantico, Virginia, began arriving in Waco late in the day on February 28. After assessing the situation, they concluded, "We're talking about . . . maybe going a week" (911.23: 17).[1] The FBI negotiators were under the impression that the situation in Waco was already being managed using a goal-rational bargaining process, and this process would continue to its logical end—i.e., the surrender of the Branch Davidians. Consequently, "March 2 was the day that many law enforcement officials believed the stand-off would end" (Justice 31), and all of the appropriate resources had been mobilized to handle the surrender of the Branch Davidians. The U.S. Attorney's Office was prepared to process the large number of individuals exiting Mount Carmel. Some would be jailed on federal charges; others would be held as material witnesses. U.S. marshals were standing by, as was a judge, to expedite initial hearings. The FBI had arranged medical care for the wounded Branch Davidians. "In short, everyone on the law enforcement side was prepared for a peaceful and orderly solution to a tense situation" (Justice 31). By March 3,

---

1. An open microphone recorded a conversation between Byron Sage, the local FBI negotiator who helped Larry Lynch on February 28, and personnel at the sheriff's office. Consequently, Tape 911.23 provides a rare glimpse into the decision making of the negotiators in Waco.

some FBI representatives were expressing frustration with what they saw as Koresh's betrayal of the negotiated agreement to end the standoff.

To understand why the FBI negotiators predicted such a speedy resolution of the Waco situation, we must attempt to "see" what they "found" when they arrived in Waco, and we must attempt to understand why they took the actions they did when they arrived. What they found was a situation already molded and interpreted for them by the first negotiators on the scene. What they did was assess the situation through the filter of their own assumptions about the problem that needed to be addressed and the correct practice to be used.

I am not accusing the FBI negotiators of wrongdoing. I am merely observing the real-life constraints on practitioners of crisis negotiation. All practitioners construct the object of their practice and develop methods for assessing the current state of affairs in order to select the most effective intervention (Schön 1983). The "assumptive world" (Frank 1973) of the practitioner is composed of tacit, unarticulated knowledge, derived from hands-on experience, combined with articulated and codified practices. The FBI negotiators' unspoken expectations about the time required to resolve a crisis barricade situation, standardized crisis negotiation practices, shared wisdom acquired during prior negotiations, and an articulated but incomplete analytical framework for assessing negotiation progress all figured into their evaluation of the standoff in Waco. Understanding the assumptive world of the FBI negotiators is key to understanding why they believed it was possible to shape the Waco negotiations into a process of "rational bargaining."

Assumptions about Time

Practitioners and scholars alike have tried to map out the phases of a typical crisis negotiation. They reach remarkably similar conclusions about the time needed to complete a barricade negotiation. The Michigan State Police model claims that most barricade negotiations will take from fourteen to twenty-three hours to resolve once the negotiators establish contact with the barricaded subject (Donohue et al. 1991). The thirteen actual cases in Abbott's study took an average of twelve hours to complete (1986, 34). The tendency to measure barricade negotiation incidents in hours rather than in days or weeks is reinforced by negotiators' real-life experience. "The Los Angeles County Sheriff's Office did a study of 29 incidents a few years ago and found that the average duration was 12 hours, but the actual time involved ranged from 1 hour to 40 hours" (Fuselier 1986b, 13).

Crisis negotiators know from experience, however, that complicating factors can impact both the development of crisis negotiation phases and the amount of time needed to reach resolution. A comparative study of the transcripts of authentic crisis negotiations and the transcripts of simulated training negotiations concluded that actual cases are less orderly and less organized than the simulations, and both are more disorderly and disorganized than a widely used conceptual model of negotiation phases (Holmes and Sykes 1993, 53). Holmes and Sykes conclude that much more attention needs to be directed toward identifying the situational contingencies that disrupt crisis negotiations.[2]

The FBI negotiators from Quantico are regularly called on to deal with the most complex crisis negotiations. Yet prior to the Waco standoff, the twelve-day-long uprising among Cuban inmates in the Atlanta penitentiary in 1987 was the longest siege they had handled. The Atlanta incident and a simultaneous nine-day uprising involving Cuban inmates in the Oakdale penitentiary were considered noteworthy enough to warrant special examination as "protracted incidents" (Fuselier, Van Zandt, and Lanceley 1989; McMains and Mullins 1996, 17; Van Zandt and Fuselier 1989). When ATF agents were planning the February 28 raid, they looked to a combined ATF and FBI siege of a radical religious group known as the Covenant, the Sword, and the Arm of the

---

2. Holmes and Sykes identify changing negotiators, working with impaired subjects, and dealing with disruptions in the communication channel as situational contingencies that interfere with the orderly development of negotiations (1993, 51–54). Other disruptive factors include: (1) the activities of tactical units (Fagan and Van Zandt 1993; Fuselier 1986a; Fuselier, Van Zandt, and Lanceley 1991; Hillmann 1988); (2) negotiator stress (Bohl 1992); (3) time pressures created by superiors not directly involved in the negotiation process (Fuselier 1986a); (4) problems arising from the biobehavioral effects of a crisis (Gilmartin and Gibson 1985); and (5) the role and appropriate use of outside experts and third parties (Fuselier, Van Zandt, and Lanceley 1989; Miron and Goldstein 1979; Van Zandt and Fuselier 1989; Wardlaw 1984). The impact of media attention on negotiations has also been a long-recognized factor in hostage negotiations (Miron and Goldstein 1979). Unfortunately, the descriptions of these problems remain anecdotal and disjointed, and the prescriptions for dealing with situational contingencies are necessarily incomplete.

Lord (CSA) for guidance (Judiciary 452; Treasury 38, 119). In conversation, FBI negotiators still point to the CSA siege as an anecdotal baseline against which to compare Waco. The CSA siege lasted four and one-half days and ended with the surrender of the barricaded group. By the FBI's own account, nothing in their prior experience prepared the negotiators for a fifty-one-day standoff in Waco.

Technically, the FBI is correct to argue that negotiators from CINT had no prior experience negotiating a protracted standoff involving a domestic group motivated by unconventional political or religious beliefs. The FBI institutionalized hostage negotiation training at Quantico in 1973 (McMains and Mullins 1996, 18), and the hostage negotiation unit went through a number of organizational iterations before CINT was established in 1985 (Botting, Lanceley, and Noesner 1995, 12). However, it is inaccurate to imply that *FBI negotiators* had never dealt directly with a barricade negotiation incident lasting longer than twelve days. In 1973, the FBI was involved in an extended barricade situation when American Indian Movement (AIM) activists occupied Wounded Knee, South Dakota, for seventy-one days (Robbins 1992; Wall 1992). By 1993, the FBI negotiators had also witnessed the 1985 MOVE crisis in Philadelphia in which a radical group and the city police became embroiled in a barricade standoff that resulted in tragedy (Assefa and Wahrhaftig 1990; Wagner-Pacifici 1994).[3] Thus, it is more accurate to say that prior to Waco the current generation of FBI negotiators had never dealt with an incident longer than twelve days.

Conceivably, the negotiators could have drawn lessons applicable to Waco from both Wounded Knee and MOVE. That they did not turn to these cases for useful lessons reveals much about the FBI negotiators' worldmaking narratives. Crisis negotiators, like other skills-based practitioners, acquire much of their "craft knowledge" from reflecting on and distilling lessons from previous cases. Which cases they study and which they ignore greatly impacts current

3. Starting in the 1970s, MOVE and the Philadelphia police engaged in a series of confrontations that ended on May 13, 1985. The police used tear gas, water canons, and ten thousand rounds of ammunition in an effort to dislodge members of MOVE from their residence. When this failed, the Philadelphia police dropped a bomb on the house, igniting a fire that destroyed 61 houses, damaged 110 others, and killed eleven MOVE members, including five children.

practices. Determining which cases are most analogous to an unfolding crisis, so that one accesses the most appropriate lessons, is critically important.

Like most practitioners, crisis negotiators spend the bulk of their time thinking about how to cope with *typical* or commonplace problems. Although the definition of typical and atypical cases is subject to change, modifications to the categorization of cases occur in response to real-life experience rather than to an analysis of "irrelevant" historical cases. For example, when negotiators noticed an increase in domestic barricade situations involving an estranged spouse or significant other who holds family members or a former lover hostage, they developed guidelines for dealing with "pseudo-hostage situations" (Fuselier, Van Zandt, and Lanceley 1991). They now use a collection of stories about actual pseudo-hostage situations as the basis for their thinking about what should be done in new situations that they encounter.

In 1993, protracted standoffs involving communities motivated by unconventional religious or political beliefs were rare occurrences. Therefore, crisis negotiators had directed almost no attention to learning lessons from earlier standoffs such as Wounded Knee and MOVE. This truncated mapping of barricade incidents may have blinded the negotiators to salient features of the Branch Davidian standoff, leading the FBI to predict a more rapid resolution of the conflict than the situation warranted.

Indicators of Progress

Although aware of the phase models of hostage negotiation, FBI negotiators prefer to use a set of assessment criteria to determine whether negotiations are progressing satisfactorily.

Negotiations are going well if:

1. No one has been killed since the negotiations started;
2. The number of emotional incidents, e.g., verbal threats against hostages, is decreasing;
3. The length of each conversation with the HT [hostage taker] increases, there is less talk of violence, and his rate of speech and pitch are lower;
4. Hostages have been released;
5. Deadlines have been passed; (Fuselier 1986a, 9)

6. The subject demonstrates increased willingness to follow negotiator suggestions;

7. Negotiators have established a relationship with the barricaded subject;

8. The subject demonstrates a willingness to discuss topics unrelated to the incident. (FBI training materials)

Using these criteria, the FBI negotiators concluded that negotiations were well under way in Waco on March 1. No one had been killed since the cease-fire was arranged. The number of emotional incidents had decreased considerably from the earliest 911 calls. Conversations between Mount Carmel residents and law enforcement agents were proceeding smoothly and were, for the most part, cordial. Children were being released. Furthermore, the Branch Davidians had apparently decided to bargain with law enforcement authorities.

According to the following log entries, the Mount Carmel residents made the first demand in the Waco negotiations (Logs 1–3, emphasis added).

Date	Time	Narrative
2/28/93	14:29	*First demand made.*
2/28/93	13:36	*Working on media deal with radio AM 1080 Dallas . . .*
2/28/93	14:43	ATF Supervisor being contacted for the go-ahead on radio broadcast . . .
2/28/93	15:11	ATF gives go-ahead for media link-up, now negotiation with radio station . . .
2/28/93	15:36	KRLD ready: Wayne says 4:00 P.M. OK . . .
2/28/93	16:08	*Passed news release deadline!*

The notion that the Branch Davidians were interested in bargaining for publicity was further reinforced by a second set of log entries (Logs 6–7, emphasis added).

Date	Time	Narrative
2/28/93	18:54	Wayne back on line—David says, "If you play message, children will be let go!" . . .
2/28/93	19:05	"1 child released every time message is played" . . .
2/28/93	20:26	2 kids out for each broadcast.
2/28/93	20:59	Wayne agreed to get rest of kids out this way—two at a time.

Assumptions about Barricaded Subjects

These log entries neatly fit with the FBI negotiators' preexisting assumptions about the needs and psychological characteristics of "religiously motivated" barricaded subjects. Next to the mass suicide in Jonestown, the most frequently cited "religious cult case" in the crisis negotiation literature is the Haigler incident (Fuselier 1986a; Powell 1989, 54–55; Van Zandt 1993, 26–27). In 1982, Keith and Kate Haigler hijacked a bus traveling from Arkansas to Kansas. The Haiglers, members of a small religious group, demanded to meet with local television reporters "to tell the world the Messiah has arrived" (Van Zandt 1993, 26). They claimed to be the two witnesses spoken of in chapter 11 of the Book of Revelation. The standoff ended when the Haiglers exited the bus pointing guns at police officers. The police shot and wounded them, and Kate Haigler killed her husband and then herself. Negotiators cite this incident as evidence of a connection between paranoid delusions and heightened religious fervor in barricaded subjects (Van Zandt 1993, 26).[4] Crisis negotiators also use the Haigler case to explain why offering access to the media is an effective bargaining strategy when dealing with religiously motivated barricaded subjects. FBI negotiators assume that subjects such as the Haiglers have an expressive need for attention that arises out of their delusions of grandeur.

Confronted with a barricaded subject using religious language, FBI negotiators set themselves three tasks. First, determine whether the person is capable of bargaining. The negotiators evaluated Koresh's mental state and concluded he was probably delusional and paranoid but was not exhibiting schizophrenic symptoms. Crisis negotiators believe that people suffering from paranoid delu-

---

4. "The delusions [of a paranoid schizophrenic hostage taker] are typically either delusions of grandeur—believing he has special qualities, abilities, or a special mission in life—or delusions of persecution—believing he is being persecuted because he has a special mission or is God's select person, etc." (Fuselier 1986a, 2). This quote is taken from one of the most widely read and frequently cited articles on crisis negotiation. Another influential author writes that a delusion is "a distortion of reality, a false belief [that] usually takes the expression of grandeur. Many, if not most, paranoid schizophrenics believe that they have an important role to play in the course of world events, and that God has entrusted them with a special skill, talent, or knowledge to complete this mission" (Strentz 1986, 13).

sions without schizophrenic symptoms are "coherent and lucid in [their] speech [so that] a 'reasonable' dialog can often be established" (Fuselier 1986a, 3). Therefore, they concluded Koresh was capable of negotiating. Second, the FBI negotiators ascertain whether the barricaded subject has a spoken or an unspoken need for publicity. This second task was short-circuited in Waco when the negotiators from Quantico read the previously cited log entries as evidence of Koresh's need for media attention. Third, if negotiation is appropriate, negotiators set the agenda for the negotiation process so as to avoid arguing with the barricaded subject about his or her beliefs. Having completed steps one and two, the FBI negotiators adopted a policy that one of the negotiators later described in the following way:

> We listened to David Koresh's theology and his points of view. We never tried to tell him that we understood that to the level that he did. But there are two consistent themes that you will hear from every mental health expert that knows anything about crisis intervention, crisis negotiation, and that is that you neither embrace someone's belief system nor do you discount it. (Judiciary 325)

The negotiators' goal was to keep Koresh focused on the instrumental bargaining process, listen to his religious ideas without engaging him in debate, and persuade him that coming out with his "flock" would advance his cause, enhance his fame, and increase his following. Unfortunately, the FBI negotiators did not actually follow this advice. They engaged in worldviewing debates with Koresh and the rest of the Mount Carmel residents, and ultimately they refused to acknowledge that the Branch Davidians' beliefs had legitimacy for the residents of Mount Carmel. Instead, they treated these beliefs as a form of mass delusion.

I have already discussed the risks associated with reducing a barricaded subject to bundles of traits or psychopathologies. The risk is significantly increased when dealing with a barricaded community motivated by unconventional beliefs. I will not revisit that issue here. Instead, I want to ponder the manner in which complex social interactions were filtered down or narrowed into the log accounts with which the negotiators from Quantico assessed early progress in Waco.

Revisiting the Negotiators' Decision to Use Bargaining

The log entries in combination with the FBI negotiators' preexisting assumptions made their efforts to impose a bargaining framework on the Waco negotiations appear logical. What happens to that logic if the log entries are inaccurate or incomplete, or both? Using the 911 transcripts that coincide with the log entries, later transcripts in which the negotiators and Branch Davidians offer competing accounts of the earliest negotiations, and a contextual analysis of events, we can tentatively reverse the filtering process by which complex interactions were distilled into the log entries. By so doing, we can answer important questions such as: Who actually initiated bargaining in Waco, and what other forms of interaction or exchange were *not* recorded in the logs? Once these questions are answered, we may fruitfully reflect on the efficacy of the attempt to impose a bargaining process on the Waco situation.

Who Initiated Bargaining in Waco?

According to the logs, the Branch Davidians started the bargaining process by demanding access to the media. This is obviously an incomplete picture of events because Martin "demanded" an immediate cease-fire when he phoned 911 (see chapter 5). The ecstatic notation about "passing the deadline" for the news release further implies that the alleged demand by the Branch Davidians was accompanied by a threat. Passing the deadline was, for the negotiators, an indication of negotiation progress and a lessening of violence. Examining the transcripts, however, we discover that whoever recorded the logs translated a complicated process of negotiating reality into the bargaining framework preferred by crisis negotiators.

The so-called first demand recorded in the logs was actually part of an effort to solidify the cease-fire at Mount Carmel.

> LARRY: No, no. They're [ATF agents] not coming back. . . . [T]here will be no more aggressive moves from ATF, okay. We're not gonna take any action . . .
> WAYNE: *However, Larry, it would reassure me a great deal if we could hear the media state that the BATF is not gonna make another aggressive move.*

LARRY: You want to hear that through the media.

WAYNE: We would like to hear that confirmed in the media. (911.5: 20, emphasis added)

The *crisis negotiators* introduced the bargaining element into this exchange.

LARRY: Alright. Let me ask you this. Are you in the position to promise me that . . . We can bring this thing together in a peaceful . . . end?

WAYNE: I'm not in that position because . . . we don't have that central communication. . . . We'll work on that.

LARRY: Okay, that [was] what I wanted to hear you say. . . . You know, that's what you and I want. . . . Okay. So . . . ATF is not gonna do anymore aggressive action, okay. I'm telling you that, I promise you that they're not gonna do that, okay.

WAYNE: Well, uhm, if they won't agree [to the radio broadcast] please let me know. (911.5: 20–22)

Later, *Lynch* suggested that media access might be something that could be traded for cooperation from the Branch Davidians.

LARRY: Alright, what do you think of . . . after the wounded have been moved out of there . . . talking to the media.

WAYNE: Ah, let me pass that on. (911.5: 23)

The ATF assurance regarding the cease-fire was broadcast twice. Then Martin told Lynch, "We want you to broadcast David's message. He's made a statement. . . . It's a speech for all of us" (911.8: 43). Lynch agreed to check into this and put pressure on Martin to get the situation resolved and get everyone out of Mount Carmel before dark (911.8: 46–47).

From the Branch Davidian perspective, their request to have Koresh's speech broadcast was the first interaction that might reasonably be interpreted as a demand for access to the media. However, this demand was not part of a bargaining effort. Rather, it was an expression of the Branch Davidians' fear that the ATF would attack them. "We got to talk to the media right away. . . .

We don't feel *secure* unless we can tell our side of the story" (911.3: 57, emphasis added). It was also a reflection of the Branch Davidians' frustration with the way they were being misrepresented and slandered by the ATF commanders and others (911.9: 4, 9–10). Access to the media was the only way the Branch Davidians could "set the record straight" about the February 28 raid and inform the world of their beliefs. "We've been given information about the Bible, that people do not know" (911.4: 36). They did not define access to the media as a commodity for which they should have to bargain, but defined it as their right. As a result, their demand was presented as a *moral claim,* not as an offer to trade goods, promises, or concessions.

When Lynch passed along the information that the ATF commanders wanted something in return for broadcasting the Mount Carmel message, the Branch Davidian moral claim was reframed as part of a bargaining process. By arguing that they had already made two broadcasts "without receiving anything," the ATF commanders unilaterally renarrated the radio broadcasts that clarified the cease-fire as part of a bargaining process. Furthermore, they described the earlier so-called exchange in a manner that put the Branch Davidians in debt to the ATF commanders. Martin's response that Lynch would "be right with God" if he played the tape can be seen as an effort to activate an exchange based on moral obligation rather than on bargaining.

> WAYNE: *Ah, Larry, please play the tape. You know, when you block the truth it puts you right in the judgment. I'm not talking about this life. I' talking about the one to come. If you're blocking God's truth.*
>
> LARRY: Okay, what . . . do we get for playing the tape? I mean . . . we need to get some folks out. Let's get the people [Branch Davidians] that are wounded. (911.9: 9–10, emphasis added)

Lynch rejected this moral appeal, along with Martin's subsequent proposal that the Branch Davidians would "stay in here peacefully" in exchange for the broadcast of their message (911.9: 15).

Finally, Martin brought a message from Koresh. "He said if you play my message, I'll let some of the children go" (911.9: 29). Martin and Lynch haggled over how many children. Lynch said all of the children. Martin said, "Every time that message is played. We'll send one child, at least one child" (911.9: 37). Ultimately, the agreement was two children for each broadcast of Koresh's message. The Branch Davidians cooperated with the bargaining framework in this instance, but not without resistance and not without offering an alternate basis for negotiation.

When Koresh said, "if you play my message, I'll let some of the children go," he confirmed the negotiators' preexisting belief that he was a manipulative, controlling, charismatic leader surrounded by brainwashed followers. The negotiators also assumed that such statements meant Koresh was the person with whom they needed to bargain. It is unclear, however, whether he initiated this language or was simply following the FBI lead. A more complete reading of the transcripts reveals a much more complex picture of negotiation strategies.

What Forms of Exchange Were Not Recorded in the Logs?

The Branch Davidian effort to negotiate on the basis of moral obligation is not noted in the logs. Yet the transcripts reveal that the Branch Davidians were not alone in making demands based on a sense of moral obligation or justice. In fact, the first demand after the cease-fire was established came not from the Branch Davidians, but from the ATF. Furthermore, that demand was formulated not as an instrumental exchange, but as a moral claim. The ATF demanded access to the Mount Carmel property to evacuate their dead and wounded agents, and the Branch Davidians *responded* to that demand out of a sense of moral obligation. They did not haggle over how many agents could be rescued, and they did not demand a concession from the ATF before they would cooperate. Mutual fear and suspicion, along with the flawed communication channels on both sides, delayed the rescue of the ATF agents.[5] The Branch Davidians and the ATF had to work out agreements about safe pas-

5. For evidence of the communication problems within Mount Carmel and between Lynch and the ATF, see the following tapes: 911.1; 911.1AA; 911.2; 911.3.

sage,[6] whether or not the rescuers could be armed,[7] and whether vehicles could be driven onto the property.[8] However, the two parties were in agreement about their moral obligation to work cooperatively on the problem of moving the agents to safety.

Worldviewing Differences That Disrupted Bargaining

We might argue that Cavanaugh and Lynch were simply unprepared to record significant events when the negotiator role was thrust upon them. Thus, the failure to note the ATF demand regarding recovery of their agents was merely an oversight. However, the complete record demonstrates the failure was not an accident, but a consequence of persistent worldviewing differences between the Branch Davidians and law enforcement negotiators.

The Branch Davidians regularly endeavored to negotiate reality and attempted to frame their issue-specific negotiations with the FBI as a search for justice. The negotiators consistently resisted or ignored both efforts and tried to force the Branch Davidians into a narrowly defined bargaining process. Although the Branch Davidians and FBI negotiators occasionally were able to execute small deals, the Branch Davidians obviously preferred a model of negotiation other than bargaining. The FBI negotiators never recognized that the Branch Davidians were, in fact, negotiating but were just framing the negotiations differently. The Branch Davidians' persistent attempts to negotiate on the basis of moral obligations or justice were not recorded at all, or they were dismissed as irrelevant, illogical, and disruptive.

6. The law enforcement agents did not trust the Branch Davidians to hold their fire during the evacuation process. Lynch and the ATF repeatedly raised the problem of guaranteeing safe passage for the ATF agents sent to remove their wounded comrades. Delays caused by this fear are documented in tapes 911.1 through 911.3.

7. The Branch Davidians did not trust the ATF to refrain from attacking them during the rescue operation. They wanted the agents who returned for the wounded to be unarmed, but quickly conceded this point (911.2) in response to Lynch's and the ATF's moral arguments.

8. The ATF suggested using an ambulance to evacuate the wounded agents. The Branch Davidians were afraid a vehicle could be used as cover during a sneak attack. See the following tapes: 911.2: 59–62; 911.3: 2–7, 19–20. Further panic was created when the medical rescue helicopter landed on the perimeter of the property (911.3: 25).

The FBI negotiators in Waco were afflicted with two types of worldview blindness that undercut their efforts to resolve the standoff. First, they were apparently unaware of their own role as initiators of demands. They did not classify a demand as such until the Branch Davidians ratified it, and then it was attributed solely to the barricaded subjects. No recognition was given to the cooperative worldnaming process behind the articulation of coherent instrumental demands. Second, the negotiators had no process for categorizing different types of demands. Every demand the Branch Davidians made was treated as an instrumental proposal, even those that were presented as moral claims. Meanwhile, law enforcement agents' moral claims were neither recorded as demands nor considered appropriate subjects for bargaining. In combination, the FBI negotiators' worldviewing impairments created an asymmetrical awareness of moral claims that offended the Branch Davidians.

Competing Rationalities

Unlike negotiating reality, issue-specific negotiation processes are goal-directed and consciously managed undertakings. Whether framed narrowly as bargaining or framed broadly as a problem-solving exercise, negotiation is partially governed by the presupposition that the participants are rational actors. Determining what constitutes rationality, however, is an exercise in negotiating reality. When the FBI negotiators pushed bargaining as the appropriate negotiation strategy in Waco, they were also reinforcing only one form of rationality and validating only one form of social action.[9]

Weber classifies social action according to four ideal types: (1) goal-rational (*zweckrational*) action, (2) value-rational (*wertrational*) action, (3) affectual action, and (4) traditionally oriented action.[10] Goal-rational actions are recognizable by their "rational orientation to a system of discrete individual ends . . .

---

9. Social action is human behavior distinguished by two critical features. All social action is *meaningful* because the actor attaches meaning to his or her own behavior (Weber 1964, 88). All social action is *interactive* because the actor orients his or her action "to the past, present, or expected future behaviour of others" (Weber 1964, 112).

10. The English translations of *zweckrational* and *wertrational* are taken from Campbell 1981 (176–77).

making use of . . . 'conditions' or 'means' for the successful attainment of the actor's own rationally chosen end" (Weber 1964, 115). In other words, the goal-rational actor chooses his or her objective and identifies the best possible means for achieving that end. Rationality is a matter of selecting a reasonable or realistic goal and discerning the most efficient methods for reaching that objective. In contrast, when an actor orients his or her actions "to an absolute value . . . involving a conscious belief in the absolute value of some ethical, aesthetic, religious, or other form of behavior, entirely for its own sake and independently of any prospects of external success," he or she is engaged in value-rational action (Weber 1964, 115). The value-rational actor works toward a goal that is determined in reference to absolute values rather than to realistic possibilities. The means for achieving a value-rational goal are selected on the basis of moral coherence and must correspond to the underlying values that determine the actor's objective. The actor's emotional states, feelings, and attachments determine affectual action. Traditionally oriented action is determined "through the habituation of long practice" or the established and accepted norms of a community (Weber 1964, 115).

When we study Waco, it is tempting to argue that the FBI negotiators were engaged in goal-rational action, whereas the Branch Davidians were engaged in value-rational action. However, the evidence paints a much more complicated picture. As Weber notes, "it would be very unusual to find concrete cases of . . . social action which were oriented *only* in one or another of these ways" (1964, 117). Parties involved in conflict, like all human actors, tend to mix various types of action.

Actors may adopt a goal in relation to an absolute value, but select the means for reaching their goal on the basis of efficiency and practicality. For example, the FBI negotiators were deeply committed to the absolute value of enforcing the law in Waco. They preferred to use nonviolent means (negotiation) to achieve that goal, but did not rule out the use of force on moral grounds. In short, the crisis negotiators in Waco were primarily but not exclusively inclined toward goal-rational action, and when diplomacy appeared to fail, they were willing to consider direct, violent action. Even those negotiators who objected to a direct attack on Mount Carmel couched their arguments in goal-rational terms (i.e., "it will not work").

The Branch Davidians, on the other hand, were primarily but not exclusively inclined toward value-rational action. As actors who were deeply committed to a set of values that reflected their understanding of ultimate reality, the Branch Davidians placed great emphasis on the moral coherence between means and ends. Actors whose means and ends must be morally coherent are less able to compromise and bargain than are goal-rational actors, who are free to choose the most efficient means to achieve their desired ends. Consequently, the Branch Davidians were able to participate in a goal-rational bargaining process only insofar as they were not required to trade goods and promises in a manner that violated their absolute values.

Does this mean the FBI negotiators were rational and the Branch Davidians were irrational? Or can we say the FBI negotiators were more rational and the Branch Davidians were less rational? Not if we take seriously Weber's invitation to displace a unidimensional concept of rationality and recognize the existence of *competing rationalities*.

I label as rational those activities that are based on or derived from reasoning. In other words, actions are rational when they can be explained logically. Goal-rational actions are rational—that is, reasonable, explainable, and logical—*within an instrumental worldview*. Goal-rational actors choose the means for achieving their goal on the basis of efficiency, expediency, and effectiveness. The instrumental worldview dominates modern societies, so most people consider the logic of goal-rational actions self-evident. By contrast, many people find value-rational, affectual, and traditionally oriented actions puzzling or illogical, particularly when the values, affectual relationships, or traditions are rooted in a worldview they do not share. However, value-rational, affectual, and traditional actions are not devoid of reason; they are not illogical. All these forms of action are rational if we understand the internal logic of the worldviews within which they originate.

If we understand the pattern of compulsions and permissions that constrain a value-rational, affectual, or traditionally oriented actor, we can discern the rationality of his or her actions. To explain the actions of someone oriented toward affectual action, we need to discover his or her emotional state, feelings, and attachments. To explain the actions of someone who is traditionally oriented, we need to fathom the expectations imposed on the actor by his or her tradition. To explain the actions of a value-rational actor, we need to comprehend his or her absolute values and the moral constraints those values impose on his or her selection of actions. Granted, it is more difficult to describe and understand the rationality of actors who are motivated by orientations other than goal rationality. That does not, however, justify privileging goal-rational actions by equating them with rationality per se.

Nevertheless, researchers as well as practitioners fall into the trap of imposing a unidimensional concept of rationality on complex cases of worldview conflict. For example, Assefa and Wahrhaftig worry about the validity of rationally analyzing the "irrational" behavior of MOVE (1990, 4). They claim to have overcome this problem by ferreting out the "consistent, explainable logic in MOVE's behavior" (4). What Assefa and Wahrhaftig have actually done, however, is assess the value-rational actions of MOVE against a goal-rational yardstick. They highlight those instances of MOVE behavior that most closely resemble goal-rational action. Consequently, they make much of MOVE's participation in the "composting agreement" as an indication that problem-solving processes can work with groups such as MOVE. MOVE's back-to-nature philosophy led the community to discard "most of the remains from their fruit and vegetable diet in their backyard so that it would be 'cycled' back to nature" (Assefa and Wahrhaftig 1990, 15). When this practice generated the inevitable odor and rodent problems, their neighbors objected. One community organization negotiated an agreement with MOVE in which MOVE members agreed to compost their refuse. This "was a mutually satisfactory solution since it was in accord with MOVE's philosophy, and at the same time reduced the odor and rat population in the neighborhood" (Assefa and Wahrhaftig 1990, 50). To argue, as do Assefa and Wahrhaftig, that this case shows an essentially irrational actor behaving rationally misses the underlying process of *worldview coordination* on which the composting agreement depended. MOVE members were able to enter into the composting agreement because it fit their own value-rational orientation, not because they adopted the goal-rational orientation of the other actors.

Recognizing the importance of worldview coordination in the composting agreement verifies the connection between negotiating reality and issue-specific negotiation. This example leads me to reformulate the practical quandary of designing an issue-specific negotiation process for use with parties who are separated by significant worldviewing differences. The predicament has typically been cast as one of getting all of the actors to "be rational"—i.e., to engage in a goal-rational process. I suggest it is more productive to think of the problem as helping diverse parties, each of whom is motivated by a complex mix of action orientations, to negotiate reality, thereby allowing them to manage their disparate rationalities during a negotiation encounter. Successful issue-specific negotiations will ensue when the parties achieve a *coordinated rationality*. Difficulties will occur when the incommensurate rationalities of the parties are poorly managed or remain uncoordinated.

As currently constructed, the practice of crisis negotiation rests on a single, unidimensional concept of rationality. Goal-rational behavior is deemed rational; all other forms of action are irrational, nonrational, or irrelevant to the process of crisis negotiation. Furthermore, negotiators identify only two types of actors: those who are motivated by a goal-rational orientation and those who are motivated by an (out of control) affectual orientation. Figure 6 (in chapter 3) shows how in common practice crisis negotiators assist a barricaded subject, who is engaged in affectual action, in moving to a more balanced emotional state so that he or she can participate in goal-rational action. Traditional action and value-rational action—and, by implication, traditionally oriented actors and value-rational actors—are completely missing from figure 6. Working with this limited conceptual model of human motivation, crisis negotiators attempt to impose goal-rational negotiation processes on barricaded subjects.

This practice works remarkably well with actors who are already predisposed toward goal-rational behaviors. Barricaded subjects who favor a goal-rational orientation (e.g., criminals or terrorists) do not resist the bargaining process, even if they do not particularly care for the limited range of options that the police place on the table. Current crisis negotiation practices also work well with barricaded subjects who are acting out of a temporarily heightened affectual orientation. These actors can, indeed, be moved from emotionality to rationality as FBI training materials suggest. On the other hand, actors who are intensely committed to value rationality or to an established set of traditions will be deeply offended if asked to treat their absolute values, ultimate concerns, or traditions as negotiable. We can understand why they are so offended only if we first examine the internal logic of the bargaining process.

Naming the World as Amenable to Bargaining

Before parties can engage in bargaining, they must identify specific objects, actions, or commitments as instrumental entities suitable for trading. Bargaining requires that parties name some features of the world as commodities. Every negotiator has his or her limits regarding what is or is not properly defined as a commodity. Parties who share cultural and worldviewing assumptions operate within an unspoken understanding of these limitations. In worldview conflicts, disagreements over the legitimacy of characterizing specific entities as commodities can easily derail the bargaining process. Each party may deeply, albeit inadvertently, offend the other by attempting to commodify "sacred" entities.

To trade people for media access, the people have to be transformed into commodities. In typical barricade situations, hostage takers treat their captives as mere bargaining chips, and the police cooperate in that worldnaming process. In Waco, the FBI negotiators designated persons as commodities, but the Branch Davidians tended to resist that naming of the world. The FBI negotiators were concerned about the safety of the women and children, so they used a bargaining process in which women and children were treated as a medium of exchange in order to remove them from danger. This worldmaking narrative worked only insofar as the Branch Davidians were willing to allow the FBI to classify women and children as commodities.

The negotiators were the first to use the language of commodities when talking about Branch Davidian women and children. Even after the Branch Davidians objected to this language, the negotiators persisted in using it. These are but a very few examples:

PN03: Supposing we do this. When . . . —you send out the two kids . . . with the tape, *give me two kids and two women.* How about that? (Tape 10b: 5, emphasis added)

PN04: Listen. *Offer me something. Women . . . and children.* Let's go with the women and children. (Tape 69: 53, emphasis added)

PN05: And if you release some of those youngsters out of there, we will play the tape. But you send the tape out, we'll listen to the tape. *Then you send the youngsters out, the tape gets played.* (Tape 78: 14, emphasis added)

PN06: We got the milk for you. . . . We'll bring the milk down. We'll drop it off . . . . *In return, we want four of your kid sto come up, and we're going to give you the milk for the kids.* (tape 78: 29, emphasis added)

Distinguishing between tradable objects and sacred entities is an exercise in categorization, one of the most basic worldviewing activities. To categorize the world is to "create islands of meaning" by simultaneously engaging in "two rather different mental processes—lumping and splitting" (Zerubavel 1991, 21). Lumping "involves grouping 'similar' items together in a single mental cluster," whereas splitting "involves separating in our mind 'different' mental clusters from one another" (Zerubavel 1991, 21). The logical bases on which a community lumps and splits the world may vary significantly. In other words, things are defined as similar or different through a complex process of identifying the salient characteristics of entities, and different communities consider different characteristics salient.

Furthermore, separating tradable objects from sacred entities is a valuing process. Conflicts over categorizing commodities and sacred objects do not lend themselves to resolution by reference to some external reality. We cannot point to the material world and prove that some objects are inherently sacred, whereas other objects are fundamentally profane. We must present a coherent argument for separating objects into any categories, including dividing the world into sacred entities and commodities; and others may accept, reject, or modify our arguments.

Conflicts over lumping and splitting sacred objects and commodities are only one type of categorization problem when bargaining is introduced into a worldview conflict. If the parties in a worldview conflict recognized the same categories of objects but valued them differently, bargaining would be difficult, but at least they could determine the overlapping categories of objects that both parties considered commodities and bargain within that shared set of objects. Unfortunately, parties involved in worldview conflicts face an even more difficult situation. They rarely recognize the same categories of objects. They lump and split the world differently even before they distinguish between commodities and sacred objects. Consequently, the FBI assumed that all Mount Carmel residents, other than Koresh and perhaps his closest associates, could be treated as commodities. The Branch Davidians, on the other hand, were willing to cooperate with the FBI bargaining process by trading children for a variety of concessions, but found it ethically offensive to label people other than children as commodities.

Difficulties were compounded when the FBI negotiators interpreted bargaining accomplishments as evidence the Branch Davidians *shared* their own goal-rational orientation and their own categories of commodities. The FBI neither recognized nor attempted to understand the internal logic of the Branch Davidian worldview that led them both to cooperate with and to resist trading people for publicity. Instead, the FBI described the Branch Davidians' inconsistent participation in the bargaining process as a sign of their bad faith or their intent to manipulate the negotiators. The entire negotiation process would have been better served if the negotiators had asked: "What classificatory distinctions are leading the Branch Davidians to behave in this apparently illogical manner?"

Why Could the Branch Davidians Trade
Some People but Not Others?

Koresh and others in the Mount Carmel community explained quite clearly why they were able to participate in a bargaining process that traded children for access to the media. The community agreed with Koresh when he said, "the children don't have [moral] decisions in them" (Tape 9: 20) and are therefore subject to their parents. Cooperating with the FBI bargaining script allowed those parents who elected to remove their children from Mount Carmel to do so. There is, however, a huge worldviewing leap between cooperating with someone else's script and actually adopting the rationality on which it is based. The Branch Davidians traded children for media access because they could do so without violating their own worldmaking narrative. Like MOVE in the composting agreement, the Branch Davidians coordinated their value-rational actions with the goal-rational activities of the outside world.

Worldview coordination collapsed when the FBI moved to commodify adult women. Neither Koresh nor anyone else at Mount Carmel considered adults, male or female, as bargaining chips. Rather, they categorized them as moral agents. Within the Branch Davidian worldmaking narrative, all adult moral agents were under a sacred obligation to choose freely between obedience to God's commands and the demands of secular authorities, which is logical, given that a moral decision-making process brought most residents of Mount Carmel to Waco in the first place. Because adult members of the Mount Carmel community could not be commodified, the FBI negotiators' insistence on trying to trade adults for media access and other concessions deeply offended the Branch Davidians.

The bargaining framework also implied that someone in Mount Carmel had the power to trade people. Koresh was the obvious candidate for this role, but he and the rest of the community vehemently resisted the idea that he controlled the other adults in the community. The following conversation, one of many similar exchanges, illustrates the disconnection between the Branch Davidian worldmaking narrative and the FBI negotiators' bargaining framework:

PN01: Listen, I want your folks to have a chance in life. And, . . .you know how we were yesterday, where we couldn't get anywhere, we didn't seem to get anywhere until you and I started to make some agreements about the children coming out. . . . What I'm trying to say is once we had an agreement about what was going to happen, you made it happen. You know, you've got a strong will, and what I'm saying—

MR. KORESH: And I explained to you why. Because the children don't have decisions in them.

PN01: I know it, but, but what I'm saying is *if you could make an agreement with your people that they're walking out of there and you could—*

MR. KORESH: *I am not going to tell them what to do. I never have and never will. I show them out of a book what God teaches. Then it's for them to decide.*

PN01: David, these, these kids need their parents and we want everybody to be safe. *How about the women? Can—Will you let them come out of there?*

MR. KORESH: Hey, haven't, haven't Sita and them already come out?

[Note: The FBI allowed Sita Sonobe to exit and reenter Mount Carmel in order to assist with turning children over to the FBI.]

PN01: Oh, yeah, but I mean, I mean come out and actually stay out.

MR. KORESH: Yeah, but the thing of it is that *if they wanted to, they, they could.*

PN01: Well, I, I think they feel like they can't because you don't want them to.

MR. KORESH: No, no, no, no. Let's stop that now.

PN01: Okay. I mean, I think your will is so strong that—and they love you so much that they, *they wouldn't go unless you sent them. You know what I mean? . . . David, give me a sign and send, send a woman with some children. . . . Give me a sign.*

MR. KORESH:—I'm not going to play that game.

PN01: Come on, give me a sign. Send a woman with some children. (Tape 9: 19–21, emphasis added)

The reader may be wondering why the Branch Davidians disagreed with the FBI's classification of women and children as a tradable commodity when Wayne Martin and Larry Lynch had earlier lumped women and children to-gether as a category of people in need of protection (see chapter 5). How we categorize the world depends in part on the task at hand and on our under-standing of the context. Protecting women and children from harm and trad-ing women and children to achieve a goal are two different activities. The FBI connected these activities in a manner the Branch Davidians did not. In the FBI negotiators' worldview, trading the women and children would remove them from a dangerous situation. Why did the Branch Davidians not validate the FBI negotiators' overlapping categories of women and children as both tradable commodities and people in need of protection? Because the concept of protection entails a definition of risk, and conceptions of risk vary greatly from one community to another.

Differing conceptions of risk led the Branch Davidians to evaluate the ne-gotiators' bargaining proposals in unanticipated ways. For example, they were not completely convinced that their children would be safer "out in the world." They did not want their children placed in foster homes or with Child Protec-tive Services. They were afraid the children would be fed food prohibited by their religious dietary laws, put under the scrutiny of psychologists and social workers whose secular values were offensive to the Mount Carmel community, and otherwise exposed to pernicious influences if sent into the world. Those children who left Mount Carmel were routinely reminded to be careful and re-member their faith. When the children were not placed with their relatives, as the Branch Davidians had requested, the parents at Mount Carmel who still had children with them reevaluated the wisdom of sending out those children. No children left the property after March 3.

The adult Branch Davidians assessed the danger of their own situation in relation to God's imminent judgment. They felt threatened by the FBI, but they felt even more endangered by the prospect of falling into sin if they failed to follow God's will. Barricade negotiation practices rely on the strategic use of threat and coercion. The tactical teams are used to remind the barricaded subject of the negative consequences of a negotiation failure, which works only if the barricaded subject believes that the tactical team poses the greatest threat to his or her survival. Steve Schneider summarized the perspective of the Mount Carmel residents very clearly.

> STEVE: . . . They're [the community members] not afraid. You could mow them down, you could shoot them down. . . . And the only reason why we're staying here together as a unit still is because of that one word, wait. It's not because we fear man. There's a higher power we have learned to fear more so that—I mean when that God says he can destroy your soul and you know what he's talking about, we actually believe that is a reality more so than this world which will pass away. (Tape 70: 12)

This conception of risk had a profound impact on the bargaining process. Given the need to decide between the dangers of the world and the peril of eternal damnation, all adults at Mount Carmel, women included, were compelled to make their own moral decisions about leaving the property. They could not be traded lest they be coerced into sinful action.

The transcripts even provide evidence of the Branch Davidians' belief regarding the age at which children became responsible for their own decisions. On March 3, Koresh offered the FBI the following "deal."

> PN01: Okay, well why can't you tell me what's going to happen next, after we wait a while? I mean, is, is something going to happen inside?
> DAVID: Well, I'm still going to send some more kids out.
> PN01: Okay, good.
> DAVID: But here's the, here's the thing now. . . . You get you . . . a Bible,—

... We'll bear with this fool just a little longer— ... —and I'll give you a Bible
study, and then I'll send another kid out to you, okay? Fair enough?

PN01: Well, wait just a second. Just one child? I'd like to—

DAVID: Well, this one wants to go. (Tape 26: 29)

The child in question was Koresh's twelve-year-old nephew, and, it is evident
from the taped conversations that the adults at Mount Carmel, including the
child's father, assumed he was capable of making a personal choice about leaving
the property. So moral agency or the capacity to make an informed decision regarding one's own response to God's will and the unfolding events in Waco was
one basis for lumping and splitting people within the Mount Carmel community.

A second distinction was made within the category of children. When Koresh announced "these are *my* babies," the negotiator heard this statement as
the concern of a protective father. Therefore, the negotiator promised, "We'll
take good care of them . . . just like they're my own." However, Koresh was not
simply expressing paternal anxiety. Given the unusual circumstances of the
children's conception, the whole community was worried about the way these
children would be treated by the outside world, and the community members
were reluctant to identify the children by name. Even discussing the number of
children at Mount Carmel was a sensitive topic, and Koresh and the others did
not like being pushed on this issue.

PN01: Why don't we—why don't we do something. Why don't you—why
don't you send out those eight children you mentioned before? [Koresh was the
father of all eight children.]

DAVID: No. Stop playing games with me or I'm going to stop talking to you
all together and you can do what you want to do. . . .

PN01: Oh, I thought you were ready to do it [send the children out].

DAVID: I didn't say that. . . . I told you I'd give you their names.

PN01: Oh, okay, I'm sorry. All right. Go ahead. I thought you were ready to
do it. (Tape 44: 8)

Beyond the concern for their well-being, these particular children were also
categorically different from the others because they were Children of the New
Light Doctrine and thus had a significant role to play in the coming Kingdom of

God (Tabor and Gallagher 1995, 68; also see Thibodeau and Whiteson 1999, 107–10, 222–23). They were the "children spoken of in prophecy that are the direct product of a truth or a doctrine which comes from heaven" (Tape 53: 44) and could not be treated as commodities in an effort to cooperate with the FBI negotiators' bargaining process. Only through "asking counsel and receiving counsel from God" (Tape 44: 9) could Koresh determine whether his children could be sent into the world. Unfortunately, the negotiators ignored Koresh when he tried to explain, "Well, there's something about those babies and prophecies you all don't know" (Tape 42: 52).

Koresh repeatedly pointed out that "My children that I have are different than the other children," but he eventually concluded that the negotiators could not understand this fact because they did not understand the Seven Seals (Tape 57: 22). Consequently, none of Koresh's biological children residing at Mount Carmel left the property during the standoff. Twelve children (ages in parentheses) who died on April 19, 1993, were fathered by Koresh: Cyrus (eight), Star (six), Bobbie Lane (two), Serenity (four), Chica and Lawan (twenty-two-month-old twins), Dayland (three), Paige (infant), Chanel (fourteen months), Startle (one); Mayanah (two); Hollywood (two). Three surviving children fathered by Koresh were not in residence at Mount Carmel in 1993.

The FBI Negotiators' Categories of Commodities

The FBI negotiators, who persisted in treating all members of the community as potential bargaining chips, did not recognize the Branch Davidians' lumping and splitting of people. Why? Obviously, they were not experts in Branch Davidian theology. Nor can we reasonably expect FBI negotiators to be familiar with the beliefs of every religiously and politically motivated unconventional group with whom they might have a confrontational encounter. On the other hand, greater attention to the language of the Branch Davidians and a more critical awareness of their own worldnaming actions would have directed the FBI negotiators' attention to the Branch Davidians' worldmaking narrative.

Instead of listening for indications of the Branch Davidians' worldmaking narrative, the FBI negotiators tried to adapt their own preexisting hostage negotiation script to fit this unusual situation. They kept attempting to squeeze some or all of the Mount Carmel residents into the category of hostages. They also directed their energies toward diagnosing Koresh. The negotiators, behavioral scientists, and commanders in Waco believed that if they could just "fine tune the assessment of who they were dealing with—a delusional religious zealot with a messianic complex, or a con man" (Justice 135), they would know how to handle the negotiations. Activities that have worked well in other barricade situations—that is, identifying hostages and diagnosing the perpetrator—led the FBI negotiators astray and prevented the development of effective negotiation strategies during the Waco standoff.

Acknowledging the fact that the Mount Carmel residents considered themselves free moral agents and not the duped victims of a deluded charismatic leader would have been far more effective than attempting to diagnose Koresh's sincerity. Pragmatically speaking, the accuracy or inaccuracy of categorizing the Branch Davidians as suffering from "low self esteem" (Justice 206) and Koresh as the manipulative con man was irrelevant. As long as the residents of Mount Carmel identified themselves as independent decision makers, they would not participate in any bargaining process that treated adult members of their community as commodities.

How then did the FBI negotiators commodify the residents of Mount Carmel? They separated people in Mount Carmel according to their purported relationship to an alleged hierarchical authority structure that was grounded more in anticult propaganda than in a careful analysis of the evidence.[11] The FBI defined Koresh and his "mighty men" as independent actors capable of exerting control over other members of the community and classified other members of the community as misguided followers who succumbed to Koresh's manipulation out of individual weaknesses.

Within the category of followers, women and children were designated as

11. The FBI negotiators insist that they did not solicit advice from anticult activists or so-called cult experts during the Waco standoff. When given unsolicited advice by such experts, the FBI "evaluated the credibility of the information and treated it accordingly" (Justice 192). Nevertheless, the transcripts bear witness to the fact that the FBI negotiators worked with a worldnaming narrative about "cults," which in the absence of detailed information about the Branch Davidians led the negotiators to make unwarranted assumptions about the internal dynamics of the Mount Carmel community.

particularly vulnerable to victimization. The reasons for thinking of children as potential victims are obvious. The logic behind assuming the women were victims is less apparent. Based on the transcripts, the logs, and personal conversations with FBI agents, I hypothesize that the negotiators categorized the women in Mount Carmel as victims on the basis of the negotiators' own normative response to the unusual (in their eyes, deviant) gender relations within the community. It was simply inconceivable to the negotiators that the women of Mount Carmel had freely chosen to engage in sexual relations with Koresh and to forego sexual relations with their husbands. Because they must have been duped or brainwashed in this regard, they were not taken seriously as decision makers during the negotiation process.

The FBI negotiators felt a strong moral obligation to protect the supposedly victimized women and children of Mount Carmel from further harm. The negotiators also surmised that, having already victimized the women and children, Koresh would be inclined to treat them as bargaining chips to advance his own ends. The negotiators persisted in this belief even when Koresh and the other adults in the community, including the women themselves, consistently denied its validity.

A visual comparison of the Branch Davidian and FBI categorizations of people in Mount Carmel illustrates the complex problems involved in identifying commodities suitable for trading when the parties are separated by profound worldviewing differences (fig. 10.). It also illustrates the very narrow range of people the Branch Davidians were willing to exchange for media attention or for any other concession from the FBI.

When Is Bargaining Inappropriate?

Confusion over which people could be commodified for the purposes of bargaining and which people could not be treated thus was only one controversy that disrupted the Waco negotiations. There were also subjects around which the Branch Davidians considered bargaining a completely inappropriate negotiation process because bargaining involved converting moral claims into instrumental entities. For example, the negotiators presumed that access to the media was a negotiable commodity over which the FBI had legitimate control.

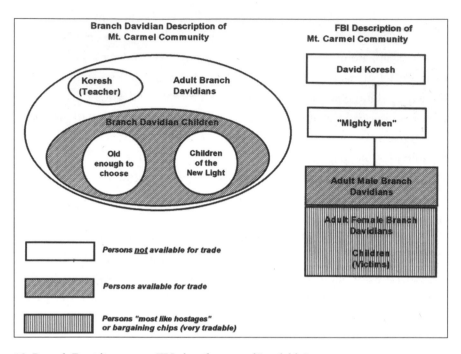

10. Branch Davidian versus FBI classification of "tradable" persons.

The Branch Davidians vehemently objected to this naming of the world because they considered access to the media their *right*. By denying them access
to the media, the FBI affirmed the Branch Davidian belief that they were being
attacked unjustifiably by a federal government that could not be trusted. However, the Branch Davidians' moral objections went unheeded and unacknowl-
edged, as in the following exchange:

> STEVE: One of the biggest impasses, . . .that we have, it's two things, which
> have been right from the beginning. . . . One of the biggest things of all things is
> that you cut us off. You cut our telephones off from talking to who we will.
>
> PN04: We, we, we do this in every . . .
>
> STEVE: Put—leave our phones—put them as they were, as is given in the
> Constitution the freedoms that we should have to be able to speak. And if you
> want to refute that—
>
> PN04: You will have those services restored eventually.
>
> STEVE: If you want to get your people to refute that, that is fine. That is fine.

PN04: I'm not going to refute that.

STEVE: Let us, let us tell our side of the story. If you think I'm going to come out and put myself in your hands without being . . . able to speak my mouth and mind. (Tape 65: 39)

Although the FBI negotiator did not refute Schneider's claim regarding free speech, the FBI continued to hold the restoration of communication as a commodity for which the Branch Davidians were required to bargain.

Thus, the agreement to exchange children for access to the media involved a major *worldviewing concession* on the part of the Branch Davidians as well as an act of *worldviewing coordination* between the FBI and the Branch Davidians. The Mount Carmel residents did not have to change their belief that they had a right to free communication with the public, but they did have to set aside their moral objections to the FBI's physical control over their access to the public. Having done that, the Branch Davidians also had to find a commodity of interest to the FBI that nevertheless did not violate their own values. Viewed thus, the simple agreement to exchange children for the broadcast of a message from Koresh represented a major accomplishment in worldview management.

I cannot emphasize enough the importance of validating the Branch Davidians' worldviewing concessions. Only by acknowledging this type of compromise can we provide a fair and balanced account of the negotiations. Thus far, every single official account, investigation, or hearing related to the negotiations has portrayed the FBI as making remarkable concessions, but the Branch Davidians as conceding nothing and remaining obstinate and belligerent. The Danforth (2000) report is an excellent example of this portrayal. To be fair, Senator Danforth was not asked to evaluate the *negotiations* in Waco. Nevertheless, I invite the reader to compare the Special Counsel's description of the Waco negotiations (appendix A) with the information presented in this book.

The parties in Waco were, unfortunately, less successful in managing other worldviewing differences. As with the issue of access to the media, the Branch Davidians demanded that the FBI tactical units be removed from the Mount Carmel property because they had a *right* to live according to their own beliefs, a *right* to protect their property, and a *right* not to be terrorized in their home by police using military-style weapons and equipment. The negotiators over-looked the moral basis of these claims and treated the Branch Davidian de-mand as amenable to goal-rational bargaining. Consequently, the negotiators expended considerable energy convincing the FBI commanders to offer the Branch Davidians a deal that would exchange the removal of armored person-nel carriers from the Mount Carmel property for the Branch Davidian surren-der. Having invested their time in bargaining with their bosses on behalf of the Branch Davidians, the negotiators were shocked and frustrated when the Mount Carmel residents summarily dismissed the deal.

> STEVE: He [Koresh] handed the phone to me. He wanted me to hear what you had to say.
>
> PN04: Okay. Well, as I proposed to him, we've had some problems over the last day or so working out a way we can get past this point where we seem to be hanging up. There's obviously a reluctance on your part to accept that *we're try-ing to do everything we can on your behalf.* So, as I was telling David, the reason I haven't called in today is because *I've gone to the commanders up here and made some requests of them* and we've been talking at length, trying to resolve this im-passe. And, *so, we're . . . offering this proposal that if you folks in there will commit to coming out . . . of the compound, we'll withdraw the Bradleys from the property, back across from the property lines.* And as we're withdrawing the Bradleys, you send four kids or four adults up the . . . path there as we're moving. So that way we know that you're going to be committed to your part of the agreement and you know that we're committed to our part of the agreement. And then once those Bradleys are off the property, then the rest of you folks go ahead and follow the kids out or those first four individuals out in the same fashion as—
>
> STEVE: Well, I should actually—*I should have you save your breath because right now you and I are so far apart . . . that there's no sense in even talking.*
>
> PN04: Okay. Well, offer me a suggestion.
>
> STEVE: You need to go back—*you need to go back to the commanders*—and *start talking sensibly* and then you can call me when you've got something worth-while to talk about. (Tape 68: 7–8, emphasis added)

The negotiators and the commanders took the Branch Davidian rejection of this deal as an indication of their unwillingness to "bargain in good faith." Because the FBI negotiators had neither recorded nor recognized the different types of claims and proposals being put on the table, they heard Schneider's response as a rejection of the deal that had been offered. However, negotiation based on moral claims (value-rational negotiation) and negotiation based on instrumental claims (goal-rational negotiation) are grounded in two different worldmaking narratives. Schneider, Koresh, and the other residents of Mount Carmel were not declining the deal. They were rejecting the legitimacy of applying the worldmaking narrative of bargaining to this particular problem.

The women at Mount Carmel were particularly incensed when the FBI attempted to trade the "release" of women and children for six gallons of milk. Koresh sent one thousand dollars in cash out of Mount Carmel with one of the children to be used to take care of the children and to purchase supplies needed at Mount Carmel. He and the rest of the community were under the impression that the FBI had agreed to send in milk for the children, a telephone, and extra phone cord. The following exchange between Kathy Schroeder and a negotiator demonstrates the Branch Davidians' objections to bargaining:

KATHRYN SCHROEDER: Give us the milk. We've already given you 21 kids.

PN06: I can only provide it to you, I can only provide it to you—

KATHRYN SCHROEDER: If we send out four more kids. That doesn't make any sense.

PN06: Listen. I'll, I'll get the milk to you for two kids.

KATHRYN SCHROEDER: You get the milk to me for the two kids that went out Friday.

PN06: Kathy, perhaps we're wasting one another's time. All right? Put somebody else on.

KATHRYN SCHROEDER: I mean, all you want, all you want to do is bargain?

PN06: Kathy!

KATHRYN SCHROEDER: Are you going to bargain with human lives?

PN06: Kathy! I've told you what we'll do and, and if that's not agreeable to you, perhaps we're wasting one another's time. All right? . . . Why don't you put somebody else on, please?

KATHRYN SCHROEDER: Look, ... There are babies here that need the milk. Are you that inhumane that you can't just send us the milk for not sending out kids, or sending out David, or sending out women[?]

PN06: Our concern, our concern is for those children first and foremost and the rest of you also. All right? The children—

KATHRYN SCHROEDER: So, your concern is that these babies get fed the milk they need?

PN06: Kathy.

KATHRYN SCHROEDER: It doesn't sound like you're concerned, . . .

PN06: Kathy, you don't want to listen to me. Okay? . . . So why don't you put somebody else on, because obviously you're not listening to what I have to say. . . . I'll be happy to talk with you—

KATHRYN SCHROEDER: Say it again, then.

PN06:—if you want to use reason. Okay?

KATHRYN SCHROEDER: I'll listen to it again.

PN06: Okay. The agreement that I tried to get David to commit to was to send the kids once we drop the milk up there. All right? Send the kids and an adult to pick the milk up and send the children out. That's the agreement. I went into my boss and he said we will do it under these conditions. We have attempted to, to work with you folks and we will continue to do so, but we have to, we have to share in this responsibility. You have to take some responsibility, we have to take some responsibility. There's a give and a take, concessions have to be made by both sides and we're willing to do this. Send the children out, the milk will be there. . . .

KATHRYN SCHROEDER: If, if I don't—. . . , what I'm saying is you're saying that we don't have anything to say to each other because I do not agree with your stipulations. That's—it's like who's controlling whose mind here? Dave is not controlling my mind. You're trying to control my mind.

PN06: I'm not trying to control anything.

KATHRYN SCHROEDER: You are—

PN06: You said you want the milk. I'm willing to give you the milk.

KATHRYN SCHROEDER: Okay. Give me the milk then.

PN06: You send the children and that's agreeable. It's a done deal. It's already there. We'll do it. We'll do it. I'm happy to do it. . . .

KATHRYN SCHROEDER: No you won't do it— . . . You won't. Even if I sent all the kids out you wouldn't.

PN06: Okay. Listen, Kathy, you're really—I know you're upset and that's fine. Why don't you give it some consideration and if you want to talk, reason, then we—you and I will talk together, but really it's, it's, it's no reason for us to go on now, because—you won't accept—

KATHRYN SCHROEDER: Because I won't accept your conditions. But you won't accept ours either.

PN06: Well, we have to meet and, and I'm willing to bring the milk out. . . .
What are you willing to do to get the milk? That's the question. What are you
willing to do?

KATHRYN SCHROEDER: I'm willing to, myself, walk out that gate and be shot
by your Bradleys if I have to and I'll go get that milk. (Tape 83: 3–7)

This exchange also illustrates the highly problematic gender dynamics that
cropped up whenever the male FBI negotiators tried to bargain directly with
the women at Mount Carmel. The negotiators tended to consider the women
highly emotional whenever they disagreed with the "logic" of the negotiators.
The negotiators also grew frustrated with male Branch Davidians whose logic
was other than their own, but they did not as readily deem the men "emotional" and "overwrought." When the negotiators felt the women in Mount
Carmel were being emotional, they requested to speak with a more reasonable
(usually male) member of the community. The negotiators also tended to speak
sharply to the women at Mount Carmel, addressing them in ways they did not
address the men.

Why Did the Branch Davidians Bargain at All?

After mapping out the Branch Davidian worldview, we might wonder why
they were willing to cooperate with the bargaining process as much as they did.
The answer can be found in the FBI's use of power and in the Branch Davidians' creative manipulation of the FBI's bargaining framework for their own
purposes. The FBI's use of power is obvious. They were clearly determined to
coerce and intimidate the Branch Davidians into negotiating an end to the
standoff. Less obvious is the manner in which Koresh and the community
members used the FBI's bargaining framework to accomplish their own ends.
This manipulation of the bargaining framework can be illustrated by revisiting
the deal in which Koresh "traded" his twelve-year-old nephew for a Bible study
with the negotiators.

Where minority communities confront a dominant discourse, they must
often adopt the language of the powerful in order to have any voice at all
(Spender 1980). However, they frequently twist that discourse to suit their own
ends (hooks 1994; Memmi 1965). Although Koresh couched his statements in

bargaining language in this conversation, he was apparently using the available discourse to further his own goals.

This type of discursive subversion is filled with risks. In initiating this bargaining exchange, Koresh endangered his identity by appearing to embrace the role of a "cult leader" who has the power to trade children for Bible studies. This is an example of attacking one's own face (Rogan and Hammer 1994), and we have to wonder what Koresh was getting out of this arrangement that made it worth incurring such damage. Having said, "nothing . . . hurts me more than being called a cult leader" (Tape 9: 13), why would Koresh taint his identity in this manner simply to advance the instrumental objectives of the FBI? That he fully recognized the identity implications of offering this deal is evident in his stipulation that the child (a moral adult) wanted to leave Mount Carmel anyway. I suggest this conversation can be understood if we start with the assumption that Koresh would endanger his identity in this bargaining exchange only if it would allow him to achieve a goal of his own choosing. That goal appears to have been to engage the FBI in a process of negotiating reality.

From this perspective, what were the costs and benefits of this exchange for each party? The cost to the FBI for getting more children out of Mount Carmel was participating in a Bible study with Koresh. The benefit to Koresh was forcing the FBI to participate in a dialogue they were scrupulously trying to avoid. In the long run, however, the cost to the community may have been very great indeed. Every time Koresh adopted the language of the FBI negotiators, he reinforced their preexisting assumption that he was a charismatic cult leader in full control of everyone in the community. The stronger their conviction that Koresh was in full control of his followers, the more they pressured him to cut a deal to end the standoff immediately.

By using the FBI's own language subversively, Koresh created an image that led the negotiators to pronounce him a con man. Having so labeled Koresh, the FBI negotiators turned their energies toward publicly exposing his "true nature" in order to persuade his followers to abandon him. Thus, the bargaining process gradually gave way to a strategy of persuasion and debate. Through direct persuasion, the negotiators attempted to convince the residents of Mount Carmel to "abandon their leader." They also tried to influence the community dynamics at Mount Carmel by urging other individuals to wrest control from Koresh.

7

"We Don't Want Anything from Your Country"

Negotiation as Diplomacy

ON MARCH 2, the Branch Davidians were supposed to exit Mount Carmel and surrender to authorities. This did not happen because David Koresh claimed he had received a message from God telling him to wait. On March 5, he surprised the FBI negotiators with the following pronouncement.

> DAVID: You see Mt. Carmel center here? You see our humble domain? . . . *Let's respect this 78 acres, 77 acres, let's respect this in this nation as Europe respects [the] Vatican, okay? . . . You came on property that is disclaimed from the United States of America* in the respect that when that United States of America who says In God We Trust steps over the boundary lines of justice and truth and it acts upon its people [with] tyranny and oppression. (Tape 57: 30–31, emphasis added)

Mount Carmel as the equivalent of the Vatican? Private property within the United States that has been "disclaimed" from the legitimate political authority? Was Koresh crazy? Was this statement a reflection of his idiosyncratic delusion? Or was it part of a coherent worldmaking narrative shared by the Mount Carmel community?[1]

The earliest indication of this attitude is recorded in the first three 911

---

1. I have been asked whether the Militia and Patriot movement members, for whom Waco has become a rallying cry, were aware of the Branch Davidians' separatist claims *during the standoff.* I do not know the answer to that question, which is an interesting one and worth further research. Some Militia groups certainly tried to rally to the Davidian cause during the standoff.

tapes. Because he was monitoring 911 calls, Lt. Lynch's immediate response to Wayne Martin's call on February 28 was to send ambulances to Mount Carmel (911.1: 3). Once Martin and Lynch initiated conversations about resolving the crisis at Mount Carmel, Lynch mentioned in a regularly repeated litany of concern the problem of getting medical assistance for the injured Branch Davidians (911.1: 8, 11, 16, 19, 20 ff.). He identified an end to the active firing of weapons and assistance for the injured as problems to be negotiated in sequence. Martin, however, was adamant that the issue of aid for the injured would not be addressed until the ATF withdrew from Mount Carmel property.

> LYNCH: Okay, okay, we'll, we're gonna resolve this issue one at a time, first of all, we, we, the firing has ceased, that's what we wanted, now we, you've got casualties, we need to start thinkin' about those casualties, let's make one step at a time . . .
> WAYNE: The next step is they start backing off. (911.1: 29)

Lynch may have forgotten that he and Martin had reconceptualized a cease-fire to include the withdrawal of the ATF from Mount Carmel (see chapter 5), but Martin had not.

After much discussion, Lynch persuaded Martin to get a head count of the wounded and an assessment of their injuries. However, Lynch was stymied in his efforts to provide aid for the wounded Branch Davidians when the Mount Carmel residents countered his efforts at instrumental problem solving with a starkly symbolic claim.

> LYNCH: OK. Wayne. Let's, here's, here's one way to look at it. OK. The most serious of your wounded, let's address them first, and figure out how many people it's gonna take to move them to safety. OK?
> WAYNE: Lynch?
> LYNCH: Yes sir.
> WAYNE: Here's the message . . .

Their activities caused some concern among the FBI commanders, who worried about related security issues.

LYNCH: I'm here. Go ahead. Give me your count.

WAYNE: We don't want anything from *your* country. (911.3: 29, emphasis added)

"We don't want anything from your country." The "we" and the careful framing of this statement as a message argue against the assumption that Martin was acting on the basis of some private delusion. Furthermore, Martin took pains to explain that the message came from those who would be most directly harmed if the Branch Davidians acted on their belief that Mount Carmel was separate from the United States.

WAYNE: That's what our wounded are telling us. They don't want your help. (911.3: 30)

"We don't want anything from your country." In one calmly delivered sentence, the Branch Davidians articulated an ontological claim and announced their separatist identity. Ontological commitments, though rarely stated this openly, are linked to a narrative logic that constrains and directs the actions of those who hold them.[2] Consequently, the Branch Davidians never did agree to send their wounded out for treatment. Their refusal to cooperate in this matter was a foreshadowing of worldviewing impasses that would plague the Waco negotiations for the next fifty-one days.

In 1996, the FBI confronted the Freemen in Montana, who claimed their property was a sovereign territory with laws and courts independent of the federal legal system. In 1997, the Texas Rangers (with FBI assistance and advice) dealt with members of the Republic of Texas who declared a house in west Texas their embassy. As an embassy, the house was pronounced sovereign territory. Dealing with groups who "disclaim" their property from the United States

2. Every culture lumps and splits the world and tells stories based on the categories so created. Formal logic as defined and used in European culture is not universal, but narrative reasoning is a universal human activity. The stories told by a community constrain and direct the practical actions of its members. When I say "ontological commitments are linked to a logic," I am referring to this type of narrative logic.

of America is an increasingly common experience for federal law enforcement negotiators. In 1993, however, the Branch Davidians did not fit any recognized pattern of barricaded subjects, so FBI negotiators in Waco had no script for dealing with a barricaded separatist group motivated by unconventional religious and political beliefs, nor did they have the conceptual or analytical tools that would enable them to make sense quickly of the separatist claims put forth by the Mount Carmel residents. Consequently, the negotiators classified the Branch Davidians' separatist proclamations as irrelevant to the negotiation process. In this approach, they were mistaken. Whether or not the negotiators acknowledged the Branch Davidians' separatist worldmaking narrative, that story about the world had implications for framing an effective negotiation process in Waco.

Categorization, Framing, and the Branch Davidians'
Separatist Identity

"There is nothing more basic than categorization to our thought, perception, actions, and speech" (Lakoff 1987, 5). Through the lumping and splitting processes of categorization, people distinguish themselves from their surroundings and differentiate those parts of their environment that are benign from those that threaten their well-being. "Any time we either produce or understand any utterance of any reasonable length, we are employing dozens if not hundreds of categories" (Lakoff 1987, 6). In Waco in 1993, the Branch Davidians were not alone in categorizing the world. The FBI negotiators, too, were using *unmarked* categories that had become invisible through long use and widespread acceptance, whereas the Branch Davidians were using categories that were *marked* because they were unusual within mainstream culture. Few citizens would embrace the notion that a religious community within the United States has the right to declare itself an independent political entity. It is important to remember, however, that the Branch Davidians' categories stood out because they deviated from the norm in terms of content, not because the Branch Davidians were engaged in some unique, defective, or deviant cognitive process.

Identity formation involves the complex manipulation of numerous conceptual categories, including but not limited to age, gender, race, ethnicity, and religious affiliation. Group or social identities are formed through processes of self-categorization (Hogg and McGarty 1990) that involve both lumping and splitting. "In order for any group to be perceived as a separate entity, it must have some nonmembers who are excluded from it" (Zerubavel 1991, 41). Conceptually, the Mount Carmel residents lumped themselves together into one meaningful category and split themselves off from their surrounding environment. There is nothing unusual about that process. All groups distinguish members from nonmembers; identity groups create deeply held personal identities for their members by distinguishing members from the surrounding culture.

Having separated themselves conceptually, identity groups also mark their boundaries by processes that include developing or maintaining a separate language, distinctive clothing, unique cultural practices, strict requirements for membership, or a strong sense of a group mission that sets group members apart from nonmembers (Cohen 1985). The Mount Carmel residents did all of these things. They spoke a language of biblical prophecy and revelation that was foreign to the FBI negotiators. They adhered to strict dietary practices and observed a rigid calendar of religious holidays. The daily lives of the Mount Carmel residents revolved around religious worship, teaching, and prayer. Their gender relations and child-rearing practices also set them apart from the surrounding society. The Branch Davidians saw themselves as carrying out a divinely inspired mission, and, more important for the purposes of this study, they laid claim to an identity that disrupted the established framework of barricade negotiation processes. This difference became apparent when they offered their own framing of the negotiation process.

If people categorize in order to sort and name the entities that occupy their world, they *frame* the world in order to explain or give meaning to the relationships that exist among the objects and persons whose existence they recognize through their categorical beliefs. Two monkeys wrestle, chase, and slap at one another. Are they playing, or are they fighting? Bateson (1972) observed that the same actions take on different meaning depending on whether they are framed as playing or fighting. The monkeys send clues or signals at a metacommunicative level that say "this is playing" or "we are fighting." People engage in similar framing processes by means of which they surround "situations, acts, or objects with mental brackets that basically transform their meaning by defining them as [for example] a game, a joke, a symbol, or a fantasy" (Zerubavel 1991, 11).

It is possible for people to agree on the contents of a situation but to disagree on the meaning of those contents because "a frame is characterized not by its contents but rather by the distinctive way in which it transforms the contents' meaning" (Zerubavel 1991, 11). The same smart remark that is a joke when shared among friends becomes an insult when made by an outsider. Thus, framing and naming are integrally related activities. Alternate framings of an interaction (playful banter with one's in-group or an unpleasant encounter with a member of an out-group) result in divergent characterizations of the same statement (joke or insult). In Waco, the Branch Davidians and FBI negotiators agreed that they were negotiating. They named their interactions using the same term. However, each group had different ideas about what counted as real negotiation; they framed the negotiation process in divergent ways.

Framing plays an important role in both conflict and efforts to resolve conflict, including negotiation. Certainly, if we take worldviewing seriously, it is logical to conclude, "mismatches in framing are sources of conflict" (Putnam and Holmer 1992, 136). We might even identify frame mismatches as one indicator of a worldview conflict. There is some hope among conflict resolution practitioners, however, that *reframing the problem* can be used to help resolve or transform conflicts. New framing of a problem may open up possibilities for action that the parties have not previously considered (Drake and Donohue 1996; Putnam and Holmer 1992; Schön and Rein 1994; Spector 1995; Stein 1989, 267). The difficult part of dealing with frames is trying to see them, especially our own frames. It is important to remember that conflict resolution practitioners also engage in framing when they design their intervention processes. Practice frames may actually complicate a conflict if they are not carefully chosen and applied. According to Schön (1983), studying the ways in which practitioners frame problems and roles can increase their critical awareness of the tacit frames that influence their actions. When analyzing the assumptions behind the FBI negotiators' practice, I have been doing this type of frame analysis.

How Does Worldviewing Impact Framing?

Susan Hunter writes, "Each of us, I contend, has a structure of existence within which we live, function, and perceive the world. The types of entities that exist for us and the relationships among these entities constitute this structure and serve to constrain our values, goals, and actions. *The structure provides the frame for our interactions with other actors and for the strategies we develop for dealing with problems*" (1989, 26, emphasis added). The nested model of framing during conflicts in figure 11 incorporates worldviews or worldmaking narratives as the largest frame (the ultimate metaframe) in anyone's world. In conflicts where the parties largely share worldviews or worldmaking narratives, their *symbolic frames* recede into the background.

Most negotiation research presumes the parties operate within the same symbolic frame. In routine confrontations or disputes, this assumption is not unwarranted. The parties usually do share a metaframe and are therefore able to focus their attention on "*substantive frames* [that] define what the conflict is about" (Putnam and Holmer 1992, 135, emphasis added). In many situations, the parties share substantive as well as symbolic frames. Management negotiators and union representatives usually begin with a shared definition of their dispute or conflict as well as with coordinated worldmaking narratives. Likewise, a customer negotiating to purchase an automobile and the salesperson share a coherent definition of their problem or dispute.

When symbolic frames and substantive frames are well coordinated or shared, the parties are free to focus on clarifying their "*aspiration frames* [that] express the disputants' underlying interests and needs" (Putnam and Holmer 1992, 135, emphasis added). When conflict resolution practitioners advise people to "focus on interests, not positions" (Fisher and Ury 1981, 41) or to clarify "interests, values, and needs" (Burton 1996, 58), they are directing attention to the parties' aspiration frames. As long as the parties experience no disruptive frame conflicts at the substantive or symbolic levels, this advice is good.

Each party also selects a *process frame* for managing their shared conflict. Although a process frame may include anything from avoidance to nuclear war, conflict resolution scholars and practitioners are most interested in the framing of nonviolent processes for managing, resolving, or transforming the conflict at hand. Negotiation is one such process. If the parties agree to adopt negotiation as their process frame, each party enters the encounter with preexisting "expectations about how the negotiation will or should proceed" (Putnam and Holmer 1992, 135). Thus, they may agree that negotiation is the way to deal

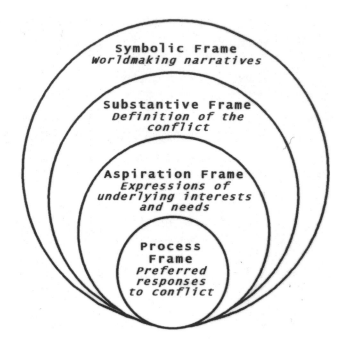

11. Types of frames the parties bring to a conflict.

with their conflict, but still disagree about how to enact the negotiation process.

Within the process frame of negotiation, we can discern *enactive frames* that the parties use to guide their interactions and decision making (fig. 12.). Enactive frames include, but are probably not limited to the following:

1. *Interaction frames* express the parties' expectations regarding the type of negotiation script that will be used in their encounter and the forms of interaction that are permissible. Examples of negotiation scripts include state-to-state diplomatic negotiations, hostage negotiations, or labor negotiations. Examples of the forms of permissible interaction include debating, bargaining, problem solving, threatening, and promising.

2. *Justice or fairness frames* reflect the parties' understanding of process justice or what constitutes a fair and equitable negotiation encounter.

3. *Issue-refinement frames* shape the parties' assumptions about which issues

may be legitimately introduced into the negotiation process and which issues are irrelevant or out of bounds.

4. *Characterization frames* are one party's "expectations and evaluations of the other disputants' behaviors, [status,] and attitudes" (Putnam and Holmer 1992, 135).

5. *Identity frames* are each party's presentation of its own character, status, behaviors, and attitudes.

6. *Language frames* delineate the language that will be used during the nego-tiations. In cross-cultural encounters, this delineation may involve making choices about whether the negotiators will speak French, Spanish, or English. It also includes assumptions about the type of language (instrumental, relational, identity, narrative, or symbolic) parties may legitimately use during negotiations.

7. *Loss-gain frames* "provide interpretations associated with the risk or ben-efits of various outcomes" (Putnam and Holmer 1992, 135).

8. *Outcome frames* "are the disputants' preferred positions or solutions" (Putnam and Holmer 1992, 135).

Parties involved in negotiation may experience mismatches in their enactive frames that disrupt or complicate even their best-intentioned efforts to negoti-ate in good faith. Differences in the parties' enactive frames may be based on prior experience. For example, unlike the FBI negotiators, the Branch Davidians had never been involved in a barricade situation and did not know the FBI ne-gotiators' script. Parties may also discover that their enactive-frame mismatches are manifestations of deep-rooted worldviewing (symbolic-frame) conflicts.

The Waco transcripts contain so many examples of frame conflicts at all levels (fig. 11) that it is difficult to select among them for analysis. However, two types of frame conflict stand out as particularly disruptive during the fifty-one-day standoff. First, symbolic-frame conflicts (worldviewing differences) disrupted the parties' efforts to create and enact a process frame for their nego-tiations. Second, when the FBI negotiators and the Branch Davidians did at-tempt to reconcile their process-frame conflicts by acknowledging the process frames each of them was offering, enactive-frame conflicts got in the way. The parties were particularly hampered by their inability to reconcile their respec-tive identity and characterization frames. These two problems explain many of the negotiation failures in Waco.

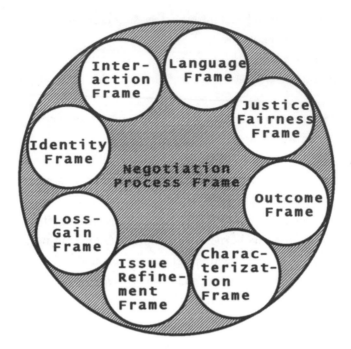

12. Enactive frames used during negotiation.

The Branch Davidians Seek a Process Frame in Waco

Negotiation "is a social process in which *collective* cognitive images are created and changed" (Morley, Webb, and Stephenson 1988, 120, emphasis added). The concept of a collective cognitive process is critically important because "frames are not free-floating but are grounded in institutions that sponsor them" (Schön and Rein 1994, 29). Very few barricaded subjects have an institutional grounding on which to advocate for a process frame other than that offered by the police. Consequently, isolated subjects almost always accept the police framing of the negotiation process as the only alternative to violent conflict. This relative disempowerment did not exist in Waco. The Mount Carmel community was an institutional entity with the capacity to articulate process frames and to present alternative collective cognitive images for consideration by the parties.

Institutions sponsor process frames when the members attempt to "find a *formula* linking what is happening now to what has happened in the past, and to what will happen in the future" (Morley, Webb, and Stephenson 1988, 120, emphasis in original). The search for a formula or script is first subject to an "intragroup bargaining process in which different people [within the group] try out different arguments, and sponsor different scripts" (Morley, Webb, and Stephenson 1988, 121). These scripts may then be tested with the other party. Although we lack adequate data to document thoroughly the intragroup negotiations among the Branch Davidians, their intergroup negotiations with the FBI shed some light on the scripts that were being tried out inside Mount Carmel.

Trying Out a Citizen-to-Government Process Frame

Although the state-to-state negotiation frame was the most dramatic process proposal offered by the Branch Davidians, it was not the only frame with which they experimented. The wounded Branch Davidians may have said "we don't want any help from your country," but Schneider, Martin, Koresh, and others also articulated moral claims based on their constitutionally guaranteed rights as *citizens* of the United States.

Although apparently contradictory, the citizen-to-government negotiation frame and the state-to-state negotiation frame both had the effect of leveling the negotiation table. Both process frames counteracted the tainted identity that normally attaches to barricaded subjects during a standoff with the police. By invoking the identity of citizens whose rights had been violated by an oppressive law enforcement organization, the Branch Davidians tried to overcome the negative identity that the police, the media, and the public normally impose on a barricaded subject. When this framing of the negotiation proved inadequate, the Branch Davidians further developed and refined the state-to-state process frame implicit in their earliest refusal to accept medical assistance from the police. The state-to-state negotiation frame allowed them to claim another untainted identity. As citizens of a different political jurisdiction, the Branch Davidians could argue that their rights under international law had been violated when the U.S. government sent armed "troops" onto the Mount Carmel property.

The citizen-to-government and state-to-state negotiation frames were also similar in that both overcame the disempowerment that normally accrues to barricaded subjects as "individuals negotiating on behalf of themselves with the representatives of commonweal constituencies" (Powell 1989, 21). In the state-to-state negotiation frame, the Mount Carmel community claimed a sovereign political status equal to that of the United States. When the Branch Davidians used the citizen-to-government negotiation frame, they were laying claim to membership in a group (citizens) that holds preeminent status in the U.S. legal tradition. The Branch Davidians were reminding the "representatives of the commonweal constituency" that the powers of the state are limited by the Constitution of the United States. Individual rights of citizens are sacrosanct, and the law enforcement agents in Waco would be held accountable for any breach of constitutional principles.

To justify the citizen-to-government negotiation frame, the Branch Davidians accused the ATF of wrongdoing on February 28. Furthermore, they argued it was not the first such violation of the Constitution. The Mount Carmel community may have led a separatist lifestyle, but they were deeply concerned about current events insofar as those events revealed God's plan for the end of history. Therefore, they looked very closely at news stories that might verify End Time prophecies by illustrating the evil actions of worldly governments. Early in the negotiations, Steve Schneider brought up the issue of Ruby Ridge and compared the Branch Davidians' situation to that of Randy Weaver.[3]

> MR. SCHNEIDER: Well, you know the truth is, you know . . . here's an Army tank over here now, armored carrier vehicle of some sort. . . . I mean, what is this going to be World War III or what? . . .
>
> PN02: Don't, don't misinterpret what that stuff means. The . . . way the federal government responds to these things—

3. In 1992, the HRT went to Idaho to "clean up" after a botched operation by the ATF and the U.S. Marshals Service (USMS). In an attempt to arrest Randy Weaver on weapons charges, the USMS engaged Weaver, his family, and a friend in a gun battle. One marshal and Weaver's teenage son were killed. During the ensuing siege, an HRT sniper shot and killed Weaver's wife. Among gun rights groups, Weaver has become a hero and symbolic victim of government agencies run amok.

MR. SCHNEIDER: Well, I do remember reading about that Weaver story and a number of other stories— . . . in the past and, you know, it definitely unsettles a person. (Tapes 4 and 5: 54)

The Branch Davidians' focus on the Weaver case was symptomatic of their suspicions about the federal government. There is clear evidence in the transcripts that Schneider, Koresh, and others at Mount Carmel had taken elements of various conspiracy theories, mixed them into a unique melange, and spiced it with their own brand of biblical prophecy. Among the Mount Carmel residents, Schneider was the most articulate when connecting the Branch Davidian beliefs to secular ideas.

On the Trilateral Commission,[4] Schneider said, "I've always wanted to see why there was a first World War, why a second World War. . . . Then I started hearing about a group called the Council on Foreign Relations, a group called the Trilateral Commission. . . . Carter being the first member, the first one to become President in '76, handpicked by Rockefeller in '73. Every cabinet member belonged to the Trilateral Commission. What on earth is this? What's happened to this country?" (Tape 40: 28–32)

About the federal government, Schneider claimed, "But your . . . agency and all those are part of that whole thing, taking away the freedoms of America . . . more legislation, more regulations, more laws, so that ultimately a person has no freedom. So taxed to death that you never have a choice with the hard earned money you make to choose to where it should be paid. . . . I've always considered myself to be a conservative, someone who is not into taxes, who's into the freedom of people so that they can express themselves" (Tape 40: 29–32).

On the risks associated with being a minority group, Schneider argued, "This country which was guaranteed by the people that came here and, and

4. The goal of the Trilateral Commission, started in 1972, was "to strengthen ties among the economic, political, and intellectual elites of the United States, Europe, and Japan" (Boyer 1992, 265). Jimmy Carter was recruited as a member and upon his election appointed a number of Trilateral Commission members to high offices in his administration. The Trilateral Commission has figured prominently in many popular books on the coming apocalypse (Boyer 1992, 265).

gained their freedoms, separated church and state . . . —in fact, this was originally called a republic, not a democracy. A republic guarantees the rights of mi-
norities. A democracy is where a majority rules" (Tape 52: 37–38).

About the repression of the free press, Schneider noted, "But you don't read
about [the Trilateral Commission] in the press. Is [the press] controlled, is the
question? Well, how come you don't get a broader view of things? . . . Who's
watching the watchdog?" (Tape 40:32).

On the ATF, the FBI, and the Constitution, various Mount Carmel residents had strong views. Schneider said, "I hate to see how this country of
America has digressed and your type of agencies are one of the biggest causes
for it. . . . [T]here is getting to be a Big Brother" (Tape 40: 27). He also questioned the constitutional basis for federal law enforcement agencies. "You . . .
don't have to tell me but I mean what do you think after your years of being
raised and living in America with this great Constitution to have such an
agency [the ATF] that originally wasn't even incorporated into the Constitution come—I mean normally isn't it a sheriff or something that brings a warrant
if there's something wrong? . . . I mean not, not like 80 or 130, you know, assault weapons with flak jackets on" (Tape 52: 34–35). Koresh indicated that the
Mount Carmel community was aware of an anti-ATF video when he said,
"there's a . . . video out on you guys [ATF]. It's called 'Breaking the Law in the
Name of the Law' " (Tape 13: 16).[5]

The citizen-to-government frame for enacting the negotiations in Waco
coincides with the Branch Davidians' "medium-term" narrative of interdependence (fig. 9 in chapter 5). In this story, the Branch Davidians offered a substantive frame that defined the conflict as a confrontation between a
community of citizens who are endowed with constitutionally protected rights
and government agents who may have overstepped their constitutionally limited authority. The Branch Davidians were primarily interested in obtaining

5. Koresh was referring to a video put out by the Gun Owners of America titled *Breaking the
Law in the Name of the Law: The BATF Story*. We know there was a copy of this video at Mount
Carmel because it was explicitly mentioned in the ATF affidavit, which has led to accusations
among members of the Patriot movement that the ATF targeted the Branch Davidians because of
their advocacy of gun ownership and their negative opinion of the ATF as much as for any actual
violations of gun laws.

guarantees that the ATF agents would be held accountable for their allegedly unconstitutional actions in the same way the Branch Davidians would be held accountable for their allegedly criminal actions.

It may be a peculiarly American phenomenon, but separatist identity groups in the United States frequently seek protection from government institutions even as they profoundly question the legitimacy of those institutions. They place tentative faith in the constitutional principles on which the government was founded even as they castigate current institutions for their corruption and abuse of power. The Branch Davidians' citizen-to-government negotiation frame followed this tradition.

The FBI Negotiators Attempt to Work with the
Citizen-to-Government Process Frame

The citizen-to-government process frame created discursive space for the FBI negotiators at least partially to coordinate their own worldmaking narratives with those of the Branch Davidians. The negotiators clearly stated that they shared the Branch Davidians' concerns about the Constitution. "We [the FBI] work within the framework of the Constitution. . . . [W]e protect the rights of those people that we deal with on . . . an everyday basis. . . . We don't take that responsibility lightly" (Tape 52: 39). Furthermore, the negotiators argued, this protection extended in every respect to the Branch Davidians. "I know this morning Steve . . . indicated to me . . . you know, once you folks leave what is going to happen? I said, one thing that we're going to tell you that's going to happen is that the Constitution is going to be strictly adhered to. . . . [N]o one is going to circumvent any of your constitutional rights, we will not allow that to happen" (Tape 53: 8–9).

On the basis of this apparent worldviewing agreement, the FBI attempted to convince the Branch Davidians that they could best satisfy their aspirations by surrendering to authorities and moving their dispute with the government into the courts and other public forums. The FBI negotiators assured the Branch Davidians that the ATF was no longer responsible for managing the current crisis.

PN03: . . . I want you to tell everybody that's in there, that their safety is guaranteed. . . . And whatever punishment is going to [happen] . . . it's not the

FBI or, or the ATF that's dishing out that punishment. I mean, everybody's going to go and stand trial. . . . Whoever is charged is going to . . . go through the judicial system. It doesn't mean that, that, that your safety, or anybody's safety is not guaranteed. Everybody's safety is guaranteed. (Tape 48: 22–23)

As part of the Department of Justice, the FBI would be conducting a full investigation. Ultimately, the Department of Justice attorneys would determine which Branch Davidians and which ATF agents should face criminal charges.

> PN04: . . . The FBI is doing an inquiry . . .
>
> KATHY [SCHROEDER]: An inquiry is not the same as a trial.
>
> PN04: But that's where it begins. . . .
>
> KATHY: But, yeah, but the same agency that's being investigated is the one doing the investigating.
>
> PN04: No, not so. The FBI was not involved in that shooting. We are doing an investigation. The Department of Justice is doing an investigation. The United States Congress is doing an investigation. Not the ATF. That's unacceptable. The ATF . . . will do their internal investigation, obviously, but that's not what's going to be the determining factor in what, in any kind of court action is taken. Not the ATF. It has nothing to do with them any longer. . . . I hope that everybody has that straight in their mind. (Tape 66: 18–20)

It is worth noting that the negotiators were often frustrated by the need to explain repeatedly the differences between the ATF, the FBI, and the Department of Justice. The negotiators would have done well to remember that parties in conflict often work with "an image [of] the enemy as a single unified entity, the members of which are all equally bent upon [one's] downfall, equally evil, and equally implacable in their pursuit of a set of unjust and immoral goals" (Mitchell 1981, 108). As a consequence of their separatist identity and apocalyptic expectations, the Branch Davidians did not hold a very multifaceted understanding of different law enforcement agencies. The FBI negotiators often failed to recognize that simply declaring themselves as separate from the ATF was not enough to make that distinction clear for many of the Branch Davidians.

In addition to clarifying the roles of various Department of Justice and law enforcement actors, the FBI negotiators also pointed to actors in other branches of the government who could be relied on to protect the Branch Davidians.

> PN04: [There will be a] congressional inquiry into the shooting. Obviously, there is absolutely no one in this country that wanted to see something like that happen. . . . And the congressional people are now making an inquiry into this thing. We're getting down to the nuts and bolts of these issues. . . . [T]he congressional inquiry is going to address just the same issues as you guys have mentioned to us. (Tape 51: 41–42)

These reassurances might have been more effective had they come directly from members of Congress, but the information that Congress was looking into the raid did elicit some positive responses from the Branch Davidians. Shortly after the statement quoted above, Schneider asked, "What would be the process and procedure of such a thing? We come walking out, what happens? Are we all taken [into custody]?" (Tape 52: 17).

The negotiators also attempted to convince the residents of Mount Carmel that the legal system was fair and just. They spent hours talking with Koresh and others about the Mount Carmel community's prior experience with the courts in 1988.[6] In an effort to overcome the Branch Davidians' skepticism about the legal system, the negotiators contrasted the federal courts favorably with local courts.

> PN05: . . . the federal judicial system it's not like a state judicial system, believe me. . . . The court meaning the judges—are certainly not the same. . . . Federal judicial system is much more thorough and I think people's rights are explained much more clearly to them and I think it's like night and day. (Tape 61: 16)

6. In 1988, local police arrested Koresh and other Branch Davidians after a violent confrontation with George Roden, who resented Koresh's selection as leader of the community. In the ensuing trial, everyone was acquitted except Koresh. The jurors were split over Koresh's guilt, and the judge declared a mistrial.

When the Branch Davidians complained about how much it had cost them to prove their innocence in 1988, the negotiators stressed that this case would be different because so many people were interested in it.

> STEVE: You know how much it cost these guys, though . . . to get justice?
>
> PN04: Well, listen, it isn't going to cost you a nickel. . . . I'm telling you, people are standing in line to get, to get to you. I mean people want to hear what happened here. (Tape 52: 29–30)

The negotiators were not authorized to discuss any reduction in charges against the Branch Davidians. However, the negotiators encouraged the Mount Carmel residents to believe they had a strong case regarding their actions on February 28. They even reminded the Branch Davidians of available material evidence that could be used to their advantage.

> DAVID: . . . the film coverage in regards to actually who shot first and— . . . And you all did fire first and everything.
>
> PN01: There's some film of that, and, and that'll get out in the court . . .
>
> DAVID: But actually there's the agents who . . . admitted to it, that's the real important thing.
>
> PN01: Well, that's . . . good for your side. And the truth needs to come out, I think, don't you? (Tape 41: 49–50)

The negotiators also encouraged the Branch Davidians to consider procedural options that might help their court case.

> PN01: So, just remember that. You know when this thing goes to court, okay, I've seen a lot of cases where judges even throw them out before they go to a jury. I've had that happen. Do you understand? . . .
>
> RACHEL [Koresh's wife]: You said something about they sometimes throw it out, excuse me, it doesn't make it to court.
>
> PN01: Well, the judge throws it out. . . . And, and also you got to remember that . . . You know a jury has to be made up of peers. . . . So, you know, in your case the people of Waco and the ranchers . . . That's who's the judge in there. . . . that's who decides what happened. And the judge would be bound by their

decision. It's not his decision. He could throw it out if he wants, you know, or parts of it. There's a whole lot of things that could happen. I just want you to keep that in mind. (Tape 39: 43–45)

The FBI negotiators actually tried to use the Weaver case as a positive example of someone in a similar situation using the legal system to make his point.

> PN04: Weaver left, okay. Weaver walked out on his own and decided let's take this to court. We'll get this resolved. And this—and there are still many of these issues are pending there. He's going to get his day in court, has already had his day in court and will continue to get that. . . . [H]e's filing a motion, somebody else has filed a motion but it will be done. It has to be. There's just absolutely no way it will not be done. (Tape 52: 23–24)

Ironically, the trial of Randy Weaver coincided with the Waco standoff. Steve Schneider, among others at Mount Carmel, did not have much faith that justice would be done in that case. At one point, he asked, "What about Weaver? What's happening with the Weaver trial? Let me see how you guys do and what kind of freedom and access he has to defend himself of that case" (Tape 40: 37). We now know that the Mount Carmel residents were receiving radio transmissions from KGBS during the entire siege, so they were able to follow the Ruby Ridge trial news. However, KGBS was not providing a mainstream slant on the Ruby Ridge trial or on the Branch Davidians' own situation. According to Thibodeau and Whiteson, KGBS announcer Ron Engelman, a spokesman for the Patriot movement, was "speaking out on our behalf when most of the media were swallowing the official version of events or pursuing their own warped agendas" (1999, 230). Engelman's incoming broadcasts, tinged as they were with "his own agenda" as a "believer in a radical interpretation of the U.S. Constitution as a bulwark against government abuse" (Thibodeau and Whiteson 1999, 230), were thus influencing the Branch Davidian interpretation of their current predicament. Although the Branch Davidians' awareness of political resistance to federal authority predated the February 28 raid, their attitude was no doubt reinforced by their experience during the standoff and by Engelman's broadcasts and efforts on their behalf.

The FBI Could Not Fully Embrace the
Citizen-to-Government Frame

Acknowledging all of these efforts to coordinate the FBI negotiators' process frame with the Branch Davidians' raises the big question: What went wrong? Why were the parties unable to craft an agreement that enabled the Branch Davidians to move their issues and concerns into the courts? From their own perspective, the FBI negotiators were bending over backwards to accommodate and address the interests and needs of the Branch Davidians. Why, then, did their efforts fail to elicit the desired response (surrender) from the Mount Carmel residents?

Process Frames Incorporate Symbolic Frames

The FBI negotiators considered the Branch Davidians' "Bible babble" irrelevant to the negotiations. They unilaterally imposed their own *language frame* on the negotiation encounter. Consequently, they did not recognize the depth of the Branch Davidians' conviction that the United States, although "blessed by God . . . above any nation" (Tape 59: 51), lacked ultimate legitimacy. As Koresh said, "this is a great nation, but . . . it's not bigger than my God" (Tape 8: 33). When the Mount Carmel residents incorporated references to the Constitution into their negotiation frame, the FBI negotiators simply presumed that both parties in Waco shared similar worldmaking narratives about the past, present, and future of the legal and political system in the United States. With the Branch Davidians, however, a belief in constitutional principles was mixed with political skepticism, and their political skepticism was a reflection of their apocalyptic religious beliefs.

The Branch Davidians and FBI negotiators may have articulated common concerns about enforcing constitutional guarantees of freedom, but they held very different ideas about the history and future of the world. The FBI negotiators worked within a *progressive view of history,* whereas the Branch Davidians adopted a *degenerative view of history.* A progressive view of history sees the future as getting better and better as a consequence of human creativity and ingenuity. A degenerative view of history, common to many apocalyptic sects, rests on the claim that the nations of the world are becoming more and more evil even as they achieve unprecedented material well-being. For the Mount Carmel community, every life experience was integrally connected to God's preordained plan for the end of human history and to the establishment of God's earthly kingdom, and, for them, that plan was coming to fruition, now! Thus, the Branch Davidians' believed their encounter with the ATF and their negotiations with the FBI could be truly understood only in relation to God's plan for the world.

> STEVE: . . . After 6,000 years of human history, we should all be able to come to the place and say, it doesn't work down here. No matter what we do and how we try to bring peace about on the earth, it just can't happen. There's just so many—
>
> PN04: But we can improve it. Can't we improve it?
>
> STEVE: Well, if anything, it's not improving. It's going downhill. If you read the prophecies—
>
> PN04: Well, let's restrict ourselves to this event, okay, to this, to this incident here. . . . Can we not improve it? And that's what I'm here to— . . . do with you.
>
> STEVE: I would sure like to. (Tape 51: 40)

This philosophical difference is important because each party's story about human history placed the U.S. Constitution in a different position. For the FBI negotiators, the Constitution represented the culmination of a progressive history in which protections for individual liberty were finally codified into a "sacred" text. For the Branch Davidians, the Constitution was a good document and useful for protecting oneself under some circumstances, but by no means the culmination of history. Indeed, the Constitution, like all man-made documents, was flawed and bound to "pass away" at the end of time.

The FBI negotiators said they understood that the concerns of the Mount Carmel residents were "both a logical issue and a spiritual, factual issue" (Tape 59: 15). However, they incorrectly assumed the philosophical differences between the parties were irrelevant to the practical problem of ending the standoff.

Process Frames Include Implicit, Contestable Enactive Frames

The divergent process frames promoted by the Branch Davidians (citizen-to-government or state-to-state) and by the FBI (hostage barricade) implicitly promoted competing enactive frames. The *identity frames* and *characterization frames* implicit in each process frame created the greatest difficulties for the parties.

In presenting the citizen-to-government process frame, the Branch David-ians were proposing an identity frame that undercut the FBI negotiators' usual assumptions about the criminal or disturbed nature of the barricaded subject. Rather than as an encounter between criminals and the police, the Branch Da-vidians cast the negotiations as an encounter between citizens and representa-tives of the government, some of whom may have acted illegally. To accept the Branch Davidians' identity frame, the FBI negotiators would have been forced to revise their preferred characterization frame by altering their assumptions about the behavior, attitudes, and disposition of the Branch Davidians. They would also have been compelled to change their own identity frame by letting go of their morally righteous self-image as blameless enforcers of the law. Logi-cally speaking, the FBI negotiators could have separated themselves from this tainting of the law enforcement identity by blaming the ATF for acting inap-propriately on February 28. However, four federal agents were killed during the initial raid, and the rhetorical process of valorizing fallen comrades had already begun. This valorization, along with a desire not to say anything negative about the ATF that might later be used in a trial setting, made it almost impossible for the FBI agents to speak ill of the ATF.

Also implicit in the Branch Davidians' descriptions of the parties were ex-pectations about an *interaction frame* and beliefs about *process justice* that ruled out some of the tactics normally used in barricade negotiations. The Branch Da-vidians considered threats, coercion, manipulative tactics, and the restriction of their opportunities to communicate with the public to be inappropriate activ-ities during negotiations between citizens and government representatives.

Tragically, even if the FBI negotiators had fully grasped the citizen-to-government process frame and all of its implied enactive frames, they might still have been baffled by some of the Branch Davidians' actions. The Branch Davidians may have claimed secular citizenship as a basis for fair treatment from federal agents, but they also saw themselves as citizens of a much different realm. From Koresh on down to the newest member of the community, they ex-perienced themselves as living under God's command. This identification is very much in keeping with Weber's observation that "when action is oriented to absolute values, it always involves 'commands' or 'demands' to the fulfillment of which the actor feels obligated" (1964, 116). Remember that value-rational actors may *see* a full range of options for action, but their own choices are constrained by the need to select behaviors that are morally coherent with their absolute value. Thus, the Branch Davidians were able to tell the FBI negotiators they understood all of the available options even though they *could not* take those actions that would have ended the standoff immediately, which frustrated the negotiators because they were working with a characterization frame that treated the Branch Davidians as if they were in full control of their own lives. In so doing, the negotiators indicated a profound disrespect for—or at least a deep misunderstanding of—the power of radical religious beliefs.

As a consequence of the mismatches in their respective identity and characterization frames, the FBI kept demanding actions from the Branch Davidians that they could not take without altering their sense of identity. The Branch Davidians were actors whose identity frames created a sense that they were controlled by the scene in which they were located (Burke 1969a, 3–20). Whatever they did was in response to their reading of a scene (the End Time) that they considered impervious to human activities. The FBI negotiators, however, insisted on using a characterization frame that treated the Mount Carmel residents as if they were capable of reshaping the scene through their freely chosen activities. As a result, the negotiators kept demanding that Koresh or someone else at Mount Carmel take control.

> PN04: Will you do me a personal favor and send out a couple more of the kids?
> DAVID: No. Not yet.
> PN04: Well, why will you not, Dave?
> DAVID: Because like I said I have a boss over me.
> PN04: Okay. And so do I. And I've made—
> DAVID: Well, my boss is—I'm going to follow my boss—
> PN04: You've—I know. You've got the big boss.
> DAVID: —as you have to follow your boss.
> PN04: Okay. But listen, I have done a number of things for you folks out there.
> DAVID: And we've done for you.

PN04: . . . As, you know, a personal consideration for me, I'd like you to send out a couple of the kids. And I'm asking you to do this for me. . . . Because David, you're the one that runs that operation there. These folks—if you tell them to leave and, and I wish you would do that for me. . . .

DAVID: I can't do that, because that's not what I received . . . from my headquarters.

PN04: You can send a child out then.

DAVID: See you don't seem to understand. You think I'm . . .

PN04: I do understand. David, I'm not—

DAVID: No. *Your statements very clearly show you think I'm here calling my own shots.*

PN04: No, *I don't think . . . that at all.* I, I couldn't listen to you for all these minutes and [not] understand a little of something about what you have told me. *But please meet me halfway . . .*

DAVID: I've been doing so. Everything that I, everything that I've been *allowed* to do, I have done everything in my power for your benefit, for the benefit of this nation. . . . For this country, to be able to comply in every detail possible that I'm *permitted* to. . . . *But there is a limit of which I'm able to operate.* (Tape 57: 2–3, emphasis added)

Even when the negotiators tried to speak in the Branch Davidians' language, they reframed the Branch Davidian concepts to fit a goal-rational action orientation, and, as a result, the negotiators ended up sounding ignorant, manipulative, or disrespectful.

PN03: Can I ask you to go beyond and stretch as far as you can stretch and please ask for Divine intervention with as much concentration, sincerity as you can. . . . *Can you please stretch and see if you can get your message now so that we can get everybody out of there now,* before people—these young people reach the limit to their patience? Please.

DAVID: Well . . . that's what I've been doing every day and every night.

PN03: David, please.

DAVID: I am. *I really, really am. And then my god says wait. See you don't know about these gods.* (Tape 49: 13–14, emphasis added)

In short, the negotiators kept trying to impose on the Branch Davidians, particularly on Koresh, a characterization frame that deeply offended the Mount Carmel community members' own sense of identity. By March 5, the conversation had degenerated to the following.

PN05: *Yeah, but the bottom line is who is it up to?* Who is going to have to make the decision?

MR. KORESH: Well, *God is.*

PN05: *You are.*

MR. KORESH: *God is—*

PN05: *No, you are.*

MR. KORESH: *—and you are.* No, *God is.*

PN05: Is that so? . . . The bottom line is you're the one that's going to hear God, right?

MR. KORESH: Yes, I'm the one listening to God and you're the one listening to the law, your system.

PN05: And I'm listening to you.

MR. KORESH: That's not true. You're listening *at* me and I'm listening *at* you. (Tape 61: 21, emphasis added)

Why did the negotiators persist in ignoring the Branch Davidians' explanations for their own actions? Why did they listen *at* rather than *to* the Branch Davidians? Because they assumed the residents of Mount Carmel were incapable of acting in their own best interests. Law enforcement agents felt they needed to protect the Branch Davidians from their own poor judgment and from Koresh's manipulation. Even Koresh needed to be protected from himself.[7]

PN05: I'm trying to do what I think is in your best interest, in the best interest of the people in there and in the best interest of the people out here to peacefully, successfully bring this to a resolution. And, and that's where the

---

7. Many critics have focused on the hostility that law enforcement agents showed to the Branch Davidians. However, the drive to protect people from themselves also contributed to the outcome in Waco. A paternalistic approach to dealing with unconventional religious and political groups may be as deadly as a hostile approach.

conflict lies, doesn't it? You know, because *you have to make up your mind when you're ready to come out of there.*

MR. KORESH: I'm ready right now. . . . I, I was ready yesterday. I was ready the past few days.

PN05: —there's, there's no question—See, there's no question in my mind that you're coming out of there and you're going to lead your flock out of there. . . . The only question is when. . . . Isn't that the bottom line?

MR. KORESH: Yeah, the bottom line is that you're denying and being— Okay, look, Psalm 75 [followed by a Bible study] . . .

PN05: You know, basically, when, when I said that, you know, you're the person that's going to make the decision, and, and there's no question in my mind that you're coming out of there. . . . It's, it's that I believe you are coming out and you are going to lead your flock out there. . . . I know it's going to happen. *But when, when I ask you to be responsible and to lead these people, you just keep passing the buck back to me and start preaching to me.* (Tape 61: 21–25, emphasis added)

The negotiators were extremely frustrated because Koresh kept trying to convert them (Justice 17, 49). Unfortunately, the negotiators never recognized that they were just as guilty of trying to convert the Branch Davidians. Conversion is not a strictly religious phenomenon. A person may be converted "from and to new religious groups, ways of life, systems of belief, and modes of relating to a deity or the nature of reality" (Rambo 1993, 3). By demanding that they "take control" of the situation and make "rational" decisions, the FBI negotiators were insisting that the Branch Davidians adopt a goal-rational action orientation—that is to say, adopt a new identity frame. The negotiators thought they were just trying to get the Branch Davidians to negotiate rationally, but they were demanding much more of the Branch Davidians. They wanted the Branch Davidians to become mainstream Christians rather than apocalyptic believers. They wanted to convert the residents of Mount Carmel by forcing them to assume a goal-rational identity frame, at least for the duration of the standoff. After that, the Branch Davidians were free to preach and believe whatever they wanted as guaranteed by the Constitution.

To be evenhanded, the disconnection between characterization and identity frames cut both ways in Waco. The Branch Davidians were also listening *at* the FBI and imposing a characterization frame on the FBI negotiators that was out of synch with the negotiators' identity frame. Whereas the negotiators saw law enforcement officials as in control and capable of shaping the barricade situation and its outcome, the Branch Davidians considered all of the federal law enforcement agents as unwitting pawns in God's End Time drama. The Mount Carmel residents saw religion as profoundly political. The End Time prophecy predicts that a nation blessed above all others, professing to be a lamb but acting as a dragon, will attack God's chosen people. The Branch Davidians kept trying to explain to the negotiators that *the system* would inevitably attack Mount Carmel. However strenuously individual agents might work against this outcome, they really had no power to redirect the system within which they worked.

> PN04: . . . We're going, we're going to get this thing straightened out.
> STEVE: Well, it probably never will be but . . . you know, you and I—
> PN04: We'll work on it.
> STEVE: —will do the best we can.
> PN04: You're darned right we will. . . . That's what I'm doing for you. I am guaranteeing—I'm giving you my personal guarantee that your rights—
> STEVE: *Well, I know you mean well and that but, of course . . .*
> PN04: Well, it's more than I mean. It will happen.
> STEVE: *One would be very naïve . . . to believe that you would have any kind of power over the forces that be . . .*
> PN04: Well, I'm not naïve but, listen, listen . . . (Tape 52: 36–38, emphasis added)

Koresh, Schneider, and others kept trying to convince the negotiators that just as God used the Jews against Christ and the Roman Catholic Church against Martin Luther, so God was using the law enforcement agencies of the United States against the Mount Carmel community. On the other hand, each law enforcement agent had the freedom to choose good or evil, and the Branch Davidians were clearly concerned about the eternal fate of individual negotiators. The residents of Mount Carmel were convinced they would be saved by God no matter what the system did, as long as they remained "in the message" regardless of the hardships. They were, however, worried about the agents who would be caught up in the coming battle between God and the evil earthly powers. The Branch Davidians expended great amounts of energy bringing the word to individual agents. Consequently, "the FBI questioned whether its negotiations with Koresh could even be characterized as 'negotiations' at all, but rather as Koresh's attempt to convert the agents before it was too late and God destroyed them" (Justice 17).

In fact, the Branch Davidians' willingness to embrace individual law enforcement agents as "souls who might be taught God's plan for the world" may even have helped lay the groundwork for the February 28 raid. By all accounts, they welcomed the ATF undercover agents, particularly Robert Gonzalez (real name Robert Rodriguez), into their community, even though the undercover operation was poorly conducted and the Branch Davidians knew their new neighbors were government agents (Treasury; Thibodeau and Whiteson 1999, 143–46). The behavior of the Mount Carmel community can be understood only in relation to their conviction that all earthly powers were under judgment and would soon pass away to be replaced by God's kingdom. As believers, they were already obligated to live according to the laws of God's kingdom, which meant they dealt with individuals as individuals, not as representatives of the system that would inevitably attack them at some point. They tried many, many times to explain this perspective to the skeptical FBI negotiators.

PN05: How come prior to that time . . . you never sat down with Robert, said I know who you are . . .

DAVID KORESH: . . . See, I loved his soul, all right? I didn't want to scare him off. I wanted to show him—

PN05: No, but you could have . . . told him . . . you didn't appreciate what was going on, huh? If you, if you truly didn't . . . like what was going on.

DAVID KORESH: —we don't mind, we didn't mind what was going on. As a matter of fact, his cover gave me the best advantage to be able to teach these young men where I'm coming from. . . .

PN05: Do you think you were successful?

DAVID KORESH: Well, you have to ask Robert, don't you? . . . [B]ut the thing of it is, when Robert saw what he saw, he was convicted. He cannot deny Psalm 45. He cannot deny Psalms 1, Psalms 2, Psalms 3, Psalms 4. (Tape 60: 28–30)

Even in the midst of the standoff, Koresh and others at Mount Carmel wanted to speak with Robert Rodriguez. They said they were not angry with him; they simply wanted to finish their "spiritual business" with him. The FBI negotiators could not understand why the Branch Davidians thought they had some special relationship with Rodriguez that needed to be straightened out, and they absolutely refused to let anyone in the community speak with the ATF agent. Quite frankly, the negotiators did not believe the Branch Davidians could be anything other than furious with the ATF undercover agents, mainly because they and the Branch Davidians evaluated the pre-February 28 interactions between the residents of Mount Carmel and the undercover ATF agents according to different sets of expectations. The negotiators found the Branch Davidians impossibly naïve because the Davidians did not understand the rules of the game when it came to the work of undercover agents. The Branch Davidians found the negotiators impossibly naïve because the negotiators did not understand the rules of the game when it came to God's plan for the world.

> PN05: . . . Why didn't you have a confrontation [with Rodriguez] and say look, I just . . . don't appreciate you being here?
> STEVE: Well, . . .because here's a possible guy, here's a soul maybe, here's someone like myself—
> PN05: Yeah, but he wasn't there to have his soul saved, right?
> STEVE: Well, who knows, though? You never can tell.
> PN05: Wait a minute. I know. . . . I worked under cover years and years ago and I wasn't there to have somebody save my soul. I was there to either prove someone was violating the law or prove they weren't violating the law. . . . And that's the same reason Robert was there.
> STEVE: I realize that. See, just like the Centurion in the Book of Acts, came to do some arresting but walked away not doing that, but himself wanting to know . . . and have salvation . . .
> PN05: So his reason for being there had absolutely no religious connotation or, or overtones.
> STEVE: That is not what he said, though . . .
> PN05: We say a lot of things when we're working in an undercover capacity.
> STEVE: And we suspected that could be true. . . . But, still, we love people

so much, you give them the opportunity. . . . Even if it's one out of a million, even if it's that, whatever it might be, he's still a person that was made, created by an authority above himself and we loved the guy. I mean . . . we spent enough time with him where we really got to appreciate the man's character and personality. (Tape 60: 32 and Tape 61: 3)

For the Mount Carmel residents, the observation that the corrupt system of the world was attacking God's chosen people was a statement of historical, political fact. It was not an assessment of the character of individual negotiators or agents. The individuals could be perfectly "good" people—well intentioned, deeply concerned, and professional—but that did not mean they would not play a pivotal role in bringing about God's earthly kingdom by attacking his faithful followers. The negotiators, on the other hand, heard these statements as personal attacks on their character and on the integrity of the legal system. When Koresh said, *"an agency, either knowingly or unknowingly, is being utilized to possibly genocide a work or a people"* (Tape 59: 24, emphasis added), he did not mean the negotiator on the other end of the phone line was consciously engaged in an act of genocide. That, however, is what the negotiator heard. "You know, something that you brought up kind of struck a nerve with me and I hope you didn't really mean it seriously, and that's when you talk about the issue of genocide. And I think that's an awful strong word to come up. . . . Certainly, certainly genocide is a strong, strong word for you to throw out. And you know better than that" (Tape 59: 28). This type of miscommunication was a routine part of the negotiations in Waco. Each party experienced its identity frame as under attack by the other party's characterization frame.

Enactive Frames Are Acted Out, Not Just Spoken

Contradictory characterization and identity frames were expressed in actions as well as in words, and the actions combined with the words escalated the confrontation in Waco, particularly when it came to each party's efforts to "defend itself" from further violence by the other party.

Within the first few days of the confrontation, the tactical units placed APCs on the Mount Carmel property, violated the agreed upon perimeter, and destroyed cars and outbuildings belonging to the community. From the comfortable position of twenty-twenty hindsight, the FBI's response to what they perceived to be verbal threats by the Mount Carmel residents seems misguided and overaggressive. We must keep in mind that *at the time* the FBI agents felt they had every reason to fear the Branch Davidians. On February 28, the residents of Mount Carmel had demonstrated both their willingness and their ability to direct deadly gunfire at law enforcement personnel, so the FBI commanders were far less willing than normal to discount anything that sounded like a threat coming from the Davidians.

FBI caution was further heightened by outside information regarding the types of weapons that the Mount Carmel community possessed. According to the event log, within the first week of negotiations, the FBI received information from a variety of sources that the Mount Carmel community possessed: (1) "a 50 cal. sniper rifle" (Logs 12); (2) "nightscopes" (Logs 15); (3) "mercury switches and plastic explosives to be applied to door and windows, as well as ammunition and 2 night vision scopes" (Logs 32); (4) "M-16 rifles and L.A.W. rockets" (Logs, 68); (5) "2 .50 cal. Barrett weapons with 10 power scopes" (Logs 71); and (5) "mustard and chlorine gas cannisters" (Logs 73). Several sources had also told the FBI that the community had a sophisticated tunnel system four hundred to seven hundred yards long that extended past the road. "The tunnel could be used as a means of escape or could present a danger to agents on [the] perimeter with exits from the tunnel to the rear" (Logs 56). Although much of this information was not immediately verified and may have been incorrect, the tactical commanders were not taking chances.

To protect their agents, the FBI commanders decided to deploy APCs or Bradleys. It was left to the FBI negotiators to persuade the Branch Davidians that this move was reasonable, necessary, and in the best interests of all involved. The Branch Davidians suspected that the APCs would be used to mount another assault on their residence. The negotiators needed to counteract this fear while justifying the presence of the APCs, so they were put in the position of having to convince the Davidians that the law enforcement agents were afraid of the Mount Carmel residents. The only way to do that was to "attack the face" of the Davidians by implying they would assault the federal agents. In other words, the negotiators had to indicate that the Branch Davidians were not to be trusted.[8] At the same time, they also had to portray the Branch Davidians as trustworthy negotiating partners in order to sustain their own diplomatic efforts. The Davidians were caught in a similar double bind. To protect their own face and to sustain the negotiations, they had to deny all hostile intentions. Yet to keep the FBI from thinking they could easily assault the Mount Carmel residence, the Branch Davidians also had to respond to the tactical activities with pugnacious rhetoric. Both parties were sending mixed messages.

Mixed messages can occur in any negotiation process, but once again the symbolic-frame differences between the parties in Waco complicated the situation immensely. Because of their worldviewing differences, each party interpreted the other party's *warnings* as *threats*. Threats and warnings are similar in that both foretell negative consequences if the other party does not comply with one's demands. However, threats and warnings explain the source of the negative consequences quite differently. In a threat, the person making the demand and issuing the threat expresses his or her explicit determination to make sure the other person suffers negative consequences for noncompliance. In a warning, the person making the demand and issuing the warning points to environmental factors that will bring inevitable negative consequences for noncompliance (Iklé 1964). "If you touch that stove, I will spank you" is a threat. "If you touch that stove, you will get burned because it is hot" is a warning. Threats and warnings can be sorted out only in relation to a particular worldmaking narrative or symbolic frame.

The Branch Davidians equated the APCs with the "chariots of flaming torches that shall jostle in the streets and run like the lightnings and sound like the thunders" described by the biblical Nahum (Tape 57: 16). They also equated the forces arrayed against them with Goliath and reminded the FBI negotiators that Goliath was killed by a much smaller and weaker David who

---

8. The negotiators used the removal of the gun barrels from the APCs as symbolic evidence of their defensive purpose. They could not, however, avoid verbally attacking the Branch Davidians when trying to explain why the APCs were needed: "PN01: They've got these vehicles that'll protect their men. We made them take the gun barrels off them. There's no gun barrels on them, okay? . . . You know, they have a big gun on them. You guys have a lot of heavy weapons in there and some of the, you know, the troops want to be protected" (Tape 8: 27).

was God's chosen one. Furthermore, they *warned* the FBI negotiators that the Mount Carmel community had the biggest defender of all: God would not tolerate those who threatened His chosen community; He would act on behalf of the Branch Davidians with powers the FBI agents could not even imagine.

RACHEL: You're trying to keep you and the people out there off of us and *he's trying to keep God and his army off of you.* God is very powerful, you know, and when he gets angry . . . (Tape 21: 5, emphasis added)

DAVID: You see, it's just like you guys. There's tanks out here and everything. Well, you know, that, that could destroy your enemies, right? . . . But you're telling me, you're saying to me, you're saying, but, Dave, they're out there. That's a show of arms but they're not there to destroy you. . . . They're just there to, to kind of emphasize that I want you to come my way. . . . *But you don't realize that there is guns a billion times bigger than yours pointed at you. . . . You see. Bigger than you, bigger, and more accurate. And the thing of it is, you can't see them.* You've got guys out here trying to camouflage themselves, trying to hide, but you don't see the camouflage that's hurled all around you guys. You don't know what's fixing to happen to you. And for your lack of knowledge, you don't have that much fear of God. I realize that. But the thing of it is Psalm 45. That threat should scare you. (Tape 28: 9–10, emphasis added)

DAVID: Yeah. Well, let's think about God on the throne too now . . .
PN01: Okay, David, I will.
DAVID: I want you all in the, in your system and all the men of this nation who have ears to hear and eyes to see to have every opportunity . . . *before you end up standing in front of guns that you have no power against.* (Tape 42: 5, emphasis added)

DAVID: You are confronting a man, an individual, who's trying to be very sober and trying to tell you very clearly . . . very sincerely, that I'm trying in all my power to bear as long as I can under God's jurisdiction . . . to have you to allow me to show you what these seals contain.
PN04: I appreciate that.
DAVID: Okay, now *you need to learn what that means before you learn the hard way.*

PN04: Before I learn the hard way.

DAVID: *The real hard way.*

PN04: The real hard way. Well, I'm, I'm willing—

DAVID: *It's not a threat. It's a promise.* (Tape 56: 29, emphasis added)

Because the FBI did not believe that God could or would intervene directly into earthly events on behalf of the Branch Davidians, they heard these warnings as threats. The FBI assumed that Koresh was saying the Branch Davidians had heavy weapons and would use them. To complicate matters further, sometimes the Branch Davidians did threaten to harm the tactical troops on their property.

DAVID: Well, if you keep getting closer, we're going to retaliate. And then you're going to have to come in, and that's just the way it is, Jim. I'm sorry. . . . You're going to keep moving your erratic finger closer and closer to our rear ends, and then finally we're going to turn around and we're going to slug you. (Tape 8: 33)

DAVID: I'm the little guy, you're the big guy. . . . You know, the Goliath, I'm the David. Remember that. Remember, David took five smooth stones. And we're in the fifth seal now, okay? . . . And Goliath does get his head sunken in with a rock. Think about that. (Tape 8: 34)

Furthermore, Koresh and the negotiators both had to contend with potential hot heads in their respective organizations. Koresh did not always know whether he could keep the younger members of the Mount Carmel community from doing something foolish, and the negotiators had to apologize repeatedly for the actions of tactical agents. Thus, the cycle of fear based on misunderstandings, half understandings, and competing symbolic interpretations of the same actions fueled the escalation of conflict in Waco.

Trying Out the State-to-State Negotiation Frame

When their constitutional rights process frame did not yield adequate results, the Branch Davidians started placing greater emphasis on a more radical framing of their encounter with federal agents. By declaring Mount Carmel an independent political entity, they named their community as separate from and *equal to* the state entity with which they were negotiating. Consequently, they invoked a process frame of state-to-state diplomatic negotiations. For the Branch Davidians, the state-to-state negotiation framing of their encounter with the FBI had the benefit of clarity. There was no confusion about whether or not the Branch Davidians granted the federal government authority to regulate their lives; they did not. The boundary between Mount Carmel and the United States was clearly marked in their minds. The state-to-state negotiation frame also provided a language for the Branch Davidians to talk openly about God's power, God's actions, and God's methods of constraining their own actions. When this framing of the negotiation process reached its most developed stage, Koresh was speaking as God's ambassador, and the rest of the Branch Davidians were attesting to his legitimacy as God's emissary, which heightened Koresh's claims to a representative identity. Like the FBI negotiators, Koresh was acting on someone else's behalf. If the FBI negotiators had to accommodate their bosses, the Branch Davidians had to do the same. If the FBI negotiators were trying to keep the tactical troops and commanders from getting angry because the negotiations were not progressing, Koresh was trying to keep God's army from destroying the FBI agents because they refused to listen to His message.

There were, however, great costs associated with the state-to-state negotiation frame. To use this frame, the Branch Davidians had to rely more heavily on the biblical language that the FBI deemed irrelevant, making the language-frame divergence between the parties even more problematic. Ultimately, the FBI declared the Branch Davidian "Bible babble" a nonlanguage that was totally irrelevant to the negotiations. They were, in effect, pushing the Branch Davidians' ultimate concerns off of the table. The interaction frame associated with state-to-state negotiation deviated so radically from the "agent-to-criminal" interaction frame associated with barricade negotiations that the FBI negotiators were often stymied. Furthermore, the state-to-state negotiation frame created a competition of legitimacy between institutions. When the FBI negotiators urged the Branch Davidians to take their case to court, the Branch Davidians responded by offering the ATF agents a chance to be tried in God's court. For every institutional forum the FBI negotiators suggested, the Branch

Davidians had a counterpart in God's coming kingdom. Their entire dialogue was transformed into a negotiation over reality; issue-specific negotiations were buried under worldmaking disputes. Obviously, the Branch Davidians' framing of the negotiation process was no more effective than the FBI's bargaining framework.

When the Parties Bring Their Gods to the Table

NEITHER SIDE in the Waco negotiations disputes that they had reached an agreement for the Branch Davidians to exit Mount Carmel on March 2. They do disagree vehemently about the reasons the surrender plan failed, and they disagree even more adamantly about why the negotiation process never got back on track. How did the FBI and Branch Davidian worldviewing differences, reflected in their advocacy for competing negotiation processes, create a situation in which they reached a surrender agreement, but were unable to bring that agreement to conclusion? To understand this problem, we need to look at the way the parties' negotiation frames changed or did not change during the course of their interactions.

Power, Resistance, and Cooperation

The March 2 surrender agreement was achieved through a process of coercive bargaining. The process was coercive because the FBI isolated the Mount Carmel community by "capturing" their phone lines while also trying to intimidate the Branch Davidians with tactical maneuvers. It was also coercive because the negotiators badgered the Branch Davidians to operate within a bargaining frame, even when participating in such a process required that the Mount Carmel residents sacrifice their deeply held value commitment to acting as free moral agents. Finally, the process was coercive because the negotiators pushed the Branch Davidians to negotiate for hours on end without time to sleep or rest.

The Branch Davidians found this last issue particularly irritating when the negotiation switched from Jim Cavanaugh of the ATF to the first negotiators from Quantico. In Tapes 4 and 5, Steve Schneider and PN02 debated the injustice of allowing Cavanaugh to sleep while PN02 took over and kept Schneider up all night. Depriving barricaded subjects of sleep is a deliberate negotiation strategy in typical barricade situations. In this case, however, it violated the Branch Davidians' sense of process justice and ultimately helped affirm their belief that "the system" was inherently unjust, evil, and arrayed against them.

The FBI negotiators also had the advantage of working with a prepared, rationally organized, goal-directed negotiation script. The Branch Davidians, by contrast, lived in a reflective community. Their lives were organized around an interpretive process of discerning God's plan for the world so they could live in accordance with His will. When the FBI negotiators stepped in with their goal-rational negotiation process, the Mount Carmel residents were still "facing [heavenly] realities that [when] they're learned in the prophecies is [sic] one thing, but now [that] they're facing [earthly] reality" are something else (Tape 6: 33–34). They were "talking about a lot of issues" (Tape 9: 30), or, in academic terms, they were engaged in intragroup negotiations over the meaning of their encounter with the ATF. The Branch Davidians were trying to find a formula that linked what was happening to them now to what had happened in the past and to what would happen in the future (Morley, Webb, and Stephenson 1988, 120). Consequently, the community had not yet developed an institutionally validated process frame with which to resist the bargaining frame advanced by the FBI negotiators.

The Branch Davidians did, however, have one immediate process request. They wanted time to rest, think, pray, and recover from their trauma.

> MR. SCHNEIDER: . . . *give it a little time, you know, don't rush it and push it.* . . . You know, we've shown to you already, we've not done anything, you, you can keep your eye on us, we'll be doing the same, you know, let's have a little trust. . . . We're going to get this—we're going to actually get this thing worked out. I mean, we, we mean that. We're going to work it right on through. . . . Okay. So

let's, let's keep the relation going, you know, but if you, if you could just give me a—boy, I'd love to just, you know, lay back maybe for an hour or two. (Tape 4–5: 79, emphasis added)

MR. KORESH: Well, I'm telling you what you'll do. Just give us some time, give us time, you know. That's all I'm asking. Give us time. You know, you've all done—you've all been enraged a lot of times, you know. Don't burn our building down.

PN01: No, we won't do that.

MR. KORESH: Don't, don't shoot us all up. *Give these people a chance before God to weigh out whether what they've learned in the scripture is the truth or, you know, whether maybe they have second thoughts.* But they've got to, they've got to have that time. (Tape 9: 17, emphasis added)

This request was perfectly logical given the Branch Davidians' need to make sense of their current situation in relation to the Bible and God's plan for the End Time.

Although the negotiators reassured the Branch Davidians there would be no attacks on Mount Carmel, they were not inclined to honor the request for time. For the FBI negotiators, there was "not much sense for this to continue on and . . . have additional people hurt" (Tape 4–5: 10). When Jim Cavanaugh went off duty, the new FBI negotiator "[didn't] think we should waste this precious time and, and not proceed with, you know, the mutually beneficial things that I hope we can accomplish" (Tape 4–5: 67). The negotiators kept pressing the Branch Davidians to participate immediately in a bargaining process. Because the bargaining frame allowed the Branch Davidians to achieve some of their own practical goals, they cooperated. Those parents who wanted to send their children out of Mount Carmel were able to do so by bargaining with the FBI or by allowing Koresh to bargain on their behalf, considering that the FBI thought he was in control of everyone.

Branch Davidian Intragroup Negotiations

Even as they worked within the bargaining frame, however, the Branch Davidians were narrating their experiences in relation to past events and future expectations. This narration was a daily worldmaking practice for the Mount Carmel residents as an apocalyptic community. "Biblical apocalypticism involves the interplay of three basic elements: (1) the sacred Text, which is fixed and inviolate; (2) the inspired Interpreter, who is involved in both transmitting and effecting the meaning of the Text; and (3) the fluid Context in which the Interpreter finds himself or herself" (Tabor and Gallagher 1995, 8–9). The Branch Davidians' context had altered radically in the space of a few hours on February 28. They needed time to interpret those changes in relation to their text, the Bible.

Discerning the meaning of their situation was not a daunting task for a community that spent most of its time focused on this meaning-creation process. Figuring out how to interact with the FBI while remaining faithful to God's will was a much more difficult undertaking. The Branch Davidians had little experience in developing process and enactive frames for negotiating with secular authorities, and the experience they did have was ill suited to their current circumstances. As a community, the Branch Davidians preferred to withdraw from "the world." They engaged in dialogue with people who were already seeking truth, or they debated those people, such as members and ministers of the Seventh-day Adventist Church, whose beliefs were similar but not identical to their own. They generally avoided interaction with secular authorities, and when officials did intrude on their lives, the Branch Davidians adopted a stance of skirting the truth while still cooperating. The community arranged phony civil marriages for Koresh's many wives and did not write Koresh's name as the father on the birth certificates of his many offspring. In this way, they hoped to avoid official attention. When the Branch Davidians were investigated for alleged child abuse, they gave social workers from Child Protective Services a tour of their home while deflecting any discussion of the paternity of the children.

Now, however, the Mount Carmel community was locked into a highly escalated *adversarial* confrontation with secular authorities that neither understood nor validated their core concerns. Consequently, they had to translate their apocalyptic interpretation of events into process-frame proposals suitable for negotiating with the FBI. This was not easy. The Branch Davidians could not placate or cajole federal agents into leaving the community in peace by employing the same tactics they had previously used with Texas Child Protective Services and other government officials. Nor could they deal with federal agents as people seeking or debating truth. Even Koresh realized the negotiators were not going to be very interested in hearing about or debating God's plan for the world.

> MR. KORESH: Well, like I was telling Jim, you know, I told Jim to, to look into that Bible. I told him to look into Revelation 4 and 5. I told him to look into those seals. Now, if you look at the, the fifth seal, if you look at the sixth seal, if you look into Isaiah 13, if you look in Joel 2, if you look into the back of Nahum, what's fixing to happen has already been foretold. I teach seven seals. . . . *I'd like to talk with you guys in full. I'd like you to grab a Bible, sit down and follow me word by word, see what the ancients have foresaw. And that way we'd have a better understanding. But I realize that, you know, most of you are not ready for that. You've got your own way of doing things.* (Tape 10a: 20, emphasis added)

Branch Davidian Framing of the Negotiations

Several critical ideas that would later influence the Branch Davidians' framing of the negotiation process took shape during the first few days of bargaining. First, Koresh and the others decided that their negotiations involved more than just the law enforcement community. In other words, they adopted a stance that would eventually lead them to develop a substantive framing of their conflict that encompassed actors other than the FBI. They did acknowledge the issue of their own accountability for the February 28 gunfight: "Those [Branch Davidians] who've done injustice, . . .they've got to give theirselves over to the judicial system" (Tape 9: 14–15). On the other hand, they also demanded the same accountability from the ATF: "You need to arrest these people. They came on our property. They shot" (911.2: 2). This formed the basis for an outcome frame that required equitable treatment for the Branch Davidians and the ATF.

A second framing narrative that later proved to be a critical factor in negotiations developed as the Branch Davidians contemplated the implications of their belief that two systems or two laws—God's and man's—were involved in a final showdown. This second narrative led the community to articulate a dilemma that would play a central role in the development of their characterization frame when dealing with the FBI. On the one hand, the Branch Davidians acknowledged that the United States was probably the nation that came closest to God's vision of justice. If any worldly government could be trusted to treat God's remnant fairly, it was the United States. On the other hand, the Bible also warned about a great nation that "acts like a peaceful lamb-like beast [but] really under its breast, speaks as a dragon" (Tape 33: 4–5). Thus, whatever their interactions with the FBI, the Branch Davidians needed to watch carefully to determine whether they could or should place themselves in the hands of the judicial system. Was the United States a safe place for God's remnant, or was it Babylon? The answer, they believed, would be found only by observing the FBI actions.

> MR. KORESH: . . . And, like I say, these people know the seals and they know that unless this country observes and sees, then they know point-blank what's going to happen according to the prophecies. That's why *our main burden is holding out here until we have an opportunity to state our cause.* . . . *[M]e and you, we kind of, kind of have a little friction, because I want to serve your laws where they coincide with God's laws. And America does. Above all of the nations.* It does. You know, it's the closest to God's laws, basic principles of common sense, you know. But, again, there are some laws in the scriptures of truth which are the laws of prophecy. (Tape 10b: 13–14, emphasis added)

> MR. KORESH: Now, that's why without you knowing where these seven seals are in the Bible, you know, you wouldn't know how to judge me. . . . Except by your law. And I respect that. See, *I'm willing to come out and be observed and judged by your . . . law.* . . . *if you allow me to first speak my law.* (Tape 10b: 14–15, emphasis added)

Having adopted the identity of the chosen remnant and believing that the End Time was imminent, the Branch Davidians also articulated an issue that the FBI never fully understood. The Branch Davidians felt morally obligated to get out to the public their message about the coming end of the world. The precise audience for this message was not clearly defined and remained vague throughout the negotiations. Sometimes they seemed interested in preaching to the whole world. At other times, residents of Mount Carmel seemed most concerned about reaching the agents with whom they were negotiating, preachers who were misinterpreting Scripture on the radio and television, or the judicial system. Assuming they had a missionary obligation to enlighten the world affected the Branch Davidians' participation in the negotiation process in two ways: they eventually adopted an interaction frame that included "converting the negotiators" as a legitimate part of negotiation, and they developed a heightened sensitivity to the process injustice of their isolation.

The themes outlined above provided a conceptual basis for the Branch Davidians' emergent citizen-to-government framing of the negotiations (see chapter 7). However, that process frame developed over time and only as a consequence of the extended encounter between the parties. Meanwhile, the Branch Davidians were being pressured to bargain. Without a clear alternative process proposal, their earliest resistance to bargaining rested primarily on their ethical objections to commodifying adult moral agents (see chapter 6). These objections only limited bargaining and did not prevent it entirely. Therefore, the parties were able to engage in some mutually satisfactory exchanges. The problems with bargaining reached crisis proportions only after the FBI and the Branch Davidians achieved an agreement to end the standoff and that deal collapsed.

The FBI (Mis)Interprets the Branch Davidians' Needs and Aspirations

How did the negotiators entice value-rational actors into a goal-rational deal that, by all appearances, violated those actors' absolute values? To turn a typical barricade standoff into a problem suitable for bargaining, crisis negotiators identify the subject's needs and use them to obtain resolution of the incident. In other words, the police try to identify the barricaded subject's aspiration frame. For this process to work, the barricaded subject must make demands, and the police negotiator must be able to establish his or her identity as someone who is able to harm the subject but is willing to help instead (McMains and Mullins 1996, 25). Confronted with a barricaded subject who makes no demands, police negotiators play "both sides of the negotiation act by supplying a vocabulary of demands" (Powell 1989, 53). They do so by interpreting and inferring the barricaded subject's needs and interests (aspirations).

If the barricaded subject resists efforts to build a relationship with the negotiators, the police compel a relationship by isolating the subject and controlling his or her environment. The police negotiator becomes the only person through whom the barricaded subject can achieve his or her aspirations. Using an interaction frame of bargaining, the police exchange fulfillment of the subject's needs and interests for compliant behavior and ultimately surrender. The subject's needs are presumed to include both instrumental needs for such things as survival, food, water, comfort, and predictability of circumstances, as well as expressive needs for acceptance, belonging, affection, and self-worth.

Negotiators are told to listen for unspoken as well as spoken needs. However, they are not cautioned that the listener's own worldmaking narratives distort the listening process. In any conversation, important information is filtered out, and those responses that conform to the listener's expectations are amplified (Fiumara 1990). For example, all of the needs listed in the crisis negotiation literature are material or psychological in nature. There is no acknowledgment of the human need to be part of a community with "shared goals, values, customs, [and] traditions," all of which provide "sacred meaning" to human life (Clark 1990, 47). Consequently, crisis negotiators are not trained to listen for indications of the one human need most salient for members of unconventional religious and political groups.

When the parties involved in conversation are separated by worldviewing differences and operating in the context of hostility and suspicion, the risks associated with filtering and amplification are greatly increased—which was a significant problem in Waco. I have already described two such problems during the negotiations. The negotiators did not listen carefully to the explanations that the Branch Davidians offered to justify "trading" children for concessions from the FBI. They filtered out symbolic and narrative language as irrelevant. Consequently, they misinterpreted Branch Davidian cooperation with the bargaining process as full acceptance of a bargaining framework. In similar fashion, the FBI negotiators later "heard" the Branch Davidians' references to the Constitution, but "filtered out" evidence that the Constitution was not their ultimate authority.

Listening carefully to the worldmaking language of another person is critical if we are attempting to identify his or her needs or interests. Because the FBI negotiators ignored symbolic and narrative language, they made several significant errors when interpreting the Branch Davidians' aspiration frame. They incorrectly characterized Koresh's motives for wanting access to the media, assuming that Koresh was a self-centered, egotistical, manipulative "cult leader" who wanted access to the public in order to fulfill his own need for acclaim. So they told him that thousands of people were interested in his message. Had the FBI negotiators attended to the Branch Davidians' symbolic and narrative language, they would have realized the futility of this persuasive argument. However much we might doubt the humility of a man who claimed to be the Lamb promised in the Book of Revelation, Koresh and the members of the community were adamant that it was the message and not Koresh that mattered. He could not appear to be openly swayed by an appeal to his ego without violating his own sense of identity. Indeed, he probably felt compelled to demonstrate that he was *not* motivated by self-interest, but rather by a humble obedience to God's message and commands, which may help explain his stubborn refusal to exit Mount Carmel after God told him to wait.

> PN03: Are you ready to do it [come out] now?
> DAVID KORESH: I cannot go beyond the commandment of my Father.
> PN03: *Can you do the right thing now?*
> DAVID KORESH: *I am doing the right thing now.* (Tape 21:35–36, emphasis added)

The negotiators also kept promising Koresh he would have plenty of time and opportunity, even if he ended up in prison, to "increase his flock." Again, the implications of self-centered motives evoked resistance from Koresh and others in the community. Furthermore, this argument made no sense within the Branch Davidians' symbolic frame; David Koresh had no grand aspiration to be the next Billy Graham. Because the world was coming to an end, time to "recruit" new followers would necessarily be short. Besides, God's remnant would be just that, a scrap, a small group of elect believers. The Branch Davidians had no interest in evangelizing and converting the masses because such an accomplishment would have been out of step with the prophecies. The FBI negotiators also incorrectly assumed that Koresh was the only person at Mount Carmel who had strong feelings about maintaining access to the media. In truth, however, the entire community was focused on the problem of finding venues for sharing their message in an appropriate manner.

The FBI Manipulates the Negotiation Context

When the FBI negotiators from Quantico arrived in Waco, the Branch Davidians were talking with other negotiators on one phone and with the press and their families on other phones. The Mount Carmel residents were deemed too independent of the FBI negotiators for bargaining to be fully effective. Byron Sage, the first FBI negotiator to arrive in Waco, explained the decision to "capture the phone lines" as follows:

> BYRON: The decision that's been made . . . and I was in on it over there with [PN02] is that . . . it's time, I think we've given this guy time after time after time what he's wanted. Not inhibited his free access to the media. He was able to get that accomplished . . . now it's time to capture the phones, which have been done and it's time to . . . basically . . . start calling the shots. Ah, still try to work with him . . . and coordinate everything and try to . . . be sensitive to his needs and interests and so forth. (911.23: 12–13)[1]

Already, the FBI negotiators were assuming that their negotiations were primarily with one person, Koresh. This naming of the problem led the negotiators to adopt several interactive frames that did not address the actual dynamics of the Branch Davidian community. As discussed in chapter 6, the negotiators believed they were bargaining with Koresh for the "release" of women and children. In fact, there is clear evidence in the transcripts that the Branch Davidian parents were making decisions about their own children.[2]

1. This transcript is misdated 2/28/93, 8:40 A.M.–9:42 A.M. It was actually recorded on the morning of March 1, 1993, and overlaps or follows Tapes 4 and 5. This is evident from internal references to Tapes 4 and 5 in which the first negotiator from Quantico (PN02) engaged "in kind of a show down with [the Branch Davidians] . . . regarding whether or not they're gonna allow them to talk to [Jim] Cavanaugh" (911.23: 11–12).

2. Koresh was not the only person at Mount Carmel who indicated the children were being sent out by their parents. Schneider discussed the difficult decisions facing mothers who were trying to determine which parents wanted to send children out and how to pair the children up so

When the FBI negotiators did interact with the members of the community, they treated them as if they were motivated by an individualist sense of self-identity. Because the Mount Carmel residents appeared to name themselves primarily in relation to their group membership, this tactic failed miserably. The FBI negotiators never created an interactive process that recognized the fact that they were negotiating with an identity group.

Sage was also clear that the FBI would be "calling the shots" when it came to naming the substantive frame or defining the problem at hand. In spite of the log entries cited in chapter 6, the Branch Davidians had not outlined any demands. They still wanted the federal authorities simply to go away, but the FBI negotiators were fully convinced that the primary problem at hand was arranging for all of the Branch Davidians to surrender to the authorities, at least temporarily, so that criminal charges could be straightened out and lodged against the appropriate persons. From the FBI negotiators' perspective, the Mount Carmel residents needed to have their attention focused on the *real* problem under negotiation and needed to be brought into a dependent relationship with the FBI so that they would be forced to bargain with the authorities.

Late in the afternoon on March 1, the FBI created a dyadic relationship with the Branch Davidians by disconnecting all but one phone line into Mount Carmel and arranging for that phone to connect only to the negotiators. Cutting off phone contact between Mount Carmel and the outside world infuriated Koresh and others inside Mount Carmel (Justice 29; Logs 14). The Branch Davidians gave two reasons for their anger. First, they could not talk with their families:

> STEVE: David is really getting upset because we were downstairs, the telephone rang, his parents are on the phone. They were saying a few words to him and he was just telling them to be cool, that everything was being worked out, and the phone went dead. . . . They couldn't call in. Nobody can and you can't call out. David said he's going to stop the children even.
>
> PN01 : Well, I don't want him to do that.

---

that an older child always accompanied a younger child. Scott and Sita Sonobe, who were the first to send their children out of Mount Carmel, both indicated the decision was their own and not Koresh's.

STEVE: I mean, there, there's no sense in doing that with the phone. Nothing's being said. He's talking to them about relaxing and . . . trying to keep these people, you know, you know, they're all upset and they don't know what's going on. . . . They want to hear the voices and we're trying to just say just look, like, you know, it's being worked out, but, you know, they like to hear it from us, of course. (Tape 8: 17–18)

Second, they could not speak with the public and the press. Whereas Schneider's focus was the issue of talking with family members, Koresh's primary objection to having the phone lines severed was his inability to address those people who wanted to hear the Branch Davidians' message. No mention was made of a constitutional right to free speech, although Koresh briefly stated "we have the right."

DAVID: Now, listen to me. . . . You guys are telling the public of this country that you don't want any blood. All right, now, I made a deal with you. You tell these boys they better get our lines back operable, okay? . . . Or they're going to go to bed every night with the knowledge that they're the one that killed these little children.

PN01: Okay, David.

DAVID: No playing around any more, okay?

PN01: I know. Listen, just hang—

DAVID: No, you listen. I've been fair with you, you've been fair with me thus far. . . . But you tell those guys that are pranking around with the innocent that there's only one thing that makes me mad, and that's when the innocent are hurt. . . . Now, I made a deal with you with the children. . . . You tell these boneheads, these bureaucrats, whatever they are, to open our lines up.

PN01: Okay. I'm going to see what I can do. *I know it's painful being cut off from the people you love.*

DAVID: *No, the thing of it is is that we have the right*—the radio stations are saying they haven't heard from me since two last night, and you know the reason why. *People are wanting to call. They want to know some things.* . . . So, you know, tell them guys if that's what they want is a big fight . . . then come on. (Tape 8: 19–21, emphasis added)

The negotiators heard the Branch Davidians' anger about the phones as a validation of their characterization of Koresh's goals, objectives, and psychological motivations. They also heard Koresh's reference to the children being killed as affirmation of a possible group suicide, although it was clear that most Mount Carmel residents believed the government might kill them. The negotiators classified access to the media as one of Koresh's "needs" and treated it as a tradable "commodity." They presumed that once they moved Koresh past his emotional response to being isolated, he would engage in rational bargaining activities in order to fulfill his expressive need for attention by regaining the public spotlight.

The negotiators apparently overlooked the fact that Koresh was not the only one being isolated from the outside world. The entire community was affected by this action. Residents could not phone extended family members to make arrangements for the care of their children should they opt to send them out of Mount Carmel. Nor could they seek counsel or advice from Branch Davidians not in residence at Mount Carmel, a group that might have been particularly helpful in convincing the community to surrender because they could speak the language of the community. Furthermore, the negotiators did not listen carefully to Koresh's worldmaking language. It annoyed him to be cut off from his loved ones, but the *real* problem was that "people . . . wanted to know things," and they could not get through to Mount Carmel to have their questions answered. The FBI was blocking the sacred message, the central organizing principle of the Mount Carmel community.

To make matters worse, the tactical team brought in the APCs at the same time the phone lines were disconnected. The negotiators justified the use of the APCs, indicated that they sympathized with the tactical agents' desire to be protected, and ultimately convinced the Mount Carmel residents to tolerate the presence of military vehicles. Or so they thought. However, the two issues—physical encroachment on Mount Carmel property with military equipment and the imposition of isolation—became inextricably intertwined in the minds of the Branch Davidians. The linkage became clear later when the two issues were connected to the same constitutional rights rhetoric in the citizen-to-government process frame. The FBI negotiators did not adequately recognize that both actions offended the community's expectations regarding process justice, and both actions only pushed the Branch Davidians closer to concluding that the United States was "the beast" that would oppose God's remnant in the End Time.

The Parties Strike a Deal

From the outset, law enforcement negotiators in Waco treated access to the media as a bargaining chip, which they were willing to exchange for the "release" of people at Mount Carmel. The ultimate goal of the negotiators was to get everyone out of "the compound." However, they opened their bargaining by asking for the release of children and women. Once the phone lines were severed, they sweetened their offer by suggesting they could give Koresh access to a *national* audience if he would give them more than just two children. They wanted everyone to exit Mount Carmel peacefully and to surrender to authorities. This proposal was first tested with Steve Schneider.

> PN01: Steve . . . I want to give you something to, to think about.
>
> STEVE: All right.
>
> PN01: Okay? I don't know if I can do this, but what I'm going to do is I'm going to go back there and talk to some commanders. . . . And I want to tell them about our conversations.
>
> STEVE: Okay.
>
> PN01: And I'm going to see if, just a possibility now—'cause I don't want you to get mad if, if I can't work it out. That *if I was able to get I mean a major, major broadcast of your word out* . . . I'm not talking about the radio station in Dallas. I'm talking about some major thing.
>
> STEVE: Okay.
>
> PN01: *Would you all come out?* I mean, would you all—
>
> STEVE: *Can I, can I put it to David, because that's what he's been talking about?*
> (Tape 9: 41–42, emphasis added)

It is unclear whether Koresh had been talking about getting everyone out, access to the media, or both. There is clear evidence that he was concerned with resuming his "conversations" with the public via the press. It is not clear that he was connecting that access to the press with having everyone exit

Mount Carmel. Koresh's initial negative response to the FBI proposal was a reflection of the Branch Davidians' naming of themselves as free moral agents.

> STEVE TO KORESH: He's not promising or anything, he doesn't know if he can even do it. If it's possible if he could put you in touch with the, the best news coverage possible—I mentioned . . . Ted Koppel—he says would you as a group come out together and—
>
> MR. KORESH: *Can't do that.*
>
> STEVE: *Well, he's saying he can't do that because he wants them [the residents of Mount Carmel] to have the choice, you know, every one of them. . . .* He wants them to be able to I guess move on their own without—Some of them, you know, they're scared and all the rest. (Tape 9: 43, emphasis added)

Several hours later, however, Koresh had apparently agreed to this suggestion. In the following exchange, he tied the continued immediate "release" of children to a repetition of his earlier message on the local radio, and the exit of everyone in Mount Carmel to a national broadcast.

> PN03: Okay. . . . Now, what I can do, or what I'd like to do is let me talk to them in terms of selling this to KRLD and maybe we can have KRLD then go national during prime time. And if we do that, will you agree to come out at that time?
>
> MR. KORESH: When you've done the national.
>
> PN03: Okay.
>
> MR. KORESH: You can do KRLD and I'll still send the children. . . .
>
> PN03: All of them?
>
> MR. KORESH: Not all of them yet. Like I say, when you go national, then they'll all come, all of us come. . . . That, that's the agreement we originally made. (Tape 10b: 4–5)

The Issue of Isolation Was Dormant, but Not Forgotten

Because the negotiators would not listen to biblical language, they thought their strategy of cutting the community off from the public was working. Furthermore, the Branch Davidians' actions affirmed their positive interpretation of progress. After an immediate angry reaction to losing phone communication

with the outside world, the Branch Davidians responded positively to the proposal to exchange national broadcast of a message from Koresh for the immediate surrender of everyone at Mount Carmel (Tape 9). The negotiators did not
recognize that prior bargaining successes rested on worldview coordination
rather than on worldview agreement, so it never occurred to them to wonder
whether Koresh and the Branch Davidians were participating wholeheartedly
in this deal or simply trying to work with the only available negotiation process.

On March 2, as the residents prepared to exit Mount Carmel, they made
little reference to their loss of contact with the outside world. However, there
were indications that the community was deeply concerned about having the
media moved back from the property. Combined with the phones being cut off,
the removal of the press from the Mount Carmel vicinity heightened the
Branch Davidians' fear that the government would attack them and there
would be no witnesses to tell the world what really happened.

> STEVE: Yeah. Wait. (Indiscernible voice in background) David, . . .believes
> that you're fixing to hit us tonight, he says.
> PN01: No, we are not fixing to hit you. That is not true. . . .
> STEVE: The news media was told to get out of the way and to back way off,
> much farther back than what they are even now. Why is that?
> PN01: Nobody's coming in there. A thousand percent absolute guarantee.
> I'm promising you, it's true, okay? . . .
> STEVE: These guys are being told to move back a half-mile more even for
> safety. Safety of what? . . . We're listening—Right now on the news all the press
> is, is being told to move back a half-mile more for their own safety. What are
> they talking about? . . . Well, their comments are, you know, for safety, that
> they don't get hurt and so forth. I mean, wow.
> PN01: Oh, yeah, but that's not—That's normal. We don't want them there.
> I mean, they've raced in real fast early and, you know, now we're just trying to
> get them back and clear the road. It's nothing, trust me. And it means nothing.
> I'd like to—Tell you what, I'd like to move them back to Arkansas, they're such
> a pain in the neck. . . . And the policemen are just glad, you know, you go out
> and the lieutenant says get rid of all the reporters. What do you think the po-
> liceman does? Tries to kick their butt back a mile, so don't—it's no big thing.
> (Tape 10a: 9–11)

Moving the press back from Mount Carmel might have been normal procedure for the police. For the Branch Davidians, however, it played into the darkest prophecies about the End Time. It also altered their loss-gain frame by changing their calculation of the risks associated with walking out of Mount Carmel.

Again, the negotiators had every reason to believe they had handled this problem effectively. Between the negotiators' reassurances that they had no intention of assaulting Mount Carmel and the distractions provided by the immediate problem of preparing Koresh's tape for broadcast, the Branch Davidians showed little interest in arguing with the FBI about the issue of their isolation.

> MR. KORESH: The press, you know, you all pulled them back because, you know, they feel that when you all come in here and, and bang us all up and everything that you don't want them to get it on footage.
>
> PN03: But the press was saying last night that we were storming the place at eight o'clock, and I told you we weren't, and we haven't. And even when you thought that somebody was on the roof, I told you that we were not.
>
> MR. KORESH: Yeah, that's true.
>
> PN03: And we didn't.
>
> MR. KORESH: And that's in your favor, I agree. (Tape 10b: 4)

Moving from Agreement to Implementation

Planning for surrender. Assuming they had an agreement for the surrender of everyone at Mount Carmel, the FBI arranged for the national radio broadcast of a taped sermon by Koresh. They also engaged the Branch Davidians in elaborate planning for their departure, specifying the order in which people would exit and arranging to send in a stretcher for Koresh. Dissolving an armed barricade is always a dangerous procedure, and crisis negotiation literature stresses the need to move very cautiously and deliberately through this phase. However, the worldnaming narratives of the parties in Waco led them to develop very different visions of the risks involved in the surrender procedure.

In Waco, four federal agents and an unknown number of Branch Davidians were already dead. The FBI tactical teams did not trust the Branch Davidians to surrender peacefully. They were wary of at least three possible violent scenarios during the surrender. First, the Branch Davidians might engineer a "suicide by cop" similar to the Haigler case. Second, they might concoct a combined murder/suicide attack by "wiring themselves" with explosives. Third, they might send out the women, children, and least-committed male members so that Koresh and a cadre of his "mighty men" could engage law enforcement agents in another deadly gun battle.[3]

For their part, the Branch Davidians were very wary of trusting the FBI. They tried to accept the distinction between the ATF and the FBI, but remained suspicious of all federal law enforcement agents. They had been expecting an apocalyptic confrontation with evil worldly forces since at least 1985. Therefore, many in the community were afraid they would be killed upon exiting the building. The fact that the FBI had removed the press from the area elevated this anxiety. The Branch Davidians wanted the media to serve as witnesses to their surrender, a request that the FBI ignored.[4] The Branch Davidians also did not believe they would receive fair treatment in court. They were fully aware that the charges related to the February 28 raid and shoot-out were capital offenses and that murder charges would be leveled against some members of the community. They also thought the FBI would deliberately destroy physical evidence on the Mount Carmel property, evidence that would exoner-

3. This summary of law enforcement fears and concerns regarding the Branch Davidian surrender is based on the transcripts, the Department of Justice report on Waco, testimony during the congressional hearings on Waco, secondary sources, and personal conversations with FBI agents.

4. The FBI failure to pay attention to this request is difficult to understand. In past negotiations, they have made arrangements for witnesses to the surrender ritual. For example, during the Atlanta prison uprising of Cuban inmates, a Catholic bishop was brought in to observe and assist with the surrender ritual, which was done in response to the inmates' request. (Fuselier, Van Zandt, and Lanceley 1989). I suspect that when thinking about this problem, the negotiators did not see the structural and psychological parallels between the surrender of barricaded inmates and the surrender of a barricaded community. Rather, the negotiators were fixated on the religious language of the Mount Carmel community and drew inferences about a possible dramatic suicide similar to the Haigler case with the media as witnesses to the carnage.

ate the Branch Davidians by corroborating their allegation that the ATF attacked first.[5]

In spite of these mutual fears and anxieties, the negotiations leading up to the broadcast of Koresh's sermon reflect a relatively harmonious relationship between the negotiators and the Branch Davidians. Children continued to leave Mount Carmel two at a time. The negotiators kept the community busy with problem-solving activities related to their impending departure, offered reassurances to those who were worried about what would happen when they left Mount Carmel, and kept the community informed about the plans for broadcasting Koresh's tape.

One critical issue for the FBI negotiators was getting Koresh to declare publicly that the Branch Davidians would leave Mount Carmel after the tape was played. They wanted to pin him down on national radio so that they could hold him to the agreement if he demonstrated any reluctance to leave Mount Carmel. Koresh agreed to this stipulation without debate and read back a statement dictated by the FBI with one meaningful symbolic revision. He recorded and attached the following statement to the beginning of his sermon tape.

DAVID: I, David Koresh, agree upon the broadcasting of this tape to come out peacefully with all the people immediately. (Tape 12a: 11)

The original statement as dictated by the FBI read, "I agree that upon the broadcasting of my tape I will immediately come out peacefully with all *my people*" (Tape 12a: 7, emphasis added). The negotiators neither noted nor commented on Koresh's revision. They only wanted to ensure that the words *peacefully* and *immediately* were included in the statement.

As the time approached for the broadcast and exodus, the community members appeared to be preparing to leave their home. The Branch Davidians and negotiators engaged in "the great puppy negotiation," when the children

5. This summary of Branch Davidian beliefs and fears is based on the transcripts, a videotape made by the Mount Carmel residents, the testimony of defense attorneys for Koresh and Schneider who were permitted to visit with the Branch Davidians during the siege, and survivors' statements. Also see Thibodeau's account of the fifty-one-day siege (Thibodeau and Whiteson 1999).

asked permission to bring their puppies out and the FBI preferred not to complicate the surrender procedure. The FBI eventually won this negotiation, but promised to make sure the puppies were well cared for. When the broadcast ended, the children were being helped into their jackets, and Koresh was changing clothes in preparation for being moved downstairs where he would be placed on a stretcher. There was no indication that the community would fail to exit the property. Even after the surrender plans collapsed, people in the community affirmed that they had been prepared to depart Mount Carmel on March 2.

> PN03: Well, you know, he had, he had told me—he had promised the world that he was going to lead everybody out. . . . I assumed, based on what he said and based on the fact that everybody is dressed and ready to leave, that everybody was going to be leaving. . . . Okay? Is that the impression that you had?
>
> RACHEL: That we were going to leave after him and the children went out the front.
>
> PN03: Uh-huh.
>
> RACHEL: Yes.
>
> PN03: Okay. Did—was everybody prepared to leave?
>
> RACHEL: Yes . . . we were. (Tape 23: 15–16)

The Surrender Plans Fail

All of the surrender planning was rendered moot when the Branch Davidians failed to leave Mount Carmel Center. The hour-long tape of Koresh's teaching was played at 1:30 in the afternoon. The FBI expected an immediate surrender, only to be left waiting while the Branch Davidians said good-bye to Koresh and to one another. Just before 5:00 P.M. the negotiators were told that Koresh was preaching and leading the group in prayer. According to an official report, "Steve Schneider came on the line at 5:45 P.M. and, in an *obvious attempt to delay,* began preaching and reading the Bible" (Justice 35, emphasis added). In response to pressure from the negotiators, Schneider informed them that Koresh had been told by God to wait.

STEVE: He says his God says that he is to wait because that which was played on the air is given for everyone to hear . . . that they might be proven or not. That's exactly what he said to me. Did you hear me? (Tape 19: 13)

Why did the carefully planned surrender never materialize? Depending on which party one asked, either God spoke to Koresh or the Branch Davidians reneged on their agreement. Suddenly, the parties were back to negotiating reality.

The Aftermath of the Failed Surrender

From Disappointment to Impasse

The Branch Davidians explain what happened. The failure of the planned surrender on March 2 evoked competing explanatory narratives from the Branch Davidians and the FBI. The Mount Carmel residents offered a *corporate apologia* that made no sense to their audience. "An apologia is not an apology (though it *may* contain one); rather it is a response to a social legitimation crisis in which an organization seeks to justify its behavior by presenting a compelling counter account of its actions" (Hearit 1995, 3).[6] The fact that they offered an apologia indicates the Branch Davidians understood that their failure to exit the center constituted a breach of widely shared social norms about honoring one's agreements. However, their apologia invoked a higher authority and moral obligation, a commitment that both preceded and superseded their agreement with the FBI.

DAVID: . . . *the truth of God and the laws of men do not harmonize in every degree.* So that when the laws of men direct men to go contrary to the laws of God, *men must take their stand to either be with God and God's law, or with man and*

6. The negotiator's explanation of the FBI decision to move the press back from Mount Carmel is also an example of an apologia. The FBI was losing legitimacy with the Branch Davidians because witnesses (the media) were being removed from the area. The negotiator offered a compelling counteraccount of the FBI's actions. An apologia works only if the audience grants it legitimacy. Like blaming narratives, apologia constitute a joint exercise in meaning creation.

man's law. That's why, in order to receive the seal of the living God, you've got to know what God's will is. You've got to understand his law, the nature of his law, and his will. (Tape 26: 19, emphasis added)

For the Branch Davidians, obedience to God's law and cooperation with His unfolding plan were more important than honoring their promise to any human being or worldly agency. Their worldmaking narrative included competing systems of law, and the most central conflict in their lives was ensuring that they acted in accordance with the more righteous system. This is a clear example of value-rational action. "The action of persons who, regardless of possible cost to themselves, act to put into practice their convictions of what *seems to them to be required* by duty, honour, the pursuit of beauty, a religious call, personal loyalty, or the importance of some 'cause' no matter in what it consists" is perfectly rational when viewed from a value-rational orientation (Weber 1964, 116, emphasis added).

The Branch Davidian explanation is rejected. This sense of compulsion and an absolute need to be obedient to God's will made no sense to the FBI agents. The notion of radical obedience to a divine will or plan was contrary to their belief in human autonomy and free will. In spite of their skepticism, the negotiators knew that a harsh rejection of the Branch Davidian apologia would endanger negotiations. Consequently, they were publicly cautious in their statements about the failed surrender. Other FBI agents and government officials were less discreet in their public response. The media hue and cry over Koresh's role as an alleged "cult leader" increased dramatically, and he was branded a liar and a coward, as well as a child abuser and murderer.

The rejection of their apologia did not surprise the Branch Davidians. They did not expect the FBI or the public to understand their explanation. That, however, did not make them any less determined to live according to God's will. If anything, rejection of their account increased their determination to withstand the test of public scorn in order to live righteous lives. The more calumnies that the FBI and the media heaped on Koresh, the more the Mount Carmel residents were convinced he was speaking God's truth.

The FBI responds to the Branch Davidian apologia. The disappointment of March 2 did not have to lead inevitably to a failed negotiation between the parties in Waco. The ensuing interactions between the negotiators and the

Branch Davidians along with the activities of the FBI tactical units created the negotiation impasse and set the stage for the April 19 fiasco. This statement may be the most controversial I have made thus far. Since April 19, 1993, the negotiators have contended that the negotiations in Waco were undermined by tactical maneuvers (Justice 140). Without tactical errors, the negotiators believe they could have convinced more Branch Davidians to leave Mount Carmel, even if Koresh and his "mighty men" or a hard-core group of believers ultimately decided to commit suicide rather than surrender. The negotiators attribute the ultimate collapse of negotiations in Waco to Koresh and his followers. Koresh, they claim, was to blame because he was manipulative, controlling, and unwilling to face giving up his status in the community. In 1996, one negotiator explained the collapse of the March 2 surrender in a congressional hearing.

> If you go back over those tapes . . . you can see how the process worked. But at the very last moment he could not do it. And Mr. Smerick [FBI behavioral scientist] . . . gave us an analysis, and I still believe that his analysis was . . . right. . . . [Smerick] said when he [Koresh] lined up with all the children and the women in the hallway, and they all came by to kiss his ring, and that is detailed in the transcript ad nauseam, that he could not leave this place where he was God, with unlimited sexual favors, unlimited being the Messiah, and walk out to a cold jail cell. (Judiciary 302)

The rest of the community members, particularly the adults, were culpable because they "believed so strongly in Koresh that the notion of leaving the squalid compound was unthinkable" (Justice 205).

The transcripts do not bear out this one-sided blaming narrative. On the contrary, they contain ample evidence that the collapse of the March 2 surrender agreement was a crisis point created *in part* by the negotiators' failure to account for the Branch Davidians' worldmaking narrative in constructing the negotiation process. Furthermore, the negotiators' continued lack of attention to worldviewing problems helped bring the negotiations to an impasse by March 15.

Immediately after the March 2 disappointment, the FBI negotiators were publicly upbeat about the possibility of resolving the standoff. They claimed to have faith in the Branch Davidians' goodwill and commitment to working things out. However, in their conversations with Koresh and others at Mount Carmel, the negotiators were less delicate. They demanded that the Branch Davidians justify or explain their failure to surrender and then rejected the explanation that was offered. When the parties clearly needed to step back and focus on negotiating reality rather than on pressing ahead with issue-specific negotiations, the FBI negotiators barely tolerated the biblical language with which the Branch Davidians tried to explain their symbolic world and aspirations. Even when residents of Mount Carmel stopped using biblical language and attempted to explain their world to the negotiators using secular language, the parties experienced moments of "language shock" (Agar 1994).

According to two people close to Koresh, Steve Schneider and Koresh's wife Rachel, the message from God telling Koresh to wait was not an unusual or unique occurrence at Mount Carmel. Koresh always made his decisions in response to God's directives. Schneider learned this the first time he met Koresh.

> STEVE: . . . When I first met him, you know, I didn't know who he was from Adam. I was dubious about the guy. And when I heard what he had to say from the Bible, I said to him, "Well, could I take you over to—I'll fly you to some friends of mine. They're scholars. And I'd like to have you share what you did with me to them." And he said to me—he looked at me. He said, *"Steve, I don't go anywhere. I don't do anything without God directing me,"* and I looked at him and I thought, well, huh? You mean if I've got an interest and my friends have an interest? And he said that and he left it at that. . . . But then the next day, the next morning, he invited me to stay overnight that night. I did. The next morning he said, "Let's go," and again I looked at him. I says, "Really?" He says, "Yeah," and I says, "Okay," and, you know, it turned out very well. (Tape 22: 36–37, emphasis added)

However normal this kind of decision making might have been for the Branch Davidians, it was incomprehensible to the FBI negotiators. How, they asked, did Koresh receive this divine inspiration? What, responded Rachel Koresh, do you mean by divine inspiration? Divine inspiration is a concept congruent with religious traditions in which every person is thought to have equal access God's will through prayer, but the Branch Davidians did not follow this tradition. David Koresh did not work through divine inspiration; he *heard* God's voice and *saw* God's plan for the world.

> RACHEL: . . . *You know, God tells him what to do.* . . .
>
> PN03: . . . I don't know if he's waiting to, to hear something or to see something or to dream something. I'm not exactly sure what it is that he's waiting for. I'd like to be able to understand that. . . . *Do you know whether he hears voices—*
>
> RACHEL: *Yes.*
>
> PN03:—*or see visions?*
>
> RACHEL: *Yes, both.*
>
> PN03: Okay. Before he—before he does something, that's what he does? He either hears a voice or, or sees a vision or something like that?
>
> RACHEL: *Well, like I said, he was praying and the voice told him to wait, God's voice.* . . . *God spoke to him, he's had visions before.* (Tape 23: 18–19, emphasis added)

Given the negotiators' predilection for "diagnosing" barricaded subjects and their tendency to label religiously motivated barricaded subjects as delusional, we can only imagine their reaction to the information that Koresh heard voices and saw visions. The important point for the Branch Davidians, however, was that other members of the community did not have similar visions because Koresh was the one spoken of in the Book of Revelation who could open the Seven Seals. The Branch Davidians were sure God would protect them as long as they were faithful to His plans. Only Koresh could unravel those plans, and if he was told to wait, the entire community waited. The Mount Carmel residents had such faith in Koresh's access to God that most of them went to sleep after he received his message to wait. They did, however, stay in their clothes, just in case God told Koresh they should leave Mount Carmel.

The negotiators thought the community members were unnaturally calm about the whole experience and kept probing their feelings in an attempt to determine what was keeping them from simply walking out of Mount Carmel as agreed.

> PN03: Okay. *Is anybody anxious* to leave that place or not?
>
> RACHEL: No.
>
> PN03: No?

RACHEL: Not at all. . . .

PN03: Okay. But—and but since he's waiting for divine inspiration, how does everybody feel about that? . . . What I mean is do people still want to come out or don't want to come out? *Is there a reluctance by some of the people left to leave?*

RACHEL: Well, we—I'm not exactly sure how to use the right words. I'm not a good spokesperson. But, *you know, we believe only he can open the seven seals and God told him to wait and that's what we're doing.*

PN03: Yes, but what I'm saying is how does everybody feel in terms of their not being—their not having left? Do they—*do you feel let down or*—

RACHEL: No.

PN03:—*are you happy* that you're not leaving?

RACHEL: *No. Neutral pretty much*, I'd say. I'm speaking for myself. *Just wait- ing. . . . I know it will all work out okay.* (Tape 23: 15–17, emphasis added)

This calm acceptance is indicative of the way the community embraced their situation as "a test of our faith and an enhanced 'withering experience,' a kind of purification under duress" (Thibodeau and Whiteson 1999, 229). Although Rachel's attitude was difficult for the negotiators to understand, it was not an indication that the Branch Davidians had conspired to trick the FBI into playing their message on the radio. Rather, it was rooted in the faith of the community. Schneider asked the negotiators to remind their bosses that "the major aspect to life for us is the spiritual" (Tape 22: 47). Furthermore, according to Schneider, when the community did follow Koresh's visions, "it's always worked out for the best" (Tape 22: 37). "I've been with him for six-and-a-half, going on seven years and I've seen God come . . . through time and time again" (Tape 22: 5).

Schneider and one of the negotiators starkly summarized the divergent ontological commitments that separated the Branch Davidians and the FBI negotiators:

PN01: But that [waiting for God's word] was not . . . our agreement, Steve.

STEVE: I understand . . . *I know in this world you don't believe that there is a su- pernatural power that speaks audibly to a person.*

PN01: *No.* (Tape 19: 14, emphasis added)

When the negotiators rejected the Branch Davidians' symbolic claims and accused them of acting unethically, the Branch Davidians acknowledged the justice of the negotiators' moral claims, but continued to invoke a higher law. In the Branch Davidian worldmaking narrative, integrity and honesty (on a human scale) were frequently placed in opposition to obedience and righteousness (on a sacred scale), and each person was called upon to choose. The Branch Davidians left no doubts about their own choice.

STEVE: If there is a God in this universe and there's the laws of man and there's the laws of God. And this God that has led him all his life says to him to wait, what do you do? . . .

PN01: What does trust mean to you?

STEVE: Exactly what it means . . . to you. Honestly. . . . I . . . That's why I'm telling you I understand what you're saying. . . . And as a human being, I want to do that also but if there's a God more powerful . . .

PN01: A man is—a man is his word, okay, a man is his word. And God's word is important, too. I mean we're talking about someone giving his word, man or God, someone gives the word. . . . Trust. . . . But the bottom line is, is he a man of his word? . . .

STEVE: It's something I, I'm aware of right now. But— . . . the only reason I ever left Hawaii in the first place was because I wanted to know God, his will . . . over my own fallible weaknesses. (Tape 19: 14–15)

The FBI negotiators would not or could not hear the Branch Davidians' ethical dilemma, and they would not or could not acknowledge the Branch Davidians' sincerity. Furthermore, the negotiators would not or could not reframe their own negotiation process to accommodate the Branch Davidians' decision-making process and worldview.

The negotiators increase their use of debate and persuasion. "Most negotiations are, to some extent, exercises in persuasive debate" (Walcott, Hopmann, and King 1977, 193). However, few negotiations are pure debates. "Processes of persuasion coexist with processes of bargaining" (Walcott, Hopmann, and King 1977, 193). In Waco, for example, the FBI negotiators were using persuasive strategies in conjunction with bargaining to convince the Mount Carmel residents that the standoff could be resolved through an agreement to exchange media access for the surrender of the Branch Davidians. Debate is a competitive activity because one is trying to bring the adversary's views into line with one's own. On the other hand, debate can also be used cooperatively to enhance problem solving and conflict resolution (Rapoport 1960). Worldview conflicts frighten many people because they tend to degenerate into unresolvable competitive debates. Pearce and Littlejohn note that in moral conflicts "rhetorically eloquent presentations of one's case sometimes intensifies, rather than settles, the conflict" (1997, 5).

When the March 2 deal fell through, the frustrated negotiators tried a number of different persuasive debating strategies. In their own minds, these efforts were simply attempts to follow through on the agreement. Given the symbolic frame differences between the parties, however, these efforts were actually attempts to exercise worldnaming control. The FBI negotiators were unilaterally trying to "define what is good or bad, acceptable or unacceptable, right or wrong" (Ramesh 1992, 37), and they were trying to reinforce those definitions by reproaching the Branch Davidians for their conduct.

The negotiators attempted to make the Branch Davidians feel guilty.

> PN01: Okay. Just listen and . . . *think about the things that we have done for you.* . . . We have played the scripture message [a short tape played on local radio]. . . . Probably 30, 40, 50 times. . . . We played the hour-long message on the Christian Broadcast Network. We played an hour-long message on KRLD. And we, *we kept every single part of our bargain.* We, we moved the snipers back from the fence. We told you before a truck would come up. We've never, ever, ever broken our word. . . . And, now, I feel, *I feel really let down by you and David.* I mean, I'm telling you, I had a lot of faith in you guys. I mean I'm around here bragging to these commanders that you guys are first rate and your word is your bond and . . . now, I mean, I just feel like, I mean, somebody has just devastated me. (Tape 19: 19–20, emphasis added)

The negotiators used the standard police negotiation tactic of setting up their commanders as a common problem to be managed cooperatively by the negotiators and the barricaded subjects.

PN01: *I now have the commanders concerned and they are losing trust and confidence.* . . . *I've got commanders who do not trust in me.* I said, look, this is going to happen. And they're starting to doubt me. And, you know, it's a problem if, if we have this go like that. I don't want that to happen. . . . I worked hard to do this. And Henry did and Gary did and a lot of people are on your side. (Tape 19: 11, emphasis added)

The negotiators warned the Branch Davidians that if they reneged on this deal, future negotiations and arrangements would be much more difficult.

PN03: Okay. We've lost some of the—you know, some of the bosses feel that we're not on a real good working relationship with you because they were anticipating getting something from David. . . . *The time may come again where he needs something,* but if we can have something that we can put our hands on to say to our bosses, look, he said this and he did this, you know.
STEVE: Right.
PN03: *But right now we're not on that kind of a relationship with the bosses.* (Tape 22: 47–50, emphasis added)

The "bosses" removed the Branch Davidians' favorite negotiator (PN01) and told them that they were punishing the negotiator because of the Davidians' failure to exit the property. Interestingly, when the Branch Davidians made no big fuss over the absence of PN01, he was allowed to return to the negotiations.

The negotiators also attempted to change the internal dynamics of the Mount Carmel community by appealing to other members to take a leadership role. Once more, the parties experienced moments of worldview opacity because they had very different concepts of leadership. Leadership among the Branch Davidians was founded on knowledge of God's will, and only Koresh was seen as having that special knowledge. Therefore, only he could lead the community. When asked what would happen if Koresh died, the community members responded as though they had never even considered this problem. Seen from the worldview of the FBI negotiators, this lack of attention to prac-

tical matters of leadership simply reinforced the notion that Koresh had mes-
merized the Mount Carmel residents.

> PN03: Okay, and, let me ask you this Rachel, if, *if he starts to deteriorate, who
> can we count on to become a person that's going to be a leader and a person of re-
> sponsibility?* Can you do that or are we going to have to depend on somebody
> else?
> RACHEL: Well, *I'm not sure if I understand,* you know, I mean *everybody will
> probably be for themself I guess.* . . . I'm not sure if I can even answer that question.
> PN03: Do you feel, do you feel strong enough to lead everybody? Can you
> talk to the group?
> RACHEL: Yeah, I can talk.
> PN03: Okay. *Do you think that they will follow your lead?*
> RACHEL: *I think they'll do whatever, I don't—I don't really know.* . . . If, you
> know, if he happens to go, I don't really know what they'll do. (Tape 20: 9–10,
> emphasis added)

The parties' worldviewing differences are clarified. Ultimately, the problem was
not the leadership among the Branch Davidians or the relationship between
the negotiators and the residents of Mount Carmel or even the relationship between the negotiators and their commanders. Rather, it was clear from their dialogue that the two parties were working with extremely different images of
God and prayer. For the negotiators, prayer was something people do; prayer
was not a dialogue between a person and God.

> STEVE: *But what if there is a higher power than you and I that speaks to an indi-
> vidual or says something—read this or pray* and—I mean what do you do? That's
> the question.
> PN01: Well, *I don't think prayer is going to end just because . . . David comes to
> the ambulance.* (Tape 19: 5–6, emphasis added)

For the Branch Davidians, prayer was an act of radical obedience. If one
prayed, then one must obey, no matter what God commanded. When the negotiators kept plaguing the Branch Davidians to leave Mount Carmel immediately, they merely demonstrated their own lack of faith.

STEVE: *He said to me, why don't you fear God?* He says, I can't go beyond what, what God has told me. He said, he gave me the seals, and that's what I have given to mankind. I have tried and, and that's been my whole mission in life. And he says, why doesn't he fear God?

PN01: No, *you tell David that I do fear God. . . . I have been a God-fearing man my whole life. . . .*

STEVE: I mean he was told to wait. He said, so *the same God that showed him the seals and gave him the seals is the same one that said, wait.* So, that's—right at this moment, *that's all he can do, right at this moment.* (Tape 19: 25–26, emphasis added)

Furthermore, those who live prayerful lives of obedience must follow God's time, not man's time. That requires patience, fortitude, and faith.

STEVE: Well, the thing is that's what he was telling you. There's a time element that we're speaking about here. . . . I mean, *when Christ says in Revelation 1*—he's talking to people 2,000 years ago and then he says, *"I come quickly."* I mean, what, what do you make out of that? He comes quickly? *2,000 years is quickly?* But, anyway, you know, no matter—even for me it's a struggle, you know. There's things like that that take a strength of . . .

PN03: *Don't tell me we're going to have to wait 2,000 years.*

STEVE: PN03, I appreciate it. Okay. Let me, you know—I'm still waiting here myself . . . and I'm anxious. *I'm just as anxious as you are. . . . But I guess I'm learning to just wait a little bit and, you know, that's the hardest thing I've ever had to do in my life.* (Tape 22: 4–25, emphasis added)

The concept of an entire community awaiting God's unfolding revelation was completely antithetical to the worldviewing assumptions of people who practice crisis management. As goal-rational actors, the negotiators in Waco focused on getting the job done quickly, efficiently, and without further violence. The Branch Davidians, on the other hand, believed that God does not follow man's sense of logic. Therefore, it was useless to ask why God would "change His mind" about having the Branch Davidians leave Mount Carmel. God does not work by man's rules. That which is irrational to man is perfectly rational to God.

STEVE TO DAVID KORESH: Did you promise, did you promise them that you'd come out immediately?

STEVE: He says yes, he did.

PN03: Okay. Then, you know, he needs to be called to task because God told him to say that. . . . That's exactly right and the promise was immediately and if God instilled in him to say that, that's exactly what he meant. Now, God does not take his word back. Now, there is some confusion and that's fine, but . . . God does not take his word back. . . . How can David expect to spread God's word if he does not live by the promise instilled in him by God? (Tape 22: 11–13)

Furthermore, at the end of history, God mandates completely new rules, new laws, and a new system. Those who want to avoid death must study the Bible to discern God's plan and to follow that plan to the letter. They must live by the laws of the coming kingdom, not the laws of the dying order, no matter how irrational the new laws seem and no matter how great the personal risk incurred by following God.

PN03: If he dies, if he dies within the place, you know . . . everything that everybody worked for will be for nothing. We can't let that happen.

STEVE TO DAVID KORESH: They're concerned that you might die and everything that has been worked for will come to nothing.

STEVE: And he's saying the word of God never dies. This is why Paul in the book of Hebrew—

PN03: That's right. And if it doesn't die—you know, his word was that he would come out immediately and lead his people out. He has not done that. . . .

STEVE: PN03, can he explain—give you an explanation for that?

PN03: I, I don't need an explanation. What I need is for him to live up to that. . . .

STEVE: After 6,000 years of human history, do you think we're somewhere near the end of time or do you think that this world will go on indefinitely?

PN03: That is not for us to know because that is for . . . that is for God to know.

STEVE: God—that's why he gave you and I a book, [PN03], so that you might know ahead of time those things which he's going to bring upon this world, that you might miss out on the catastrophes. (Tape 22: 11–14)

The Branch Davidians believed God wanted to save His chosen people from catastrophe and death, but that did not mean they expected Him to follow our human sense of compassion. They did not even expect Him to live up to the mainstream Christian concept of a loving God.

> PN01: But listen, there's another issue, okay? . . . And that is that you and I both know God is a loving and caring being, right?
>
> SCOTT [SONOBE]: Oh, yeah.
>
> PN01: Here you are suffering and you need medical attention [Scott was wounded on February 28]. . . . Okay. God would support you to go out. David supports you to go out. You know what I mean? That is the only message that could come from a *real* God, right? (Tape 19: 24–25, emphasis added)

There it was; the gods had arrived at the table.

The Battle of the Gods

When the worldviewing aspects of their conflict became more obvious, the parties fell into the trap of framing their conflict as the God of the negotiators versus the God of the Branch Davidians. It was the private, personal God of mainstream Christianity versus the biblical God who takes an active part in human political and social affairs.

> STEVE: . . . *He said* his present position is he still promises to [come out] and—but *you have to deal with his God.*
>
> PN03: *Everybody has to deal with God within himself.* Okay? And—
>
> STEVE: Wait, wait, wait. That's—*not according to the Bible, not according to the Bible.* You do it God's way or like in the days of Moses when Coradathian and Nebyrum raised their voices because they didn't like the way Moses was doing it, God opened up the earth, swallowed up these men alive with thousands of others. The earth closed up while they were yet screaming and they were stuck in a position and that's the way they suffocated. *God throughout history has given many examples. When he speaks, he means what he says.* (Tape 22: 10–14, emphasis added)

Of course, the FBI negotiators rarely acknowledged this debate as openly as PN01 did when he pitted the "real" God against the Branch Davidian God. As far as they were concerned, the only people bringing God to the negotiation table were the Branch Davidians, whereas they were just being logical and reasonable. They considered themselves perfectly justified in refusing to listen to biblical language, even though their own instrumental language frame effectively silenced the Branch Davidians, who could explain their actions only in biblical terms.

> PN03: Okay. *I need to know, are you going to live up to your promise? What are you planning to do?*
> DAVID KORESH: Let me explain. *See, in verse 2—*
> PN03: Yes, I know. *Please tell me what you're going to do.*
> DAVID KORESH: *I am trying. Please look at verse 2 of Nahum.*
> PN03: *Let's not talk in those terms, please.*
> DAVID KORESH: No. Then you don't understand my doctrine. You don't want to hear the word of my God.
> PN03: I have listened to you and listened to you, and I believe in what you say. . . . For God's sake, you know, give me an answer, David. I need to have an answer. Are you going to come out? (Tape 21: 29–30, emphasis added)

"You don't want to hear the word of my God," and therefore you don't want to hear me. What kind of language was left for the parties in this interaction?

How Do We Negotiate When Gods Are at the Table?

In desperation, the negotiators sought to revive the language of the marketplace. They reactivated their bargaining frame.

> PN03: Okay. Is he going to let any other people out?
> STEVE: He said the only thing he can do right now is wait.
> PN03: Okay. And I can understand that. He wants to wait. . . . But I'm not asking for himself. . . . Does he not want to let any, any other people out? (Tape 22: 33–34)

PN03: If we could have two children every hour or every couple of hours, be-lieve me, it would go a long ways towards if we wound up in some kind of a situ-ation where then we need to give you something, you know, to you, as we did before. That is, in making all the arrangements that we did in trying to get his message out, you know, we were very hopeful and it took a lot, you know, for us to make all of those arrangements. (Tape 22: 49)

The parties were right back where they started. Or were they?

After the March 2 exit plans fell apart, the negotiators faced people inside Mount Carmel who were actively redefining the conflict. Suddenly, everyone the negotiators spoke with was talking about how the FBI abused their power and violated the rights of the Branch Davidians by severing their contact with the outside world and placing "chariots with flaming torches" on their property.

STEVE: . . . Just take a little time and see how that cannot be the greatest nation that God has ever risen up, the United States of America with the sepa-ration of church and state and the great Constitution allowing for our freedoms which are quickly being eroded. You know that because of the very agency you're in. Even though there's a higher bureaucracy over yourselves, you see yourself in a very decent job and so forth, and you probably are, in your sincer-ity, a very decent person, but the truth of the matter is all— (Tape 22: 8–9)

RACHEL: . . . And he [Koresh] would like for the whole world to be saved.

PN03: Well, see, and I think a lot, and I think a lot of—millions of people lis-tened to his, to his word and we facilitated that. We helped him to get that mes-sage out, and part—

RACHEL: Um-hum, and then you cut us off. We couldn't even talk to the media.

PN03: Wait a second. We made all of that available to him, you know. I made that available for him.

RACHEL: Yeah, but I'm saying . . . we were calling them on the phone. They were calling us on the phone before. (Tape 23: 21–22)

DAVID: . . . this is the United States of America, and we may be just chalked up as one more cult group. . . . But there are seven seals and as long as you do not permit me to show you. . . . You're trying to understand why our actions have been so dramatic in regards to your systematic, bureaucratic system of government. . . . We have gone against you. The big guy, the little guy's come up and pushed at you. We told you, you're not going to come here and push your little ATF butt around. We are Americans too. . . . We have bothered no one. We will serve and believe God. (Tape 26: 12–14)

This nascent rights-based substantive framing of the conflict was coming from multiple sources inside the Mount Carmel community. Thus, it did not seem to be the product of a single person's beliefs. It was also mixed in with many other narrative explanations for the decision not to leave Mount Carmel and thus was easily overlooked. Nevertheless, it was a critical turning point in the negotiations because it reinforced the conceptual groundwork for the Branch Davidians' citizen-to-government process frame.

Where did this story come from, and why did it become a powerful basis for Branch Davidian resistance to the FBI negotiators' bargaining process? The themes of government tyranny, oppression, and persecution were already present in the community before February 28. The Branch Davidians knew that God's chosen remnant would be persecuted and hounded by a nation that spoke as a lamb but acted as dragon. The symbolic themes had been laid. All that was needed to make the connection to their present situation was evidence that the United States was the nation spoken of in prophecies, that the Branch Davidians were the chosen remnant, and that the government's behavior was oppressive, tyrannical, and persecutory. The community already believed they were God's chosen people. Like many gun rights advocates, they saw the ATF as an oppressive agency. The question was whether the FBI was also a tool of the evil system arrayed against God's faithful. Or could the Branch Davidians trust the FBI and the federal courts? Apparently the case *against* the United States and the FBI had gained authority and credibility among the Branch Davidians while Koresh prepared the tape for national broadcast.

How did this happen? Without recorded evidence of the internal dynamics of the Branch Davidian community during the siege, we cannot answer this question with certainty. Given the evidence from the negotiation tapes, testimony of survivors and observers regarding the Mount Carmel community Bible study practices, and an awareness of processes of symbolic convergence in isolated communities, we can offer a reasonable speculative explanation for the Branch Davidians' newfound clarity of vision after March 2.

We know from the transcripts that Koresh did not withdraw into a private room to prepare the recording for national broadcast. We know from Branch Davidian Thibodeau (Thibodeau and Whiteson 1999) as well as from the transcripts that Koresh continued to teach the community during the siege. Every member of the community was privy to his message and listened avidly as it was prepared. Just as President Bush garnered public support when he hit on the terrorist narrative to describe Saddam Hussein, so Koresh found a theme around which the Branch Davidians could organize a response to their current predicament. That theme caught hold and became a point of symbolic convergence around which the community members began to develop a coherent substantive frame and related process frames.

> DAVID: . . . *there's one little group, one little remnant, and all they do is talk about Seven Seals*, which is the knowledge of the authority of the heavens, you know. . . . And it says that the heathen will regard and they'll wonder. They won't know what's going on. The prophets say the heathen will not understand. Daniel foretold the same event in the latter days. Daniel says, and there's a small remnant. Daniel says, *the wicked will be doing wickedly and none of the wicked will understand* but the righteous, they shall understand. (Tape 27: 45, emphasis added)

Then came the crisis. God spoke to Koresh and the community obeyed, but the negotiators rejected God's message and did not understand. By debating the Branch Davidians' theology after the collapse of the March 2 agreement, the negotiators demonstrated to the Davidians their own ignorance of God's truth. By questioning Koresh's integrity and the authenticity of his vision, they demonstrated their refusal to fear the one true God. By pressuring the Branch Davidians to act according to the goal-rational orientation of the world, they demonstrated their lack of respect for a people of faith. When the tactical units responded to the situation by moving the perimeter onto Mount Carmel property, destroying outbuildings, and running their "tanks" over the Branch Davidians' vehicles, the Mount Carmel residents knew for certain they were in the presence of "the beast." When the FBI commanders began insulting Koresh and the others during press conferences, the Branch Davidians recognized the voice of Babylon. Once they were isolated by the negotiators' decision to sever their phone lines, this fantasy theme became a self-reinforcing narrative in the Mount Carmel community. The one outside source of information they trusted, Ron Engelman's radio broadcasts, only served to validate their negative image of the FBI and other federal agents.

Trying to Bridge the Worldview Gap

As their worldnaming narrative gained clarity, the Branch Davidians were better able to delineate their aspirations. For example, they were more articulate about their desire to see the ATF agents held accountable for their part in the February 28 raid. They had not yet settled on a radically separatist process proposal, but they began testing their citizen-to-government negotiation frame, which was clearly an effort to overcome some of the worldviewing differences that separated them from the FBI.

From the Branch Davidian perspective, however, using this process approach was a great risk because it was predicated on the belief that the United States was not "the beast" or "Babylon." Therefore, the effort at a rapprochement contained in the citizen-to-government negotiation frame was very fragile. As discussed in chapter 7, the negotiators responded positively in their attempt to nurture the constitutional rights theme in the Branch Davidian narrative. Unfortunately, they undermined their own efforts to meet the Branch Davidians halfway by appropriating the constitutional language but rejecting the rest of the Branch Davidians' process proposals. They also undercut these positive, face-building efforts by interspersing them with the types of face-attacking debates just described.

In addition to the constitutional rights-framing efforts, the two parties made several other attempts to establish conceptual or worldviewing connections, which are worth noting because they illustrate the benefits and dangers associated with such activities.

First, some FBI negotiators tried to use biblical concepts to construct persuasive arguments for the Branch Davidians to exit Mount Carmel.

PN03: Now, everybody is still thinking that *he is going to lead his people out just like Moses did and just like David slew the giant. They feel that he needs to slay fear, that he is just afraid.* That's what the thinking is. . . . *We need for him to take on the giant.* He needs to lead the people out of the compound. . . . [T]he people need to know that he is not hiding. If he is going to die [of his wounds], so be it, but he need not die isolated because it's important. He gave his word. He needs to come out.

RACHEL: Well, like you said . . . *if you're comparing him to Moses leading the children of Israel out and God directed Moses, right? Well, then we relay the message to you that God told him to wait,* the same God that revealed to him the seven seals, so that was our message to you. *So you're trying to tell me something different than what God is leading him to do.* (Tape 21:2–4, emphasis added)

In a similar fashion, Koresh tried to use terms the negotiators would understand by comparing his own position with theirs. The negotiators had "bosses" to whom they had to answer, but Koresh also had a "boss," and his boss had given him an important job to teach the negotiators God's law so they could make a choice about their eternal lives.

DAVID: I still have full intentions of doing what I said, but the thing of it is, you got to remember, *I have a headquarters too.* . . . The case is, is that as long as I am able to, I am to remain, and God has strengthened me, my pulse and everything went up, and *God has strengthened me for this one last thing, for one last opportunity, and that is for you and all of the agents and all of these individuals who are risking their, not just their carnal lives, but the lives hereafter.* (Tape 26: 6, emphasis added)

Most important, Koresh was to wait for further instructions from his boss. He understood the negotiators' anxiety and tried to reassure them, but was clear about his obedience to headquarters.

DAVID: Well, as soon as I get the message from the headquarters I'll be out.
PN03: I hope the message of the headquarters comes—
DAVID: Soon.
PN03: Now.

DAVID: Well, it's not now. Okey-doke?

PN03: It could be now though, right? I mean if, if it comes now, you're not going to wait?

DAVID: Well, yeah, if it came now I would not wait.

PN03: Okay.

DAVID: See, I please my Father, okay, that's all I can do. . . . You see, it's his law. He has written a manuscript, and I do not have the power, even in heaven, to go above his word. I am subject to the Father. You read the Hebrews, that when the Father gives all things to Christ, and the son is subject to the Father? . . . I cannot go beyond the commandment of the bounds that God has given me in the fields. . . . I cannot stand above my God and state that I have jurisdiction above his own word. (Tape 36: 2–3)

Why Borrowed Symbolic Language Does Not Always Work

The FBI negotiators' attempts to use biblical imagery and symbols sometimes trapped them in ways they did not anticipate. First, their lack of knowledge about *apocalyptic* theology and biblical interpretation sometimes made them look ignorant. This problem was compounded by the fact that they were trying to use biblical symbols and concepts to effect instrumental goals. When PN03 compared Koresh to Moses in order to argue that he should "lead his people out of Mount Carmel," he was focused on one small part of the story about Moses but ignoring the fact that Moses led his people into the desert in obedience to God's command, where they wandered for *forty years*. The second risk associated with using biblical language was that it led the Branch Davidians to assume the negotiators were really open to conversion. Symbols the negotiators were using to achieve an instrumental goal entangled them in the very theological discussions they were trying so hard to avoid.

On the other hand, Koresh's portrayal of God as his boss led the negotiators to assume that Koresh could "bargain with God." Because the negotiators were debating and negotiating with their own bosses about how best to achieve the instrumental end of concluding this standoff, they assumed Koresh could do the same with God. The repeated explanations from the Mount Carmel residents that God was "not that kind of a boss" went unheeded or were treated as efforts to avoid real negotiation, to stall for time, and to mislead the negotiators about the Branch Davidians' true intentions.

The negotiators were particularly concerned about a potential Jonestown-style suicide at Mount Carmel. After March 2, these fears increased. They kept pressing Koresh and others to tell them how long the wait would be and what would happen at the end of it. When pressured, the Branch Davidians could not or would not tell the negotiators how long God was going to have them wait, and they could not or would not indicate what was going to happen at the end of the waiting period. From within their own worldmaking narrative, the Branch Davidians *could not* answer these questions for the FBI because the answers would be revealed when the time was right. The FBI negotiators, with their belief in human autonomy and instrumental action, assumed that Koresh and the others simply *would not* share this information.

"You Are More Deluded Than We Thought!"

More than the failure to end the siege on March 2, the parties' subsequent apologia and blaming narratives, their debates, and even their attempts to bridge their worldview divisions soured the relationship between them. Seeking a *logical* explanation for Koresh's erratic cooperation with the negotiation process, the FBI negotiators were inclined to think he was faking his revelation for his own purposes. On the other hand, the notion that the FBI was a tool of Babylon was gaining strength at Mount Carmel.

Much has been made of the Branch Davidian theological interpretation of the FBI and the United States as Babylon.

> In Koresh's theology, the government, particularly the federal law enforcement agencies, were the "Assyrians" or the "Babylonians" who were bent on destroying the true believers—the Branch Davidians. Koresh had predicted to his followers well before the February 28 ATF raid that law enforcement agents planned to kill him and his followers. Koresh planned for the predicted apocalyptic showdown with the government by massively arming himself and his followers beginning in early 1992 and continuing through early 1993. (Justice 208–9)

Negotiators who were at Waco speak in pained and puzzled tones when they describe the way Koresh classified them as "Babylonians" or "Assyrians." They truly do not understand why the Branch Davidians thought so badly of them when they were only trying to end a dangerous situation without further bloodshed. The FBI personnel with whom I have spoken have not yet recognized that this negative description of the United States and the FBI was not set in stone. Rather, the FBI *became* the Assyrians and the United States *became* Babylon during the course of the negotiations in Waco; furthermore, the period just subsequent to March 2 was critical to this development.

When negotiations started, relationships were relatively cordial, considering the violence of the initial raid and gun battle. Koresh made it clear that "God always gives two ways out," and the Branch Davidians were willing to find a peaceful solution as long as it could be done in keeping with God's truth. But the actions of the FBI, including their coercive and worldview-insensitive negotiation efforts, led the Branch Davidians to conclude they were indeed dealing with "the beast" of the Book of Revelation.

Even then, the Branch Davidians remained deeply concerned about saving those agents with whom they were negotiating. All of the individual agents were seen as victims of the system in which they were embroiled. The Branch Davidians did not consider them evil people, just ignorant and in need of conversion. If this paternalistic attitude offends the FBI negotiators, they should keep in mind that it was identical to their own belief that the Branch Davidians needed to be saved from Koresh or from themselves.

If at First You Fail, Just Do More of the Same,
But Do It More Forcefully

I recently received a joke over the Internet. "Ancient wisdom says that when you discover you are riding a dead horse, the best strategy is to dismount. Organizations, however, often try many other strategies." Among the listed strategies: "Buy a stronger whip. Fall back on the declaration, 'This is the way we've always ridden.' Harness several dead horses together to increase speed." In other words, when embarked on a course of action that is not working, organizations frequently assume they just need to do more of the same, but do it better or louder or more forcefully.

The FBI negotiators did not step back after March 2 and ask whether there was a problem with their bargaining framework. They simply decided it had not worked because their bargaining partners were acting in bad faith or did not understand the process. The Branch Davidians needed to be persuaded that bargaining was effective. Consequently, the FBI negotiators continued to turn every problem into an opportunity to "get something" from the Branch Davidians. To be fair, there is a great deal of evidence that the commanders were pushing the bargaining model of negotiation. The negotiators have told me they would have liked to try granting some unilateral concessions in order to build trust. However, even with unilateral concessions included, the model was still one of dealing and bargaining. The negotiators have not yet recognized the importance of demands based on moral claims (chapter 6), the difficulties associated with negotiating across worldview differences, or the role of negotiating reality in relation to issue-specific negotiation.

As demonstrated in the following examples, the Mount Carmel residents often deemed the negotiators' efforts at bargaining morally offensive.

Peter Gent/Michael Schroeder. On March 5, the Branch Davidians located the body of Peter Gent, who had been killed outside the main building on February 28. At about the same time, the FBI finally admitted that Michael Schroeder had been killed on February 28 in a firefight on the property but away from the main house. In the initial cease-fire agreement, the Branch Davidians and law enforcement negotiators had agreed that the dead and wounded would be taken away for proper burial or treatment. The wounded Branch Davidians had refused treatment, but the community now wanted the FBI to take Gent's body to his parents, who had arrived in Waco from their home in Australia. The FBI refused to grant this request unless they received something in return. Specifically, they wanted Kathy Schroeder (Michael's wife) or some other adult to accompany the body. Kathy refused to participate in this exchange and was deeply offended by the suggestion, as were the rest of the Branch Davidians, who concluded that, for the FBI, the cease-fire agreement to treat the dead with respect and dignity applied only to dead ATF agents.

Milk and telephones. At their press conferences and on the phone, the FBI professed concern about the well-being of the children at Mount Carmel. The community was running out of milk and asked that some be sent in. They had also indicated very early in the negotiations that they were having difficulty with their telephone equipment. In order to make a wire long enough to bring a phone to the wounded Koresh, the Branch Davidians had strung together a bunch of small phone cords. Early in the negotiations Koresh sent one thousand dollars in cash out with one of the children. He asked that some of that money be used to buy a telephone and about 150 feet of phone cord. Later he requested some of the money be used to buy milk. Probably because they assumed the situation would be resolved in relatively short order, the FBI did nothing about the telephone and cord. When they did start to work on the problem, they wanted to haggle over what it would "cost" the Branch Davidians. On the milk issue, the FBI tried to exchange the milk for children, which made no sense to the Branch Davidians because the milk was for the children. The Branch Davidians were offended by the commodification of what they considered reasonable requests.

The FBI negotiators adopt themes for persuasive action. On March 5, the FBI negotiators summarized their persuasive strategies using five themes. Each theme was highly problematic because it was either based on a misunderstanding of the Branch Davidian worldview and community dynamics or, when implemented in a coercive bargaining framework, resulted in actions the Branch Davidians found morally offensive. A few brief examples of these themes demonstrate why each strategy helped ensure that negotiations would not succeed in Waco.

> • Appeal to the parents inside to join their released children by sending photographs and videotapes of the children into the compound, passing messages from the children to their parents and vice versa, and demonstrating that the children needed the parents, missed them, and awaited their reunion. (Justice 129)

The original agreement regarding the children was that they would be sent to live with extended family members. Instead, the children were placed as a group under the care of Texas Child Protective Services. Furthermore, the FBI negotiators *initiated* the sending of photos and videos of the children into Mount Carmel so that the parents would realize their children needed them. They then treated the photos as a "concession" and asked the Branch Davidians for something in return.

KATHY: We even asked for milk for our babies and you didn't bring it. . . . You brought something we didn't ask for. You brought something to pull on my heartstrings, you showed me my kids pictures,—

PN04: Now hold it. We brought that at the request of . . . Now, listen. I want to addressed that issue because what you're doing is telling me that I'm a liar, and I'm not a liar.

KATHY: Yes, I am telling you that because no, we did not ask for the video . . .

PN04: No, you didn't ask specifically. What you said was that you were concerned that the kids were being farmed out . . . to foster homes.

KATHY: Okay.

PN04: We wanted to indicate to you that that was not being done and that the kids are together.

KATHY: Okay, but we specifically asked for the six gallons of milk, didn't we? (Tape 66: 28)

The negotiators argued that it was not their decision to place the children with social workers rather than with their relatives. That decision was made by other experts, who thought the children should be kept together. This claim may have been an honest statement of the negotiators' preferences with regard to the children, but their instrumental use of the children to lure their parents out of Mount Carmel made the Branch Davidians suspect otherwise. Media reports that the children had been examined by psychologists who concluded the children were abnormal and the Branch Davidians' fears that their children were being subjected to deprogramming effectively convinced the other parents to keep their children safely inside Mount Carmel.

- Continue to reassure those inside the compound that they would not be harmed and would be treated fairly if they came out. (Justice 129)

The Branch Davidians found it difficult to believe that "the system" would treat them fairly if they came out when that same system was abusing them in their own home. Military vehicles in their yard were destroying their property even though the original agreement with the FBI prohibited this activity. They were cut off from the public in violation of their rights and had to listen while they were publicly abused and maligned in the media. Furthermore, there were no witnesses should the FBI decide to assault the community, destroy evidence, and kill the Branch Davidians.

> RACHEL: Well I notice they feel pretty bold in bringing their tanks onto our property. . . . When the agreement was made that, you know, nobody would come on to the perimeter. . . . And it's just not being upheld. . . . I mean they were right here practically in our back yard. (Tape 39: 11)

> STEVE: But you guys have got it your one way right now, because of course, we can't speak to the press but—I don't know if we can or can't yet. . . . I mean, you know, you guys, of course, I don't—what are you trying to hide, you know. What are you got planned, what are you up to? What are you gonna do? What have you done to people in the past? That's why I raised those questions with you about your agency earlier. I've heard—anything I've ever heard about that agency, it's not been too good. (Tape 41: 40)

• Use the twice daily press conferences to accentuate the positive reasons for the individuals to come out, to demonstrate concern for their safety, to clarify press distortions or inaccurate speculation about persons inside the compound, and to use psychology to get the Davidians to doubt Koresh's leadership. (Justice 129)

This persuasive strategy was rendered ineffective because it was internally inconsistent, it was misused, and it violated the Branch Davidians' sense of justice. Any attempt to get the community to doubt Koresh's leadership involved implicitly or explicitly ridiculing and denigrating him. Because the Branch Davidians were a community organized around Koresh's prophetic leadership, attacking Koresh amounted to attacking the community members' fundamental beliefs and moral commitments. Because the Branch Davidians derived their identities from their group membership, the FBI was attacking the members themselves. Furthermore, rather than "clarifying press distortions or inaccurate speculation about persons inside the compound," the commanders often perpetuated the cult stereotype and atrocity narratives directed against the Branch Davidians. The level of anger this entire strategy generated was evidenced by Schneider's response to press conferences in which the FBI spokesperson appeared to be mocking Koresh.

STEVE: Well, you mean to tell me these agencies with all the evidences, all the different equipment at hand and everything else, they can't get the facts together before they go on national, international?

PN01: Well, they should.

STEVE: I mean, yeah. Well, that sounds nice, you telling me that they should, but you're in a position where you—you know, I'm cut off. I can't talk to anybody but yourself, so you can sympathize with me and say nice things to me like this, but when it keeps on coming out on the TV and like what was said about David in this conference earlier today, "Well, he's miraculously recovering," and then, of course, all the laughter. If you got to see what you guys did to him—I did. I thought—he thought I thought he would have been dead within hours of that. He was laying on the floor. We dragged him along. He's never moved from that place. . . . And when—you showed concern because you thought like yourself as there may be Gary and Henry that he would die and I tell you the truth, we thought more than likely originally he would.

PN01: I'm glad he's better.

STEVE: Well, yeah, I am too, but, you know, it's the way it was stated even to the press like, you know, it's a, it's a sarcasm to his—you know, the lamb and the seven seals. Only the lamb can open up the seven seals. And then he's never claimed to be Jesus Christ. He never said he was.

PN01: I agree. He's never said that. . . .

STEVE: But it's these kind of sarcastic comments, the way they're, you know, put out. . . . to tell you the truth, I'm really teed off. I hate to see how this country of America has digressed and your type of agencies are one of the biggest causes for it. . . . Read the writings on the statements of people like Abraham Lincoln or Jefferson or Madison, the great principles laid down, so things that are happening now that—which you are more a part of than anybody, would never take place. Like I can't talk to the outside world. You've taken care of that, your kind of people. . . . The press are so far back that you guys could come and blow us away and they wouldn't—and you could write—give any kind of a story you wanted. (Tape 40: 24–28)

- Negotiate with Steve Schneider in order to "drive a wedge" between Koresh and . . . his second-in-command. The negotiators constantly urged Schneider to take charge and to bring the people out. (Justice 129)

Once again, the FBI negotiators were simply not listening to the Branch Davidians' worldmaking narratives. It was obvious from their conversations that Koresh's leadership was grounded in his unique access to special knowledge. As long as the community valued that knowledge and as long as no one else in the community was seen as privy to God's plan for the world, no alternate leader would step forward. The negotiators received this message from every single person they tried to entice into assuming leadership. For example:

> PN03: Okay. Okay. If something were to happen to him, that is if his health were to fail him, you know, and you and I spoke about this before, I would like to feel that you can take a position of leadership within the, within the compound.
> RACHEL: Why is that?
> PN03: Because we need for everybody to follow the lead—
> RACHEL: Follow a person? You mean, follow, follow me and I, I don't—I wouldn't know, you know. I don't have communication with God. I don't . . . You know, people do what they feel would be right to do. (Tape 23: 23)

The FBI negotiators refused to listen to the Branch Davidians' explanation of Koresh's leadership. Instead, they concluded that no one inside Mount Carmel was *capable* of assuming leadership because all of the Branch Davidians were under Koresh's control and suffering from low self-esteem. Once the FBI negotiators reached that conclusion, it was only one short step to deciding that the Branch Davidians needed to be saved from Koresh and from themselves. Forcing them out of Mount Carmel for their own good looked more and more justified.

- Entice Koresh to come out by discussing and implying weaknesses in the prosecution of Koresh, and pointing out to Koresh the opportunity to expand his following and promote his views through book and movie deals. (Justice 129)

I have already explained why this strategy was flawed and won't repeat the argument here.

The Branch Davidians decide to preach. The FBI was not alone in continuing an ineffective negotiation strategy. The Branch Davidians kept negotiating reality, preaching, and attempting to convert the negotiators in spite of ample evidence that such activities were ineffective and counterproductive to resolving the situation at hand. Of course, the Branch Davidians were never convinced that resolving the situation at hand was the primary purpose for the negotiations. They were more focused on God's End Time drama.

It Was All Over but the Shouting

As the Branch Davidians used more biblical language and resisted the persuasive and bargaining strategies that they deemed morally offensive, the FBI concluded the Branch Davidians were more deluded than they had originally thought. As the FBI responded with harsher measures, the Branch Davidians concluded that the United States was more evil than they had originally thought. They started using more radically separatist rhetoric, building on the state-to-state negotiation frame in order to create space for talking about their rights and about their conviction that the United States was acting under a system of evil laws. The FBI negotiators found no theme in the state-to-state negotiation frame that allowed them to advance the objective of ending the standoff. The parties were driven farther and farther apart by their inability to, first, adequately comprehend the worldview of the other and, second, create conceptual linkages with which to craft a mutually satisfactory resolution to their immediate crisis. Once their cycle of miscommunication was in place and neither party was willing to opt out of it, the fiery conclusion of the standoff on April 19 was all but inevitable. After March 15, only outside intervention or a major shift in worldviewing assumptions and related process frames by one party or the other might have prevented the tragic outcome in Waco.

Working with Worldview Conflicts

Lessons from Waco

WORKING FOR ALMOST TWO YEARS with the Waco negotiation tran-scripts was the emotional equivalent of watching a massive train wreck in v-e-r-y s-l-o-w m-o-t-i-o-n. Reading and rereading the transcripts, I had the opportunity to become acquainted with almost all of the occupants of the "Mount Carmel car" and the "negotiators' car" of a train I knew was doomed. As I became engaged with those on board—listening to their deepest hopes and fears, laughing at their jokes, and sympathizing with their frustrations—it was very difficult to remember that most of the people who seem so vibrant, compelling, and alive in the transcripts died in 1993. The tragedy of Waco can-not be undone. No one can bring back the ATF agents or the Branch Davidi-ans who died on February 28, 1993. No one can bring back the Branch Davidians who perished on April 19. Nor can anyone erase the trauma experi-enced by the survivors.

I count among the survivors people from both sides of the barricade, for in my examination of the *negotiation* process leading up to the Waco train wreck, I found no villains, no mechanical failure, and no single glaring error of judg-ment. I did find flawed organizational structures, which have since been re-paired.[1] I also found something much more difficult to document and much

---

1. In 1993, the HRT and negotiation team from Waco did not have an overarching command structure. On-scene commanders were selected from the nearest FBI field office whenever the units were deployed. I also have a sense from talking with agents that the cross-training that was supposed to be taking place with the HRT and the negotiators had been somewhat neglected

more difficult to "fix." I discovered a worldmaking narrative that is blind to the existence of worldviewing. This particular worldmaking narrative dominates our culture, and it is the cornerstone of an intolerant, judgmental approach to any group that refuses to name the world in keeping with mainstream values, ontological commitments, and categories. During the Waco standoff, the media and some FBI commanders actively nurtured this worldview-insensitive narrative and succeeded in drowning out voices of tolerance and reason with atrocity tales about a crazed "cult leader" and his "brainwashed" followers.

Even those negotiators and behavioral scientists who advocated greater tactical restraint and more respectful interactions with the Branch Davidians were significantly impacted by this worldview that does not recognize world-viewing. By April 19, the FBI decision to *force* the Branch Davidians out of Mount Carmel was supported by members of the negotiation team, much of the general public, the commanders and tactical team leaders on the ground in Waco, and Department of Justice and FBI personnel in Washington.

In the subsequent round of investigations, hearings, and court trials related to Waco, it is easy to forget that the initial response to the April 19 raid was *not* negative. The evening news on April 19, 1993, included "man on the street in-terviews" that were largely supportive of the FBI decision to force the Branch Davidians to leave Mount Carmel. One news clip even showed patrons in a bar cheering as Mount Carmel went up in flames. The public correspondence on file in the public reading room at FBI headquarters in Washington, D.C., also af-firms that the initial public response to the April 19 action was congratulatory.

It was only after passions died down and the full horror of the casualties be-came apparent that mainstream public sentiment changed. Then the FBI crisis management team was taken to task for its decisions and practices. When ex-amining the FBI *negotiators'* actions in Waco, this judgment seems unfair. The

---

under the growing list of mandates given to each team. They were under pressure to train and keep abreast of new developments, teach their techniques to other police officers from around the world, conduct research, and be prepared to go into action as needed. After Waco, the unit was reorganized, and a permanent commander was appointed to oversee both the HRT and the nego-tiation units. Greater emphasis is now being placed on making sure the units act in a coordinated manner. Their first major field test after Waco was the Freemen standoff in Montana, and the new command structure appeared to work well.

practices used by the negotiators were, in large measure, a reflection of the cultural milieu in which they were working. They did not invent the worldview-insensitive worldmaking narrative that shaped their thinking about negotiation practice. They merely tried to apply commonly used and heretofore largely successful negotiation practices to the problem of resolving an armed standoff between federal law enforcement agents and a millennialist religious community.

At the heart of the FBI's negotiation practices, we find an obsession with control that is reflected in the negotiators' desire to diagnose correctly the barricaded subject while structuring the negotiation encounter as a goal-rational decision-making process. In 1993, crisis negotiation practice included no recognition that "rhetoric and narrativity constitute an alternative way of knowing with different conceptions of rationality" (O'Leary 1994, 25). Therefore, the crisis negotiators in Waco were blind to their own worldmaking narratives as well as to those used by the barricaded subjects.

Many of the same biases toward control of process, goal-rational decision making, and instrumental rather than narrative language that dominate crisis negotiation are also found in other areas of conflict resolution practice. Those of us who practice in arenas other than barricade standoffs are usually more subtle than the FBI negotiators in our exclusion of "unacceptable language" or "irrelevant issues," but we do make similar judgments about including or excluding specific worldviews—often, in my opinion, to the detriment of the long-term goals of conflict resolution, reconciliation, and peace building. Our mistakes are not measured in lives lost, and no one records our every word, so we do not have to deal with Monday morning quarterback academics peering over our shoulders and telling us what we did wrong.

All of which is to say that I sympathize with any resistance to "learning lessons from Waco" that the FBI negotiators may feel, particularly when the person articulating the lessons is an outsider. However, the lessons of Waco must be learned. Anyone who has done even a cursory survey of the separatist movements and identity groups taking shape in this country knows there will be other Wacos (Aho 1990; Barkun 1994b). Anyone who knows the history of apocalyptic beliefs and has studied the increase of millennialist fervor in this country recognizes the same problem (Barkun 1993; Boyer 1992; Chandler

1993; Hall 1995; O'Leary 1994; Wessinger 2000a, 2000b). It is with these realities in mind that I offer the following practical lessons from Waco.

Rethinking the Analysis of Barricade Standoffs

Lesson One: Identify a New Category of Barricaded Subjects

Crisis negotiators confronted with barricaded belief communities such as the Branch Davidians must revisit their basic assumptions about the actors who become involved in barricade situations. Not all barricaded subjects can be convinced to participate in problem-solving and bargaining activities that are framed within the dominant social understanding of what constitutes rationality. For barricaded belief communities, value-rational commitments are likely to take precedence over peacefully resolving a potentially deadly standoff. Such actors may engage in bargaining and problem-solving activities, but only insofar as those activities allow them to reach agreements that do not include sacrificing, denying, or betraying their ultimate concern.

The good news is that we know crisis negotiators are capable of and willing to expand their understanding of distinct types of barricaded subjects. The not so good news is that adding barricaded belief communities to the existing typology of barricaded subjects will be more complicated than were previous additions. Adding disturbed subjects involved in pseudo-hostage situations was relatively easy in comparison.

Barricaded communities, by their very existence, pose a threat to the *identities* of law enforcement agents. Unconventional political or religious groups that refuse to recognize the legitimacy of the state are denying the state's status as a "compulsory association with a territorial basis" that holds the right to "monopolize the use of force" within its territorial jurisdiction (Weber 1964, 156). Law enforcement agencies are the coercive arm of the state. In order to function in their jobs, law enforcement agents must *assume* the legitimacy of the state, and they must believe in their right to wield force on behalf of the state. Facing barricaded subjects who do not grant that legitimacy compels law enforcement agents to acknowledge the fragility of the "negotiated order" that grants them role legitimacy, which threatens the identities of law enforcement agents at a deeply personal level. It also requires a high level of self-reflection while one is engaged in doing dangerous and difficult work.

Even if police negotiators are able to cope with the identity threats created by barricaded belief communities, they still need to develop effective practices for dealing with such groups. Again, this task is not going to be easy. To the extent that they persist in withholding legitimacy from the state, unconventional groups will have difficulty negotiating with the police who are acting to enforce the laws of the state. One does not negotiate with illegitimate opponents. This truism, which has stalled peace negotiations in the Middle East, Northern Ireland, and elsewhere for decades, is equally relevant in domestic U.S. conflicts involving unconventional groups.

*Lesson Two: Understand That Worldview Is Not
Another Word for Ideology*

Faced with barricaded subjects that deny the legitimacy of law enforcement officials, police negotiators must pay attention to the internal logic—the worldview—of these actors. Only then will they be able to understand and predict the barricaded group's likely response to their own actions. Consequently, crisis negotiators will need to revisit their conclusion that ideological commitments have little or no impact on a barricaded subject's willingness to engage in goal-rational negotiations.

Based on their experience negotiating with terrorist hostage takers, FBI negotiators have concluded that ideology does not matter when dealing with barricaded subjects (Fuselier and Noesner 1990). When I say "worldviews matter," many of the FBI negotiators with the greatest experience dealing with terrorist situations think I am unnecessarily reopening the closed issue of ideology. However, the logic of my argument regarding worldviewing differs significantly from the problem (or nonproblem) of ideology as defined by the FBI negotiators. According to crisis negotiators, the ideology of a terrorist hostage taker matters only if it causes his or her behavior to *differ* from that of other people who take hostages. Because their experience shows that terrorist hostage takers are usually willing to engage in goal-rational bargaining, these negotiators have concluded that ideology or religion is not important. I agree that most terrorist hostage takers—whether using religious or political language to justify their actions—are goal rational in their orientation. However, not all barricaded subjects who use religious or political language are goal-rational hostage takers.

The Branch Davidians held no hostages and made very few demands. In fact, the Branch Davidians very deliberately did not take a hostage even when the opportunity presented itself. Undercover ATF agent Robert Rodriguez visited Mount Carmel on the morning of the raid, and while he was there, Koresh was called out of the room and informed that the ATF was on its way. Although the Branch Davidians could have taken Rodriguez hostage and used him as a shield against an ATF assault, they did not. Instead, they sent him out with a message they hoped would prevent the raid.

Furthermore, the Davidians' demands arose out of the violent encounter in which they were embroiled, not out of some goal-oriented plan to bring their message to the world or to force the government to make concessions. For example, it is probably accurate to say the Branch Davidians "demanded" that ATF personnel involved in the February 28 confrontation be held accountable for their actions. They did not, however, initiate their confrontation with federal authorities in order to force the government to release prisoners, change its policies, or acknowledge the legitimacy of Branch Davidian beliefs.

Terrorist hostage takers who speak the language of religion have clear objectives in mind when they confront government authorities. The Branch Davidians were a millennial group who believed they were under assault by worldly forces determined to prevent them from living in accordance with God's plan for the End Time. To distinguish between actors using similar language with very different intentions, it is helpful to recognize that worldview and ideology are not interchangeable concepts. The verbal noun *worldviewing* helps make this distinction clear. Worldviewing is a largely unconscious universal human activity; worldviewing matters precisely because *everybody*—including every crisis negotiator—does it.

Conflicts are no less shaped by symbolic activities than are any other human endeavor. Consequently, each party comes to a crisis negotiation process with expectations regarding the appropriate methods for managing, resolving, or transforming the situation. When worldviewing differences confound standard crisis negotiation procedures, the problem does not rest with the "deviant worldview" of the barricaded subjects. Rather, it can be traced to mismatches in the worldviewing expectations of the barricaded subjects and the crisis negotiators. Because worldviewing is a largely unconscious process, the nature and extent of those mismatches will become apparent only during the negotiation process. That means any script brought to bear on such a confrontation must necessarily be tentative and subject to improvisation during the confrontation. As part of the improvisational work required by a confrontation with a barricaded belief community, crisis negotiators must develop an ability to reflect on their own worldviewing activities.

Lesson Three: Provide Symmetrical Attention
to Worldviewing

Scholars who want to study worldview conflicts must use a symmetrical anthropology (chapter 3). Likewise, practitioners who want to resolve, to manage, or to transform worldview conflicts should begin with a symmetrical approach to practice.[2] All conflict resolution practitioners, including crisis negotiators, should begin with the recognition that their own actions are also shaped by worldviewing activities. Their worldviews are reflected in their practice decisions—i.e., how they go about doing their work and framing the processes they apply to a conflict. Conflict resolution practitioners working with parties who have not managed their worldview differences will need to develop new practices for negotiating reality while simultaneously addressing the problem at hand. In the case of law enforcement negotiators, this combination creates a significant cognitive challenge. While acting as the enforcement arm of the established order (i.e., the dominant worldview), they must develop and apply crisis negotiation practices that both respect alternate worldviews and

2. Of all the people who have criticized the FBI actions in Waco, Stone (1993) is the most symmetrical in his approach. He claims, and I agree, that some FBI behavioral scientists and negotiators understood a great deal about the group psychology of the Branch Davidians, but even the most astute FBI agents were inadequately aware of their own group psychology. According to Stone, preventing future Wacos may depend as much on improving the FBI's self-awareness as it does on hiring outside experts who can explain unconventional groups. I would take exception only to the fact that Stone does not adequately recognize the role of *meaning-creating* activities among the negotiators and the barricaded unconventional group. Stone's report on Waco can also be found at http://www.pbs.org/wgbh/pages/frontline/waco/stonerpt.html.

create the space for hostile parties to manage their worldview differences, even as they work to defuse a potentially violent situation.

The only way to overcome the cognitive dissonance created by this situation is to adopt a symmetrical approach to practice that replaces the concept of "technical rationality" with a more provisional approach that Schön (1983) calls "reflection-in-action." Technical rationality assumes that "professional activity consists of instrumental problem solving made rigorous by the application of scientific theory and technique" (Schön 1983, 21). Reflection-in-action recognizes that practitioners do more than merely *apply* technical knowledge to concrete cases. Rather, They employ frames that shape their interpretation of the problem at hand and their selection of possible responses. Through a process of frame analysis, practitioners can recognize "that they actively construct the reality of their practice," which allows them to reflect-in-action (Schön 1983, 311). "When someone reflects-in-action, he becomes a researcher in the practice context. He is not dependent on the categories of established theory and technique, but constructs a new theory of the unique case" (Schön 1983, 68). This approach permits a flexibility and creativity that are missing in a practice dominated by technical approaches to knowledge.

Crisis negotiation, as currently framed, reflects a preference for technical rationality. Crisis negotiators diagnose the situation and apply the interactive techniques most likely to yield compliance from the barricaded subject. The operative concept is gaining control of the situation by correctly matching the negotiators' activities with the barricaded subject's characteristics. As long as the barricaded subjects concede to the police the authority to define the negotiation encounter, the technical rational approach works well. However, when barricaded subjects persist in presenting an alternative framing of the barricade encounter, technical rationality breaks down.

The Branch Davidians never fully accepted their encounter with federal authorities as a typical barricade standoff between criminal suspects and legitimate law enforcement authorities. In fact, they articulated at least two alternative narratives about the standoff, each of which contained a coherent framing of the negotiation encounter. (See figure 9 in chapter 5.) Unconventional religious and political groups operating out of a very different sense of reality are far more likely than typical barricaded subjects to persist in holding onto their own framing of any negotiations with law enforcement authorities. Therefore, crisis negotiators need to reconsider the effectiveness of relying on technical rational approaches to managing barricade confrontations involving unconventional religious and political groups.

Introducing a symmetrical attention to worldviewing into crisis negotiation entails redesigning the established norms and standards of practice. Such changes will emerge over time, but it is possible to direct attention to the types of changes that will need to be considered.

Redesigning the Practice of Crisis Negotiation

Lesson Four: Develop a New Metaphor for Crisis Negotiation

When practitioners construct the reality of their practice, they do so by using metaphors to describe the object or problem at hand. Foresters talk about the forest as a farm, and their practice enacts this metaphorical naming of the forest. Crisis negotiators describe a barricade standoff as a dangerous situation, and they frame their own practice as one of controlling the danger and preventing violence. Control is achieved through manipulating the environment, accurately assessing the psychological state and motivations of the barricaded subject, and managing his or her behavior. These control-oriented practices work remarkably well with barricaded subjects who accept mainstream worldview assumptions, but the alternate motivational imperatives created by unconventional groups render ineffective many such practices associated with crisis negotiation as currently framed and practiced.

People who do not participate in the mainstream worldview respond in unexpected ways to pressure, manipulation, isolation, and proposals for moving their conflict into another forum. Moving armored personnel carriers onto the Mount Carmel property did not lead the Branch Davidians to surrender in order to preserve their lives. Instead, the presence of "tanks" on their property affirmed their belief that in the End Time God's chosen remnant would be challenged by the fire-spitting chariots of an evil, worldly authority. Surrendering to the human judicial system was not an automatically logical option for the Branch Davidians, who believed they would be judged in *God's court* if they surrendered to worldly authorities against God's will.

Police negotiators are inclined to consider such responses irrational or bizarre. However, the Branch Davidians, like other millennial groups, were "intensely involved in interpreting apocalyptic texts in esoteric ways that . . . [were] actually quite systematic" (Rosenfeld 1998, n.p.). Members of millennial groups will not readily concede their systematic—if esoteric—worldmaking narrative during a barricade negotiation. Consequently, a crisis negotiation practice that depends for its success on the ability of the police to exercise worldnaming control unilaterally will not work in such a standoff.

A better metaphor for crisis negotiations involving unconventional communities is "crisis negotiation as adaptive management." Adaptive management is one of several recently popularized concepts used to describe a "process of linking management with monitoring within a research framework" (Noss and Cooperrider 1994, 298).[3] I first encountered the concept of adaptive management when working with natural resource management conflicts, but it can also be applied to other areas of practice. The critical term is *adaptive*. In adaptive ecosystem management, "the 'adaptive' concept underscores that knowledge and societal values are changing ever more rapidly and that management must keep abreast of these changes" by quickly incorporating new knowledge, information, and perspectives into practice (Maser 1994, 334). Applied to crisis negotiation, the term *adaptive management* directs attention to the need for interactive processes that allow the parties to learn from one another, for only when the parties have learned together and cooperatively named the reality of their encounter can they incorporate their shared knowledge into concrete proposals for managing, resolving, or transforming their conflict.

To employ adaptive management, crisis negotiators will need to alter their reliance on diagnostic techniques for evaluating barricaded subjects. The adaptive management of a worldview conflict is a practice based on dialogue rather than on diagnosis. Instead of treating those inside the barricade as objects to be analyzed, controlled, and labeled, crisis negotiators who use an adaptive management approach would treat barricaded people as subjects with whom they must cooperatively create meaning.

Would an adaptive management approach have helped the negotiators in

---

3. Similar concepts have been advanced by those who talk about "reflective management" (Schön 1983) and "learning organizations" (Senge 1990).

Waco? Hindsight is always twenty-twenty, and I do not claim that an adaptive management model would have worked flawlessly in Waco. However, I believe such an approach could have yielded a better outcome in at least three situations described in this book.

The FBI negotiators labeled the Branch Davidians a "cult," complete with manipulative leader and brainwashed members. Had they used an adaptive management model, they would have been more attuned to the fact that the Mount Carmel residents saw themselves otherwise. Therefore, any concrete problem-solving activity that depended on getting the Mount Carmel residents to define themselves, *through their words or through their actions,* as members of a cult was doomed to fail.

The FBI negotiators in Waco attempted to drive a wedge between Koresh and the rest of the Mount Carmel community. An adaptive management model would have helped the negotiators recognize that Koresh's authority rested on his access to a sacred and highly valued knowledge. Therefore, the strategy of driving a wedge between leader and followers required the Mount Carmel residents to abandon the sacred knowledge around which their lives were organized. This effort was tantamount to "deprogramming" or conversion and was destined to fail because it demanded that Mount Carmel residents alter their identities as well as their ontological and epistemological commitments.

The FBI negotiators persisted in trying to bargain for the release of women at Mount Carmel. An adaptive management practice would have alerted them to the fact that this approach was highly offensive to everyone inside Mount Carmel, especially the women, who identified themselves as free, adult moral agents rather than as bargaining chips in some power struggle between Koresh and the FBI. If exiting the property entailed denying their responsibility as moral agents, they would not leave.

Lesson Five: Develop Provisional Typologies of
Unconventional Religious and Political Groups

Even if crisis negotiators concede that worldview is not another name for ideology, they are still likely to resist implementing an adaptive form of crisis management. In the 1970s, they did not relish the prospect of having to approach every terrorist hostage taking as a unique encounter. Today, they do not relish the prospect of approaching every encounter with an unconventional religious or political group as a unique encounter. Fortunately, adaptive management includes the term *management* as well as the term *adaptive*. It is therefore possible to incorporate the judicious use of typologies, conceptual models, and analytic tools into an adaptive crisis negotiation process.

Those analytical models must, however, focus on the *group* rather than on individuals, and they must be models that get at the genuine experience of unconventional groups. Analyzing the psychological and emotional state of each group member does not yield adequate information for negotiating with the group as a whole. Crisis negotiators do recognize that they must understand the organizational structure and dynamics of unconventional groups. However, the organizational models they have used thus far focus almost entirely on the dynamics of power, control, and manipulation that are the alleged hallmarks of unconventional groups. This model is rooted in an anticult perspective and is more a projection of the anticult worldview than a reflection of the real-life experiences of unconventional belief groups. Any model adopted by crisis negotiators must account for the meaning-creating activities of group members as well as for the internal power dynamics of the group, for it is the worldmaking narrative of an unconventional belief group to which members are attracted and through which they then shape their identities.

The good news is that it is possible to develop typologies of unconventional groups that account for their meaning-creating activities as well as for the power and control dynamics within them. Such typologies can be used as heuristic devices to facilitate the crisis negotiators' learning process during a standoff. Rosenfeld, for example, has developed a set of "ideal types" or "simplified models of social activities which [may be] used in interpreting [the actual] human behavior" (Campbell 1981, 175) of unconventional millennialist groups:

> Type one includes relatively few millennial groups that believe they must act as the 'hand of God' to bring about world destruction and renewal through extralegal violence. . . . Type two groups expect to see armies of light and darkness fight a cosmic battle in heaven and earth while they watch and wait. . . . Groups of the third type withdraw from ordinary space and society to establish their own little kingdom that is modeled after their religious interpretation of the millennial kingdom. (Rosenfeld 2000, 349)

Each type of millennial group that Rosenfeld describes here may come into conflict with civil authorities, but under very different circumstances.

Type-one groups engage in militant behavior and are likely to foster terrorist activities that bring them to the attention of law enforcement officials. A contemporary example of a millennial group that turned to terrorism is Aum Shinrikyo, the Japanese group responsible for releasing Sarin gas in the Tokyo subway system. Under the current FBI reorganization, much greater attention is being devoted to antiterrorism work, and there is considerable focus on identifying this type of unconventional belief group. There is a real danger that this antiterrorism focus will lead law enforcement agencies down the path of attempting to identify "the religiously dangerous,"[4] so it is all the more critical that they develop and learn to apply analytical models that do not project images of danger where such dangers do not exist.

Type-two groups tend to be pacifist or nonviolent. Included in this category are many Christian fundamentalists who believe they will be caught up in the "rapture" or "God's rescue of all true Christians from this tortured earth" (Boyer 1992, 299). Boyer argues that this belief has "diluted the impetus to political activism" among fundamentalist Christians (Boyer 1992, 299). However, Rosenfeld points out that the pacifist or acquiescent stance of type-two millennial groups "may change if they receive revelation from God that instructs them to take on a militant defensive or offensive role in endtime events" (1998, n.p.). In the absence of such a revelation, type-two groups are unlikely to end up confronting police negotiators across a barricade as long as law enforcement agents do not initiate a confrontation.

That does *not* mean such groups will eschew all violence, but violence may well be turned inward to the group rather than outward against society. For example, Heaven's Gate can probably be categorized as a type-two group. They lived quiet lives that did not attract the attention of law enforcement officials

---

4. The phrase "the religiously dangerous" was used at the AAR meeting in 1999 and was probably in reference to the FBI report titled *Project Megiddo* (http://www.cesnur.org/testi/FBI_004.htm) or to the FBI effort to poll religious studies scholars about the characteristics of unconventional religious groups. It captures the concerns of religious studies scholars who want to work with law enforcement to prevent future Waco-type tragedies but are worried about how information they offer will be used.

until they received a revelation telling them to commit suicide—or, in their worldview, to abandon their earthly bodies for a higher level of existence. Here, the most likely problem for law enforcement agencies will be coping with their own drive to protect people. If family members approach the police looking for help because they are worried that their relative will participate in some ritual suicide like that of the members of Heaven's Gate, the police may take action that inadvertently triggers precisely the outcome that the family most fears.

Type-three groups may engage in "magical" behavior in order to transform society. Their magical behavior may include unusual gender relationships, family practices, and rituals that are considered suspect, illegal, or immoral. Consequently, type-three groups may find themselves in a confrontation with authorities. In these cases, however, the confrontation may be highly complicated by the ambiguity of the laws the group is alleged to have violated. The laws broken by type-three groups may not involve *overt* criminal activity such as armed robbery or murder.

Indeed, it may not be clear that a type-three group has broken a *law* rather than simply violated cultural norms. For example, in the state of Texas, it is legal for a fourteen-year-old girl to marry with parental permission. The Branch Davidian community had a long history of older men marrying very young women with the blessings of the bride's family. Within that context, the community saw the "new light" marriages of Koresh and girls in their early teens merely as an extension of long-established community practices. Outsiders saw their behavior as sexual abuse of minors, although these same outsiders had not objected when, in their own world, individual older men married quite young women.

Type-three groups are also more likely to see themselves as "under the authority" of an alternative set of laws and consequently are highly protective of their boundaries. Therefore, a critical factor when dealing with a type-three group is recognizing the importance they attach to the boundaries that separate them from a profane world. If law enforcement officials breach the perimeter around the sacred space of a type-three group, the response is very likely to include violent resistance. The difficulty is in understanding where the community boundaries are located and what constitutes a breach of the boundaries.

It is critical to remember that Rosenfeld's ideal types are not discrete categories. Furthermore, millennial groups transform themselves, sometimes very quickly. A group undergoing metamorphosis may exhibit the characteristic behaviors and attitudes of more than one ideal type. What is more important, unconventional religious groups may mutate as a consequence of their interactions with civil authorities.

The ATF treated the Branch Davidians as if they were a type-one or militant millennial group, which appears to have been an overreaction. It is possible, of course, that the Mount Carmel community might have evolved into a type-one group had they been left alone with a growing stockpile of weapons. However, such an evolutionary trajectory was by no means inevitable. The community had been in existence for almost sixty years by the time of the ATF raid. Other than a few internal quarrels, the Branch Davidians had not exhibited tendencies toward violence, and Koresh's teaching seemed to reserve apocalyptic violence for God alone, which has led some scholars to conclude that "the Davidians were armed, but they were not planning to attack members of society outside their community" (Wessinger 2000b, 19). Prior to the ATF raid, the Branch Davidians handled the scrutiny of government agencies nonviolently. However, when heavily armed ATF agents breached their sacred space, they responded with deadly force, which placed them in a more direct confrontational relationship with the federal government. At that point, the problem became one of nudging the Branch Davidians toward a less-resistant posture.

Even after their violent confrontation with the ATF, the Branch Davidians were far more concerned about God's ultimate judgment of their behavior than they were about the judgment of secular courts. Thus, it would seem most logical to categorize the Branch Davidians as a type-three group determined to live in accordance with the laws of God's coming kingdom. Understanding the Branch Davidians' radical commitment to an alternate authority and the implications of such a commitment for predicting the actions of Mount Carmel residents would surely have argued against the April 19 effort to *force* the community out of their sacred space.

Lesson Six: Recognize That Unconventional Belief Groups
Are Drawing on Themes from the Dominant Culture

Waco was certainly not the first confrontation between state officials and a millennialist group. The MOVE crisis comes to mind as another recent example of such an encounter. A recently published book edited by Catherine Wessinger (2000b) includes studies of fifteen millennialist groups that became caught up in violence. The case studies occurred around the world and during different historical periods, making it clear that Waco is not a type of confrontation peculiar to the United States in the late twentieth century.

In her introduction, Wessinger notes that "contrary to popular stereotypes, millennial groups that become involved in violence are not all the same. It is important to distinguish between millennial groups that are assaulted . . . fragile millennial groups . . . and revolutionary millennial groups" (2000b, 3). Assaulted millennial groups are those communities attacked by law enforcement agents who perceive them as dangerous. This section of the book contains studies of past attacks on the Mormons and on the Lakota Sioux Ghost Dancers at Wounded Knee in 1890 and the persecution of "Dreads" in Dominica, in addition to a discussion of the Branch Davidians. "Fragile millennial groups initiate violence due to a combination of internal stresses and weaknesses and the experience of 'cultural opposition' " (Wessinger, personal correspondence). Wessinger classifies four case studies as examples of fragile millennial groups: the Peoples Temple at Jonestown, the Solar Temple, Heaven's Gate, and Aum Shinrikyo. Most important from a law enforcement perspective is Wessinger's observation that the fragility of some of these groups was created by a combination of internal weaknesses and quite real and coordinated cultural opposition or persecution (2000b, 25). Wessinger's third category (revolutionary millennial movements) includes the Old Believers in late-seventeenth-century Russia, the Taiping Revolution and Mao's Great Leap Forward, Nazism as a millennialist movement, Japanese lotus millennialism, the Khmer Rouge, the American Nationalist Socialist subculture, and the Montana Freemen.

It is immediately apparent that some of these millennial movements were not minority groups persecuted by state authorities; they *were* the state authorities. Furthermore, the revolutionary millennialist movements occupy the entire political spectrum from conservative or nativist movements that seek to (re)capture a threatened identity to progressive efforts to move entire societies forward to embrace a new identity. Identifying millennialist themes in mainstream political and social activity helps break down the categorical gulf between unconventional religious groups and the rest of society. We can begin to recognize that millennialist communities are acting on themes that originate in mainstream culture. Even if they play out those themes in ways more radical than most of us would embrace, acknowledging the existence of millennialist motifs in mainstream culture works against categorizing the members of unconventional religious communities as "wholly other," which can help prevent the dehumanization of community members and thereby reduce the chance of a violent outcome in any standoff with state officials.

Lesson Seven: Learn to Listen for Indicators of Worldviewing Differences

Given the interactive sources of violence in many of the cases described in Wessinger's book, law enforcement officials who find themselves required to deal with millennialist groups desperately need information that will help them avoid instigating violent responses from such groups. I suggest law enforcement agents also need *interpretive tools* that help them understand the beliefs and internal dynamics of the millennialist communities with whom they interact. Ideally, these interpretive tools should be useful before a confrontation as well as during any barricade standoff that may result from a confrontation. Prior to an encounter with an unconventional group, worldview analysis of the group's documents, teachings, and other texts can help the police anticipate the group's response to law enforcement activities. During a confrontation, worldview analysis provides an analytical template that can help negotiators effectively use insights obtained during their dialogue with the barricaded community.

Can the theoretical frameworks I have used to analyze the Waco negotiation standoff be converted into heuristic devices that will help crisis negotiators during a confrontation involving a group motivated by unconventional beliefs? I believe they can, if crisis negotiators are willing to relearn the art of listening. They have learned to listen for expressive and instrumental language; now they must learn to listen for narrative, symbolic, and identity language.

There is nothing radical about suggesting that crisis negotiators need to expand their range of listening skills. In every field of practice, specialized ways of seeing and hearing separate trained practitioners from laypersons. When medical students are handed their first set of chest x-rays, they see masses of black, white, and gray. Only after they have been trained to "read" the x-rays do they find meaningful information in these images. Similarly, a novice geographer handed her first set of geographic information system (GIS) images must be taught to discern their meaning, and a psychiatrist-in-training listens to his patients' stories but learns to hear information with which to make a diagnosis.

As disciplines change, practitioners learn to see and hear new things. Twenty years ago, data generated through GIS technology was not applied to the study of landscape ecology. Now scientists are learning to read GIS-generated images in order to study large-scale ecosystems. Ecologists are learning not only to see the world differently, but also to ask different questions of GIS systems in order to obtain information relevant to their purposes and interests (Haines-Young, Green, and Cousins 1993). In many cases, fields of practice are radically transformed when practitioners learn to see and hear new things. Some psychologists and psychiatrists are rediscovering the power of their patients' narratives (Coles 1989; White and Epston 1990). They are relying less on theory and diagnostic labeling and more on "learning to *listen responsibly* to stories people tell about their experiences" (Code 1991, 169).

How would incorporating new ways of listening into crisis negotiation practice transform that practice? Who would take responsibility for implementing the changes, and for what specifically would they be listening?

As currently organized, crisis negotiators work in teams. The primary negotiator speaks with the barricaded subject, and a secondary or support negotiator makes note of significant information from the conversation, which is part of the information that goes into the logs. The secondary negotiator listens primarily for demands, concessions, spoken and unspoken needs or interests, threats, and verbal indicators of stress. Some negotiation teams also use a psychologist or psychiatrist, who assesses the psychological state of the barricaded subject and monitors stress in both the barricaded subject and the negotiator (Bohl 1992; Rueth 1993). Because Waco was such a complex operation, the FBI used even more personnel than a typical barricade standoff that lasts a matter of hours. In Waco, the negotiators were assigned to negotiation "cells," with each cell assigned to a twelve-hour (later reduced to an eight-hour) shift. "The negotiation cell for each shift consisted of the following positions: a team leader, a primary negotiator, a secondary negotiator, a scribe-historian, and a situation report (SITREP) preparer" (Justice 125).

However, the critical factor is not how many negotiators and support personnel are monitoring conversations with the barricaded subjects, but the types of information for which they are listening. The support staff and the primary negotiator are listening for information that they deem important or relevant to the negotiation process. If worldviewing is a significant factor in negotiations, someone trained to listen for worldmaking narratives, images, categorization schema, metaphors, and other forms of worldviewing language should also be monitoring the conversation.

Something like figure 8 (in chapter 4) might be used to direct the negotiators' attention to an expanded array of language types. Using transcripts or (preferably) tapes from Waco and other negotiations, crisis negotiators can be trained to identify narrative, symbolic, and identity language.[5] During a real standoff, the negotiation teams can use a set of questions to determine whether a barricaded group is operating with an unconventional worldview. Sample questions that would help reveal worldviewing complications in a crisis negotiation include the following:

• What forms of language (narrative, symbolic, instrumental, relational, or identity) did the barricaded subjects use when *they* initiated conversations about the standoff?

• When negotiators directed attention to instrumental problem-solving or bargaining activities, did the barricaded subjects respond in kind, or did they respond primarily with narrative, symbolic, or identity language?

• When the barricaded subjects cooperated with an instrumental process such as bargaining or problem solving, did they offer *explanations* for their cooperation? Did they use narrative or symbolic language to explain why they *could* participate in this process? If they refused to cooperate, did they use narrative or symbolic language to explain why they *could not* participate in the process?

• Did the barricaded subjects use unfamiliar metaphors or imagery?

• Did the barricaded subjects use the same words as the negotiator, but give them an atypical meaning?

• Did the barricaded subjects misunderstand or ask for clarification of

5. I have not systematically studied transcripts from barricade standoffs other than Waco. However, in my reading of portions of transcripts that were included in other research studies, I have seen evidence of worldview management and negotiating reality even in standard barricade standoffs.

"simple" questions or requests? This misunderstanding is an indication that the barricaded subjects think the *negotiators* are using common language in abnormal ways.

After an initial assessment of the situation, the negotiators and behavioral scientists should be able to tell the commanders whether or not they are dealing with a conflict in which worldview differences are a significant factor. Everyone—including the on-scene commanders, tactical unit commanders, and behavioral scientists as well as the negotiators—should be trained well enough in worldview analysis at least to recognize the presence of a significant worldview conflict. Unless everyone involved in managing a barricade incident recognizes the importance of worldviewing differences in standoffs involving unconventional groups, the commanders or tactical units will become impatient with the slow pace of negotiations. Furthermore, if these other units do not understand the symbolic significance of their own actions, they may also inadvertently overrun the negotiation process. If, after an initial assessment, the negotiators and behavioral scientists determine that a standoff involves worldviewing problems, the entire intervention team should be reminded that the situation is likely to take longer than usual to resolve.

Appropriate staffing plans should be made for the tactical team and the negotiation team. In Waco, the tactical commanders did not rotate their personnel. Consequently, the tactical agents who had been trained for rapid "get in and get out" hostage rescue operations were assigned to just watch the Mount Carmel "compound." They grew frustrated with the slow pace of negotiations and, in keeping with their training, "just wanted to get this thing over." In Montana, tactical personnel from around the country were brought in and out of the area on two-week rotations, which helped to prevent the development of hostile feelings against the Freemen.

Unlike the tactical team, the negotiation team in Waco was too disjointed. The FBI used a total of twenty-five negotiators during the standoff, and because no attention was given to recording worldviewing problems and accomplishments, the Branch Davidians had to renegotiate the parameters of the discussion with each new negotiator. Some negotiators were willing to listen to biblical language. Others were not. Some negotiators were comfortable negotiating reality. Others were not. The Branch Davidians never knew what to expect. Recording worldviewing issues and transferring information about the state of "reality negotiations" from one negotiator to the next would alleviate this problem to some extent. However, there is a great deal of tacit understanding between people who have negotiated a shared reality, so new negotiators should be introduced to the process very carefully.

Incorporating a New Set of Experts into Crisis Negotiation

When working with an unconventional barricaded community, it is essential that law enforcement personnel continually monitor their own assessment of the group. It is very easy to become enamored of one's own understanding of "what is really going on" in a complex situation. Outside experts can help law enforcement negotiators better understand a barricaded group and keep a watchful eye on their own worldviewing activities as those impact the negotiation effort.

Lesson Eight: Incorporate Religion Scholars into Crisis Negotiation

In the post-Waco review process, a great deal of friction has been generated around the FBI negotiators' use or misuse of outside experts. Religious studies scholars have argued that the FBI consulted with anticult activists who lack the necessary credentials to understand new religious groups. The negotiators have been accused of turning down the expert assistance of religion scholars who could have helped, even when the Branch Davidians asked for those scholars to serve as "mediators."[6] For their part, the negotiators have complained about the "fax meltdown" created by unknown "experts" offering to tell them how to end the Waco standoff. Not surprisingly, given the pressures they were operating under, the negotiators turned to those experts with whom

6. After hearing Phillip Arnold discuss the Bible on a radio show, Steve Schneider asked that Arnold be permitted to serve as a mediator in the standoff. At the very least, the Branch Davidians wanted to discuss the biblical prophecies with Arnold. The FBI ignored these process suggestions, although they eventually sent an audiotape made by Arnold into Mount Carmel (Justice 186).

they already had a working relationship: psychologists and psychiatrists. Some of these experts were hostile to "cults," and many of them did not take seriously the motivational power of religious beliefs.

During the Freemen standoff in Montana, the FBI did bring in experts on religion, who contend that they provided the FBI negotiators with information that was incorporated into the final resolution of the standoff.[7] However, some FBI negotiators have argued that the religion scholars "provided no useful information" and have expressed concern about the drain on their resources created when the religious studies scholars kept requesting masses of information. In the opinion of many agents involved with the Freemen standoff, the religion scholars "thought everything was religion," when, in fact, the Freemen were not religious at all. They were just criminals.[8]

Some of these disagreements are reflections of standard organizational problems. The negotiators are held responsible for the outcome of barricade situations and are therefore reluctant to cede any authority to outsiders. Also, like functionally different units in a large corporation (sales and production, for example), neither the negotiators nor the scholars adequately understand the other's practice. The scholars do not fully recognize the constraints under which the negotiators work; the negotiators do not understand why the scholars cannot provide useful information based on small amounts of data. This problem is exacerbated by the negotiators' experiences with expert consultants who have been quite willing to render opinions on the basis of very little information. For example, one expert consultant with no knowledge of theology or biblical interpretation used five letters sent out of Mount Carmel as the basis for his analysis. He concluded, "the first and third letters bore 'all the hallmarks of rampant, morbidly virulent paranoia.' The frequent Biblical references indicated to him that Koresh wished to confront and destroy the authorities (the 'Babylonians' or 'Assyrians'). . . . With regard to the second and fourth letters [he] found nothing significant, *given that those letters consisted largely of Biblical*

7. Jean Rosenfeld (1997) and Catherine Wessinger (2000a) describe their experiences consulting with the FBI during the Freemen standoff in Montana.

8. My summary of the FBI agents' perceptions regarding the use of religious scholars in Montana is based on personal conversations with negotiators, behavioral scientists, and an HRT commander who were in Montana.

quotations. With regard to the fifth letter, [he] noted that the letter appeared to be a ploy designed to buy more time for Koresh" (Justice 175–76, emphasis added). No wonder the FBI negotiators in Montana were impatient with the religion scholars' requests for substantially more data.

Additionally, even if they could reconcile their differences over how much information is necessary to make useful recommendations, the negotiators and scholars have no common language for sharing information with one another. The FBI negotiators do not know how to ask the scholars questions that will yield useful information, and the scholars do not know how to frame their information so that the negotiators can hear it. Theoretically, however, there is no reason why religion scholars and crisis negotiators cannot work together. They simply need to construct a process of mutual education and to clarify their respective roles and responsibilities, which has been done before. When police negotiators and psychologists started working together, many similar issues were raised. The two groups had to iron out roles, responsibilities, and relationships. They also had to educate one another. Many psychologists and psychiatrists who work with the police attend hostage negotiation training, and crisis negotiators frequently obtain some training in psychology.

The primary obstacle to arranging a similar process of mutual education between the negotiators and religion scholars is the fact that they have a worldview conflict (Docherty 1999). In Montana, these worldview differences played themselves out in several ways. The religion scholars felt the FBI negotiators were asking poorly framed questions based on a flawed understanding of religion.

> Almost everyone outside the field of religious studies, including FBI analysts, is unfamiliar with the sectarian expression of religion and how it makes people act differently from "con men" and "hostage-takers." For example, we were initially asked to assess who among the twenty-one individuals on the ranch were "religious" and who were not, on the assumption that those who had written fraudulent checks were nothing more than common criminals. (Rosenfeld 1997, 75–76)

On the other hand, the religion scholars irritated the FBI agents by offering process advice and thereby overstepping the established boundaries for expert consultants working with the FBI negotiators. Unless specifically asked to do so, psychologists and psychiatrists who work with the FBI do not give advice regarding tactical activities, and, generally speaking, they do not make suggestions about how to negotiate with the subject.

The role confusion and conflict between the negotiators and scholars may have been exacerbated when religion scholars suggested that they play the role of "mediators" in conflicts involving millennial groups. The FBI negotiators may have resented what they heard as the scholars' attempt to engage in process mediation, shuttle diplomacy, or some other endeavor in which control of the dialogue would be taken out of FBI negotiators' hands, or they may have been unable to envision scholars in the role of intermediaries. Although the FBI did use a wide variety of third-party intermediaries in Montana, they did not employ scholars in that role, and they still seem particularly averse to considering that option. This aversion is, I believe, a reflection of the high level of distrust that the agents seem to feel toward scholars, combined with their very apparent fear that scholars are simply not prepared to deal with the "real-life" potential for violence when working with unconventional groups. The intermediaries that the FBI used in Montana included family members of the Freemen, militia movement sympathizers who shared some of the Freemen beliefs, and a state official whom the Freemen trusted. In short, the FBI used only intermediaries the Freemen were unlikely to harm (family members) or intermediaries the FBI felt were prepared to deal with the potential violence of the Freemen. I believe the FBI agents in Montana genuinely feared that if they involved some well-meaning, scholarly person in the face-to-face negotiations on the Freemen property, or sent some scholar into the ranch to "just talk," they would end up with a hostage situation or a dead professor.

The irony is that the scholars were not suggesting that control of the process be handed over to someone other than the FBI, nor were they suggesting that scholars be used as shuttle diplomats. Rather, they were suggesting that scholars be allowed to *mediate concepts or worldviews* (Wessinger 2000a, 185).

Lesson Nine: Develop a Practice of Worldview Translation

Religious studies scholars have argued that whenever law enforcement agents "must negotiate with a religious community whose members understand the world in a way that is largely incomprehensible to them . . . the situation resembles an encounter between persons who speak different languages" (Lucas 1994, 209). The idea of "worldview translators" is a new one for crisis negotiators, and FBI agents may not be ready to concede that their practice needs to include worldview translation or interpretation. Nor is it completely clear what scholars mean when they talk about worldview translation. In defining who might be worldview translators, Lucas points to "scholars who have studied individual religious communities in contemporary America and who have, therefore, learned the 'language' of their worldviews" (1994, 210). I agree that a scholar who has studied the community in question is an excellent source of information. However, I would suggest that far more is required of a worldview translator than familiarity with one particular religious group.

If we want to think of conflict resolution as worldview translation, we must first understand the nature of translation. "If language is an integral part of culture, the translator needs not only proficiency in two languages, he must also be at home in two cultures" (Snell-Hornby 1995, 42). The cultural aspect of translation is equally significant when the parties for whom one is translating speak the same language but use divergent narratives to organize their worlds. Worldview translators need to mediate between two ways of seeing and enacting the world, and therefore need to be familiar with both worldviews. In short, translation involves an "additive process": the translator adds cultural meaning to the translation in order to account for the worldviewing gaps between the parties. This additive process happens even in supposedly simple language translations. For example, the task of translating nursery rhymes from English to Chinese requires an awareness that "contemporary speakers of English will, in reading 'candlestick,' unwittingly supply the candle and the flame" upon hearing about the adventures of nimble Jack (Eoyang 1993, 137), which dictates the use of a Chinese word that does not mean candlestick, but which communicates to the Chinese reader the candle and flame, not just the candle holder. The translator provides extra information because he or she understands the "gaps of meaning" that exist between the English and Chinese languages/cultures. Worldview translators must do the same.

To account for the active contribution of the translator, theorists have started describing translation "not as an act of transcoding, but as an *act of communication*" (Snell-Hornby 1995, 43). The greater the distance between languages (for example, Finnish to Chinese as opposed to English to German), the more involved is the translator in an act of communication (Snell-Hornby 1995, 46). The same is true of worldviews. The greater the distance between the crisis negotiators' worldview and that of the barricaded group, the more involved worldview translators will be in an act of communication, and part of that act of communication will involve holding a mirror up to the negotiators' worldview. Thus, crisis negotiators should be aware that worldview translators working with them may sound "critical" in ways that other expert consultants do not.

Worldview translators during a crisis negotiation encounter can be of assistance only if they are allowed to demonstrate the *interaction* of the law enforcement worldview and the worldview of the barricaded subjects. The worldview translator must overstep established boundaries for expert consultants in order to explain how the barricaded group will perceive or respond to particular tactical activities or to proposals for resolving the conflicts. Otherwise, the information they provide will be of no value to the negotiators. In short, worldview translators should be used in crisis negotiation only if the crisis negotiators are willing to change the way they think about their own practice, redefine the problem they are facing, and reconsider the role assigned to expert consultants. If these changes are made, then worldview translators can be incorporated into an *adaptive crisis management team* that cooperatively attempts to move the barricaded subjects and law enforcement negotiators from a position of dangerous worldview divergence to a safe resolution of the standoff.

*Lesson Ten: Construct Negotiation Processes That
Accommodate Worldview Divergence*

An adaptive crisis management team should focus on discerning the worldviews of each party—the law enforcement agents and the barricaded subjects. Everyone on the team makes a contribution, but the team members cannot work separately from one another and then just put the various pieces together. Religion scholars who are brought in as interpreters have special insights into the symbolic frame of the barricaded group, but they need to connect those insights to the process of negotiation. Otherwise, they are giving the negotiators useless information. On the other hand, the information provided by worldview translators is useful only within a practice that involves a *symmetrical analysis* of symbolic, substantive, aspiration, and process frames. The entire adaptive crisis management team needs to focus on connecting the analysis of each party's worldviews (symbolic frames) to a clear analysis of their respective definitions of the conflict (substantive frames), goals and objectives (aspiration frames), and assumptions about process (process frames and enactive frames).

The first goal is to monitor the frames of both parties and determine where they diverge and converge. In Waco, an adaptive crisis negotiation team would have noticed that the parties seemed to share an outcome frame preference for ending the standoff peacefully, but placed different *conditions* on that goal. The negotiators wanted to end the standoff peacefully while enforcing the law. The Branch Davidians wanted to end it peacefully if the ATF agents involved in the February 28 raid would also be brought to justice and if God approved. An adaptive crisis negotiation team would also have paid attention to the competing narratives of interdependence between the parties. (See figure 9, chapter 5.) Even the lowest-level frame divergence (such as differences in identifying the relevant issues, parties, forms of interaction, or outcomes) reflect symbolic framing differences between the parties. Having noticed and recorded these frame differences, what should the crisis negotiation team do?

First, let me explain what they should *not* do. Resolving or managing frame differences between the parties involves (re)negotiating reality. (See figure 4, chapter 2.) However, it is not the goal of a crisis negotiation team to reach complete worldview convergence with a barricaded unconventional group. The negotiators should not succumb to conversion by the barricaded subjects, nor should they try to convert or deprogram the group members back to a mainstream worldview. The negotiators in Waco fell into this trap with predictable results. So the question is how can parties involved in a substantive worldview conflict renegotiate reality without succumbing to mutual conversion efforts?

The negotiation team should break the worldviewing problem down into manageable chunks. They should identify those issues, objectives, and process expectations around which the parties are having difficulty managing their worldview differences. Figure 3 (chapter 2) can be used to map the parties' worldview convergence/divergence in relation to specific issues and problems. In Waco, trading children for various concessions would have been located at the top of figure 3 because the parties had successfully managed their worldviews in order to participate in this exchange. Notice that I am not saying the parties *shared* a worldview in order to trade children for concessions from the FBI. The negotiation team should always ask themselves whether a negotiation success is built on worldview convergence or worldview coordination. The team should also never presume that worldview coordination or convergence will transfer to a different issue, problem, or interaction. Thus, trading women for concessions from the FBI would have been located at the bottom of figure 3.

Had they consciously mapped the problem in this manner, the negotiation team in Waco would have recognized the need either to drop the proposal to trade women for various concessions or to negotiate reality with the Branch Davidians in order to support this bargaining proposal. Personally, I would have advocated very strongly for dropping the proposal to trade women for concessions from the FBI. The worldviewing basis for the Branch Davidians' refusal to participate in such an exchange was directly linked to their identities. Trying to get people to change their sense of self is a conversion process and is unlikely to succeed. As the transcripts demonstrate, the consequence of trying to renegotiate reality on the issue of treating women as victims or bargainable commodities was a worldviewing impasse that led to a loss of rapport between the negotiators and the Branch Davidians.

While cooperating on those issues, goals, and processes for which they have managed their worldview differences with the barricaded subjects, the adaptive crisis negotiation team should pay particular attention to the areas where the parties have been only partially successful in managing their worldviewing differences (the middle of figure 3). This area is a very difficult one in which to work. There is a great risk that the parties will recognize their shared language and overlook the differences in their meaning systems. For example, both parties in Waco validated the importance of the U.S. Constitution, and both parties spoke the language of constitutional rights. These worldnaming agreements formed a natural foundation on which to build substantive agreements. However, the FBI negotiators presumed that the Branch Davidians shared their own deep faith in the Constitution and in the legal system based on that document. With the help of worldview translators, the negotiators would have been better able to locate the Branch Davidians' use of constitutional rhetoric within their millennialist symbolic frame. The Branch Davidians felt they owed only provisional loyalty to the Constitution, with loyalty to

God being their ultimate concern. Had the FBI negotiators understood this, they would have been less confident about the efficacy of using constitutionally grounded concepts of justice to convince the Branch Davidians to leave Mount Carmel. The Branch Davidians were also deeply pessimistic about the ability of the U.S. government to live up to the Constitution. Had the FBI negotiators acknowledged this pessimism, they might have been more inclined to bring in members of Congress or higher-ranking members of the Department of Justice to reassure the Branch Davidians that evenhanded justice would be served after they left Mount Carmel.

An adaptive crisis negotiation process that incorporates worldview analysis would also work slowly and self-reflectively. Thus, any impasse or failed proposal would be examined carefully for worldviewing problems that might be located in the negotiators' own framing of the problem or process. The Branch Davidians agreed to trade (some) children for concessions, but refused to trade women in the same manner. An adaptive crisis negotiation team would have asked whether there was something about the worldnaming basis of bargaining that caused this apparent inconsistency. When the Branch Davidians failed to emerge from Mount Carmel on March 2, the same question would have been asked.

Lesson Eleven: Recognize That Worldview Analysis Is Not the "Magic Bullet"

Worldview analysis is only marginally useful in many barricade situations, and it does not hold the missing answer to every standoff with a barricaded community. Worldview analysis does not replace other forms of listening, but it does transform them. Crisis negotiators should still listen for demands, interests, and needs, but when dealing with a millennialist group or other unconventional community, they also need to recognize that the *meaning* of those demands, interests, and needs will be transformed by the community's worldmaking narrative.

Thus, Koresh and the rest of the Mount Carmel community needed or were interested in obtaining access to the press, but that did not mean they wanted to use media access to recruit masses of followers or to acquire fame and fortune. One of the religion scholars in Montana "advised negotiators that if they viewed the behavior of the Freemen merely as a means to the end of money or power or ego, they would be out of step with the Freemen perception of reality" (Rosenfeld 1997, 81). In Waco, the negotiators made the mistake of framing their persuasive arguments as if Koresh and the others were primarily interested in fame and power. They made it impossible for the community to cooperate without attacking their own sense of identity as God's humble remnant. In Montana, the negotiators did not make this error.

In spite of their success in Montana, for which they should receive full credit, the FBI Critical Incident Response Group should not assume that all of the problems from Waco have been repaired. The Freemen were not the Branch Davidians. The Freemen were less cohesive, had a less clearly developed belief system, were shorter-lived as a community, and lacked a leader that had been elevated to charismatic status. Another community such as the Branch Davidians will be far more difficult to negotiate with than were the Freemen. At the same time, there must be a clear recognition among government officials that standoffs involving law enforcement authorities and unconventional groups that deny the legitimacy of the government are not just law enforcement problems.

Creating Law Enforcement Negotiation Processes for Diplomatic Encounters

Most negotiation research, including this study to some extent, looks primarily at microlevel interactive processes. Such an approach runs the risk of artificially constructing negotiations as isolated encounters. However, we must never lose sight of the fact that processes of negotiation occur within particular institutional and historical contexts from which they cannot be separated. Because context matters, there are inherent differences between typical barricade negotiations and confrontations involving communities that are organized around alternative religious and political worldmaking narratives.

The biggest difference between a typical barricade standoff and a confrontation involving a group motivated by unconventional beliefs is a factor of *legitimacy*. When the state is legitimate in the eyes of its citizens and the police operate within the constraints of law, most citizens support police actions even when those actions include the use of deadly force. For example, law enforcement officers in Los Angeles recently engaged a group of heavily armed bank robbers in what looked like a modern-day shootout at the O.K. Corral. This violent street confrontation was televised when reporters captured it on film. In spite of the deadly violence (two people were killed), there were very few objections from citizens. By contrast, the televised video of the Los Angeles Police officers beating Rodney King did evoke outrage among many citizens. Police legitimacy is undermined when the police operate outside of the law. However, the legitimacy of police actions is also subject to change depending on the level of legitimacy attributed to the government as a whole. The legitimacy of the state waxes and wanes with changing historical circumstances, and when the legitimacy of the state or of particular laws is in question, the normal practices of police work become suspect.

The growing number of groups motivated by unconventional religious and political beliefs is indicative of a crisis of legitimacy in the United States today. This crisis of legitimacy is not evenly distributed across the country, nor is it a response to the same issues and factors everywhere it appears. In the western states, for example, much of the unrest focuses on changes in the management of federally owned lands. In counties and states where the majority of the land is owned and managed by the federal government, changes that originate in Washington, D.C., have tremendous impact on the daily lives of local residents. A growing number of citizens in this region feel disenfranchised and angry that their lives are being controlled by "Washington bureaucrats" and "outside interest groups" whose determination to "save the environment" has led to policies that negatively affect the quality of these citizens' lives. Radical protests against federal authority are likely to increase in response to a recent Supreme Court decision validating the right of federal officials to make far-reaching changes in policies related to grazing, logging, and other forms of resource use on federal lands. In Hawaii, Alaska, and Texas, nascent secessionist movements are gaining adherents. In South Carolina, the day the Confederate flag was removed from the capitol dome in Columbia was also the opening day of the Southern Party convention in Charleston. The Southern Party has vowed to seek independence using lessons learned from the experience of Quebec in Canada. In the Midwest, both farming communities still suffering from the impact of the farm crisis in the 1980s and factory towns abandoned by companies that have moved overseas feel threatened by the new global order.

Accusations that powerful people in Washington and on Wall Street have benefited from the pain inflicted on small communities by large corporations lead some people to join unconventional groups. Everywhere, Second Amendment advocates are outraged by federal moves to outlaw or restrict the ownership of weapons. All around the country, religiously oriented groups have created enclaves of believers who wish to live according to their own beliefs.

In this context, federal law enforcement agents are more likely to meet with violent resistance as they carry out their mandated duties. It is also in this context that every mistake in the application of force creates a feedback loop that exacerbates the problems related to state legitimacy. Every Ruby Ridge and every Waco reinforces the beliefs of the most radical skeptics in unconventional groups. In such an environment, each confrontation with a group motivated by unconventional beliefs is a *diplomatic encounter* with long-term implications for the legitimacy of the government. Such encounters cannot be treated successfully as just a matter of enforcing the law.

Law enforcement officers are not, however, equipped to manage single-handedly the diplomatic facets of their encounters with unconventional groups, and they should not be expected to do so. The on-scene commander in a crisis encounter cannot both manage the incident and scan the sociopolitical horizon to ascertain the diplomatic implications of each and every practical decision he or she makes. During the Freemen standoff in Montana, for example, law enforcement personnel were wearing full protective gear while manning roadblocks. This decision was made by their commander, whose obligation was to protect his personnel while accomplishing the mission he was given. It was not his job to think about the *symbolic* impact of having federal agents in full protective gear supervising roadblocks in rural Montana. That problem was noticed by the attorney general, who alerted the FBI commanders in Montana so that a suitable compromise between safety and diplomacy could be reached. On the other hand, the diplomatic monitoring task should not fall solely to the attorney general, either, and it should not depend on the fact that she happened to see pictures of the federal agents on the morning news. There is, at present, a missing diplomatic management and coordination function in the handling of crisis barricades incidents involving unconventional political and religious groups. Looking at the Waco case along with several post-Waco incidents, one can discern a number of different diplomatic tasks that must be accomplished during a standoff involving an unconventional religious or political community.

*Lesson Twelve: Provide Diplomatic Monitoring During
Critical Incidents*

The Waco standoff coincided with the Randy Weaver trial for the events at Ruby Ridge. Citizen Militia groups and members of the Patriot movement scrutinized both situations. During the Waco standoff, Linda Thompson, the "self-styled adjutant General of the Militia, called for hundreds of people to attend" a demonstration in support of the Branch Davidians (Justice 153). "Approximately twenty-seven individuals with extremist background . . . arrived in Waco" after March 1. "The FBI became concerned that because of these individuals' support of Koresh, they might pose a threat, either individually or as a group, to law enforcement" (Justice 151). In other words, the FBI agents on the scene were aware of sympathizers who might try to support the Branch Davidians in some manner, but they treated this situation as a security problem rather than as a diplomatic dilemma. Two years later, with the April 19, 1995, Oklahoma City bombing, the country became aware of the long-term ramifications of treating a diplomatic situation such as the Waco standoff as a straight law enforcement problem.

The agents were correct to be concerned about security, but someone in the Department of Justice or the White House should have been thinking about the long-term diplomatic implications of this problem. Unfortunately, the White House and the top-level offices in the Department of Justice—those jobs held by political appointees—were both in upheaval as a result of the transition from twelve years of Republican control to the newly elected Democratic administration. Attorney General Janet Reno was sworn in on March 12, at about the time the Waco negotiations were reaching an impasse. To avoid this type of problem, flexible policy guidelines should be developed in preparation for future encounters with unconventional religious and political groups. Furthermore, a specific office in the Department of Justice should be tasked with overseeing the diplomatic and policy aspects of any future extended standoff with an unconventional group. The most logical office to fulfill this function is the Community Relations Service.

Lesson Thirteen: Improve Coordination and Communication
among Government Actors

The lack of coordination between the tactical and negotiation units during the Waco standoff has been well documented. This problem was, in large part, created by the absence of an adequate command structure. At the time of the Waco standoff, the FBI policy was to draw on-scene commanders from the nearest FBI regional office. As long as the situation did not involve barricaded subjects motivated by unconventional beliefs, this system worked well. In Waco, however, the standard script was inadequate for managing the standoff, and the on-scene commander was ill-prepared to engage the negotiation and tactical teams in the type of creative problem solving required for improvising a new script (Docherty 1996a). Instead, he persisted in using standard crisis management procedures, and, even worse, he exhibited a strong tendency toward favoring tactical options over the negotiators' recommendations. After Waco, the crisis intervention team was reorganized. Now, the CIRG based in Quantico, Virginia, includes its own command structure. This group received its first test during the standoff with the Freemen in Montana. The improved integration of the tactical, negotiation, and command functions permitted the CIRG to respond creatively to the unfolding events in Montana.

However, coordinating the FBI units is only one of several similar problems that need to be managed during confrontations with unconventional groups. Political and religious communities that end up across a barricade from federal agents can be expected to espouse an alternative authority structure. At the very least, they will be highly skeptical about the legitimacy of the established legal system. For example, the Freemen refused to recognize any law other than that of their own courts. Groups who espouse such beliefs certainly complicate the negotiators' task of convincing the barricaded subjects to move their grievances into the established court system. In the case of apocalyptic religious groups, the problem is even more profound. "Active millennial, apocalyptic, and messianist groups present a unique challenge to civil authorities because they proclaim allegiance to the allegedly 'higher law' of a divine Power that may contravene the mores of society and the statutes of the state" (Rosenfeld 2000, 349).

Negotiations are not entirely hopeless under such circumstances, however.

Barricaded unconventional communities may be *willing* to die for their belief in an alternate authority, but they do not necessarily *want* to die. Even deeply committed apocalyptic groups may demonstrate some flexibility when it comes to cooperating with state authorities. For example, the Branch Davidians were determined to follow God's commands, but they saw room to maneuver and negotiate as long as the government did not act in ways that reinforced their fears that the United States was the evil empire predicted by the prophets and the Book of Revelation.

To build on the fragile negotiating flexibility of barricaded unconventional communities, law enforcement negotiators must somehow convince them that it is safe to move their grievances into the courts. Yet the negotiators have no control over other actors in the judicial system. They cannot make commitments regarding plea bargains or a reduction in charges. They cannot make promises on behalf of a judge to permit certain types of evidence or testimony. They cannot control even the decision making of the local U.S. attorney during the standoff. In Waco, for example, the U.S. attorney unnecessarily complicated negotiations when he brought murder charges against Margaret Lawson and Catherine Matteson even though they were almost certainly not involved in the February 28 shootout. The decision to bring these charges created a crisis of confidence among the Branch Davidians and complicated the negotiators' efforts to persuade those still in Mount Carmel that they would be treated fairly by the judicial system. This problematic relationship between the negotiation team and the U.S. attorney is not always present. For example, Coulson describes the very cooperative relationship between the U.S. attorney in Arkansas and the FBI when they successfully negotiated an end to a standoff with the radical group the CSA (Coulson and Shannon 1999). However, this coordination of activities is too important to be left to chance and the possibility that both the on-scene commander and the U.S. attorney will act sensibly and in a coordinated manner. Again, the institutional solution to this problem lies outside of the FBI. Someone in the Department of Justice needs to assume responsibility for coordinating the activities of the U.S. attorney and other actors in the Department of Justice with the activities of the negotiators.

A third communication problem involves working with other unconventional groups during a crisis situation. In post-Waco confrontations, Citizen Militia and Patriot groups have formed a highly relevant, potentially volatile, self-selected "concerned audience." Proclaiming "No more Wacos," these groups have appointed themselves to monitor the actions of law enforcement negotiators and tactical units. Barricaded subjects have also appealed to militia groups for support. Under such circumstances, rumor control is critical. It is also important that the crisis management personnel be kept apprised of how their actions are perceived by this relevant audience.

One effort to accomplish this task was the establishment of a "hotline" between the CIRG commander and the National Confederation of Citizen Militias (NCCM) (Witkin 1997). The hotline is a useful undertaking, but the FBI negotiators, commanders, and tactical units should not assume this mechanism alone can handle the diplomatic (as opposed to security) issues related to groups that sympathize with a barricaded community. The Militia and Patriot movements are extremely diverse, and the FBI is well aware that the NCCM represents the moderate faction of a diffuse and ill-defined social movement. Therefore, putting information out through the NCCM may or may not reach the full range of groups concerned about the handling of a specific incident. Furthermore, the CIRG commander has little time to spare for diplomacy while trying to manage a critical incident. A rumor-control center such as those usually established by the Community Relations Service during periods of unrest in urban communities has more hope of reaching the widest possible audience and would take the pressure off of the CIRG commander. This solution still would not address the problem of reaching out to the most disenfranchised groups, those who are unlikely to trust *any* information coming out of a federal agency.

Lesson Fourteen: Assume That Prevention Is the Best Cure

The best way to handle critical incidents is to prevent them from happening in the first place. This is much easier said than done, but looking at the most likely scenarios that could trigger another Waco-like standoff directs attention to preventive measures that federal law enforcement agencies should institute.

The Waco standoff started when the ATF went to Mount Carmel to serve a search-and-arrest warrant. ATF commanders opted for a dynamic entry raid assuming that the Branch Davidians, like typical criminal suspects, would simply give up in the face of overwhelming force. Unconventional communities—

even if they have engaged in criminal activities—cannot be expected to behave like typical criminal suspects. If they have broken the law, they have often done so out of a commitment to a higher law, and they may well be willing to kill or die or both in defense of that higher law. Careful arrest planning is critical and must involve an assessment of the community's worldmaking narrative.

In the federal system, agencies as diverse as the Environmental Protection Agency, the Forest Service, the Bureau of Land Management, the Internal Revenue Service, or the United States Marshals Service are tasked with enforcing a variety of regulations, serving warrants, or making arrests. Employees of any one of these federal agencies or a dozen others could inadvertently instigate an armed standoff. All federal personnel who might be required to deal with unconventional groups should be made aware of the diplomatic implications of their enforcement activities. They should receive basic conflict resolution training that includes education about the importance of beliefs as a motive for conflict. Furthermore, because the FBI is tasked with cleaning up any confrontation arising out of efforts to enforce federal laws, it seems only fair that FBI personnel should be consulted during the enforcement planning phase in any case involving unconventional groups.

In Montana, the FBI intervened because federal laws were broken. However, many people in the local community thought the intervention should have occurred earlier. The Freemen had allegedly threatened their neighbors, the local judge, elected officials, and the sheriff. In rural communities, where many unconventional political and religious groups are forming, local officials frequently lack adequate resources for handling a complex, protracted conflict. The Department of Justice would be wise to think about ways to help these communities before conflicts escalate. Consideration should be given to using mediators and facilitators from the Community Relations Service to assist communities that ask for help with conflicts involving unconventional religious and political groups.

Appendixes

References

Index

The Special Counsel's Summary of the Waco Negotiations

THE FOLLOWING ACCOUNT of the negotiations in Waco is taken from the interim report of the Special Counsel (Danforth 2000, 97–99). The full text of the report was downloaded from http://www.osc-waco.org on July 21, 2000.

F. The FBI Attempts to Negotiate a Peaceful
Resolution of the Standoff

37. As the reports of other Waco investigations have set forth in detail, the FBI negotiation teams and the tactical teams ran different and sometimes conflicting operations. Most of this information is irrelevant to the charter of the Office of Special Counsel, but the following narrative provides some context relevant to the Special Counsel's conclusions. The negotiators centered their activities in a Negotiations Operations Center at the rear TOC [Tactical Operations Center]. The FBI negotiators worked with negotiators from ATF, the Texas Department of Public Safety, the Austin Police Department, and the McLennan County Sheriff's Department. Their principal objective was to secure the release of the children in the complex and eventually effectuate the peaceful arrest and departure of the adults. They worked in 12-hour shifts. Each shift utilized a primary negotiator and a secondary "coach" who maintained notes of the negotiations and provided prompts to assist the primary negotiator. FBI personnel recorded and, if possible, transcribed the contents of negotiation sessions. Each shift kept a negotiations log and handwritten chronology. The negotiators regularly prepared "situation reports" summarizing the status of negotiations. The negotiators also relied upon behavioral psychologists and religious experts for advice concerning the likely reaction of the Davidians to their negotiation strategy.

38. Over the 51 days, more than 40 law enforcement officers participated in nego-

tiations, the objective of which was to get the Davidians to leave the complex peacefully. In order to effectuate a peaceful resolution to the standoff, [Jeff] Jamar made numerous concessions to Koresh based upon the recommendations of the negotiators. On March 1, the negotiators arranged the radio broadcast of a scripture message recorded by Koresh. Two days later, based on Koresh's promise to come out, they arranged for a one-hour message from Koresh to be aired nationally on television and radio. The negotiators also allowed Davidians to exit the complex for such matters as the burial of Davidian Peter Gent, to dispose of their dead dogs, and to retrieve Bible study materials from one of their cars. The negotiators sent in medical supplies for the wounded, made multiple deliveries of milk and food for the children, and provided the Davidians communications from family members outside the complex, as well as legal documents that Davidians had requested. Moreover, the negotiators took the unprecedented step of permitting criminal defense lawyers to enter the complex on several occasions to meet with Koresh and Schneider, even though the crime scene was unsecured.

39. The negotiators had some early success. Between February 28 and March 23, Koresh allowed 35 people to exit the complex. But Koresh also made repeated, well-chronicled and unfulfilled promises to exit the complex with the remaining Davidians, allowing only two people to exit after March 23. As early as March 3, a key behavioral psychologist, Dr. Park Dietz, advised the negotiators that Koresh would not leave the complex and would not allow anyone about whom he truly cared to leave, including his numerous biological children. FBI negotiators also obtained conflicting opinions on the likelihood of a mass suicide by the Davidians. The negotiators considered the possibility of a mass suicide either within the complex or as part of an assault against the FBI by exiting Davidians. On March 27, Schneider told negotiators that the FBI should set the building on fire. Eventually, after meetings with his attorney, Koresh promised that he would exit the complex after he had written an interpretation of the Seven Seals referenced in the Book of Revelation. The negotiators concluded that this was another empty promise because Koresh failed to turn over an interpretation of any of the Seven Seals.

Defining the Coding Categories

POLICE NEGOTIATORS and most researchers have ignored the meaning-creation function of language. I have identified two forms of language that are particularly salient in conflicts that revolve around worldviewing differences: *narrative* and *symbolic* language. Because applying these categories to crisis negotiation is innovative, I want to introduce them first.

Narrative Language [NARRAT]

Barricade negotiation transcripts in general have not been coded for narrative language. Yet the Waco transcripts are filled with examples of narrative and storytelling. The barricaded subjects tell *autobiographical stories* to explain their presence at Mount Carmel and their determination to stay. The police tell *visionary stories* about what will happen when the barricade standoff ends. Storytelling is also evident in the excerpts from other barricade negotiation transcripts included in previous studies, and Ramesh (1992) uses symbolic convergence theory (SCT) to examine a number of narratively grounded fantasy themes common to crisis negotiation. So the neglect of narrative language is a reflection of the researchers and the police negotiators' analytical frameworks, not an indication that Waco was unique in this respect. The following is a list of the most common types of stories I coded as narrative language in the Waco transcripts:

- Individual autobiographical stories
- Group autobiographical stories (chapter 3)
- Speculative stories about future consequences of the raid and standoff
- Biblical stories and parables [1]
- Stories that served as accounts, excuses, or reasons for particular actions [2]

1. Even prior to their dramatic confrontation with federal authorities, the Branch Davidians relied on narratives drawn from the Bible as a form of sacred knowledge. According to their the-

Symbolic Language [SYMBOL]

The category *symbolic language* raises a potential problem. Because language is, by definition, the manipulation of symbols, what language is not symbolic? I acknowledge this dilemma, but nevertheless find it useful to identify specifically language that references such symbolic constructs as *values, ontological claims,* and *epistemological assertions.* Both the police and barricaded subjects use symbolic language. In most barricade standoffs, the parties use similar symbolic constructs, so their symbolic language remains largely unproblematic and unnoticed. In Waco, the parties were each trying to impose a distinct set of values, ontological claims, and epistemological assertions on the negotiation process. Narrative and symbolic language are often linked because symbols are woven into meaningful stories. However, every community develops shorthand references to more complex symbol systems. I coded the following types of language as symbolic:

- Value-laden terms such as *justice, truth, fairness, responsibility,* and *morality*
- References to authoritative texts such as the Bible, the U.S. Constitution, and federal or state laws
- References to authority figures such as God, the president of the United States, the attorney general, the prophets, and Jesus

Instrumental Language [INSTRUM]

Based on concepts of instrumentality used by crisis negotiators and by communication-based researchers who study hostage negotiations, "instrumental message behav-

---

ology, all current events were already explained and predicted in the Bible. As God's faithful followers, they were compelled to discern the true meaning of their daily lives by reference to Scripture, including biblical stories about past believers, apostates, and villains. Some of the FBI negotiators also tried to use stories from the Bible to persuade the Branch Davidians to take particular actions. In chapter 8, I explain why these laudable attempts to speak the language of the Branch Davidians frequently foundered when the Branch Davidians took them as signs of the negotiators' willingness to negotiate reality.

2. *Apologia,* explanations for one's own failure to fulfill the expectations of another, play a significant role in all negotiations. So do *blaming narratives,* or stories about the wrongdoing of the other party. The Branch Davidians and the FBI negotiators used both forms of narratives.

ior arises in crisis negotiations as the hostage taker and negotiator bargain with one another regarding the incompatibility of their respective objective concerns" (Hammer and Rogan 1997, 15). It is easy to assume that instrumental messages are strictly efforts at direct bargaining. "I'll give you one pizza for two hostages." There are, however, many forms of interactive exchanges involved in arriving at the point where bargaining, in this limited sense of the word, becomes possible. *Issues* need to be defined, *information* needs to be shared, and both parties need to be persuaded that bargaining is the appropriate *process* for resolving their confrontation. Other forms of language used in negotiation are also instrumental because they are goal-directed and designed to contribute to reaching the final "bargaining" stage of negotiation. Thus, I coded the following types of messages as instrumental language:

- The statement of demands or identification of issues to be addressed
- Problem-solving activities
- Information sharing
- Attempts to persuade the other party to participate in bargaining or other issue-specific negotiation processes
- Efforts to frame an issue in a manner that makes it amenable to problem solving or bargaining
- Bargaining

Relational Language [RELAT]

Researchers and some practitioners have now divided into two forms of expressive communication what crisis negotiators once thought of as a single type of language (expressive): *relational* language and *identity* language. "Relational message behavior denotes an individual's concern for the nature of the relationship between self and other. Power, trust, and affiliation represent three core elements of relational message behavior" (Hammer and Rogan 1997, 15). Donohue and Roberto have given the relational language used by police negotiators and barricaded subjects two primary dimensions, interdependence and affiliation. *Interdependence* is "the extent to which individuals can demand rights and impose obligations on one another" (Donohue and Roberto 1993, 177). *Affiliation* is "the extent to which individuals are attracted to, like, and accept one another" (Donohue and Roberto 1993, 177). A relational message may express either high or low affiliation and high or low interdependence. Relational messages also express *relative power* between the speaker and the listener. Relational language is also used to express *empathy* by acknowledging the other person's perspective (Borum and

Strentz 1992; DiVasto, Lanceley, and Gruys 1992; Froman and Glorioso 1984). Crisis negotiators use expressions of empathy to build rapport with barricaded subjects. Hence, I have marked the following types of exchanges as relational language:

- Statements of affiliation
- Statements of interdependence
- Statements of relative power
- Efforts to express empathy or build personal rapport or both

Identity Language [IDENT]

Rogan and Hammer have established the importance of facework or *identity* language in barricade negotiations (Hammer and Rogan 1997; Rogan 1990; Rogan and Hammer 1994). Relational language is distinguished from identity language by its focus on the relationship between the parties. Identity-oriented language focuses attention on one party alone. Rogan and Hammer argue that facework is particularly important in crisis negotiations in which "an important part of reducing the perpetrator's level of emotional excitation is to stabilize the suspect's sense of self (i.e., face)" (1994, 217). When discussing the ways in which they attempt to stabilize and enhance the hostage taker's sense of self, hostage negotiators talk about "beefing up" the subject. Rogan and Hammer (1994) have developed a coding schema that differentiates defending self's face, attacking self's face, restoring self's face after an attack, defending other's face, attacking other's face, and restoring other's face after an attack. When coding the Waco negotiations, I merely noted the use of facework without distinguishing attacking, defending, or restoring activities.

When the Waco transcripts are coded for all five types of language—narrative, symbolic, instrumental, relational, and identity—the worldviewing features of identity language are clarified. Identity language straddles the divide between negotiating reality and issue-specific negotiation, particularly when one recognizes that the self is not universally defined in individualistic terms. Some people may choose to activate group membership rather than individuality as an expression of identity (Abrams 1990), which seems particularly relevant in the case of a barricaded unconventional community with a sense of identity defined in opposition to the dominant culture. When identity is tied to an unconventional group and to an oppositional stance vis-à-vis society, identity language is closely tied to narrative and symbolic language that names the world, self, and other. Therefore, I coded two types of identity messages:

- Positive and negative face messages
- Symbolic or narrative statements of self-identity or other-identity

References

Abbott, Thomas E. 1986. Time-Phase Model for Hostage Negotiation. *The Police Chief* (April): 34–35.

Abrams, Dominic. 1990. "How Do Group Members Regulate Their Behaviour? An Integration of Social Identity and Social Awareness Theories." In *Social Identity Theory: Constructive and Critical Advances,* edited by Dominic Abrams and Michael A. Hogg, 83–112. New York: Springer-Verlag.

Abrams, Dominic, and Michael A. Hogg. 1990. "An Introduction to the Social Identity Approach." In *Social Identity Theory: Constructive and Critical Advances,* edited by Dominic Abrams and Michael A. Hogg, 1–9. New York: Springer-Verlag.

Agar, Michael. 1994. *Language Shock: Understanding the Culture of Conversation.* New York: William Morrow.

Aho, James A. 1990. *The Politics of Righteousness: Idaho Christian Patriotism.* Seattle: Univ. of Washington Press.

Ammerman, Nancy T. 1995. "Waco, Federal Law Enforcement, and Scholars of Religion." In *Armageddon in Waco: Critical Perspectives on the Branch Davidian Conflict,* edited by Stuart A. Wright, 282–96. Chicago: Univ. of Chicago Press.

Assefa, Hizkias, and Paul Wahrhaftig. 1990. *The MOVE Crisis in Philadelphia: Extremist Groups and Conflict Resolution.* Pittsburgh: Univ. of Pittsburgh Press.

Augsburger, David W. 1992. *Conflict and Mediation Across Cultures: Pathways and Patterns.* Louisville, Ky.: Westminster, John Knox.

Avruch, Kevin. 1991. "Introduction: Culture and Conflict Resolution." In *Conflict Resolution: Cross-cultural Perspectives,* edited by Kevin Avruch, Peter W. Black, and Joseph A. Scimecca, 1–17. New York: Greenwood.

Avruch, Kevin, and Peter W. Black. 1993. "Conflict Resolution in Intercultural Settings: Problems and Prospects." In *Conflict Resolution Theory and Practice: Integration and Ap-*

plication, edited by Dennis J. D. Sandole and Hugo van der Merwe, 131–45. New York: Manchester Univ. Press.

Avruch, Kevin, Peter W. Black, and Joseph A. Scimecca, eds. 1991. *Conflict Resolution: Cross-cultural Perspectives.* New York: Greenwood.

Bailey, B., and B. Darden. 1993. *Mad Man in Waco.* Waco, Tex.: WRS.

Baird, Robert D. 1971. *Category Formation and the History of Religions.* The Hague: Mouton.

Barker, Eileen. 1983. "With Enemies Like That: Some Functions of Deprogramming as an Aid to Sectarian Membership." In *The Brainwashing/Deprogramming Controversy: Socio-logical, Psychological, Legal, and Historical Perspectives,* edited by David G. Bromley and James T. Richardson, 329–44. New York: Edwin Mellen.

Barkun, Michael. 1993. "Reflections after Waco: Millennialists and the State." *Christian Century* (June 2–9): 596–600.

———. 1994a. "Millenarian Groups and Law Enforcement Agencies: The Lessons of Waco." *Terrorism and Political Violence* 6: 75–95.

———. 1994b. *Religion and the Racist Right.* Chapel Hill: Univ. of North Carolina Press.

Bateson, Gregory. 1972. *Steps to an Ecology of Mind.* New York: Ballantine.

Bazerman, Max H., and Margaret A. Neale. 1992. *Negotiating Rationally.* New York: Free Press.

Berger, Peter L., and Thomas Luckmann. 1966. *The Social Construction of Reality.* New York: Doubleday.

Berman, Morris. 1984. *The Reenchantment of the World.* New York: Bantam.

Black, Peter W. 1991. "Surprised by Common Sense: Local Understandings and the Management of Conflict on Tobi, Republic of Belau." In *Conflict Resolution: Cross-cultural Perspectives,* edited by Kevin Avruch, Peter W. Black, and Joseph A. Scimecca, 145–64. New York: Greenwood.

Blake, Robert R., and Jane Srygley Mouton. 1984. *Solving Costly Organizational Conflicts.* San Francisco: Jossey-Bass.

Blechman, Frank, Jarle Crocker, Jayne Docherty, and Steve Garon. 2000. *Finding Meaning in a Complex Environmental Policy Dialogue: Research into Worldviews in the Northern Forest Lands Council Dialogue, 1990–94.* Working Paper. Fairfax, Va.: Institute for Conflict Analysis and Resolution, George Mason Univ.

Blumer, Herbert. 1969. *Symbolic Interactionism: Perspective and Method.* Berkeley: Univ. of California Press.

Bochner, Arthur P., Kenneth N. Cissna, and Michael G. Garko. 1991. "Optional Metaphors for Studying Interaction." In *Studying Interpersonal Interaction,* edited by Steve Duck and Barbara M. Montgomery, 16–34. New York: Guilford.

Boggs, Stephen T., and Malcolm Naea Chun. 1990. "*Ho'oponopono:* A Hawaiian Method of

Solving Interpersonal Problems." In *Disentangling: Conflict Discourse in Pacific Societies*, edited by Karen Ann Watson-Gegeo and Geoffrey M. White, 122–60. Stanford: Stanford Univ. Press.

Bohl, Nancy K. 1992. "Hostage Negotiator Stress." *FBI Law Enforcement Bulletin* (August): 23–26.

Bormann, Ernest G. 1996. "Symbolic Convergence Theory and Communication in Group Decision Making." In *Communication and Group Decision Making*, edited by Randy Y. Hirokawa and Marshall Scott Poole, 81–113. Thousand Oaks, Calif.: Sage.

Borum, Randy, and Thomas Strentz. 1992. "The Borderline Personality: Negotiation Strategies." *FBI Law Enforcement Bulletin* (August): 6–10.

Bothamley, Jennifer. 1993. *Dictionary of Theories*. Washington, D.C.: Gale Research International.

Botting, James M., Frederick J. Lanceley, and Gary W. Noesner. 1995. "The FBI's Critical Incident Negotiation Team." *FBI Law Enforcement Bulletin* (April): 12–15.

Boulding, Kenneth. 1956. *The Image: Knowledge in Life and Society*. Ann Arbor: Univ. of Michigan Press.

Boyer, Paul. 1992. *When Time Shall Be No More: Prophecy Belief in Modern American Culture*. Cambridge, Mass.: Harvard Univ. Press.

Breault, Marc, and Martin King. 1993. *Inside the Cult*. New York: Penguin.

Bromley, David G., Anson Shupe Jr., and J. C. Ventimiglia. 1979. "Atrocity Tales, the Unification Church, and the Social Construction of Evil." *Journal of Communication* 29, no. 3: 42–53.

Bromley, David G., and Edward D. Silver. 1995. "The Davidian Tradition: From Patronal Clan to Prophetic Movement." In *Armageddon in Waco: Critical Perspectives on the Branch Davidian Conflict*, edited by Stuart A. Wright, 43–72. Chicago: Univ. of Chicago Press.

Brown, Richard Harvey. 1989. *Social Science as Civic Discourse*. Chicago: Univ. of Chicago Press.

Bruner, Jerome. 1990. *Acts of Meaning*. Cambridge, Mass.: Harvard Univ. Press.

Burke, Kenneth. 1969a. *A Grammar of Motives*. Berkeley: Univ. of California Press.

———. 1969b. *A Rhetoric of Motives*. Berkeley: Univ. of California Press.

Burton, John. 1987. *Resolving Deep-Rooted Conflict: A Handbook*. Lanham, Md.: Univ. Press of America.

———. 1990. *Conflict: Resolution and Provention*. New York: St. Martin's.

———. 1996. *Conflict Resolution: Its Languages and Processes*. Lanham, Md.: Scarecrow.

Bush, Robert A. Baruch, and Joseph P. Folger. 1994. *The Promise of Mediation: Responding to Conflict Through Empowerment and Recognition*. San Francisco: Jossey-Bass.

Campbell, Tom. 1981. *Seven Theories of Human Society*. New York: Oxford Univ. Press.

Carnevale, Peter J., and John A. Hilty. 1992. "Black-Hat/White-Hat Strategy and Bilateral Bargaining." *Organizational Behavior and Human Performance* 55: 444–69.

Carpenter, Susan L., and W. J. D. Kennedy. 1991. *Managing Public Disputes*. San Francisco: Jossey-Bass.

Carr, David. 1991. *Time, Narrative, and History*. Bloomington: Indiana Univ. Press.

Carstarphen, Nike. 1995. "Third Party Efforts at Waco: Phillip Arnold and James Tabor." Unpublished paper, Institute for Conflict Analysis and Resolution.

Carstarphen, Nike, Jarle Crocker, Jayne S. Docherty, and Steve Garon. 1995. "The Impact of World Views on Managing Diversity." In *At the Frontier of Managing Diversity: Integrating Practice and Research*, edited by AIMD Staff, n.p. Global Conference on Managing Diversity. Atlanta: American Institute for Managing Diversity.

Chandler, Russell. 1993. *Doomsday: The End of the World, a View Through Time*. Ann Arbor, Mich.: Servant.

CIAG. *See* Critical Incident Analysis Group. 2000.

Clark, Mary E. 1989. *Ariadne's Thread: The Replace for New Modes of Thinking*. New York: St. Martin's.

———. 1990. "Meaningful Social Bonding as a Universal Human Need." In *Conflict: Human Needs Theory*, edited by John Burton, 34–59. New York: St. Martin's.

Clifton, Chas S. 1994. "The Crime of Piety: Wounded Knee to Waco." In *From the Ashes: Making Sense of Waco*, edited by James R. Lewis, 1–5. Lanham, Md.: Rowman and Littlefield.

Cobb, Sara. 1993. "Empowerment and Mediation: A Narrative Perspective." *Negotiation Journal* (July): 245–59.

Cobb, Sara, and Janet Rifkin. 1991. "Practice and Paradox: Deconstructing Neutrality in Mediation." *Law and Social Inquiry* 16: 35–62.

Code, Lorraine. 1991. *What Can She Know? Feminist Theory and the Construction of Knowledge*. Ithaca: Cornell Univ. Press.

Cohen, Anthony P. 1985. *The Symbolic Construction of Community*. New York: Routledge.

Coles, Robert. 1989. *The Call of Stories: Teaching and the Moral Imagination*. Boston: Houghton Mifflin.

Combs, Gene, and Jill Freedman. 1990. *Symbol, Story, and Ceremony: Using Metaphor in Individual and Family Therapy*. New York: W. W. Norton.

Conrad, Charles, and Lucinda Sinclair-James. 1995. "Institutional Pressures, Cultural Constraints, and Communication in Community Mediation Organizations." In *Conflict and Organizations: Communicative Processes*, edited by Anne Maydan Nicotera, 65–99. Albany: State Univ. Press of New York.

Corcoran, James. 1990. *Bitter Harvest: Gordon Kahl and the Posse Comitatus: Murder in the Heartland.* New York: Viking.

Costantino, Cathy A., and Christina Sickles Merchant. 1996. *Designing Conflict Management Systems: A Guide to Creating Productive and Healthy Organizations.* San Francisco: Jossey-Bass.

Coulson, Danny O., and Elaine Shannon. 1999. *No Heroes: Inside the FBI's Secret Counter-Terror Force.* New York: Pocket.

Covert, Lori Anne Schmid. 1984. "A Fantasy-Theme Analysis of the Rhetoric of the Symbionese Liberation Army: Implications for Bargaining with Terrorists." Ph.D. diss., Univ. of Denver.

Cragan, John F., and Donald C. Shields. 1995. *Symbolic Theories in Applied Communication Research: Bormann, Burke, and Fisher.* Cresskill, N.J.: Hampton.

Critical Incident Analysis Group (CIAG). 2000. "CIAG: Critical Incident Analysis Group." Available at: http://www.uvace.virginia.edu/cup/ciag.htm. Cited July 22.

Cross, John G. 1996. "Negotiation as Adaptive Learning." *International Negotiation* 1: 153–78.

Crowfoot, James E., and Julia M. Wondolleck. 1990. *Environmental Disputes: Community Involvement in Conflict Resolution.* Washington, D.C.: Island.

Czarniawska, Barbara. 1997. *Narrating the Organization: Dramas of Institutional Identity.* Chicago: Univ. of Chicago Press.

D'Andrade, Roy. 1995. *The Development of Cognitive Anthropology.* Cambridge: Cambridge Univ. Press.

D'Andrade, Roy, and Claudia Strauss, eds. 1992. *Human Motives and Cultural Models.* Cambridge: Cambridge Univ. Press.

Danforth, John C. 2000. *Interim Report to the Deputy Attorney General Concerning the 1993 Confrontation at the Mount Carmel Complex Waco, Texas.* Available at: http://www.osc-waco.org. Cited July 21.

Dennis, Edward S. G. 1993. *Evaluation of the Handling of the Branch Davidian Stand-off in Waco, Texas: February 28 to April 19, 1993.* Report to the Deputy Attorney General. Washington, D.C.: U.S. Department of Justice, October 8.

Denzin, Norman K. 1992. *Symbolic Interactionism and Cultural Studies.* Cambridge, Mass.: Blackwell.

de Reuck, Anthony. 1990. "A Theory of Conflict Resolution by Problem Solving." In *Conflict: Readings in Management and Resolution,* edited by John Burton and Frank Dukes, 183–98. New York: St. Martin's.

DiVasto, Peter, Frederick J. Lanceley, and Anne Gruys. 1992. "Critical Issues in Suicide Intervention." *FBI Law Enforcement Bulletin* (August): 13–16.

Docherty, Jayne S. 1996a. "Managing Diversity During Law Enforcement Siege Management: The Lessons of Waco." In *AIMD Research Notes*, Research Newsletter nos. 6–7, 1–10. Atlanta: American Institute for Managing Diversity.

——. 1996b. "The Stewardship Metaphor in Forest Resource Management Conflicts: A Common Language Does Not Guarantee Consensus." In *Conflict Analysis and Resolution: Challenges for the Times*, edited by D. McFarland, 191–208. Fairfax, Va.: Institute for Conflict Analysis and Resolution.

——. 1999. "Bridging the Gap Between Scholars of Religion and Law Enforcement Negotiators." *Nova Religio* 3, no. 1: 8–26.

Donohue, William A., and Closepet N. Ramesh. 1992. "Negotiator-Opponent Relationships." In *Communication and Negotiation*, edited by Linda L. Putnam and Michael E. Roloff, 209–32. Newbury Park, Calif.: Sage.

Donohue, William A., Closepet Ramesh, Gary Kaufmann, and Richard Smith. 1991. "Crisis Bargaining in Intense Conflict Situations." *International Journal of Group Tensions* 21, no. 2: 133–53.

Donohue, William A., and Anthony J. Roberto. 1993. "Relational Development as Negotiated Order in Hostage Negotiation." *Human Communication Research* 20, no. 2: 175–98.

——. 1996. "An Empirical Examination of Three Models of Integrative Bargaining." Unpublished paper.

Douglas, Mary. 1996. *Natural Symbols: Explorations in Cosmology.* New York: Routledge.

Downey, Mary Josephine. 1996. "Without Mittens: Religious Atrocity Narratives of Nineteenth and Twentieth Century America." Ph.D. diss., State Univ. of New York at Buffalo.

Drake, Laura E., and William A. Donohue. 1996. "Communicative Framing Theory in Conflict Resolution." *Communication Research* 23, no. 3: 297–322.

Druckman, Daniel, ed. 1977. *Negotiation: Social-Psychological Perspectives.* Beverly Hills: Sage.

Druckman, Daniel, and Kathleen Zechmeister. 1973. "Conflict of Interest and Value Dissensus: Propositions in the Sociology of Conflict." *Human Relations* 26: 449–66.

Duck, Steve. 1994. *Meaningful Relationships: Talking, Sense, and Relating.* Thousand Oaks, Calif.: Sage.

Duck, Steve, and Barbara M. Montgomery. 1991. "The Interdependence among Interaction Substance, Theory, and Methods." In *Studying Interpersonal Interaction*, edited by Steve Duck and Barbara M. Montgomery, 3–15. New York: Guilford.

Dugan, Maire A. 1996. "A Nested Theory of Conflict." *Women in Leadership: Sharing the Vision* 1 (July): 9–20.

Dukes, E. Franklin. 1996. *Resolving Public Conflict: Transforming Community and Governance.* New York: Manchester Univ. Press.

Ellwood, Robert S. 1996. *Many Peoples, Many Faiths.* 5th ed. Saddle River, N.J.: Prentice Hall.

Eoyang, Eugene Chen. 1993. *The Transparent Eye: Reflections on Translation, Chinese Literature, and Comparative Poetics.* Honolulu: Univ. of Hawaii Press.

Experts. *See* United States Department of Justice, comp. 1993.

Fagan, Thomas J., and Clinton R. Van Zandt. 1993. "Lessons from Talladega: Even in 'Nonnegotiable' Situations, Negotiation Plays an Important Role." *Corrections Today* (April): 132–38.

FBI Law Enforcement Bulletin. 1992. Editorial (August): 2.

Federal Bureau of Investigation. 1993. Waco event log 1; Box 25I/Folder 1. FBI Reading Room (Headquarters), Washington, D.C., May 24.

Femenia, Nora A. 1996. *National Identity in Times of Crisis: The Scripts of the Falklands-Malvinas War.* Commack, N.Y.: Nova Science.

Ferrell, Jeff, and Clinton R. Sanders. 1995. *Cultural Criminology.* Boston: Northeastern Univ. Press.

Fine, Gary Alan. 1995. "Public Narration and Group Culture: Discerning Discourse in Social Movements." In *Social Movements and Culture,* edited by Hank Johnston and Bert Klandermans, 127–43. Minneapolis: Univ. of Minnesota Press.

Fisher, Roger, and Scott Brown. 1988. *Getting Together: Building Relationships as We Negotiate.* New York: Penguin.

Fisher, Roger, and William Ury. 1981. *Getting to Yes: Negotiating Agreement Without Giving In.* Boston: Houghton Mifflin.

Fisher, Roger, William Ury, and Bruce Patton. 1991. *Getting to Yes: Negotiating Agreement Without Giving In.* 2d ed. New York: Penguin.

Fisher, Ronald J. 1990. "Needs Theory, Social Identity, and an Eclectic Model of Conflict." In *Conflict: Human Needs Theory,* edited by John Burton, 89–112. New York: St. Martin's.

Fisher, Walter R. 1984. "Narration as a Human Communication Paradigm: The Case of Public Moral Argument." *Communication Monographs* 51 (March): 1–22.

———. 1987. *Human Communication as Narration: Toward a Philosophy of Reason, Value, and Action.* Columbia: Univ. of South Carolina Press.

Fiumara, Gemma Corradi. 1990. *The Other Side of Language: A Philosophy of Listening.* New York: Routledge.

Fogarty, Robert S. 1995. "An Age of Wisdom, an Age of Foolishness: The Davidians, Some

Forerunners, and Our Age." In *Armageddon in Waco: Critical Perspectives on the Branch Davidian Conflict,* edited by Stuart A. Wright, 3–19. Chicago: Univ. of Chicago Press.

Fouraker, L. E., and S. Siegel. 1963. *Bargaining Behavior.* New York: McGraw Hill.

Frank, Jerome D. 1973. *Persuasion and Healing: A Comparative Study of Psychotherapy.* Baltimore: Johns Hopkins Univ. Press.

Froman, Larry, and John Glorioso. 1984. "Applying Communications Theory to Hostage Negotiations." *The Police Chief* (May): 59–60.

Fuselier, G. Dwayne. 1986a. *A Practical Overview of Hostage Negotiations.* Reprinted with revisions from the *FBI Law Enforcement Bulletin* (June-July 1981). Washington, D.C.: Federal Bureau of Investigation, U.S. Department of Justice.

———. 1986b. "What Every Negotiator Would Like His Chief to Know." *FBI Law Enforcement Bulletin* (March): 12–15.

Fuselier, G. Dwayne, and Gary W. Noesner. 1990. "Confronting the Terrorist Hostage Taker." *FBI Law Enforcement Bulletin* (July): 1–6.

Fuselier, G. Dwayne, Clinton R. Van Zandt, and Frederick J. Lanceley. 1989. "Negotiating the Protracted Incident: The Oakdale and Atlanta Prison Sieges." *FBI Law Enforcement Bulletin* (July): 1–7.

———. 1991. "Hostage/Barricade Incidents: High Risk Factors and the Action Criteria." *FBI Law Enforcement Bulletin* (January): 6–12.

Geertz, Clifford. 1973. *The Interpretation of Cultures.* New York: Basic.

Geist, Patricia. 1995. "Negotiating Whose Order? Communicating to Negotiate Identities and Revise Organizational Structures." In *Conflict and Organizations: Communicative Processes,* edited by Anne Maydan Nicotera, 45–64. Albany: State Univ. Press of New York.

Gibbons, Pamela, James J. Bradac, and Jon D. Busch. 1992. "The Role of Language in Negotiations: Threats and Promises." In *Communication and Negotiation,* edited by Linda L. Putnam and Michael E. Roloff, 156–75. Newbury Park: Sage.

Gilmartin, Kevin M., and Robert J. Gibson. 1985. "Hostage Negotiation: The Biobehavioral Dimension." *The Police Chief* (June): 46–48.

Goffman, Erving. 1986. *Frame Analysis: An Essay on the Organization of Experience.* Boston: Northeastern Univ. Press.

Goldaber, Irving. 1979. "A Typology of Hostage-Takers." *The Police Chief* (June): 21–22.

Goode, Erich, and Nachman Ben-Yehuda. 1994. *Moral Panics: The Social Construction of Deviance.* Cambridge, Mass.: Blackwell.

Goodman, Nelson. 1978. *Ways of Worldmaking.* Indianapolis: Hackett.

Gulliver, P. H. 1979. *Disputes and Negotiations: A Cross-cultural Perspective.* New York: Academic.

Gusfield, Joseph, ed. 1989. *Kenneth Burke on Symbols and Society.* Chicago: Univ. of Chicago Press.

Hacker, Frederick J. 1976. *Crusaders, Criminals, and Crazies.* New York: W. W. Norton.

Haines-Young, Roy, David R. Green, and Stephen H. Cousins, eds. 1993. *Landscape Ecology and Geographic Information Systems.* New York: Taylor and Francis.

Hall, John R. 1995. "Public Narratives and the Apocalyptic Sect: From Jonestown to Mt. Carmel." In *Armageddon in Waco: Critical Perspectives on the Branch Davidian Conflict,* edited by Stuart A. Wright, 205–35. Chicago: Univ. of Chicago Press.

Hammer, Mitchell R., and Randall G. Rogan. 1997. "Negotiation Models in Crisis Situations: The Value of a Communication-based Approach." In *Dynamic Processes of Crisis Negotiations: Theory, Research, and Practice,* edited by Randall G. Rogan, Mitchell R. Hammer, and Clint Van Zandt, 9–23. Westport, Conn.: Praeger.

Hammer, Mitchell R., and Gary Weaver. 1989. "Cultural Considerations in Hostage Negotiations." Paper presented at the American Society of Criminology Conference, November 8–12, Reno, Nevada.

Hancock, Lee. 2000. "U.S. Not Responsible, Davidian Jury Says." *Dallas Morning News,* July 15. Available at: http://www.cesnur.org/testi/waco108.htm.

Hare, Anthony. 1997. "Training Crisis Negotiators: Updating Negotiation Techniques and Training." In *Dynamic Processes of Crisis Negotiation: Theory, Research, and Practice,* edited by Randall G. Rogan, Mitchell R. Hammer, and Clinton R. Van Zandt, 151–60. Westport, Conn.: Praeger.

Hayles, N. Katherine. 1995. "Narratives of Evolution and the Evolution of Narratives." In *Cooperation and Conflict in General Evolutionary Processes,* edited by John L. Casti and Anders Karlqvist, 113–32. New York: John Wiley and Sons.

Hearit, Keith Michael. 1995. " 'Mistakes Were Made:' Organizations, Apologia, and Crises of Social Legitimacy." *Communication Studies* 46 (spring): 1–56.

Heymann, Philip B., Deputy Attorney General. 1993. *Lessons of Waco: Proposed Changes in Federal Law Enforcement.* Government Report. Washington, D.C.: U.S. Government Printing Office, October 8.

Hillmann, Michael. 1988. "Tactical Intelligence Operations and Support During a Major Barricade/Hostage Event." *The Police Chief* (February): 18–30.

Hocker, Joyce L., and William W. Wilmot. 1995. *Interpersonal Conflict.* 4th ed. Madison, Wisc.: Brown and Benchmark.

Hoffman, Lynn. 1992. "A Reflexive Stance for Family Therapy." In *Therapy as Social Construction,* edited by Sheila McNamee and Kenneth J. Gergen, 7–24. Newbury Park, Calif.: Sage.

Hogg, Michael A., and Craig McGarty. 1990. "Self-categorization and Social Identity." In

Social Identity Theory: Constructive and Critical Advances, edited by Dominic Abrams and Michael A. Hogg, 10–27. New York: Springer-Verlag.

Holland, Dorothy, and Naomi Quinn, eds. 1987. *Cultural Models in Language and Thought.* New York: Cambridge Univ. Press.

Holmes, Michael E. 1997. "Processes and Patterns in Hostage Negotiations." In *Dynamic Processes of Crisis Negotiation: Theory, Research, and Practice,* edited by Randall G. Rogan, Mitchell R. Hammer, and Clinton R. Van Zandt, 77–93. Westport, Conn.: Praeger.

Holmes, Michael E., and Richard E. Sykes. 1993. "A Test of the Fit of Gulliver's Phase Model to Hostage Negotiations." *Communication Studies* 44, no. 1: 38–55.

hooks, bell. 1994. "Language: Teaching New Worlds/New Words." In *Teaching to Transgress: Education as the Practice of Freedom,* edited by bell hooks, 167–75. New York: Routledge.

Hopmann, P. T. 1995. "Two Paradigms of Negotiation: Bargaining and Problem Solving." *Annals of the American Academy of Political and Social Science* 542: 24–47.

Hunter, Susan. 1989. "The Roots of Environmental Conflict in the Tahoe Basin." In *Intractable Conflicts and Their Transformation,* edited by Louis Kriesberg, Terrell A. Northrup, and Stuart J. Thorson, 25–40. Syracuse: Syracuse Univ. Press.

Iklé, Fred Charles. 1964. *How Nations Negotiate.* New York: Harper and Row.

———. 1993. "Bargaining and Communication." In *Negotiation: Readings, Exercises, and Cases,* edited by Roy J. Lewicki, Joseph A. Litterer, David M. Saunders, and John W. Minton, 237–44. Boston: Irwin.

"Judge Smith's Comments." 2000. *Dallas Morning News,* July 15. Available at: http://www.cesnur.org/testi/waco107.htm.

Judiciary. *See* United States Congress. 1996.

Justice. *See* Scruggs, Richard, Steven Zipperstein, Robert Lyon, Victor Gonzalez, Herbert Cousins, and Roderick Beverly. 1993.

Katz, Neil H., and John W. Lawyer. 1985. *Communication and Conflict Resolution Skills.* Dubuque, Iowa: Kendall/Hunt.

Kelman, Herbert C. 1990. "Applying a Human Needs Perspective to the Practice of Conflict Resolution: The Israeli-Palestinian Case." In *Conflict: Human Needs Theory,* edited by John Burton, 283–97. New York: St. Martin's.

———. 1996. "Negotiation as Interactive Problem Solving." *International Negotiation* 1: 99–123.

Kirk, Stuart A., and Herb Kutchins. 1992. *The Selling of DSM: The Rhetoric of Science in Psychiatry.* New York: Aldine De Gruyter.

Kolb, Deborah. 1997. *When Talk Works: Profiles of Mediators.* San Francisco: Jossey-Bass.

Kopel, David B., and Paul H. Blackman. 1997. *No More Wacos: What's Wrong with Federal Law Enforcement and How to Fix It.* Amherst, N.Y.: Prometheus.

Lakoff, George. 1987. *Women, Fire, and Dangerous Things: What Categories Reveal about the Mind.* Chicago: Univ. of Chicago Press.

———. 1992. "Metaphors and War: The Metaphor System Used to Justify War in the Gulf." In *Thirty Years of Linguistic Evolution: Studies in Honor of René Dirven on the Occasion of His Sixtieth Birthday,* edited by Martin Pütz, 463–81. Philadelphia: John Benjamins.

Lanceley, Frederick J. 1981. "The Antisocial Personality as Hostage-Taker." *Journal of Police Science and Administration* 9 (March): 28–34.

Laszlo, Ervin, Ignazio Masulli, Robert Artigiani, and Vilmos Csányi. 1993. *The Evolution of Cognitive Maps: New Paradigms for the Twenty-first Century.* Langhorne, Pa.: Gordon and Breach Science.

Latour, Bruno. 1993. *We Have Never Been Modern.* Translated by Catherine Porter. Cambridge, Mass.: Harvard Univ. Press.

Laue, James. 1987. "The Emergence and Institutionalization of Third Party Roles in Conflict." In *Conflict Management and Problem Solving: From Interpersonal to International Applications,* edited by Dennis J. D. Sandole and Ingrid Sandole-Staroste, 17–29. New York: New York Univ. Press.

Lederach, John Paul. 1995. *Preparing for Peace: Conflict Transformation Across Cultures.* Syracuse: Syracuse Univ. Press.

Lehrer, Adrienne. 1974. *Semantic Fields and Lexical Structure.* New York: American Elsevier.

Lewicki, Roy J., Joseph A. Litterer, John W. Minton, and David M. Saunders. 1994. *Negotiation.* Boston: Irwin.

Lewis, James R., ed. 1994. *From the Ashes: Making Sense of Waco.* Lanham, Md.: Rowman and Littlefield.

———. 1995. "Self-fulfilling Stereotypes, the Anticult Movement, and the Waco Confrontation." In *Armageddon in Waco: Critical Perspectives on the Branch Davidian Conflict,* edited by Stuart A. Wright, 95–110. Chicago: Univ. of Chicago Press.

Littlejohn, Stephen W. 1995. "Moral Conflict in Organizations." In *Conflict and Organizations: Communicative Processes,* edited by Anne Maydan Nicotera, 101–25. Albany: State Univ. Press of New York.

Logs. *See* Federal Bureau of Investigation. 1993.

Lucas, Phillip. 1994. "How Future Wacos Might Be Avoided: Two Proposals." In *From the Ashes: Making Sense of Waco,* edited by James R. Lewis, 209–12. Lanham, Md.: Rowman and Littlefield.

Lutz, Catherine A. 1988. *Unnatural Emotions: Everyday Sentiments on a Micronesian Atoll and Their Challenge to Western Theory.* Chicago: Univ. of Chicago Press.

———. 1990. "Engendered Emotion: Gender, Power, and the Rhetoric of Emotional Control in American Discourse." In *Language and the Politics of Emotion,* edited by Catherine A. Lutz and Lila Abu-Lughod, 69–91. New York: Cambridge Univ. Press.

Maruyama, Magorah. 1992. *Context and Complexity: Cultivating Contextual Understanding.* New York: Springer-Verlag.

Maser, Chris. 1994. *Sustainable Forestry: Philosophy, Science, and Economics.* Delray Beach, Fla.: St. Lucie.

McCarthy, Ronald M. 1993. "An Evaluation of the Special Response Capabilities of the U.S. Department of Justice, Federal Bureau of Investigation." In *Recommendations of Experts for Improvement in Federal Law Enforcement after Waco,* compiled by U.S. Department of Justice, n.p. Washington, D.C.: U.S. Government Printing Office.

McGee, M. 1984. "Secular Humanism: A Radical Reading of 'Culture Industry' Productions." *Critical Studies in Mass Communications* 1: 1–33.

McMains, Michael J., and Wayman C. Mullins. 1996. *Crisis Negotiations: Managing Critical Incidents and Hostage Situations in Law Enforcement and Corrections.* Cincinnati, Ohio: Anderson.

Memmi, Albert. 1965. *The Colonizer and the Colonized.* New York: Orion.

Minsky, Marvin. 1975. "A Framework for Representing Knowledge." In *The Psychology of Computer Vision,* edited by Patrick H. Winston, 211–77. New York: McGraw Hill.

Miron, Murray S., and Arnold P. Goldstein. 1979. *Hostage.* New York: Pergamon.

Mitchell, Christopher. 1981. *The Structure of International Conflict.* New York: St. Martin's.

——. 1990. "Necessitous Man and Conflict Resolution: More Basic Questions about Basic Human Needs Theory." In *Conflict: Human Needs Theory,* edited by John Burton, 149–76. New York: St. Martin's.

Mitchell, Christopher, and Michael Banks. 1996. *Handbook of Conflict Resolution: The Analytical Problem-Solving Approach.* New York: Pinter.

Mittelstadt, Michelle. 2000. "Jury's Findings Reverberate Across Capital, Country." *Dallas Morning News,* July 15. Available at: http://www.cesnur.org/testi/waco107.htm.

Moore, Carol. 1995. *The Davidian Massacre: Disturbing Questions about Waco Which Must Be Answered.* Springfield, Va.: Gun Owners Foundation.

Moore, Christopher W. 1996. *The Mediation Process.* 2d ed. San Francisco: Jossey-Bass.

Morley, Ian. 1986. "Negotiating and Bargaining." In *A Handbook of Communication Skills,* edited by Owen Hargie, 303–24. New York: New York Univ. Press.

Morley, Ian, and Geoffrey Stephenson. 1977. *The Social Psychology of Bargaining.* London: George Allen and Unwin.

Morley, Ian, Janette Webb, and Geoffrey M. Stephenson. 1988. "Bargaining and Arbitration in the Resolution of Conflict." In *The Social Psychology of Intergroup Conflict: Theory, Re-*

search, and Applications, edited by Wolfgang Stroebe, Arie W. Kruglanski, Daniel Bar-Tal, and Miles Hewstone, 117–34. New York: Springer-Verlag.

Neimeyer, Robert A. 1993. "An Appraisal of Constructivist Psychotherapies." *Journal of Consulting and Clinical Psychology* 61, no. 2: 221–34.

Noesner, Gary W., and John T. Dolan. 1992. "First Responder Negotiation Training." *FBI Law Enforcement Bulletin* (August): 1–4.

Northrup, Terrell A. 1989. "The Dynamic of Identity in Personal and Social Conflict." In *Intractable Conflicts and Their Transformation,* edited by Louis Kriesberg, Terrell A. Northrup, and Stuart J. Thorson, 55–82. Syracuse: Syracuse Univ. Press.

Noss, Reed F., and Allen Y. Cooperrider. 1994. *Saving Nature's Legacy: Protecting and Restoring Biodiversity.* Washington, D.C.: Island.

Nudler, Oscar. 1993. "In Replace of a Theory for Conflict Resolution: Taking a New Look at World Views Analysis." *Institute for Conflict Analysis and Resolution Newsletter* (summer): 1, 4–5.

Oakeshott, Michael. 1994. *Experience and Its Modes.* 1933. Reprint. Cambridge: Cambridge Univ. Press.

O'Leary, Stephen D. 1994. *Arguing the Apocalypse: A Theory of Millennial Rhetoric.* New York: Oxford Univ. Press.

Ozawa, Connie P. 1991. *Recasting Science: Consensual Procedures in Public Policy Making.* Boulder, Colo.: Westview.

Paden, William E. 1988. *Religious Worlds: The Comparative Study of Religion.* Boston: Beacon.

Palmer, Gary B. 1996. *Toward a Theory of Cultural Linguistics.* Austin: Univ. of Texas Press.

Palmer, Susan Jean. 1994. *Moon Sisters, Krishna Mothers, Rajneesh Lovers: Women's Roles in New Religions.* Syracuse: Syracuse Univ. Press.

Pearce, W. Barnett, and Stephen W. Littlejohn. 1997. *Moral Conflict: When Social Worlds Collide.* Thousand Oaks, Calif.: Sage.

Pepper, Stephen C. 1961. *World Hypotheses: A Study in Evidence.* Berkeley: Univ. of California Press.

Pitts, William L., Jr. 1995. "Davidians and Branch Davidians: 1929–1987." In *Armageddon in Waco: Critical Perspectives on the Branch Davidian Conflict,* edited by Stuart A. Wright, 20–42. Chicago: Univ. of Chicago Press.

Pitzer, Donald E. 1997. *America's Communal Utopias.* Chapel Hill: Univ. of North Carolina Press.

Polkinghorne, Donald E. 1988. *Narrative Knowing and the Human Sciences.* Albany: State Univ. of New York Press.

Powell, Joel Ovid. 1989. "Negotiation Processes in Hostage and Barricaded Incidents." Ph.D. diss., Univ. of Iowa.

Prince, Gerald. 1987. *Dictionary of Narratology.* Lincoln: Univ. of Nebraska Press.

Pruitt, Dean G., and Peter J. Carnevale. 1993. *Negotiation in Social Conflict.* Pacific Grove, Calif.: Brooks/Cole.

Pruitt, Dean G., and Steven A. Lewis. 1977. "The Psychology of Integrative Bargaining." In *Negotiation: Social-Psychological Perspectives,* edited by Daniel Druckman, 161–92. Beverly Hills: Sage.

Putnam, Linda, and Majia Holmer. 1992. "Framing, Reframing, and Issue Development. In *Communication and Negotiation,* edited by Linda L. Putnam and Michael E. Roloff, 128–56. Newbury Park: Sage.

Putnam, Linda, and T. Jones. 1982. "The Role of Communication in Bargaining." *Human Communications Research* 8: 262–80.

Putnam, Linda L., and Michael E. Roloff, eds. *Communication and Negotiation.* Newbury Park, Calif.: Sage.

Quinn, Naomi. 1991. "The Cultural Basis of Metaphor." In *Beyond Metaphor: The Theory of Tropes in Anthropology,* edited by James W. Fernandez, 56–93. Stanford: Stanford Univ. Press.

Quinn, Naomi, and Dorothy Holland. 1987. "Culture and Cognition." In *Cultural Models in Language and Thought,* edited by Dorothy Holland and Naomi Quinn, 3–40. New York: Cambridge Univ. Press.

Rambo, Lewis R. 1993. *Understanding Religious Conversion.* New Haven, Conn.: Yale Univ. Press.

Ramesh, Closepet Nagaraj. 1992. "The Influence of Power on Hostage Negotiation Outcomes: A Contextual, Descriptive, and Fantasy-Theme Analysis." Ph.D. diss., Michigan State Univ.

Rapoport, Anatol. 1960. *Fights, Games, and Debates.* Ann Arbor: Univ. of Michigan Press.

Reavis, Dick J. 1995. *The Ashes of Waco: An Investigation.* New York: Simon and Schuster.

Rifkin, Janet, Jonathan Millen, and Sara Cobb. 1991. "Toward a New Discourse for Mediation: A Critique of Neutrality." *Mediation Quarterly,*9, no. 2: 151–64.

Robbins, Rebecca L. 1992. "Self-determination and Subordination: The Past, Present, and Future of American Indian Governance." In *The State of Native America: Genocide, Colonization, and Resistance,* edited by M. Annette Jaimes, 87–121. Boston: South End.

Rogan, Randall Gage. 1990. "An Interaction Analysis of Negotiator and Hostage-Taker Identity Goal, Relational Goal, and Language Intensity Message Behavior Within Hostage Negotiations: A Descriptive Investigation of Three Negotiations." Ph.D. diss., Michigan State Univ.

———. 1997. "Emotion and Emotional Expression in Crisis Negotiation." In *Dynamic Processes of Crisis Negotiation: Theory, Research, and Practice*, edited by Randall G. Rogan, Mitchell R. Hammer, and Clinton R. Van Zandt, 9–23. Westport, Conn.: Praeger.

Rogan, Randall Gage, and Mitchell R. Hammer. 1994. "Crisis Negotiations: A Preliminary Investigation of Facework in Naturalistic Conflict Discourse." *Journal of Applied Communication Research* 22 (August): 216–31.

———. 1995. "Assessing Message Affect in Crisis Negotiations: An Exploratory Study." *Human Communication Research* 21, no. 4: 553–74.

Rogan, Randall Gage, Mitchell R. Hammer, and Clinton R. Van Zandt, eds. 1997. *Dynamic Processes of Crisis Negotiation: Theory, Research, and Practice.* Westport, Conn.: Praeger.

Roloff, Michael E., and Jerry M. Jordan. 1992. "Achieving Negotiation Goals: The 'Fruits and Foibles' of Planning Ahead." In *Communication and Negotiation*, edited by Linda L. Putnam and Michael E. Roloff, 21–45. Newbury Park, Calif.: Sage.

Rosaldo, Renato. 1989. *Culture and Truth: The Remaking of Social Analysis.* Boston: Beacon.

Rosenfeld, Jean E. 1997. "The Importance of the Analysis of Religion in Avoiding Violent Outcomes: The Justus Freemen Crisis." *Nova Religio* 1, no. 1: 72–95.

———. 1998. "A Brief History of Millennialism: An Address to the Los Angeles Police Department with Practical Recommendations." March 11.

———. 2000. "A Brief History of Millennialism and Suggestions for a New Paradigm for Use in Critical Incidents." In *Millennialism, Persecution, and Violence: Historical Cases*, edited by Catherine Wessinger, 347–51. Syracuse: Syracuse Univ. Press.

Ross, Marc Howard. 1993a. *The Culture of Conflict: Interpretations and Interests in Comparative Perspective.* New Haven, Conn.: Yale Univ. Press.

———. 1993b. *The Management of Conflict: Interpretations and Interests in Comparative Perspective.* New Haven, Conn.: Yale Univ. Press.

Rubenstein, Richard E. 1993. "The Analyzing and Resolving of Class Conflict." In *Conflict Resolution Theory and Practice: Integration and Application*, edited by Dennis J. D. Sandole and Hugo van der Merwe, 146–57. New York: Manchester University Press.

Rubin, Jeffrey Z., and Bert R. Brown. 1975. *The Social Psychology of Bargaining and Negotiation.* New York: Harcourt Brace Jovanovich.

Rueth, Thomas W. 1993. "Onsite Psychological Evaluation of a Hostage Taker." *Psychological Reports* 73: 659–64.

Runes, Dagobert D., ed. 1960. *Dictionary of Philosophy.* New York: Philosophical Library.

Sandole, Dennis J. D. 1990. "The Biological Basis of Needs in World Society: The Ultimate Micro-Macro Nexus." In *Conflict: Human Needs Theory*, edited by John Burton, 60–88. New York: St. Martin's.

Sargent, Lyman Tower, ed. 1995. *Extremism in America.* New York: New York Univ. Press.

Schank, Roger C., and Robert P. Abelson. 1977. *Scripts, Plans, Goals, and Understanding: An Inquiry into Human Knowledge Structures*. Hillsdale, N.J.: Lawrence Erlbaum.

Schön, Donald A. 1983. *The Reflective Practitioner: How Professionals Think in Action*. New York: Basic.

Schön, Donald A., and Martin Rein. 1994. *Frame Reflection: Toward the Resolution of Intractable Policy Controversies*. New York: Basic.

Scruggs, Richard, Steven Zipperstein, Robert Lyon, Victor Gonzalez, Herbert Cousins, and Roderick Beverly. 1993. *Report to the Deputy Attorney General on the Events at Waco, Texas: February 28 to April 19, 1993*. Government Report. Washington, D.C.: U.S. Government Printing Office, October 8.

Senge, Peter M. 1990. *The Fifth Discipline: The Art and Practice of the Learning Organization*. New York: Doubleday.

Sergeev, Victor M. 1991. "Metaphors for Understanding International Negotiation." In *International Negotiation: Analysis, Approaches, Issues*, edited by Victor Kremenyuk, 58–64. San Francisco: Jossey-Bass.

Shupe, Anson D., Jr., and David G. Bromley. 1983. "The Moonies and the Anti-cultists: Movement and Countermovement in Conflict." In *Religion and Religiosity in America*, edited by Jeffrey K. Hadden and Theodore E. Long, 70–83. New York: Crossroads.

Sillars, Malcolm O. 1991. *Messages, Meanings, and Culture: Approaches to Communication Criticism*. Vol. 2 of the Rhetoric and Society series. New York: Harper Collins.

Simmel, Georg. 1955. *Conflict and the Web of Group Affiliations*. New York: Free Press.

Slatkin, Arthur. 1996. "Enhancing Negotiator Training: Therapeutic Communication." *FBI Law Enforcement Bulletin* (May). Available at: http://www.fbi.gov/leb/may961.txt.

Snell-Hornby, Mary. 1995. *Translation Studies: An Integrated Approach*. Philadelphia: John Benjamins.

Somers, Margaret R., and Gloria D. Gibson. 1994. "Reclaiming the Epistemological 'Other': Narrative and the Social Constitution of Identity." In *Social Theory and the Politics of Identity*, edited by Craig Calhoun, 37–99. Cambridge, Mass.: Blackwell.

Spector, Bertram I. 1995. "Creativity Heuristics for Impasse Resolution: Reframing Intractable Negotiations." *Annals of the American Academy of Political and Social Science* 542: 81–99.

———. 1996. "Metaphors of International Negotiation." *International Negotiation* 1, no. 1: 1–9.

Spender, Dale. 1980. *Man Made Language*. London: Pandora.

Stein, Janice Gross. 1989. "Getting to the Table: The Triggers, Stages, Functions, and Consequences of Prenegotiation." In *Getting to the Table: The Processes of International Prenegotiation*, edited by Janice Gross Stein, 239–68. Baltimore: Johns Hopkins Univ. Press.

Stone, Alan A., M.D. 1993. *Report and Recommendations Concerning the Handling of Incidents Such as the Branch Davidian Standoff in Waco, Texas.* Report. Cambridge, Mass.: Harvard University.

Strauss, Anselm. 1978. *Negotiation: Varieties, Contexts, Processes, and Social Order.* San Francisco: Jossey-Bass.

Strentz, Thomas. 1986. "Negotiating with the Hostage-Taker Exhibiting Paranoid Schizophrenic Symptoms." *Journal of Police Science and Administration* 14, no. 1: 12–16.

——. 1993. "The Inadequate Personality as a Hostage Taker." *Journal of Police Science* 11: 363–68.

Sullivan, Lawrence E. 1993. "Recommendations Concerning Incidents Such as the Branch Davidian Standoff in Waco, Texas, Between February 28, 1993 and April 19, 1993." In *Recommendations of Experts for Improvement in Federal Law Enforcement after Waco,* compiled by the U.S. Department of Justice, n.p. Washington, D.C.: U.S. Government Printing Office.

Susskind, Lawrence. 1994. *Environmental Diplomacy: Negotiating More Effective Global Agreements.* New York: Oxford Univ. Press.

Susskind, Lawrence, and Jeffrey Cruikshank. 1987. *Breaking the Impasse: Consensual Approaches to Resolving Public Disputes.* New York: Basic.

Tabor, James D. 1995. "Religious Discourse and Failed Negotiations: The Dynamics of Biblical Apocalypticism at Waco." In *Armageddon in Waco: Critical Perspectives on the Branch Davidian Conflict,* edited by Stuart A. Wright, 263–81. Chicago: Univ. of Chicago Press.

Tabor, James D., and Eugene V. Gallagher. 1995. *Why Waco? Cults and the Battle for Religious Freedom in America.* Berkeley: Univ. of California Press.

Tannen, Deborah, ed. 1993a. *Framing in Discourse.* New York: Oxford Univ. Press.

——. 1993b. "What's in a Frame? In *Framing in Discourse,* edited by Deborah Tannen, 14–56. New York: Oxford Univ. Press.

Thibodeau, David, and Leon Whiteson. 1999. *A Place Called Waco: A Survivor's Story.* New York: Public Affairs.

Thompson, Damian. 1996. *The End of Time: Faith and Fear in the Shadow of the Millennium.* Hanover: Univ. Press of New England.

Treasury. *See* United States Department of the Treasury. 1993.

Turner, Victor. 1974. *Dramas, Fields, and Metaphors.* Ithaca: Cornell Univ. Press.

——. 1981. "Social Dramas and Stories about Them." In *On Narrative,* edited by W. J. T. Mitchell, 137–64. Chicago: Univ. of Chicago Press.

United States Congress. 1996. Committee on the Judiciary. Subcommittee on Crime of the Committee on the Judiciary House of Representatives and the Subcommittee on National Security, International Affairs, and Criminal Justice of the Committee on Government Reform and Oversight. *Activities of Federal Law Enforcement Agencies Toward the Branch Davidians.* 104th Cong., 1st sess.

United States Department of Justice, comp. 1993. *Recommendations of Experts for Improvements in Federal Law Enforcement after Waco.* Report. Washington, D.C.: U.S. Government Printing Office.

United States Department of the Treasury. Waco Administrative Review Team. 1993. *Report of the Department of the Treasury on the Bureau of Alcohol, Tobacco, and Firearms Investigation of Vernon Wayne Howell, also Known as David Koresh.* Report. Washington, D.C.: U.S. Government Printing Office, September.

Ury, William. 1981. *Getting Past No: Negotiating with Difficult People.* New York: Bantam.

Ury, William, Jeanne M. Brett, and Stephen B. Goldberg. 1989. *Getting Disputes Resolved: Designing Systems to Cut the Costs of Conflict.* San Francisco: Jossey-Bass.

Van Zandt, Clinton R. 1993. "Suicide by Cop". *The Police Chief* (July): 24–30.

———. 1997. "Negotiating with Cults: A Practitioner's Perspective." In *Dynamic Processes of Crisis Negotiation: Theory, Research, and Practice,* edited by Randall G. Rogan, Mitchell R. Hammer, and Clinton R. Van Zandt, 143–49. Westport, Conn.: Praeger.

Van Zandt, Clinton R., and G. Dwayne Fuselier. 1989. "Nine Days of Crisis Negotiations: The Oakdale Siege." *Corrections Today* (July): 16–24.

von Bertalanffy, Ludwig. 1968. *General System Theory: Foundations, Developments, Applications.* New York: George Braziller.

Wagner-Pacifici, Robin. 1994. *Discourse and Destruction: The City of Philadelphia Versus MOVE.* Chicago: Univ. of Chicago Press.

Walcott, Charles, P. Terrence Hopmann, and Timothy D. King. 1977. "The Role of Debate in Negotiation." In *Negotiation: Social-Psychological Perspectives,* edited by Daniel Druckman, 193–211. Beverly Hills: Sage.

Wall, Jim Vander. 1992. "A Warrior Caged: The Continuing Struggle of Leonard Peltier." In *The State of Native America: Genocide, Colonization, and Resistance,* edited by M. Annette Jaimes, 291–310. Boston: South End.

Wardlaw, Grant. 1984. "The Psychologist's Role in Hostage Negotiations." *The Police Chief* (May): 56–58.

Watson-Gegeo, Karen Ann, and Geoffrey M. White. 1990. *Disentangling: Conflict Discourse in Pacific Societies.* Stanford: Stanford Univ. Press.

Weber, Max. 1964. *The Theory of Social and Economic Organization.* Translated by A. M. Henderson and Talcott Parsons. New York: Free Press.

Wessinger, Catherine. 2000a. *How the Millennium Comes Violently: From Jonestown to Heaven's Gate.* New York: Seven Bridges.

————, ed. 2000b. *Millennialism, Persecution, and Violence: Historical Cases.* Syracuse: Syracuse Univ. Press.

White, Geoffrey M. 1991. "Rhetoric, Reality, and Resolving Conflicts: Disentangling in a Solomon Islands Society." In *Conflict Resolution: Cross-cultural Perspectives,* edited by Kevin Avruch, Peter W. Black, and Joseph A. Scimecca, 187–212. New York: Greenwood.

White, Michael, and David Epston. 1990. *Narrative Means to Therapeutic Ends.* New York: W. W. Norton.

Wiener, Morton, and David Marcus. 1994. "A Sociocultural Construction of 'Depressions.' " In *Constructing the Social,* edited by Theodore R. Sarbin and John I. Kitsuse, 213–31. Thousand Oaks, Calif.: Sage.

Wierzbicka, Anna. 1992. *Semantics, Culture, and Cognition: Universal Human Concepts in Culture-Specific Configurations.* New York: Oxford Univ. Press.

Williams, Raymond. 1983. *Keywords: A Vocabulary of Culture and Society.* Rev. ed. New York: Oxford Univ. Press.

Wilson, Steven R., and Linda L. Putnam. 1990. "Interaction Goals in Negotiation." In *Communication Yearbook,* edited by J. A. Anderson, 374–406. Newbury Park: Sage.

Winkler, Carol K. 1995. "Narrative Reframing of Public Argument: George Bush's Handling of the Persian Gulf Conflict." In *Warranting Assent: Case Studies in Argument Validation,* edited by Edward Schiappa, 33–55. Albany: State Univ. of New York Press.

Winslade, John, and Gerald Monk. 2000. *Narrative Mediation: A New Approach to Conflict Resolution.* San Francisco: Jossey-Bass.

Wisenberg, Solomon L. 2000. "Waco Civil Trial Preview." At FindLaw Legal News: http://legalnews.findlaw.com. Cited July 15.

Witkin, Gordon. 1997. "The Secret FBI-Militia Alliance: How Onetime Adversaries Have Joined to Defuse Some Crises." *U.S. News & World Report* (May 12): 40–41.

Womack, Deanna F., and Kathleen Walsh. 1997. "A Three-Dimensional Model of Relationship Development in Hostage Negotiations." In *Dynamic Processes of Crisis Negotiation: Theory, Research, and Practice,* edited by Randall G. Rogan, Mitchell R. Hammer, and Clinton R. Van Zandt, 57–75. Westport, Conn.: Praeger.

Wondolleck, Julia M. 1988. *Public Lands Conflict and Resolution: Managing National Forest Disputes.* New York: Plenum.

Wright, Stuart A., ed. 1995a. *Armageddon in Waco: Critical Perspectives on the Branch Davidian Conflict.* Chicago: Univ. of Chicago Press.

————. 1995b. "Construction and Escalation of a Cult Threat: Dissecting Moral Panic and Official Reaction to the Branch Davidians." In *Armageddon in Waco: Critical Perspectives on the Branch Davidian Conflict,* edited by Stuart A. Wright, 75–94. Chicago: Univ. of Chicago Press.

Zerubavel, Eviatar. 1991. *The Fine Line: Making Distinctions in Everyday Life.* Chicago: Univ. of Chicago Press.

Index

dollar only if the interest were free of income tax. A person in
the 20 per cent income tax bracket would have required a taxable
interest rate of 4.3 per cent; in a 40 per cent bracket 5.7 per
cent; in an 80 per cent bracket 17 per cent. And all this simply
to hold even with the depreciation of the dollar and avoid
actual loss."

RATES OF INTEREST AND DEPRECIATION OF MONEY

Country	Indexes of Value of Money*		Annual Rate of Deprec. (comp'd.)	Rates Offered on Gov't. Bonds†	
	1946	1956‡		1946	1956‡
Switzerland	100	86	1.5%	3.10%	3.23%
Germany	100	72	3.2	n.a.	4.90
India	100	72	3.2	2.88	3.98
United States	100	71	3.4	2.19	3.27
Venezuela	100	70	3.5	n.a.	3.63
Netherlands	100	67	4.0	2.99	4.10
Canada	100	65	4.2	2.61	3.88
South Africa	100	65	4.2	2.89	4.75
Sweden	100	65	4.3	3.01	3.74
United Kingdom	100§	65	4.6	2.76§	4.86
New Zealand	100	59	5.2	3.01	4.73
France	100¶	58	6.5	4.26¶	5.48
Mexico	100	47	7.4	10.44	10.12
Australia	100	46	7.5	3.24	5.04
Brazil	100	26	12.7	n.a.	12.00
Chile	100	5	25.3	9.22	13.82

Note: depreciation computed from unrounded data. n.a. not available.
*measured by rise in official cost of living or consumers' price index.
‡latest month available. †except for mortgage bond yield in Germany,
commercial paper in Venezuela and Mexico, and commercial bank loan
rate in Brazil and Chile. §1947. ¶1948.

Over a lifetime, common stocks have basic advan-
tages over fixed-dollar investments. They benefit from
growth and human effort. They enjoy a certain amount
of compounding of savings by reason of reinvestment
in the business of retained earnings. They are hurt less
by inflation, and inflation is politically always more
popular than deflation or even sound financial policies.
Nevertheless, there are times when people pay too
much for them or incorrectly appraise the future.

When people ask me whether to buy stocks or wait, I know that I can do them as much financial harm telling them to wait in a rising market as telling them to buy in a falling one. The idea that buying nothing, or staying on the sidelines is "safe" is completely fallacious.

There is no storm cellar on this earth for investors save one—that is, knowledge of what you are doing.

NEVER ACCEPT WITHOUT CHECKING

I think I started writing about securities I liked as far back as 1921. I started at the same time reading what others wrote about securities *they* liked. The first one I ever wrote was about United States bonds which in those days were called "Liberty Bonds." The ones I wrote about were gold bonds totally exempt from all taxes except state and inheritance. Their yield to maturity averaged about 4% at the prices then prevailing.

I vaguely remember around that time selling Goodyear Tire & Rubber First Mortgage 8% bonds at a discount and each and every one was payable at 120% at par. Those were the days when the private investor received a good return for the use of his money. The high take-home income that was left bought plenty because the cost of things was low and the cost of living was low. The loss to the conservative dollar saver from artificially lowered interest rates, increased taxes and the decreased value of money has been astronomical.

Shortly after the United States bond story, I started writing for a column then known as "Talks by Men Who Know." One of the earliest subjects was the ailing and failing Maxwell-Chalmers automobile company. I said Walter Chrysler, who was just taking over, would rescue it, and he did.

In all these years reading what others wrote about securities they liked, I never accepted their ideas without checking. Some were interesting; some were not. It seemed logical to me to look up those I liked and see if I agreed. There is always a time lag between when something is written and when something is printed and when it is read. Markets change, situations change, and opinions change. All these factors have to be considered. I think the present feature column of the "Commercial and Financial Chronicle" is one of the most valuable sources of ideas I know and I read it religiously. I think to act on it blindly would be a mistake.

I think the caption of the column "The Security I Like Best" is a fine one but it can mean many things to many people. To begin with, it runs every week, and who among us can possibly think that a "security I like best" at the "time I like best" at the "price I like best" can all occur week after week. I consider myself very lucky if once every year or two I can find in conjunction all the elements that make for an ideal stock purchase. The time to put forward such an idea is when it occurs rather than when space for its printing happens to be available. With this in mind, I think I have to look at the caption as having a little literary license and the reader will do well to do the same.

I think, too, it is logical to ask "best for what." In my day, I have had stocks I liked best for the backbone of an investment account. I have had stocks I liked best for those that insist on income. I have had stocks I liked best for those that want some special tax advantage. In fact, I am sure every contributor who responds with a story when asked is thinking of it in one of these ways. It is only once in a few years that any of us really have a stock we like best on all counts taking the strict dictionary meaning.

HOW TO GET THE MOST OUT OF
YOUR INVESTMENTS

The investment experience and view of "inside Wall Street" given in "The Battle For Investment Survival" covers a wide and varying field.

It can be valuable to the individual reader in precise proportion to his success in appraising his personal resources, abilities, opportunities and aims.

There will be many who should learn from this book that trying to find their own way in Wall Street will prove unprofitable. They will benefit, however, by what they save rather than by what they make. I do not think anybody with savings in excess of their emergency backlog, however, should avoid owning equities. The modern investment trust gives the person with no knowledge of investment whatever a very safe, satisfactory and rewarding stake in the future of our country. It should be realized that most people who feel themselves incapable of selecting securities or dealing with the stock markets are usually equally incapable of making other types of investments. The simple system of splitting investable savings in half between government bonds and top quality investment trusts is an ideal solution for this type of person. The government bonds are a reserve against hard times and deflation. Investment trusts are a stake in good times and a hedge against the rising cost of living. Both the bonds and investment trusts are a protection against promotors and swindlers of all types in all fields—real estate, general business, or securities. This combination in my opinion is basically a much sounder approach to the problem than salting everything away in some form of dollar investment such as cash, bank accounts, mortgages, savings and loan deposits and bonds.

Most readers of this book will feel that they can go further on their own. What they do and how they go about it will vary a great deal, depending upon many personal factors, such as age, wealth, goal, ability, contacts and occupation.

The important point is that someone with a full time occupation of his own should not attempt a professional type of short-term trading which itself requires full time attention. It is essential that the ideas selected from the book match one's personal proclivities.

In the course of thirty-five years as a stock broker, as well as an investor, I have seen all types of people and all types of accounts in action. Some have made money—some have lost it. A few almost always made money in the stock market. I have even seen fabulous fortunes built up. While I have seen many losses I have luckily not seen much in the way of complete catastrophe such as attracted so much publicity in the 1929-1932 period.

So, do not be "afraid" of Wall Street. Losses in other directions simply do not get the advertising Wall Street losses receive. They are just as real, however.

I believe that whenever possible the time to run risks is when one is young. It is also the time for testing and appraising one's own abilities. This means taking a job which seems to have a future. It means living relatively frugally and renting a home rather than buying one. All one's efforts should be pointed in one direction, which is to build up capital. When I was young I invested on margin and looking back, I am glad I did so. I had a lot to gain and really little to lose. It is time enough to be conservative and safe after your ship has come in and when you have much more to lose and less to gain. It is also time enough to be conservative if you find your efforts are not successful and that saving rather than building is your obvious course.

I know as I write this that only a few who try will succeed. This is equally true of every phase of life and is certainly not an argument against trying.

There will be the practical question of how to go about it. Those few young readers of this book who are making a career in some form of the investment business will naturally try completely on their own. The majority of readers engaged in different businesses or professions will simply have to make investment an avocation or, on their own, find someone successful to help them.

Occasionally among their families or friends they may know an outstandingly successful person who can help them or who has connections of his own available for introduction. Where this is not the case, it comes down to searching for the right person in the investment business itself.

I lean to a broker rather than the average banker or investment counsellor, not because I happen to be a broker myself but because the objective of most of the readers of this book will be capital appreciation. The objective of bankers and most investment counsellors is orthodox diversification for income, safety and moderate growth.

Incidentally, this does not necessarily mean always attempting to find somebody at the top of the business.

Often such a man being older and having achieved success is no longer as free to devote himself solely to investing for appreciation as he could do in his accumulative years. Executive duties and other activities deprive him of his time. An investor seeking help in this direction must conduct himself correctly or he will not be quick to find it. Time is money, particularly in the higher income brackets.

Actually, the greatest portion of a broker's efforts should be devoted to determining what to do. In other words, what to buy—what to sell—when—etc. Once these decisions are reached translating them into policy for individual accounts is very simple. Thus, whether or not a top man can handle an account does not really depend, as most often thought, upon the size of the account but upon the amount of time which will be required to satisfy the client.

Most people outside of Wall Street incorrectly think "insiders" find profits easy to secure. Everybody has heard the story about the brokers owning the yachts rather than the customers. If Wall Street profits were easy to secure I am sure that those who have the key would willingly share it with all whom they come in contact with. This book is called *The Battle for Investment Survival* because protecting and increasing capital is in fact a "battle." In addition to experience, flair and contacts, matters like this need uninterrupted time and attention and also a need to succeed. Thus, success can often very likely be achieved if one finds some bright young broker who is going up in the world and with his help can go up with him.

Going back to the subject of selecting assistance, I apply this principle personally when venturing into fields that are unfamiliar to me. At times, I have applied it to investing in the theater, in real estate and in oil ventures.

It is equally applicable to personal matters. Years ago, I needed medical assistance. I could not operate on myself any more than I think the butcher, the baker or the candlestick maker can invest for himself. I turned my attention to appraising a half dozen surgeons before making a decision. The success of the operation resulted from my being fortunate in choosing the right doctor among the six.

The success of many accumulative programs similarly comes from the correct choice of someone in the field with whom to consult.

The type of investor I find in the majority are those who have achieved some degree of success in their own careers and who make the handling of their funds a major avocation. This is seen most often starting at about age 35. I think it is a very fundamental and worthwhile thing to do. I can only guess at the time which is required by many of this type but perhaps it is at least an hour a day. Anyone who can successfully save money or inherit it will be exceedingly well paid for giving at least this much time and attention to his affairs. In fact, it can make the difference between actually losing money and making a great deal of it. This is the man who can make the most use out of this book.

If the first period of an individual's investment life falls between the ages of 21 and 35, this second period runs from 35 to 50. After 50, people are more apt to be on the defensive. However, if they are successful in the manner indicated they will know that the best defense is a good offense. Thus, actually there will be less change in the way they do things investment-wise than in how much they do. The successful investor may show less interest in his mature years but his very success will have taught him not to change his basic tactics. Thus, investing for retirement as it is often termed, in real life is not much different for the successful man than investing for appreciation.

Some people feel there is safety in numbers. They always check the opinion of one person against that of another. I don't find this works out very well. A banker, for example, is very apt to disapprove of a list worked out by a broker. The difference may be one of objective, which is as it should be, but yet the banker may simply disapprove because it doesn't fit his personal patterns. Thus, in the final analysis, no matter what one does the investor when selecting help must depend on his own judgment.

As a broker myself, the question I am asked frequently is, "Do you know something good?"; or, perhaps a variation, "Let me know when you hear something good." I don't think the people who ask this will get much real help or find much real lasting success in Wall Street. Wall Street is not a place to try to make an isolated profit. Rather it is where one goes to set up a continuing and consistent investment or speculative program.

Another question that I am asked frequently is, "How do I make a killing?" This can be done but it involves a great deal of risk all along the line. To make a killing these days one needs to buy the maximum amount of the most volatile high leverage shares using the largest amount of credit. This means that if a person is wrong he will lose with the same supercharged speed as he had hoped to gain. In other words, he runs the risk of being "killed" as well as of making a "killing." It is also something that one probably will have to do for himself. It will take a great deal of effort to find a conscientious and intelligent broker who will share the moral responsibility of guiding such a program.

In closing, let me repeat that this book is principally a chronological review of what I have experienced and witnessed in the field of investments. It should be very obvious that the methods outlined are not equally useful to every reader. It has been said that "one man's meat is another man's poison," and this quotation is completely applicable here.

However, every reader should close the book knowing more about the hazards of preserving capital and why the book is entitled, *The Battle for Investment Survival.* To quote again, "forewarned is forearmed," and a knowledge of true investment objectives and the great difficulty in their achievement is half the battle and of great value in itself.

Printed in the United States
100292LV00002B/141/A